3

Rot

Logo!

Teacher's Guide

Harriette Lanzer

Heinemann

Heinemann Educational Publishers,
Halley Court, Jordan Hill, Oxford OX2 8EJ
Part of Harcourt Education Ltd.

Heinemann is the registered trademark of Harcourt Education Ltd.

First published 2002

04 05 06 10 9 8 7 6 5 4 3

A catalogue record is available for this book from the British Library on request.

ISBN 0 435 36693 9

Produced by **AMR** Ltd

Cover photo provided by Getty Images

Printed in the UK by Athenaeum Press Ltd.

Tel: 01865 888058 www.heinemann.co.uk

Contents

Introduction

Logo! offers a lively, communicative approach underpinned by a clear grammatical progression.

The course is suitable for pupils of a wide range of ability and includes differentiated material in the Pupil's Books as well as differentiated workbooks, and differentiated Pupil's Books in year 9. *Logo!* is specifically written for pupils learning German as a first foreign language but a fast route helps teachers to use the materials to deliver a shorter course (see below).

The components

Logo! 3 Rot (AT Levels 4–7) consists of:
Pupil's Book
Cassettes
Workbook
Resource and Assessment File
Teacher's Guide

Pupil's Book

The Pupil's Book consists of six theme-based chapters which are subdivided into seven double-page units (five in Chapter 6) covering AT Levels 4–6. The seventh unit (*MEHR*) is a consolidation and extention unit (up to AT Level 7) which can be left out if you are short of time or if it is not suitable for your pupils. It contains activities in all four skill areas and is to be used with whole classes in the same way as the other units. The activities tend to be slightly more difficult than in the core units, with longer reading and listening passages which bring together the language of the chapter.

Halfway through each chapter there is a *Mini-Test* for quick self-assessment on material covered up to that point. At the end of each chapter there is a checklist of key functions and structures (*Lernzieltest*) and revision activities which can be used as a practice test (*Wiederholung*). There are also German–English word lists (*Wörter*) covering the key language from the chapter.

At the back of the Pupil's Book there are three sections of further practice and reference. The *Extra* section contains self-access differentiated reading and writing activities. *Extra A* is for reinforcement and *Extra B* for extension. There is also a grammar reference and practice section where all the grammar points introduced in the core units are explained fully and accompanied by practice activities. Finally, there is a comprehensive German–English word list and a shorter English–German word list.

Cassettes

There are three cassettes for *Logo! 3 Rot*. The cassettes contain listening material for both presentation and practice. The material includes dialogues and interviews recorded by native speakers. **The listening material for each *Kontrolle* from the *Resource and Assessment File* is at the end of the relevant chapter.**

Currency

The activities in the Pupil's Book which involve money transactions generally include prices in Deutschmarks and euros (the legal tender in Germany after February 2002). Listening material for these activities is recorded in two versions: 'Version 1' with Deutschmarks and 'Version 2' with euros. The tape transcripts in the Teacher's Guide have euro prices in brackets (€) after the Deutschmarks.

Workbook

The workbook provides self-access reading and writing tasks which are designed to be fun. The workbook is ideal for homework. There is a page of activities for each double-page unit in the Pupil's Book. There is also a page of grammar (*Grammatik*), two pages of revision (Wiederholung) and a self-assessment page (*Lernzieltest*) at the end of each chapter.

Resource and Assessment File

The *Resource and Assessment File* contains the following photocopiable resources:

1 Worksheets (*Arbeitsblätter*) including:

a Visuals or picture sheets consisting of pictures with the matching German words/phrases. These can be used in the following ways:

- You can put them onto an OHT for presentation purposes. Introduce one at a time and then turn the OHP off. Put two or three on the OHP. Pupils guess which ones they are. Turn the OHP back on to check. You could also play Kim's game. Place the visuals on the OHP. Turn the OHP off and remove one. Pupils guess which one has been taken away.
- Give each pupil a copy of the sheet. They write the right phrases under each picture.
- Give each pair of pupils a sheet. They cut up the pictures and the phrases and make a pile of each. They pick up a picture and then pick up a phrase/word. They read the words and they keep both cards if the word matches the picture.
- Give each pair of pupils a sheet. They cut up the phrases and the pictures and play a game of pairs. The pieces are placed face down on their desk and they pick up two pieces. They keep the pair if they have the picture and the phrase that match.
- Pupils cut up the pictures and place them in a pile face down. They pick up a picture and have to say the phrase in German. They keep the card if they are right. This can be played in pairs or groups. The person with the most cards wins.
- The pictures can be used in a dice game. The visuals are placed face up on the desk and numbered. This can be played in pairs or groups. One or two dice are thrown and pupils say what is on the picture which has the same number as their score. They score a point for each picture described correctly.
- A variation on the pairs game can be played in groups of four. Each group of pupils is given two sheets so there are two of each visual. They are cut up and all the pictures are dealt out. The aim is to get a pair of cards. One player starts and says a phrase in German to his/her neighbour. If they have the card they must give it up. The player with the most pairs wins.

b Speaking sheets for extra pracice (e.g. information-gap tasks)

c Skill sheets practising language learning skills (e.g. dictionary work) introduced in the Pupil's Book. These sheets cover skills which are relevant to learning in general and can thus be used at any point during the course where the teacher feels they are applicable.

2 Grammar worksheets (*Grammatik*) for more practice of grammar points introduced in the Pupil's Book. The Teacher's Guide gives guidance on where these sheets fit into the Scheme of Work. They can clearly be used at any later point in the scheme (see page x for a complete list of grammar worksheets).

3 Chapter word lists (*Wortschatz*) organized in topics to help with vocabulary and learning and revision

And for assessment:

4 *Lernzieltest*: checklist for self/peer assessment

5 *Kontrollen*: end-of-chapter (and end-of-year) tests for formal assessment together with the teaching notes and the answers for the tests

Teacher's Guide

The *Teacher's Guide* contains:

- general overview of *Logo! 3 Rot*
- overview grids for each chapter
- clear teaching notes and full tape transcript
- mapping of activities to the National Curriculum
- guidance on using the materials with pupils of varying abilities
- suggestions for additional differentiated practice
- help with using German in the classroom

Using *Logo! 3 Rot* with pupils of varying abilities

After initial teacher-led presentation work with the whole class, pupils move on to a range of individual, pair and group activities which allow them to work at different levels. There is much scope in the core material for differentiation by pace and outcome. Suggestions are provided in the Teacher's Guide. The activities in the Pupil's Book are supplemented by those in the *Extra* section at the back of the book. For each chapter there is a double page of activities: the A page activities are at reinforcement level and the B page activities are at extension level. For ease of use these activities are clearly flagged in the Teacher's Guide.

In order to help pupils focus on the underlying structure of the language, the grammar and grammar revision boxes in the teaching units are backed up by full explanations and practice in the grammar section at the back of the Pupil's Book as well as in the grammar worksheets. These activities can be done at any appropriate point. You may want learners to do some or all of this section, depending on their ability.

Grammar

The key structures being used in a unit are presented in a grid on the Pupil's Book page, providing support for speaking and writing activities. A summary of the key structures of each chapter is given in the *Lernzieltest* at the end of each chapter. Key grammar points are highlighted in *Grammatik* and *Wiederholung* (grammar revision) boxes on the page and there is a reference and practice section at the back of the Pupil's Book. In addition there are worksheets in the *Resource and Assessment File* which specifically focus on grammar.

Skills

Key language learning skills, including reading and writing strategies, speaking, listening, pronunciation and dictionary skills, are highlighted by Ludwig, the pupil-friendly mascot. There are also worksheets in the *Resource and Assessment File* for extra practice.

Progression

There is a clear progression within each chapter of the Pupil's Book and language is constantly recycled through all chapters in a systematic spiral of revision and extension. Clear objectives are given in the Teacher's Guide at the beginning of each unit to help teachers plan the programme of work which is appropriate for different ability groups.

Fast route

For those teachers who have less time, a fast route through the material in each chapter has been plotted in the Teacher's Guide. The route is indicated by the symbol ▶, which points to the activities which can be **left out**. This fast route ensures that all the objectives and grammar are covered and that there is a reasonable balance of skills. If teachers want to miss out some of the grammar, further activities could be omitted – as could the *Wiederholung* pages, if teachers did not want to assess every chapter.

Assessment

Revision and self-assessment

Logo! 3 Rot encourages learners to revise and check their own progress regularly. Mid-way through each chapter is a *Mini-Test* in the form of a checklist focusing on recently covered work. Pupils can work in pairs, revising for the test and then testing each other. At the end of each chapter is a *Lernzieltest* – a checklist of key language covered. There is a photocopiable version of the *Lernzieltest* in the *Resource and Assessment File* with boxes for pupils and partner/teacher to initial. There is also a version of the *Lernzieltest* in the workbooks in the form of a gap-filling task.

Teacher assessment

The assessment scheme consists of ongoing assessment as well as more formal periodic assessment. The scheme in *Logo! 3 Rot* focuses on Levels 4 to 6/7 in the four National Curriculum Attainment Targets.

All activities have been matched against National Curriculum levels to assist teachers in carrying out continuous assessment. It must be stressed that performance in an individual activity can only contribute towards evidence that a pupil is achieving that level. Pupils must successfully carry out a range of activities at a particular level in order for the level to be awarded.

The end-of-chapter (and end-of-year) tests or *Kontrollen* in the *Resource and Assessment File* provide a more formal means of assessment. The *Wiederholungen* in the Pupil's Book provide activities which will help pupils to prepare for the tests. The tests cover all four skills and can be used with pupils of all abilities. Again, the tasks are matched against level descriptions.

The teaching sequence

Presentation

New language can be presented using the cassettes, ensuring that pupils have authentic pronunciation models. To set the new language in a purposeful context, pupils usually engage in a simple matching activity. This method of presenting new language also supports the non-specialist teacher.

The range of resources in the scheme enables the teacher to vary the way new language is presented.

Visuals or picture sheets: The *Resource and Assessment File* contains picture sheets for each chapter. These can be photocopied and cut up for games or copied onto an overhead transparency and used for presentation work. Suggestions on how to use the picture sheets are given on page iv.

Practice

Pupils move on to a variety of activities in all four skills in which they practise the new language, sometimes in pairs or groups. Ideas for additional practice are presented in the teaching notes for each unit.

Reinforcement and extension

The units often end with a more extended activity of an open-ended nature. Some of these activities are aimed at a slightly higher level than the core material in the unit, in order to give higher ability learners freer, more challenging practice.

However, to cope with the range of ability in a class, additional reinforcement and extension activities are also provided in the Pupil's Book (*Extra*).

Using the target language in the classroom

Instructions in the Pupil's Book are in German. They have been kept as simple and as uniform as possible.

Incorporating ICT

Appropriate use of Information and Communication Technology (ICT) to support modern foreign language learning is a requirement of the National Curriculum. It is an entitlement for all pupils.

References to e-mail and websites occur throughout the course. Students should be encouraged to e-mail contemporaries in German-speaking countries and to research authentic information in German on the internet. A selection of useful websites is given below, but please refer to the Heinemann website (www.Heinemann.co,uk/secondary/languages) for the most up-to-date information.

Organisations for teachers of German:
www.linguanet.org
www.cilt.org.uk
www.all-languages.org.uk
www.goethe.de/london
www.centralbureau.org.uk

On-line services for teachers in England, with Modern Languages sections:
www.standards.dfee.gov.uk
www.becta.org.uk
www.qca.org.uk

German search engines:
www.de.yahoo.com
www.web.de
www.hurra.de
www.lycos.de
www.ocr.org.uk

Symbols used in the teaching notes

E extension material / suggestion for extending an activity for the more able

R reinforcement material / suggestion for simplifying an activity for the less able

► fast route (see note on page v)

Useful addresses

Association for Language Learning:
150 Railway Terrace, Rugby CV21 3HN, 01788 546443

Centre for Information on Language Teaching and Research (CILT):
20 Bedfordbury, Covent Garden, London, WC2N 4LB, 020 7379 5110
http://www.cilt.org.uk/

Central Bureau for Educational Visits and Exchanges (CBEVE)
10 Spring Gardens, London SW1A 2BN, 020 7389 4004

The International Pen Friend Service, via Torino 256, 10015 Ivrea, Italy

European Bookshop
5 Warwick St, London W1B 5LU, 020 7734 5259

Goethe Institut
50 Princes Gate, Exhibition Road, London SW7 2PH, 020 7596 4000

Solutions to *Grammatik* exercises
(Pupil's Book pp. 122–136)

1 **2** Annabel ist Engländerin. **3** Roberto ist Italiener. **4** Miguel ist Spanier. **5** Sophie ist Österreicherin. **6** Françoise ist Französin. **7** Scot ist Schotte. **7** Harry ist Ire.

2 **2** unsere, **3** ihr, **4** Ihr, **5** meine, **6** seine, **7** eure

3 **2** Welche Hose gefällt dir? Diese Hose gefällt mir. **3** Welche Actionfilme gefallen dir? Diese Actionfilme gefallen mir. **4** Welches T-Shirt gefällt dir? Dieses T-Shirt gefällt mir. **5** Welche Schuhe gefallen dir? Diese Schuhe gefallen mir. **6** Welcher Bierkrug gefällt dir? Dieser Bierkrug gefällt mir.

4 **2** Ich finde sie ziemlich unfreundlich. **3** Ich finde dich lustig. **4** Ich finde sie sehr streng. **5** Ich finde sie total doof. **6** Ich finde ihn O.K.

5 **2** dir, **3** ihr, **4** ihm, **5** mir, **6** euch, **7** ihnen

6 **2a** Wie heißt du? **b** Wie heißt ihr? **c** Wie heißen Sie? **3a** Wo wohnst du? **b** Wo wohnt ihr? **c** Wo wohnen Sie? **4a** Was machst du gern? **b** Was macht ihr gern? **c** Was machen Sie gern? **5a** Was hast du gestern gemacht? **b** Was habt ihr gestern gemacht? **c** Was haben Sie gestern gemacht? **6a** Welche Nationalität hast du? **b** Welche Nationalität habt ihr? **c** Welche Nationalität haben Sie?

7 **2** ich wohne, du wohnst, er/sie/es wohnt, wir wohnen, ihr wohnt, Sie/sie wohnen **3** ich heiße, du heißt, er/sie/es heißt, wir heißen, ihr heißt, Sie/sie heißen **4** ich trinke, du trinkst, er/sie/es trink, wir trinken, ihr trinkt, Sie/sie trinken **5** ich gehe, du gehst, er/sie/es geht, wir gehen, ihr geht, Sie/sie gehen **6** ich mache, du machst, er/sie/es macht, wir machen, ihr macht, Sie/sie machen **7** ich kaufe, du kaufst, er/sie/es kauft, wir kaufen, ihr kauft, Sie/sie kaufen

8 **2** Er fährt gern Ski. **3** Wir sehen gern fern. **4** Sie fahren nach Hamburg. **5** Isst du gern Pommes? **6** Sie liest gern Comics.

9 **2** haben, sind, **3** ist, ist, **4** hast, bist, **5** haben, sind, **6** seid, seid, **7** sind, haben

10 **2** Claudia und Micki sollten ins Bett gehen. (Claudia and Micki should go to bed.) **3** Ich sollte meine Hausaufgaben machen. (I should do my homework.) **4** Du solltest umweltfreundliches Papier kaufen. (You should by environmentally friendly paper.) **5** Wir sollten unsere Großmutter besuchen. (We should visit our grandmother.) **6** Ihr solltet mehr Äpfel und Orangen essen. (You should eat more apples and oranges.) **7** Jenny sollte öfter mit dem Rad fahren. (Jenny should go more by bike.)

11 **2** darf (You aren't allowed to smoke.) **3** dürfen (We aren't allowed to bring cigarettes to school.) **4** darf (Her isn't allowed to sit next to me.) **5** dürfen (Claudia and Felix aren't allowed to go on the school trip.) **6** darf (Oliver isn't allowed to bully me.) **7** dürfen (We aren't allowed to play computer games in the computer room.)

12 **2** Thomas und Axel können sehr schnell schwimmen. (Thomas and Axel can swim very fast.) **3** Petra kann nicht ins Kino gehen, weil sie kein Geld hat. (Petra can't go to the cinema because she hasn't got any money.) **4** Ich kann nicht schwimmen gehen, weil ich Fieber habe. (I can' t go swimming because I have a fever.) **5** Harald kann sehr gute Bilder am Computer zeichnen. (Harald can draw very good pictures on the computer.) **6** Wir können Ski fahren, wenn es schneit. (We can go skiing if it snows.)

13 **2** Sie muss eine Uniform tragen. (She has to wear a uniform.) **3** Du musst viel zu Hause helfen. (You have to help a lot at home.) **4** Wir müssen pünktlich zur Schule kommen. (We have to get to school on time.) **5** Ich muss Hausaufgaben immer rechtzeitig machen. (I always have to do my homework on time.) **6** Ihr müsst mehr Sport treiben. (You have to do more sport.) **7** Ich muss einen Job finden. (I have to find a job.)

14 **2** Er will Eis laufen gehen. (He wants to go ice skating.) **3** Wir wollen fernsehen. (We want to watch TV.) **4** Ihr wollt Ski fahren. (You want to go skiing.) **5** Sie wollen Musik hören. (They want to listen to music.) **6** Du willst einkaufen gehen. (You want to go shopping.)

15 **2** Mark sieht gern fern. David sieht nicht gern fern. **3** Mark fährt nicht gern Ski. David fährt gern Ski. **4** Mark geht nicht gern einkaufen. David geht gern einkaufen. **5** Mark liest nicht gern Comics. David liest gern Comics.

16 **2** gefällt, **3** gefällt, **4** gefallen, **5** gefällt, **6** gefallen, **7** gefällt

17 **2** Ich habe keinen Bruder. **3** Ich trinke nichts. **4** Ich gehe nie schwimmen. **5** Ich spiele nicht gern Tennis. **6** Ich fahre nicht gern nach London. **7** Ich habe keinen Computer.

18 **2** Sophie ist Ski gefahren. **3** Petra hat ferngesehen. **4** Kai hat Computerspiele gespielt. **5** Jens hat ein Buch gelesen. **6** Alex ist ins Kino gegangen.

19 **2** Letztes Trimester habe ich gute Noten bekommen. **3** Letzte Woche bin ich Ski gefahren. **4** Letztes Jahr bin ich nach England geflogen. **5** Gestern habe ich meinen Freund besucht. **6** Vorgestern bin ich ins Kino gegangen.

20 **2** Im Winter bist du Ski gefahren. **3** Am Abend haben wir Musik gehört. **4** Am Wochenende haben Sie Computerspiele gespielt. **5** Am Samstag seid Ihr einkaufen gegangen. **6** Am Nachmittag haben sie ferngesehen.

21 **2** Er hat einen Hamburger gegessen. **3** Sie ist im Internet gesurft. **4** Ich bin Eis laufen gegangen. **5** Du bist nach England gefahren. **6** Ihr habt Musik gehört.

22 **2** gefahren, **3** gekommen, **4** gelesen, **5** gehabt, **6** geschrieben, **7** verdient, **8** gezeichnet, **9** gesurft, **10** gesehen

23 **2** hatte, **3** waren, **4** warst, **5** hatten, **6** war, **7** hattest, **8** war, war

24 **2** Nächstes Trimester werde ich ein Fahrrad kaufen. **3** Nächstes Trimester werden wir nicht rauchen.

4 Nächstes Trimester wird Ralph mehr zu Hause helfen. **5** Nächstes Trimester werden Peter und Kirstin höflich sein. **6** Nächstes Trimester wirst du pünktlich zur Schule kommen. **7** Nächstes Trimester werden Sie bessere Noten bekommen.

25 2 Wir essen viele Bananen. **3** Ich spiele gern Tennis. **4** Sie hat drei Brüder. **5** Du siehst viel fern.

26 2 Ich mag Physik-Chemie nicht, weil es schwierig ist. **3** Ich mag Sport nicht, weil es anstrengend ist. **4** Ich mag Biologie, weil die Lehrerin nett ist. **5** Ich mag Kunst, weil ich gern zeichne. **6** Ich finde Deutsch langweilig, weil ich nichts verstehe. **7** Ich mag die Schule, weil ich viele Freunde dort habe.

27 2 Wenn es schneit, fahre ich Ski. **3** Wenn es heiß ist, gehe ich schwimmen. **4** Wenn es kalt ist, gehe ich ins Kino. **5** Wenn es regnet, gehe ich einkaufen. **6** Wenn es kalt ist, gehe ich Eis laufen.

28 2 Meine Schwester fährt nach Italien, um ihren Freund zu besuchen. **3** Wir fahren nach Paris, um den Louvre zu besichtigen. **4** Du fahrst nach Spanien, um Urlaub zu machen. **5** Sie fahren nach England, um London zu besichtigen. **6** Meine Eltern fahren nach Österreich, um die frische Luft zu genießen.

29 2 Am Dienstag bin ich mit dem Rad nach Köln gefahren. **3** Am Mittwoch bin ich mit dem Bus nach Hamburg gefahren. **4** Am Donnerstag bin ich mit dem Rad zur Schule gefahren. **5** Am Freitag bin ich mit Dieter ins Kino gefahren. **6** Am Samstag bin ich mit dem Auto zum Schwimmbad gefahren.

30 2 meiner, **3** dem, **4** deinem, **5** der, **6** meinen

31 2 Zwei Mädchen sparen auf ein Fahrrad/Mofa. **3** Zehn Jungen sparen auf einen Wagen. **4** Vier Jungen sparen auf eine Stereoanlage. **5** Zwölf Jungen sparen auf einen Computer. **6** Acht Mädchen sparen auf Kleidung.

32 2 acc. (movement towards the library), **3** dat. (in school, i.e. no movement), **4** dat. (in the library, i.e. no movement), **5** acc (movement towards the cinema), **6** dat. (in the computer room, i.e. no movement)

33 **b** Das schwarze T-Shirt gefällt mir (nicht). **c** Die grünen Schuhe gefallen mir (nicht). **d** Die gelbe Jacke gefällt mir (nicht). **e** Die blaue Hose gefällt mir (nicht). **f** Der karierte Hut gefällt mir (nicht).

34 **b** Es gibt ein schwarzes T-Shirt. **c** Es gibt grüne Schuhe. **d** Es gibt eine gelbe Jacke. **e** Es gibt eine blaue Hose. **f** Es gibt einen karierten Hut.

35 2 100 cm sind länger als 50 cm. **3** Sport ist antrengender als Kunst. **4** Ein Hund ist kleiner als ein Pferd. **5** Äpfel sind gesunder als Chips. **6** Ein Auto ist schneller/größer als ein Fahrrad. **7** 25 cm sind kürzer als 125 cm.

36 2 Der größte Elefant ist c. **3** Die längste Socke ist c. **4** Das beste Bild ist c.

List of grammar worksheets (*Grammatik*) in the *Resource and Assessment File*

Resource and Assessment File	Grammar	Teacher's Guide
Chapter 1		
Grammatik 1 p. 9	The present tense	p. 40
Grammatik 2 p. 10	The perfect tense	p. 40
Grammatik 3 p. 11	The accusative case; plurals	p. 40
Chapter 2		
Grammatik 1 p. 31	The future tense	p. 63
Grammatik 2 p. 32	Comparatives and superlatives	p. 63
Grammatik 3 p. 33	Word order (1): *weil*	p. 64
Chapter 3		
Grammatik 1 p. 52	Word order (2): *um ... zu*	p. 87
Grammatik 2 p. 53	Word order (3): *wenn*	p. 88
Grammatik 3 p. 54	Word order (4): ordering ideas	p. 89
Chapter 4		
Grammatik 1 p. 73	Expressing opinions (adjectives, *gern, gefallen*)	p. 110
Grammatik 2 p. 74	Modal verbs: *dürfen, können, sollen*	p. 111
Grammatik 3 p. 75	*War* and *hatte* (inverted word order)	p. 111
Chapter 5		
Grammatik 1 p. 96	*Dieser* and *Welcher*	p. 135
Grammatik 2 p. 97	Adjective endings (after *der/die/das* and *ein/eine*)	p. 136
Grammatik 3 p. 98	Prepositions	p. 136
Chapter 6		
Grammatik 1 p. 116	Personal pronouns (nom., acc., dat.)	p. 155
Grammatik 2 p. 117	Negatives (*kein/nicht*)	p. 155
Grammatik 3 p. 118	Possessive adjectives (*mein, dein*, etc.)	p. 156

Covering the Programmes of Study

The table on page xi indicates where in *Logo! 3 Rot* pupils have the opportunity to develop the skills and understanding prescribed in the National Curriculum Programmes of Study. For each area we have indicated where these appear in the core units of the Pupil's Book. There are further opportunities both in the Pupil's Book and the supplementary components. More detail is provided in the grids at the beginning of each chapter in this Teacher's Guide.

Some opportunities, especially in section 4, are beyond the scope of a coursebook. We have used the symbol *** to denote these.

1 Acquiring knowledge and understanding of the target language	
a the principles and interrelationships of sounds and writing in the target language	Ch. 1 Unit 1; Ch. 2 Unit 2; Ch. 6 Unit 1
b the grammar of the target language and how to apply it	Ch. 1 Unit 4; Ch. 2 Unit 4; Ch. 3 Unit 2
c how to express themselves and using a range of vocabulary and structures	Ch. 2 Unit 4; Ch. 4 Unit 6; Ch. 6, Unit 4
2 Developing language skills – pupils should be taught:	
a how to listen carefully for gist and detail	Ch. 2 Unit 6; Ch. 3 Unit 3; Ch. 5 Unit 4
b correct pronunciation and intonation	Ch. 1 Unit 3; Ch. 2 Unit 2; Ch. 4 Unit 3
c how to ask and answer questions	Ch. 1 Units 1 & 5; Ch.4 Unit 3
d how to initiate and develop conversations	Ch. 1 Units 1 & 3; Ch. 4 Unit 6; Ch. 6 Unit 6
e how to vary the target language and to suit context, audience and purpose	Ch. 1 Unit 6; Ch. 3 Unit 6; Ch. 6 Unit 6
f how to adapt language they already know for different contexts	Ch. 1 Unit 5; Ch. 4 Unit 5; Ch. 6 Unit 4
g strategies for dealing with the unpredictable	Ch. 2 Unit 3; Ch. 4 Unit 2; Ch. 5 Unit 6
h techniques for skimming and for scanning written texts for i nformation, including those from ICT-based sources	Ch. 1 Unit 5; Ch. 5 Units 1 & 5; Ch. 6 Unit 2
i how to summarise and report the main points of spoken and written texts, using notes where appropriate	Ch. 3 Unit 2; Ch. 1 Unit 7; Ch. 4 Unit 1
j how to redraft their writing to improve its accuracy and presentation, including the use of ICT	Ch. 3 Unit 1; Ch. 4 Unit 5; Ch. 5 Unit 1
3 Developing language-learning skills – pupils should be taught:	
a techniques for memorizing words, phrases and short extracts	Ch. 1 Unit 2; Ch. 5 Unit 3; Ch. 6 Unit 2
b how to use contexts and other clues to interpret meaning	Ch. 2 Unit 3; Ch. 4 Unit 4; Ch. 5 Unit 5
c to use their knowledge of English or another language when learning the target language	Ch. 2 Unit 6; Ch. 3 Unit 5; Ch. 4 Unit 1
d how to use dictionaries and other reference materials appropriately and effectively	Ch. 1 Unit 6; Ch. 2 Unit 4; Ch. 3 Unit 1
e how to develop their independence in language learning and using the target language	All *Extra* pages
4 Developing cultural awareness – pupils should be taught about different countries and cultures by:	
a working with authentic materials in the target language, including some from ICT-based sources	Ch. 3 Unit 7; Ch. 4 Unit 7; Ch. 5 Unit 7
b communicating with native speakers	***
c considering their own culture and comparing it with the cultures of the countries and communities where the target language is spoken	Ch. 2 Units 1 & 5; Ch. 3 Unit 1; Ch. 6 Unit 3
d considering the experiences and perspectives of people in these countries and communities	Ch. 2 Unit 5; Ch. 5 Unit 7; Ch. 6 Unit 3
5 Breadth of study – during key stages 3 and 4, pupils should be taught the knowledge, skills and understanding through:	
a communicating in the target language	Ch. 1 Unit 4; Ch. 2 Unit 6; Ch. 3 Unit 5
b using everyday classroom events as an opportunity for spontaneous speech	Ch. 2 Unit 7; Ch. 4 Unit 2; Ch. 5 Unit 6
c expressing and discussing personal feelings and opinions	Ch. 2 Units 1 & 2; Ch. 3 Unit 4; Ch. 4 Unit 1
d producing and responding to different types of spoken and written language, including texts produced using ICT	Ch. 4 Unit 7; Ch. 5 Unit 2; Ch. 2 Unit 3
e using a range of resources, including ICT, for assessing and communicating information	Ch. 3 Units 4 & 7; Ch. 4 Unit 5
f using the target language creatively and imaginatively	Ch. 2 Unit 7; Ch. 4 Unit 2; Ch. 5 Unit 4
g listening, reading or viewing for personal interest and enjoyment, as well as for information	Ch. 1 Unit 3; Ch. 3 Unit 7 Ch. 4 Unit 7
h using the target language for real purposes	Ch. 4 Unit 2; Ch. 5 Unit 6; Ch. 6 Unit 5
i working in a variety of contexts, including everyday activities, personal and social life, the world around us, the world of work and the international world	All chapters

Logo! 3 Rot for Scotland

The following table shows where the coverage of Standard Grade topics in Logo! 3 Rot.

Topic areas	Chapter and Unit
Self	Chapter 1, Units 1–2; Chapter 6, Units 3 & 5
Home	Chapter 3, Unit 4; Chapter 6, Unit 2
Family/Daily routine	Chapter 2, Unit 5; Chapter 5, Unit 1;
	Chapter 6, Unit 1
School	Chapter 2, all units
Work	Chapter 5, all units
Leisure	Chapter 1, Units 2, 4, 5 & 7; Chapter 4, all Units
Holidays and travel	Chapter 3, Units 1–3 & 6–7
Environment, places and facilities	Chapter 3, Units 3–7
Food and drink	
Goods and services	Chapter 1, Unit 6; Chapter 5, Unit 4
Accidents and emergencies	Chapter 1, Unit 5
Events (past, present, future) concerns and ideas of adolescent and general interest	Chapter 1, Units 4 & 5; Chapter 2, Unit 4; Chapter 3, Unit 3; Chapter 4, Unit 3 & 5; Chapter 6, all units
Clothes and fashion	Chapter 5, Units 4 & 5
People	
Personal belongings/Pets/Money	Chapter 5, Units 3–6
Places	Chapter 3, all units
Immediate plans	Chapter 2, Unit 4; Chapter 4, Unit 2
Times/dates	Chapter 2, Unit 5; Chapter 3, Unit 6; Chapter 4, Unit 2
Weather	Chapter 3, Unit 2
Morale (happy, bored etc.)	Chapter 2, Units 2 & 3; Chapter 6, Unit 1–4
Physical state (hungry, ill etc.)	

Logo! 3 Rot for Northern Ireland

The table below provides an overview of coverage of the Contexts for Learning 1, 2 & 3 for *Logo! 3*.

Contexts for Learning and Associated Topics

Context 1: Everyday Activities	*Logo! 3*
a Home & school life	Chapter 1, Unit 2 Chapter 2, all units
b Food & drink	
c Shopping	Chapter 1, Unit 6 Chapter 5, Unit 4
d Eating out	
Context 2: Personal Life & Social Relationships	***Logo! 3***
a Self, family & friends	Chapter 1, Units 1, 2, 3 & 7 Chapter 5, Units 1, 2 & 3 Chapter 6, all units
b Health	
c Holidays & leisure	Chapter 1, all units Chapter 3, Units 1–3, 6 & 7 Chapter 4, all units
d Celebrations & special occasions	Chapter 5, Unit 5
Context 3: The World Around Us	***Logo! 3***
a House & home	Chapter 6, Unit 2
b Town & countryside	Chapter 3, Units 3, 4 & 5
c Getting around	Chapter 2, Unit 6
d Weather	Chapter 3, Unit 2

Logo! 3 Rot Overview

Main topics	Grammar	Skills
1 Austausch personal details (revision) nationalities hobbies useful expressions for a visit activities in the past buying souvenirs	present tense verbs: regular and irregular, sing. + plural (revision) nationalities: masculine and feminine word order in the perfect tense (revision) perfect tense: sing. + plural with *haben* or *sein* (revision) 'the' and 'this' (*der/dieser*)	learning vocabulary note-taking while listening pronunciation: imitating tape using German–English dictionary for plurals extended reading
2 Bei uns – bei euch school subjects: likes and dislikes comparing school subjects school rules plans for next term comparing German and British schools directing someone around school	word order after *weil* comparatives and superlatives *dürfen* + infinitive future tense (*werden*)	using German–English dictionary pronunciation of *ä, ö, ü* scanning texts for key words listening and repeating for intonation using English–German dictionary for new words extended reading
3 Österreich und die Umwelt activities in Austria and all weathers past tense activities where you live environmental issues letter to a tourist office	*um … zu* present tense of fahren (all forms) word order with *wenn* word order: inversion in perfect tense word order: time, manner, place *weil* (revision) *gefallen* (revision) *man sollte* + infinitive present tense: sing. + plural (revision)	using the grammar reference section adapting a text and redrafting on computer taking notes whilst listening preparing a short presentation on computer and cassette learning set phrases to reuse in writing adapting/redrafting letter on computer groupwork
4 Medien films going to the cinema music and concerts reading habits activities on computer media project week	*weil* (revision) *gefallen* (revision) perfect tense with inversion (revision) *können* + infinitive (revision) perfect tense sing. with *haben* and *sein* (revision) *war, hatte* in + dative (no movement) (revision)	using fillers to gain time while speaking asking questions pronunciation of cognates compound nouns listening: predicting what you might hear using a computer to redraft written work and to find out information useful short words for writing extended reading
5 Jobs und Geld part-time work qualities for different jobs reasons for saving buying clothes describing clothes spending money	present tense sing.: irregular verbs (revision) *in* + dative *gefallen* (revision) *dieser/diese/diese* (revision) *sparen auf* + acc. *der, dieser, welcher* adjective endings after definite article (revision) adjective endings after indefinite article (revision) future tense with *werden* (revision)	drafting/redrafting text on computer learning and revising vocabulary understanding speech at normal pace using pictures to guess words vocabulary for playing board games coping with new vocabulary in a text
6 Kein Problem family things you are and are not allowed to do at home problems resolutions writing a letter	*mein, dein, sein, ihr* with nominative and accusative personal pronouns (*nicht*) dürfen negatives: *kein, nicht* *wenn* (revision) future tense with *werden* (revision) *mit* + dative *weil* (revision) 'you': *Sie/du/ihr* (revision)	learning a short passage by recording it on tape building up longer sentences making notes and listening more than once to a recording

1 Austausch (Pupil's Book pp. 6–23)

Topic area	Key language	Skills	Grammar	PoS
1.1 Ich komme aus Europa (pp. 6–7) Ask for and give personal details	*Wie heißt du? Ich heiße ... . Wie alt bist du? Ich bin ... Jahre alt. Woher kommst du? Ich komme aus England, Frankreich, Deutschland, Spanien, Österreich, Italien, Schottland, Irland, Wales. Wo wohnst du? Ich wohne in ... .*		Present tense singular (revision)	1a, 2c, 2d
1.2 Ich bin Deutscher (pp. 8–9) Name some nationalities Talk about what you like doing	*Welche Nationalität hat ... ? Er/Sie ist Engländer/in, Italiener/in, Spanier/in, Österreicher/in, Waliser/in, Ire/Irin, Schotte/Schottin, Franzose/Französin, Deutscher/Deutsche. Was machst du gern? Ich spiele (nicht) gern Fußball/Computerspiele. Ich höre (nicht) gern Musik. Ich lese gern. Ich sehe gern fern. Ich gehe gern einkaufen / ins Kino. Ich fahre gern Ski.*	Learning vocabulary Note-taking while listening	Nationalities (m/f) Present tense plural (revision)	1b, 2a, 2i, 3a
1.3 Emilys Austausch (pp. 10–11) Understand and use everyday expressions for a visit	*Hallo. Guten Tag. Wie geht's? Gut danke. Schönes Wochenende. Gute Nacht. Gute Reise. Das war lecker. Bis bald. Tschüs. Auf Wiedersehen. Sprechen Sie Englisch? Danke sehr / Vielen Dank. Bitte sehr. Guten Appetit! Wie bitte? Entschuldigung.*	Pronunciation – use tape to imitate carefully		2b, 2d, 5g
1.4 Was hast du gemacht? (pp. 12–13) Talk about what you did on a trip	*Was hast du heute gemacht? Ich habe Fußball gespielt. Ich habe Musik gehört. Ich habe ferngesehen. Ich habe gelesen. Ich habe Computerspiele gespielt. Ich bin ins Kino gegangen. Ich bin Ski gefahren. Ich bin einkaufen gegangen.*		Word order in perfect tense (revision)	1b, 5a
1.5 Was hat er gemacht? (pp. 14–15) Talk about what other people have done	as 1.4 but third person forms		Perfect tense with *haben* or *sein* (revision)	2c, 2f, 2h
1.6 Souvenirs (pp. 16–17) Buy souvenirs	*Hallo, kann ich dir helfen? Ja, haben Sie Kulis? Ja, sie sind dort drüben. Nein, es tut mir Leid, wir haben keine ... . Danke. Was kostet dieser Kuli? 00 Euro. Geht das? Soll ich den Kuli als Geschenk einpacken? O, ja, vielen Dank.* Presents: *der Kuli/der Bierkrug, die Kassette/die Pflanze, das Buch/das T-Shirt*	German-English dictionary for plurals	'the' and 'this'	2e, 3d
1.7 Partnersuche (pp. 18–19)		Extended reading		2i, 3b
Lernzieltest und Wiederholung (pp. 20–21)	Revision			3b, 5d
Wörter (pp. 22–23)	Word list			
Extra (pp. 110–111)	Differentiated reading and writing			3e

1 Ich komme aus Europa
(pp. 6–7)

Pupils will learn how to:
- ask for and give personal details

Key language
Revision of personal details:
Wie heißt du?
Ich heiße Rudi.
Wie alt bist du?
Ich bin 14 Jahre alt.
Wo wohnst du?
Ich wohne in München.
Woher kommst du?
Ich komme aus …
England
Frankreich
Deutschland
Spanien
Österreich
Italien
Schottland
Irland
Wales

Grammar focus
- present tense singular (revision)

Resources
- Cassette A, Side A
- Workbook p. 1
- R & A File: Arbeitsblatt 1, 4 (pp. 4, 7), Grammatik 1 (p. 9)

This chapter has the topic of exchange friendships as its context.

This unit revises personal details, including stating one's name and age and where one lives. It also revises some European countries with the new expression: *Ich komme aus … .*

Copy the visuals on Arbeitsblatt 1 onto an OHT to introduce/revise the countries. *Irland, Schottland* and *Wales* are provided here in addition to the countries featured in the Pupil's Book. Point to a visual and ask, for example: *Kommst du aus Spanien oder aus Frankreich?* Pupils reply: *Aus* + name of country. Then move on to show one visual only and ask: *Woher kommst du?* Pupils reply: *Ich komme aus* + country. Encourage pupils to take over the questioning role once they are familiar with the vocabulary.

For further pairwork practice, give each pair of pupils a copy of the visuals so that they can continue the question-and-answer practice.

1a Hör zu. Wer spricht? (1–8) (AT1 Levels 2–3)
Pupils listen to short interviews and decide which teenager is speaking each time. Make sure pupils have familiarised themselves with the characters on the map before they hear the recording. You could do some basic questioning in the class to do this: *Wo wohnt Rudi? Wie alt ist Nicolas? Woher kommt Lisa?* etc.

Answers
1 Rudi, **2** Lucas, **3** Lisa, **4** Nina, **5** Nicolas, **6** Emily, **7** Nicolas, **8** Emily

1 – Wie alt bist du?
– Ich bin vierzehn Jahre alt.
– Wo wohnst du?
– Ich wohne in München.
2 – Woher kommst du?
– Ich komme aus Spanien.
3 – Wie heißt du?
– Ich heiße Lisa.
4 – Woher kommst du?
– Ich komme aus Italien.
5 – Wo wohnst du?
– Ich wohne in Bordeaux, in Frankreich.
– Und woher kommst du?
– Ich komme aus Bordeaux, in Frankreich.
6 – Wie alt bist du?
– Ich bin fünfzehn Jahre alt.
– Und woher kommst du?
– Ich komme aus England.
7 – Wie alt bist du?
– Ich bin sechzehn Jahre alt.
8 – Wo wohnst du?
– Ich wohne in Malton, in Yorkshire.

1b Hör zu und wiederhole. Findest du jeweils einen Fehler? (1–4) (AT1 Level 3)
Pupils listen to and repeat four longer interviews and then spot a mistake in each interview, based on the information in the book. Pupils might need to listen more than once to each interview to spot the mistake.

Answers
Mistakes shown in bold in tapescripts, correct answers:
1 15, **2** Salzburg, **3** Dresden, **4** Frankfurt

1 – Wie heißt du?
– Ich heiße Nina.
– Wie alt bist du?
– Ich bin **vierzehn** Jahre alt.
– Woher kommst du?
– Ich komme aus Rom, in Italien.
– Wo wohnst du?
– Ich wohne in Villach, in Österreich.
2 – Wie heißt du?
– Ich heiße Lisa.
– Wie alt bist du?
– Ich bin vierzehn Jahre alt.
– Woher kommst du?
– Ich komme aus Salzburg, in Österreich.
– Wo wohnst du?
– Ich wohne in **Deutschland**.
3 – Wie heißt du?
– Ich heiße Rudi.
– Wie alt bist du?
– Ich bin vierzehn Jahre alt.
– Woher kommst du?
– Ich komme aus **Köln**, in Deutschland.
– Wo wohnst du?
– Ich wohne in München.
4 – Wie heißt du?
– Ich heiße Lucas.
– Wie alt bist du?
– Ich bin fünfzehn Jahre alt.

– Woher kommst du?
– Ich komme aus Barcelona, in Spanien.
– Wo wohnst du?
– Ich wohne in **Spanien**.

2 Lies die Sätze. Wer ist das? (AT3 Level 2)
Pupils read sentences about the teenagers on p. 6 and identify each one.

Answers
1 Nicolas, **2** Lucas, **3** Nina, **4** Rudi

E A pupil makes a statement in the *ich* form about one of the teenagers and the rest of the class guesses who it is. The first person to guess correctly makes the next statement.

Wiederholung: The present tense (singular)
Look at the grammar revision box, which summarises the conjugation of verbs in the present tense (first, second and third person singular). Point out the endings to pupils and remind them of the importance of learning the irregular verbs *haben* and *sein*.

R Refer to p. 126 of the Pupil's Book for further information. More practice of this grammar point is also provided on Grammatik 1 (R & A File p. 9).

3 Kopiere und ergänze die Sätze. (AT4 Level 2)
Pupils copy the gapped sentences to practise the present tense third person singular form of the verb.

Answers
1 Lisa <u>kommt</u> aus Österreich. **2** Nicolas <u>ist</u> sechzehn Jahre alt. **3** Rudi <u>wohnt</u> in München. **4** Emily <u>ist</u> fünfzehn Jahre alt. **5** Lucas <u>kommt</u> aus Spanien. **6** Nina <u>wohnt</u> in Österreich. Sie <u>ist</u> fünfzehn Jahre alt. **7** Das Mädchen aus England <u>heißt</u> Emily. **8** Lucas <u>wohnt</u> in Frankfurt. Das <u>ist</u> in Deutschland.

4a Mach Interviews mit Lisa, Emily, Nicolas, Rudi, Lucas und Nina. (AT2 Levels 3–4)
Pupils use the personal details of the teenagers on p. 6 to conduct interviews.

4b Wer ist der beste Austauschpartner / die beste Austauschpartnerin für dich? Beschreib ihn/sie. (AT4 Level 4)
Pupils pick the teenager from p. 6 who they think would be the best exchange partner for them. They then write a short text to explain their choice.

E Pupils carry out interviews with three other people in the class to find out their names, ages, where they live and where they come from.

5 Mach einen Steckbrief für eine berühmte Person und schreib die Details auf. (AT4 Level 3–4)
Pupils choose a famous person and write his/her personal details in the *ich* form. Pupils also make an ID card for him/her. Pupils could research their famous person on the internet before they do this activity, finding out information about a German, Austrian or Swiss person if possible.

R The pairwork activity on Arbeitsblatt 4 (R & A File p. 7) provides further oral practice of the language used in this unit.

2 Ich bin Deutscher (pp. 8–9)

Pupils will learn how to:
- name some nationalities
- talk about what they like doing

Key language
Welche Nationalität hat Rudi/Emily?
Er/Sie ist …
Engländer/in
Italiener/in
Spanier/in
Österreicher/in
Waliser/in
Ire/Irin
Schotte/Schottin
Franzose/Französin
Deutscher/Deutsche
Was machst du gern?
Ich spiele (nicht) gern Fußball/Computerspiele.
Ich höre (nicht) gern Musik.
Ich lese (nicht) gern.
Ich sehe (nicht) gern fern.
Ich gehe (nicht) gern einkaufen/ins Kino.
Ich fahre (nicht) gern Ski.

Grammar focus
- nationalities (masculine/feminine)
- present tense plural (revision)

Skill focus
- learning vocabulary
- note-taking while listening

Resources
- Cassette A, Side A
- Workbook p. 2
- R & A File: Arbeitsblatt 1, 2, 5 (pp. 4, 5, 8), Arbeitsblatt 5 (p. 72)

This unit introduces the masculine and feminine forms of nouns of nationality. Copy Arbeitsblatt 1 onto an OHT to introduce the new vocabulary. Invite one male and one female pupil to stand at the front of the class and one of them to hold a visual, which you then describe, for example: *Er ist Waliser.* Then pass the visual to the other pupil and give the new description: *Sie ist Waliserin.* Work your way through the countries, encouraging pupils to start taking over the description.

For further oral practice of nationalities, give each pair of pupils two copies of the visuals. They mark a blue cross (for a male) on one set and a red cross (for a female) on the other and then cut them all up and place them in a pile. As they pick a visual up, they give the appropriate sentence such as: *Er ist Spanier. Sie ist Deutsche.* If they say the sentence correctly, they can keep the visual.

1a Hör zu. Wer ist das? (1–9) (AT1 Levels 1–2)

Pupils look at the speech bubbles and pictures and listen to nine people being described. They identify the correct person each time.

Answers

1 Nicolas, **2** Lucas, **3** Ryan Giggs, **4** Lisa, **5** Nina, **6** Rudi, **7** Robert Burns, **8** Emily, **9** Sonia O'Sullivan

1 – Ich bin Franzose.
2 – Ich bin Spanier.
3 – Er ist Waliser.
4 – Ich bin Österreicherin.
5 – Ich bin Italienerin.
6 – Ich bin Deutscher.
7 – Er war Schotte.
8 – Ich bin Engländerin.
9 – Sie ist Irin.

1b Partnerarbeit. (AT2 Level 2)

Pupils do a pairwork quiz on the identities of the people in activity 1a. Remind them of the pronouns *er* and *sie*.

2 Hör zu. Spricht man über einen Mann oder eine Frau? (1–8) (AT1 Level 2)

Pupils listen and decide whether the person being described is a man or a woman.

Answers

1 eine Frau, **2** einen Mann, **3** eine Frau, **4** einen Mann, **5** einen Mann, **6** einen Mann, **7** einen Mann, **8** eine Frau

1 – Sie ist Spanierin.
2 – Er ist Deutscher.
3 – Jean ist Französin.
4 – Micki ist Österreicher.
5 – Sam ist Engländer.
6 – Camillo ist Italiener.
7 – Charlie ist Schotte.
8 – Sie ist Irin.

Grammatik: Talking about nationalities

Point out the grammar box to the class, showing them the additional *-in* ending for the feminine form. Ask them if they can think of any similar words they have come across in Logo! – *Schüler/Schülerin, Lehrer/Lehrerin, Partner/Partnerin.*

Ludwig: Learning vocabulary

Remind pupils that the foundation of language learning is learning the vocabulary. Start a list on the wall of pupils' own ideas for learning vocabulary and add to it as the term goes on. Here, Ludwig suggests that pupils should carry their vocabulary books with them wherever they go. Ensure that pupils are in the habit of keeping their vocabulary books up-to-date and that they take pride in them.

R Further practice on learning vocabulary is provided on Arbeitsblatt 5 (R & A File p. 8).

► 3 Welche Nationalität hatten diese Leute? Schreib Sätze. (AT4 Level 2)

Pupils decide which nationality each of the eight famous people was and write a sentence to describe it. Point out that *war* means 'was', but that otherwise the structure is the same as before: *er/sie* + nationality.

Answers

1 Mozart war Österreicher. **2** Elizabeth I. war Engländerin. **3** Napoleon war Franzose. **4** Goethe war Deutscher. **5** Florence Nightingale war Engländerin. **6** Marie Antoinette war Französin. **7** Robert Burns war Schotte. **8** Salvador Dali war Spanier.

The next part of the unit deals with hobbies, which are mostly revised from Logo! 1 and 2. Go over the vocabulary orally using the visuals on Arbeitsblatt 2. First of all, just concentrate on the hobby, e.g. *Ich spiele Fußball.* Then introduce the concepts of 'like' and 'dislike' with the *gern / nicht gern* symbols.

The context here is that Rudi (p. 6) is writing to Emily in England to tell her about his hobbies before she visits him in Germany.

4a Hör zu und lies. Ordne die Bilder. (AT1 Level 4, AT3 Level 4)

Pupils listen to a recording of Rudi's e-mail while they read it. They then put the pictures in the order in which they are mentioned.

Answers

f, e, a, b, g, d, c, h

Hallo Emily!
Bald kommst du nach München – hurra! Vielen Dank für die Informationen über deine Lieblingshobbys. Hier unten findest du alles über meine Lieblingshobbys!
Mein Hobby Nummer eins ist Fußball! Ich spiele sehr gern Fußball. Am Wochenende mache ich das mit meinen Freunden im Park. Ich sehe auch gern fern. Seifenopern und Krimis gefallen mir am besten. Ich spiele gern Computerspiele. Ich habe einen Computer im Zimmer und manchmal spiele ich auch bei meinem besten Freund, Peter. Ich gehe gern ins Kino – gestern habe ich einen Film gesehen, aber er war sehr langweilig. Was sonst? Ach ja, ich höre gern Musik. Meine Lieblingsgruppe ist „Die Größten". Magst du sie auch? Ich lese ziemlich gern, aber meistens nur Comics. Und was mache ich nicht gern? Tja, ich fahre nicht gern Ski – das finde ich zu anstrengend. Und ich gehe nicht gern einkaufen – das ist stinklangweilig!
Bis bald, Rudi.

4b Hör zu. Was macht Emily gern? (AT1 Levels 4–5)

Pupils listen to Emily talking about her likes and dislikes and note down what she says.

Answers

Fußball ✓, fernsehen ✓, Computerspiele ✗, Kino ✓, Musik ✗, lesen ✓, Ski ✗, einkaufen ✓

- Hallo, Emily, wie geht's?
- Ach, sehr gut, danke.
- Sag mal, Emily, spielst du gern Fußball?
- Fußball? Ja, klar, ich spiele sehr gern Fußball.
- Und siehst du gern fern?
- Sehe ich gern fern? Ja, jeder sieht gern fern, oder? Ich sehe sehr gern fern, besonders Talkshows. Die liebe ich!
- Und spielst du gern Computerspiele?
- Computerspiele? Nein, Computerspiele finde ich so langweilig. Ich spiele nicht gern Computerspiele.
- Gehst du auch gern ins Kino, Emily?
- Ja, ich gehe sehr gern ins Kino und am liebsten mag ich Zeichentrickfilme – sie finde ich so lustig.
- Und wie steht's mit Musik? Hörst du gern Musik?
- Nein, eigentlich nicht. Ich höre nicht gern Musik. Das mache ich nur selten.
- Also, liest du vielleicht lieber?
- Ja, ich liebe Bücher und ich lese jeden Tag.
- Fährst du gern Ski?
- Nein! Das habe ich nur einmal gemacht, aber es war schrecklich und so kalt.
- O je. Gehst du gern einkaufen, Emily?
- Ja, ich gehe sehr gern einkaufen! Das mache ich samstags mit meinen Freundinnen.

Ludwig: Note-taking while listening

Point out Ludwig's advice before pupils do activity 4b and encourage them to jot down abbreviated notes, rather than try to write full sentences. After the activity, pupils could compare their notes with a partner to see whether they used the same abbreviations or not, and whether they can learn some useful hints from their partner.

R Further practice on coping with listening activities is provided on Arbeitsblatt 5 (R & A File p. 72).

► 4c Was machen Emily und Rudi (nicht) gern? (AT4 Level 3)

Pupils bring together their information from activities 4a and 4b to work out what Rudi and Emily both like or dislike.

Answers

Sie spielen gern Fußball. Sie sehen gern fern. Sie gehen gern ins Kino. Sie lesen gern. Sie fahren nicht gern Ski.

Wiederholung: The present tense (plural)

Work through the grammar revision box with pupils, pointing out that the *wir/sie/Sie* form is identical with the infinitive of the verb and ends in *-en*. The *ihr* form is provided here for reference, but pupils are not expected to use it productively.

5 Partnerarbeit. Seht euch die Bilder zu Übung 4a an. (AT2 Level 3)

Pupils work in pairs to question each other about the pictures in activity 4a. Encourage pupils to ask questions with both *gern* and *nicht gern* to practise both forms.

6 Was machst du gern? Was machst du nicht gern? Schreib eine E-Mail wie in Übung 4a. (AT4 Level 4–5)

Pupils copy the example provided by Rudi at the top of the page to write an e-mail outlining their likes and dislikes.

Further practice of this unit's language is to be found on p. 110 of the Pupil's Book, activity 1.

Further practice of this unit's language is to be found on p. 111 of the Pupil's Book, activity 1.

3 Emilys Austausch (pp. 10–11)

Pupils will learn how to:
- understand and use everyday expressions for a visit

Key language	
Hallo!	Bitte sehr.
Guten Tag!	Guten Appetit!
Wie geht's?	Wie bitte?
Gut danke.	Entschuldigung!
Schönes Wochenende!	**Skill focus**
Gute Nacht!	• pronunciation
Gute Reise!	
Das war lecker.	**Resources**
Bis bald!	• Cassette A, Side A
Tschüs!	• Workbook p. 3
Auf Wiedersehen!	• R & A File:
Sprechen Sie Englisch?	Arbeitsblatt 5 (p. 51)
Danke sehr. / Vielen Dank.	

This unit introduces useful expressions for a visit to Germany in the context of Emily's arrival in Munich to stay with Rudi. Go through the dialogues presented here with the class and then practise them, perhaps using simple sketches of a waving hand (*Wie geht's? Gut danke. Wie geht's dir?*), a knife and fork (*Guten Appetit!*) and a bed (*Gute Nacht!*) as prompts.

1a Hör zu und wiederhole. Welches Bild ist das? (1–14) (AT1 Level 2)

Pupils listen to extracts taken from three dialogues between Rudi and Emily and identify each extract.

Answers

1 b, **2** a, **3** b, **4** c, **5** b, **6** c, **7** c, **8** b, **9** a, **10** b, **11** a, **12** c, **13** b, **14** b

1 – Guten Appetit, Emily!
2 – Hallo. Wie geht's?
3 – Äh, was ist das?
4 – Gute Nacht, Rudi.
5 – Danke. Guten Appetit!
6 – O.K., gute Nacht.
7 – Ja, aber ich bin sehr müde und morgen machen wir viel!
8 – Aber ich bin Vegetarierin.
9 – Sehr gut! Gehen wir nach Hause?
10– Also, hier ist Brot und Käse für dich.
11– Gut, danke. Wie geht's dir?
12– Aber es ist erst neun Uhr.
13– Das ist Weißwurst. Eine Spezialität aus München.
14– O, isst du gern Brot und Käse?

1b Hör zu und lies die Dialoge. Beantworte die Fragen. (AT3 Level 3)

Pupils listen to and read the dialogues in full and then answer the questions about them. There is no need for them to write full sentences.

Answers

1 München, **2** mit dem Flugzeug, **3** gut, **4** eine Spezialität aus München, **5** Emily, **6** Brot und Käse, **7** um neun Uhr, **8** gute Nacht

– Emilys Austauschpartner ist Rudi. Er wohnt in München, in Süddeutschland. Letzte Woche hat Emily Rudi besucht. Am Samstag ist sie nach München geflogen.

– Hallo. Wie geht's?
– Gut, danke. Wie geht's dir?
– Sehr gut! Gehen wir nach Hause?
– Ja.

– Guten Appetit, Emily.
– Äh, was ist das?
– Das ist Weißwurst. Eine Spezialität aus München.
– Aber ich bin Vegetarierin.
– O, isst du gern Brot und Käse?
– Ja.
– Also, hier ist Brot und Käse für dich.
– Danke. Guten Appetit!

– Gute Nacht, Rudi.
– Aber es ist erst neun Uhr.
– Ja, aber ich bin sehr müde und morgen machen wir viel!
– O.K., gute Nacht.

E Pupils translate the dialogues into English, noting how many of the German words are similar to English words.

1c Partnerarbeit. Lest die Dialoge zu zweit vor. Ändert die Details, wenn ihr wollt. (AT2 Levels 3–4)

Pupils work in pairs to create their own dialogues along the lines of those on p. 10. The best examples could be performed to the whole class.

At this point introduce the remaining useful expressions (see 'Key language' above) using mime or simple sketches.

2 Rudi hat eine Liste von Ausdrücken für Emily gemacht. Was passt zusammen? (AT3 Level 2)

Pupils read the list of expressions as prepared by Rudi and match each one to its English equivalent.

Answers

1 k, **2** h, **3** a, **4** j, **5** i, **6** d, **7** n, **8** c, **9** l, **10** e, **11** g, **12** m, **13** b, **14** f

► 3a Hör zu und wiederhole. Wie heißt das auf Englisch? (1–14) (AT1 Level 2)

Pupils listen to and repeat the expressions and note down their English meanings.

Answers

1 Hello. How are you? **2** Good night. **3** Enjoy your meal. **4** Do you speak English? **5** Hello. **6** Have a nice weekend. **7** Have a good trip. **8** That was tasty. **9** See you soon. **10** Bye. **11** Goodbye. **12** Thank you. You're welcome. **13** Pardon? **14** Sorry.

1 – Hallo. Wie geht's?
2 – Gute Nacht.
3 – Guten Appetit!
4 – Sprechen Sie Englisch?
5 – Guten Tag.
6 – Schönes Wochenende!
7 – Gute Reise!
8 – Das war lecker.
9 – Bis bald.
10 – Tschüs.
11 – Auf Wiedersehen.
12 – Danke sehr.
– Bitte sehr.
13 – Wie bitte?
14 – Entschuldigung.

Ludwig: Pronunciation – imitate the recording carefully

Point out Ludwig's advice about improving one's German pronunciation by copying the speaker on the cassette. Play each expression on the cassette once more and ask pupils to imitate it as closely as possible.

Further practice on coping with speaking activities and pronunciation issues is provided on Arbeitsblatt 5 (p. 51) in the R & A File.

3b Partnerarbeit. Testet einander. (AT2 Level 2)

Pupils test each other on the expressions with an English–German quiz. Pupils could also do this activity the other way round, asking: *Wie heißt ... auf Englisch?*

4 Was kann Emily sagen? Pass auf – manchmal gibt es zwei oder drei Antworten. (AT3 Level 2)

Pupils read seven scenarios and choose the appropriate responses.

Answers

1 Gute Nacht. **2** Guten Appetit. / Das war lecker. **3** Wie bitte? **4** Schönes Wochenende. **5** Hallo. / Guten Tag. **6** Gute Reise. / Auf Wiedersehen. **7** Tschüs. / Bis bald. / Auf Wiedersehen.

Pupils write mini-dialogues based on the language they have learned on this spread. Encourage them to act them out to the class with expression.

MINI-TEST

At the end of the third unit in every chapter, there is a *Mini-Test*. This is intended as a half-way checkpoint for pupils to check that they are familiar with the key language of the chapter so far. Pupils could revise the language with a partner in class or for homework.

4 Was hast du gemacht?
(pp. 12–13)

Pupils will learn how to:
- talk about what they did on a trip

Key language	Ich bin ...
Was hast du heute gemacht?	ins Kino gegangen
Ich habe ...	Ski gefahren
Fußball gespielt	einkaufen gegangen
Musik gehört	**Resources**
ferngesehen	• Cassette A, Side A
gelesen	• Workbook pp. 4, 7
Computerspiele gespielt	• R & A File: Arbeitsblatt 2 (p. 5), Grammatik 2 (p. 10)

This unit revises the perfect tense with *haben* and *sein* from Logo! 2. Copy Arbeitsblatt 2 onto an OHT. Introduce the hobbies in the perfect tense by saying what you did yesterday. Then ask pupils to complete your sentences: *Ich habe Computerspiele* ... and finally ask pupils: *Was hast du gestern gemacht?* while pointing to a visual.

For further oral practice, give each pair of pupils a copy of the visuals. One partner says a sentence and the other one indicates which visual matches the sentence. Alternatively, one partner points to a visual, asking: *Was hast du gestern gemacht?* and the other pupil supplies the answer.

1a Hör zu und lies. (AT1 Level 4, AT3 Level 4)
Pupils listen to and read a dialogue between Emily and Rudi's father, in which Emily explains what she did today.

– Na, Emily? Was hast du heute gemacht?
– Ach, ich hatte einen hektischen Tag! Ich habe Fußball gespielt – das war anstrengend! Ich bin einkaufen gegangen und ich habe viele Souvenirs gekauft. Was habe ich sonst alles gemacht? Tja, ich habe ferngesehen, gelesen und Musik gehört und ich habe Computerspiele gespielt. Ach, ja, und ich bin ins Kino gegangen! Was haben Sie denn gemacht, Herr Stein?
– Ich? Tja, ich bin nach Österreich gefahren und ich bin Ski gefahren!
– Wie bitte?
– Ja, ich bin Ski gefahren – Österreich ist nur achtzig Kilometer von München!

1b Beschrifte die Fotos. Was haben sie heute gemacht? Was sagen sie? (AT4 Level 3)
Pupils look at the photos and label each one with a perfect tense expression to explain what Emily or Mr Stein did today.

Answers

a Ich habe gelesen. **b** Ich bin einkaufen gegangen. **c** Ich bin ins Kino gegangen. **d** Ich bin Ski gefahren. **e** Ich habe Musik gehört. **f** Ich habe Computerspiele gespielt. **g** Ich habe ferngesehen. **h** Ich habe Fußball gespielt.

2 Hör zu. Was haben sie heute gemacht? Mach Notizen. (1–2) (AT1 Level 5)
Pupils listen and make notes about what two people did today. Remind pupils of the importance of just jotting down abbreviated notes rather than writing full sentences while they listen. After they have done the listening activity, pupils could expand on their notes to write sentences in the *ich* form.

Answers

1 Computerspiele gespielt, Comics gelesen, ins Kino gegangen, einkaufen gegangen (Souvenirs gekauft);
2 Ski gefahren, ferngesehen, Fußball gespielt, Musik gehört.

1 – Was hast du heute gemacht?
– Also, am Vormittag habe ich Computerspiele gespielt. Das war wunderbar.
– Und was hast du danach gemacht?
– Tja, dann habe ich fünf Comics gelesen. Comics lese ich besonders gern.
– Und nach dem Lesen? Was hast du dann gemacht?
– Also, um zwei Uhr bin ich ins Kino gegangen. Ich habe den neuen Disney-Film gesehen und er war toll.
– Ach, schön. Hast du dann sonst noch was gemacht?
– Ja, ich bin einkaufen gegangen und ich habe einige Souvenirs gekauft.
– Ach, das war ein voller Tag!

2 – Und du? Was hast du heute gemacht?
– Ich? Am Vormittag bin ich Ski gefahren. Das war echt klasse.
– Super. Und was hast du dann gemacht?
– Am Nachmittag habe ich ferngesehen. Ich war sehr müde!
– Ja, das glaube ich. Also hast du sonst nichts gemacht, oder?
– Doch, ich habe Fußball gespielt.
– Fußball gespielt? Aber du warst müde, nicht?
– Ja, aber meine Freunde haben Fußball gespielt, also habe ich mitgespielt.
– Meine Güte! Was hast du nach dem Fußball gemacht? Bist du vielleicht schwimmen gegangen?
– Nein, ich habe Musik gehört. Das war toll.

3 Was hat Rudis Schwester heute gemacht? Ordne die Bilder. (AT3 Level 5)
Pupils read an account by Rudi's sister of what she has done today and put the pictures in the order in which the activities are mentioned.

Answers

c, g, f, d, b, a, e

4 Partnerarbeit. Memoryspiel: Wer hat den aktivsten Tag gehabt? (AT2 Levels 4–5)
Pupils play a chain game in which they each add a new activity and remember those which went before.

Refer to pp. 130–31 of the Pupil's Book for information on word order in the perfect tense. More practice of this grammar point is also provided on Grammatik 2 (R & A File p. 10) and on p. 7 of the Workbook.

5a Schreib eine Präsentation über deinen Tag wie im Text zu Übung 3 (mindestens acht Sachen). (AT4 Levels 4–6)
Pupils write a text about a busy day they have had, including at least eight activities. Encourage pupils to use the expressions provided to make their work more interesting and also remind them that the form of *haben* or *sein* must come in second place.

5b Nimm deine Präsentation auf Kassette auf und vergleiche sie mit einem Partner / einer Partnerin. (AT2 Levels 4–5)
Pupils record their texts on a cassette, making sure that they speak clearly and with a good German accent. They then swap their recordings with a partner and give each other feedback.

5 Was hat er gemacht?

(pp. 14–15)

Pupils will learn how to:

- talk about what other people have done

Key language as the previous unit, but third person forms **Grammar focus** • perfect tense with *haben* or *sein* (revision)	**Resources** • Cassette A, Side A • Workbook pp. 5, 7 • R & A File: Arbeitsblatt 2 (p. 5)

This unit practises the perfect tense in the third person singular. Remind pupils that *er/sie hat* and *er/sie ist* are the forms they will need to use. Distribute the visuals from Arbeitsblatt 2 around the class and ask questions such as: *Was hat Josh gemacht?* to elicit the answer: *Er hat Musik gehört.*

The context of this unit is a newspaper report of an accident which Emily had while out on a bike ride with Rudi.

1a Hör zu und lies. Hörst du sechs Fehler auf der Kassette? (AT1 Levels 5–6, AT3 Levels 5–6)

Pupils listen to and read the report about the bike accident and see if they can spot six mistakes in the recorded version.

Answers

England = „Schottland", Um zwei Uhr = „Um <u>ein</u> Uhr", auf der linken Seite des Radwegs = „auf der <u>rechten</u> Seite des Radwegs", er hat seinen Vater angerufen = „er hat seine <u>Mutter</u> angerufen", Herr Stein = „<u>Frau</u> Stein", Kopfschmerzen = „<u>Magen</u>schmerzen"

Emily Lloyd, 14, aus Yorkshire, **Schottland**, hat gestern einen Unfall gehabt. Emily hat eine Radtour mit ihrem deutschen Brieffreund, Rudi Stein, 14, gemacht. Um **ein** Uhr haben sie Picknick gemacht und dann sind sie im Starnberger See schwimmen gegangen. Das Wasser war sehr kalt und nachher ist Emily bald wieder mit dem Rad gefahren. Leider hat die Engländerin etwas vergessen – in Deutschland fährt man rechts. Emily ist auf der **rechten** Seite des Radwegs gefahren. Ein anderer Radfahrer ist gekommen und rums!, die zwei sind zum Boden gefallen. Zum Glück hatte Rudi sein Handy dabei und er hat **seine Mutter** angerufen. **Frau** Stein ist sofort mit dem Auto gekommen und hat Rudi und Emily gefunden. Die Engländerin hat sich den Arm wehgetan und sie hatte **Magen**schmerzen. „Das nächste Mal fahre ich rechts", sagte sie.

1b Richtig, falsch oder nicht im Text? (AT3 Level 5)

Pupils read ten statements about the report and decide if they are true, false or not mentioned in the text.

Answers

1 nicht im Text, **2** richtig, **3** falsch, **4** falsch, **5** nicht im Text, **6** richtig, **7** falsch, **8** nicht im Text, **9** falsch, **10** nicht im Text

► 1c Lies den Artikel noch mal. Finde das Perfekt von folgenden Verben. Wie heißen sie auf Englisch? (AT2, Level 5)

Pupils read the report again and pick out the perfect tense phrases.

Answers

1 sind gegangen – went, **2** hat vergessen – forgot, **3** hat gefunden – found, **4** hat gemacht – did, **5** hat gehabt – had, **6** ist gefahren – drove/went, **7** sind gefallen – fell, **8** ist gekommen – came, **9** hat angerufen – phoned **10** hat (sich) wehgetan – hurt

► 1d Mach ein Interview mit Emily und Rudi für die Lokalnachrichten. (AT2 Levels 4–6)

Pupils work in pairs to conduct an interview with Emily and Rudi for the local news. Encourage them to use their imagination and include a certain amount of media sensationalism in their interview. The best examples can be performed for the rest of the class to enjoy and recorded on video, if video equipment is available.

2a Hör zu. Wer hat das auf Austausch gemacht? (1–6) (AT1 Level 2)

Pupils look at a grid giving details of what some of the other teenagers from p. 6 did on their exchange visits and decide who is being described each time.

Answers

1 Lucas, **2** Nicolas, **3** Lisa und Lucas, **4** Nicolas und Lucas, **5** Lisa und Nina, **6** Nina

1 – Er hat einen Unfall gehabt.
2 – Er ist Ski gefahren.
3 – Sie sind schwimmen gegangen.
4 – Sie sind einkaufen gegangen.
5 – Sie sind mit dem Rad gefahren.
6 – Sie hat eine Radtour gemacht und sie hat Musik gehört.

Wiederholung: The perfect tense with *haben* or *sein*

This grammar revision box brings together all the parts of the perfect tense and most participles met to date. Ask pupils to write six sentences in the perfect tense, using a different form of *haben* and *sein* and a different participle each time.

2b Ergänze die Sätze mit *haben* oder *sein*.
Pupils copy and complete the gapped sentences with the correct form of *haben* or *sein*.

Answers
1 Nicolas ist Ski gefahren. **2** Lucas hat einen Unfall gehabt. **3** Lisa und Lucas sind schwimmen gegangen. **4** Lisa und Nina haben eine Radtour gemacht. **5** Nicolas hat ein Buch gelesen. **6** Lucas hat Computerspiele gespielt.

An exercise on this grammar point is provided on p. 7 of the Workbook.

2c Partnerarbeit. Stellt Fragen und beantwortet sie. (AT2 Level 3)
Pupils question each other about the teenagers featured above. The language grid below gives them the constructions they will need.

3 Gestern hast du einen Unfall gesehen. Beschreib den Unfall für die Lokalzeitung. (AT4 Levels 4–6)
Pupils imagine that they witnessed an accident yesterday and write a report about it for the local newspaper. Encourage pupils to look back at the article on p. 14 in their books and pick out any expressions they could use in their own writing. Brainstorm ideas together as a class if necessary.

Further practice of this unit's language is to be found on p. 110 of the Pupil's Book, activity 2.

Further practice of this unit's language is to be found on p. 111 of the Pupil's Book, activity 2.

6 Souvenirs (pp. 16–17)

Pupils will learn how to:
- buy souvenirs

Key language Hallo, kann ich dir helfen? Ja, haben Sie … ? Kulis Bierkrüge Kassetten Pflanzen Bücher T-Shirts Ja, sie sind dort drüben. Nein, es tut mir Leid, wir haben keine … Was kostet dieser/diese/dieses … ? Kuli Bierkrug Kassette Pflanze Buch T-Shirt	Geht das? Soll ich den/die/das … als Geschenk einpacken? Danke. / Vielen Dank. *Prices in Euros* **Grammar focus** • 'the' and 'this' **Skill focus** • German–English dictionary for plurals **Resources** • Cassette A, Side A • Workbook p. 6 • R & A File: Arbeitsblatt 3 (p. 6), 6 (p. 30), Grammatik 3 (p. 11)

This unit introduces and practises a dialogue for buying souvenirs while in Germany. Introduce the souvenirs orally by copying the visuals on Arbeitsblatt 3 onto an OHT. Introduce the concept of 'this', by pointing to one of a group of items, e.g. one of the beer mugs, saying: *dieser Bierkrug.*

For further oral practice, distribute a set of the visuals to each pair of pupils. They cut them up, shuffle them and take six each. One pupil then asks: *Haben Sie … ?* If the other pupil has one of that item, he/she hands it over, saying: *Ja, hier ist der/die/das …* . If he/she has more than one of the item, he/she answers: *Ja, hier sind …* . If the pupil does not have the item, he/she answers: *Nein, es tut mir Leid.*

1 Hör zu und wiederhole. Ordne die Fotos. (AT1 Level 3)

Pupils listen to and repeat the shopping dialogue and then put the photos in the correct order.

Answers

d, b, a, c

– Hallo, kann ich dir helfen?
– Ja, haben Sie Bierkrüge?
– Ja, sie sind dort drüben.
– Danke … Was kostet dieser Bierkrug?
– Fünfzehn Euro zehn. Geht das?
– Ja.
– Soll ich den Bierkrug als Geschenk einpacken?
– O ja, vielen Dank.

2a Was passt zusammen? (AT3 Level 2)

Pupils read the sentences and match them to the artwork.

Answers

1 c, **2** a, **3** d, **4** e, **5** b, **6** f

2b Beschrifte die Bilder a–f – Singular und Plural.

Pupils label the artwork, giving the singular and plural form each time with *dieser*. A grammar box is provided to support them in the task.

Answers

a dieses Buch – diese Bücher, **b** dieser Bierkrug – diese Bierkrüge, **c** dieser Kuli – diese Kulis, **d** dieses T-Shirt – diese T-Shirts, **e** diese Kassette – diese Kassetten, **f** diese Pflanze – diese Pflanzen

Ludwig: German–English dictionary for plurals

Point out Ludwig's advice to pupils. It shows them how to find out the plural of a German noun. Remind pupils that German nouns all form their plurals individually; thus the plural form needs to be learned along with the gender when they come across a new noun. Also remind pupils that if they are looking up the plural of a compound noun, they will need to look up the final part of the compound. So, for *Bierkrug*, they will need to look up the plural of *Krug*. Give pupils a few more nouns to look up in a dictionary as a timed exercise.

R Further practice in using reference sources is provided on Arbeitsblatt 6 (p. 30) in the R & A File.

Grammatik: 'The' and 'this'

This grammar box shows the declension of *der* and *dieser* in the nominative and accusative cases. Remind pupils that they need to use the accusative case after *es gibt* … and whenever a noun is the direct object of a verb. Point out to pupils that *dieser* has similar endings to *der*.

R Refer to pp. 123–124 of the Pupil's Book for further information. More practice of this grammar point is also provided on Grammatik 3 (R & A File p. 11).

3a Hör zu. Schreib die Tabelle ab und füll sie aus. (1–5) (AT1 Level 4)

Pupils listen to five dialogues in a souvenir shop and note down what each person bought, how much it cost and whether it was a present or not. Remind pupils to listen carefully to the pronunciation in the dialogues, as they will shortly be practising their own dialogues. Version 1 of the tape has prices in Deutschmarks while Version 2 uses Euros.

Answers

	hat gekauft	hat gekostet	Geschenk?
1	Kassette	€6,25	nein
2	Buch	€20	ja
3	Pflanze	€4	ja
4	T-Shirt	€10	ja
5	Kuli	(€9,99	ja

1 – Hallo, kann ich dir helfen?
– Ja, haben Sie Bücher?
– Nein, es tut mir Leid, wir haben keine Bücher.
– O, haben Sie Kassetten?
– Ja, sie sind dort drüben.
– Danke ... Was kostet diese Kassette?
– Sechs Euro fünfundzwanzig.
Geht das?
– Ja.
– Soll ich sie als Geschenk einpacken?
– O nein, es geht so.

2 – Hallo, kann ich dir helfen?
– Ja, haben Sie Bücher über München?
– Ja, sie sind dort drüben.
– Danke ... Was kostet dieses Buch?
– Moment mal ... also das Buch kostet zwanzig Euro.
Geht das?
– Ja.
– Soll ich das Buch als Geschenk einpacken?
– O ja, vielen Dank.

3 – Hallo, kann ich dir helfen?
– Ja, haben Sie Pflanzen?
– Ja, sie sind dort drüben.
– Danke ... Was kostet diese Pflanze hier?
– Vier Euro.
– Super – ich nehme sie für meine Mutter. Sie hat heute Geburtstag!

4 – Hallo, kann ich dir helfen?
– Ja, haben Sie Sweatshirts?
– Nein, es tut mir Leid, wir haben keine Sweatshirts, aber wir haben viele T-Shirts.
– O, was kostet dieses T-Shirt hier?
– Moment mal ... es kostet zehn Euro.
– Wie bitte?
– Zehn Euro.
– O.K., ich nehme es für meinen Bruder.
– Soll ich das T-Shirt als Geschenk einpacken?
– O ja, vielen Dank.

5 – Hallo, kann ich dir helfen?
– Ja, haben Sie Kulis?
– Ja, sie sind dort drüben.
– Danke ... Was kostet dieser Kuli?
– Neun Euro neunundneunzig. Geht das?
– Ja, O.K.
– Soll ich ihn als Geschenk einpacken?
– O ja, der ist für meine Großmutter.

3b Was haben sie gekauft? Schreib Sätze. (AT4 Levels 3–4)

Pupils write sentences to describe the outcome of each shopping dialogue. Remind pupils that they will need to use the accusative case to do this, so *ein* (masculine, not neuter) becomes *einen* when they describe the object each person has bought.

Answers

Nummer eins hat eine Kassette gekauft. Die Kassette hat €6,25 gekostet. Nummer zwei hat ein Buch gekauft. Das Buch hat €20 gekostet. Nummer drei hat eine Pflanze gekauft. Die Pflanze hat €4 gekostet. Nummer vier hat ein T-Shirt gekauft. Das T-Shirt hat €10 gekostet. Nummer fünf hat einen Kuli gekauft. Der Kuli hat €9,99 gekostet.

4 Partnerarbeit. Macht Dialoge. (AT2 Level 4)

Pupils conduct their own dialogues in a souvenir shop. Encourage them to use expression and to be as lively as possible when they perform them. Pupils could bring along suitable souvenirs they have bought on holiday or they could use the visuals on Arbeitsblatt 3 to make a mock shop counter.

5 Schreib einen Dialog für diese Geschenke. (AT4 Level 4)

Pupils write a dialogue based on one of the items in the clouds. Remind pupils that they will probably need to look up the plural form in a dictionary.

► 7 Partnersuche (pp. 18–19)

Resources
- Cassette A, Side A

The *MEHR* unit is intended as extension material for more able pupils. Pupils will be more challenged by the longer reading texts and by exercises which draw together all the language of the chapter.

The context of this unit is a teenage friendship service on the internet.

1a Lies die Texte. Wer macht das gern? (AT3 Level 5)

Pupils read the personal information provided by four teenagers and decide who enjoys doing each of the hobbies depicted.

Answers

a Sonja, Dirk, **b** Sonja, **c** Miguel, **d** Dirk, Veronika, **e** Miguel, **f** Miguel, Veronika, **g** Dirk, Veronika, **h** Miguel

1b Mach Steckbriefe für die Jugendlichen aus Übung 1a. (AT4 Level 2–3)

Pupils prepare ID cards for each of the teenagers in activity 1a.

Answers

Name: Miguel, **Nationalität**: Spanier, **Alter**: 15, **Wohnort**: Barcelona, **Hobbys**: Ski fahren, lesen, fernsehen, einkaufen gehen
Name: Dirk, **Nationalität**: Deutscher, **Alter**: –, **Wohnort:** Jena, **Hobbys**: Computerspiele spielen, Musik hören, ins Kino gehen, Videos ansehen
Name: Veronika, **Nationalität**: Französin, **Alter**: –, **Wohnort**: Bordeaux, Frankreich, **Hobbys**: Musik hören, fernsehen, Computerspiele spielen
Name: Sonja, **Nationalität**: Österreicherin, **Alter**: 14, **Wohnort**: Wien, **Hobbys**: Fußball und Tennis spielen, ins Kino gehen

1c Beantworte folgende Fragen. (AT3 Levels 5–6)

Pupils answer ten comprehension questions on the texts in German. Point out to pupils that in questions 5 and 10 they will have to change 'my' (e.g. *mit meiner Familie*) in the text to 'her' (e.g. *mit ihrer Familie*) for the answer. They should answer in complete sentences.

Answers

1 Er ist Ski gefahren. **2** Er kann nicht viel kaufen – er hat kein Geld. **3** Die Hauptstadt von Österreich heißt Wien. **4** Sie ist an die italienische Küste gefahren. **5** Sie ist mit ihrer Familie gefahren. **6** Sie hat die Liga gewonnen. **7** Er bekommt immer schlechte Noten in Englisch. **8** Er besucht eine Hauptschule. **9** Sie findet Deutsch schwierig. **10** Sie hat viele Computerspiele mit ihrem kleinen Bruder gespielt.

2a Hör zu. Schreib die Tabelle ab und füll sie aus. (1–4) (AT1 Level 5)

Pupils listen to four teenagers talking about themselves and they note down the details in a grid.

Answers

	Alter	kommt aus	wohnt in	Hobbys	in den Ferien
1	15	Österreich	Deutschland	fernsehen, Musik	nach Spanien gefahren
2	14	Italien	Deutschland	Fußball, Tennis, Kino	Großmutter in Berlin besucht
3	16	Deutschland	München	Ski, lesen, einkaufen	zu Hause spielt Fußball
4	15	England	Yorkshire	Musik, Computerspiele, Kino	ins Kino gegangen

1 – Ja, hallo. Tja, ich bin jetzt fünfzehn Jahre alt ... ja, und ich komme aus Österreich. Ich wohne jetzt in Deutschland und ich höre gern Musik und ich sehe gern fern. Ja, in den Ferien bin ich nach Spanien gefahren, na ja ... und das war total toll.
2 – Hallo. Tja, ich bin vierzehn Jahre alt und ich komme aus Rom, in Italien. Aber jetzt wohne ich in Deutschland. Ansonsten in meiner Freizeit spiele ich gern Fußball und Tennis und ich gehe gern ins Kino. In den Ferien habe ich meine Großmutter in Berlin besucht, aber das war ziemlich langweilig.
3 – Ja, hallo erstmal. Ja, ich bin gerade 16 Jahre alt geworden und komme aus Deutschland. Ich bin in München geboren, aber ich will da so schnell wie es geht weg. Ich will in die Schweiz. Ich fahre sehr gerne Ski. Ja, das macht mir einfach Spaß. Ich lese gerne. In den Ferien bin ich zu Hause. Ja. Ich spiele jeden Tag Fußball.
4 – Ja, hallo. Ich bin jetzt fünfzehn Jahre alt und ich komme aus Gloucestershire. Das liegt in England. Aber jetzt wohne ich in Yorkshire, und meine Hobbys sind Musik hören und Computerspiele spielen. Ich gehe aber auch ziemlich gern ins Kino. In den Ferien bin ich sehr oft ins Kino gegangen und das war sehr super.

2b Finde einen passenden Partner / eine passende Partnerin auf Seite 18 für sie. (AT3 Levels 5–6)

Pupils look at their answers from the listening activity and match each of the speakers to the most compatible teenager from p. 18.

Answers

Nummer 1 und Veronika, Nummer 2 und Sonja, Nummer 3 und Miguel, Nummer 4 und Dirk

3a Erfinde eine Identität und mach einen Steckbrief dafür. (AT4 Level 2)

Pupils complete an ID card for themselves, assuming a false identity.

3b Gruppenarbeit. Finde den besten Partner / die beste Partnerin für dich in der Klasse. (AT2 Level 4)

Pupils circulate in the class and try to find somebody who would make a compatible partner.

3c Schreib eine E-Mail über deine neue Identität wie auf Seite 18. Beschreib auch das, was du neulich gemacht hast. (AT4 Levels 5–6)

Pupils write an e-mail to the friendship service on the internet giving personal details and also information about what they have done recently.

Lernzieltest and Wiederholung (pp. 20–21)

Resources
- Cassette, A, Side A
- Workbook pp. 8–10
- R & A File: Wortschatz pp. 12–13

Lernzieltest p. 14
Kontrolle 1 pp. 15–24 (including teacher's notes)

At the end of each chapter there is a revision unit for pupils to use before the assessment materials. The unit begins with a *Lernzieltest* (like the *Mini-Test*) for pupils to test themselves on key language from the chapter. This is also provided as a checklist for pupils to write on (R & A File p. 14) and some related gapped sentences are also provided on p. 10 of the Workbook.

If pupils are unsure of any of the language, they should be encouraged to revise the relevant unit in the chapter. A complete wordlist containing key words and phrases from the whole chapter is provided on the *Wortschatz* sheets (R & A File pp. 12–13).

Wiederholung provides pupils with revision exercises in the four skills. The listening exercises should be done in class, but the other exercises could be done either in class or for homework. Further revision exercises are provided on pp. 8–9 of the Workbook.

Wiederholung

Hören

1 Hör zu. Schreib die Tabelle ab und füll sie aus. (1–5) (AT1 Level 3)

Pupils listen to five teenagers being interviewed and note down their names, ages, places of residence and nationalities.

Answers

	Name	Alter	Wohnt in	Nationalität
1	Judith	14	Madrid	Spanierin
2	Ulrich	16	Bremen	Deutscher
3	Miriam	15	Rom	Deutsche
4	Wanda	17	Paris	Französin
5	Erik	14	Linz	Österreicher

1 – Wie heißt du?
– Ich heiße Judith. J.U.D.I.T.H.
– Und wie alt bist du, Judith?
– Ich bin vierzehn Jahre alt.
– Und wo wohnst du?
– Ich wohne in Madrid.
– Ach, bist du dann Spanierin?
– Ja, ich bin in Spanien geboren.
2 – Wie heißt du?
– Ich heiße Ulrich. U.L.R.I.C.H.
– Und wie alt bist du, Ulrich?
– Ich bin sechzehn Jahre alt.
– Wie bitte?
– Ich bin sechzehn Jahre alt.
– Danke. Und wo wohnst du?
– Ich wohne in Bremen.
– Und kommst du auch aus Bremen?
– Ja.
– Du bist also Deutscher?
– Ja.
3 – Wie heißt du?
– Ich heiße Miriam. M.I.R.I.A.M.
– Wie alt bist du, Miriam?
– Ich bin fünfzehn Jahre alt.
– Fünfzehn Jahre alt. Sehr gut. Wo wohnst du?
– Ich wohne in Rom.
– Ach, sehr schön. Bist du dort geboren?
– Nein, ich komme aus Deutschland. Ich bin Deutsche.
4 – Wie heißt du?
– Ich heiße Wanda.
– Wanda?
– Ja, Wanda – W.A.N.D.A.
– Alles klar. Wie alt bist du, Wanda?
– Ich bin siebzehn Jahre alt.
– Siebzehn Jahre. ... Und wo wohnst du?
– Ich wohne in Paris.
– Ach, Paris ist eine sehr schöne Stadt, nicht? Hast du immer dort gewohnt?
– Ja, ich komme aus Paris – ich bin Französin.
5 – Wie heißt du?
– Ich heiße Erik. E.R.I.K.
– Gut. Erik, wie alt bist du?
– Ich bin vierzehn Jahre alt.
– Und wo wohnst du?
– Ich wohne in Linz, in Österreich.
– Sehr gut. Bist du denn Österreicher?
– Ja, das bin ich.

2 Hör zu. Was hat Georg heute gemacht? Mach Notizen. (AT1 Level 5)

Pupils listen to Georg describing what he has done today and note down the activities he mentions.

Answers

Fußball gespielt, gefrühstückt, Musik gehört, ferngesehen, gelesen, Computerspiele gespielt, in die Stadt gefahren, einkaufen gegangen, ins Kino gegangen

Also, heute habe ich sehr viel gemacht. Um acht Uhr in der Früh habe ich mit meinem Freund Fußball gespielt. Das war sehr lustig, aber ein bisschen anstrengend. Also habe ich nachher gefrühstückt und auch Musik gehört. Um elf Uhr kam meine Lieblingssendung im Fernsehen, also habe ich sie gesehen und dann habe ich ein Buch gelesen – das war ein englisches Buch, das ich für meine Hausaufgaben lesen musste. Langweilig! Nach dem Mittagessen habe ich Computerspiele gespielt. Das finde ich immer total spannend und ich habe drei Stunden lang gespielt. Dann bin ich schnell in die Stadt gefahren und ich habe meine Freundin getroffen. Wir sind zusammen einkaufen gegangen und dann sind wir ins Kino gegangen. Leider war der Film total langweilig und doof, also bin ich eingeschlafen.

Sprechen

3 Partnerarbeit. Wie viele Informationen kannst du herausfinden? (AT2 Levels 4–5)

Pupils interview each other to find out as much personal information about their partner as possible.

esen

4 Lies den Brief und ordne die Bilder. Beantworte dann die Fragen. (AT3 Levels 4–5)

Pupils read a letter from Jochen and put the pictures in the order in which they are mentioned in the letter. Pupils then answer ten comprehension questions in German. They should answer in full sentences where appropriate.

Answers

, b, d, c, a

1 Er heißt Jochen. **2** Er ist fünfzehn Jahre alt. **3** Er kommt aus St. Johann, Österreich. **4** Er wohnt in Leipzig, Deutschland. **5** Er hat Hockey gespielt. **6** Nein. **7** Er war sehr spannend. **8** Er hat sein Portemonnaie verloren. **9** Er ist Ski gefahren (und hat sich das Bein gebrochen). **10** Nein.

Schreiben

5 Schreib eine Antwort an. (AT4 Levels 4–5)

Pupils write a reply to Jochen in which they answer the questions at the bottom of his letter.

► EXTRA

The EXTRA pages at the back of the Pupil's Book are intended to provide consolidation/reinforcement activities (EXTRA A) and more challenging / extension activities (EXTRA B). The exercises concentrate on the skills of reading and writing only. They could be used for differentiated work in class or at home. The best place to use each activity is clearly indicated in these notes, just above the exercise rubric, e.g. [after pp. 8–9].

EXTRA A (p. 110)

[after pp. 8–9]

1a Ergänze die Steckbriefe für Olaf, Gabi und Frank. (AT3 Level 3)

Pupils read the speech bubbles and complete the ID forms for Olaf, Gabi und Frank.

Answers

Name: Olaf Schmidt, **Alter**: 15, **Geburtsort**: Dresden, Deutschland, **Nationalität**: Deutscher, **Wohnort**: München, **Hobbys**: Tennis, Ski fahren
Name: Gabi Ross, **Alter**: 14, **Geburtsort**: Hull, **Nationalität**: Engländerin, **Wohnort**: Wien, **Hobbys**: fernsehen, Musik
Name: Frank Max, **Alter**: 16, **Geburtsort**: Paris, Frankreich, **Nationalität**: Franzose, **Wohnort**: Berlin, **Hobbys**: Kino, einkaufen

1b Mach einen Steckbrief für dich. Kannst du auch einen kurzen Text schreiben? (AT4, Levels 3–4)

Pupils write their own ID form. Some pupils might also like to write a short text about themselves, giving their name, age, nationality and place of residence, as in activity 1a.

[after pp. 14–15]

2a Was passt zusammen? (AT3 Level 2)

Pupils match the pictures to the perfect tense sentences.

Answers

1 g, **2** d, **3** h, **4** b, **5** c, **6** f, **7** e, **8** a

2b Ergänze die Sätze.

Pupils complete the sentences in the perfect tense, using the help box.

Answers

1 Er hat ein Buch gelesen und er hat ferngesehen.
2 Marti ist einkaufen gegangen. Sie hat ein Buch gekauft.
3 Ich habe Tennis im Park gespielt. Ich bin auch ins Kino gegangen. **4** Ich bin einkaufen gegangen und ich habe Computerspiele gespielt. **5** Kai und Marti haben ferngesehen und sie haben Musik gehört. **6** Kai und Marti sind Ski gefahren. Sie haben auch Fußball gespielt.

2c Was hast du letztes Wochenende gemacht? Schreib mindestens sechs Sätze. (AT4 Levels 4–5)

Pupils write at least six sentences to explain what they did last weekend.

EXTRA B (p. 111)

[after pp. 8–9]

1a Beantworte die Fragen für Hannes, Lisa und Nicole. (AT4 Levels 2–3)

Pupils read the ID forms and answer the questions about Hannes, Lisa and Nicole. They should answer in complete sentences.

Answers

Hannes: **1** Ich heiße Hannes Becker. **2** Ich bin fünfzehn Jahre alt. **3** Ich komme aus Deutschland. **4** Ich bin Deutscher. **5** Ich wohne in Frankfurt. **6** Ich spiele gern Tennis und ich fahre gern Ski.
Lisa: **1** Ich heiße Lisa Kemp. **2** Ich bin vierzehn Jahre alt. **3** Ich komme aus England. **4** Ich bin Engländerin. **5** Ich wohne in Linz. **6** Ich sehe gern fern und ich höre gern Musik.
Nicole: **1** Ich heiße Nicole Lehmann. **2** Ich bin sechzehn Jahre alt. **3** Ich komme aus Frankreich. **4** Ich bin Französin. **5** Ich wohne in Berlin. **6** Ich gehe gern ins Kino und ich gehe gern einkaufen.

1b Beantworte die Fragen für dich. (AT4 Levels 2–3)

Pupils answer the questions (in complete sentences), giving their personal details.

[after pp. 14–15]

2a Lies die E-Mail und ergänze die Tabelle mit Ausdrücken im Perfekt. Wie heißt das auf Englisch? (AT3 Level 5)

Pupils read the e-mail about a hectic weekend and gather together all the perfect tense phrases in a table.

Answers

ich bin gefahren (I went), wir sind gefahren (we went), er hat vergessen (he forgot), wir sind gekommen (we came), er ist gegangen (he went), ich habe ferngesehen (I watched TV), ich habe gehört (I listened to), ich bin gegangen (I went), er ist geblieben (he stayed), er hat gegessen (he ate), er hat getrunken (he drank), er hat gespielt (he played), ich habe gemacht (I did), ich bin gesurft (I surfed), ich habe gefunden (I found), du hast gemacht (you did)

2b Beantworte die Fragen. (AT3 Level 5)
Pupils then answer questions about the hectic weekend. They should answer in complete sentences.

Answers
1 Er ist am Samstag Ski gefahren. **2** Karls Bruder kann nicht gut Ski fahren. **3** Er hat seine Jacke vergessen. **4** Sie sind um fünf Uhr nach Hause gekommen. **5** Er hat ferngesehen und ein bisschen Musik gehört. **6** Karls Bruder hat Computerspiele gespielt. **7** Er hat Informationen über Sommercamps in Italien gefunden. **8** Er will nach Italien fahren.

2c Was hast du am Wochenende gemacht? Schreib eine E-Mail an Karl. (AT4 Levels 5–6)
Pupils write a reply to Karl's e-mail, describing their activities last weekend in as much detail as they can.

Workbook

p. 1

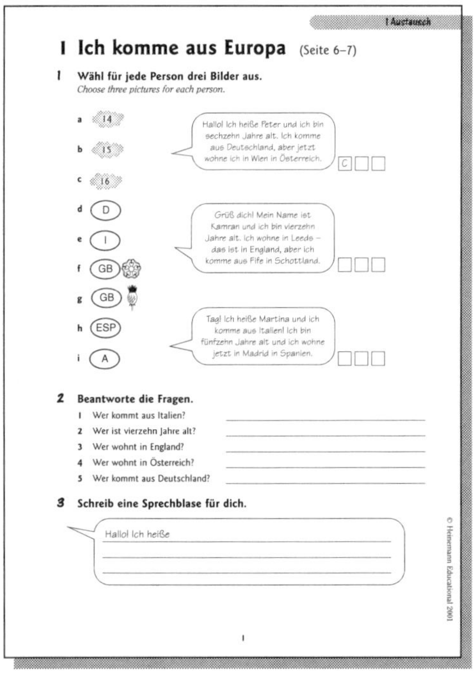

1 (AT3 Level 3)
Peter: c, d, i; **Kamran:** a, f, g; **Martina:** e, b, h
2 (AT3 Level 3)
1 Martina, **2** Kamran, **3** Kamran, **4** Peter, **5** Peter
3 (AT4 Level 3)
individual answers

p. 2

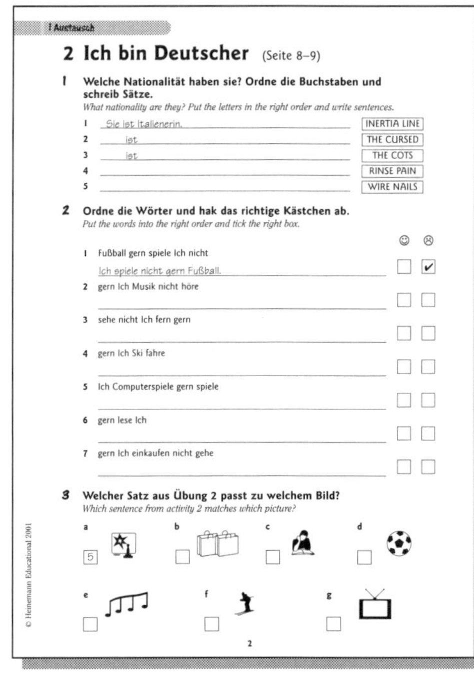

1 (AT4 Level 2)
1 Sie ist Italienerin. **2** Er ist Deutscher. **3** Er ist Schotte. **4** Sie ist Spanierin. **5** Sie ist Waliserin.
2 (AT4 Level 2)
1 Ich spiele nicht gern Fußball. ☹ **2** Ich höre nicht gern Musik. ☹ **3** Ich sehe nicht gern fern. ☹ **4** Ich fahre gern Ski. ☺ **5** Ich spiele gern Computerspiele. ☺ **6** Ich lese gern. ☺ **7** Ich gehe nicht gern einkaufen. ☹
3 (AT3 Level 2)
a 5, **b** 7, **c** 6, **d** 1, **e** 2, **f** 4, **g** 3

p. 3

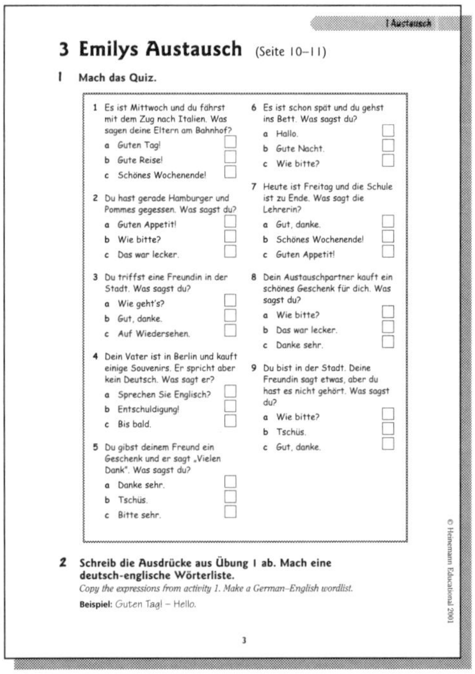

1 (AT3 Level 4)
1 b, **2** c, **3** a, **4** a, **5** c, **6** b, **7** b, **8** c, **9** a
2 (AT4 Level 3)
Guten Tag! – Hello; Gute Reise! – Have a good trip! / Bon voyage!; Schönes Wochenende! – Have a good/nice weekend!; Guten Appetit! – Enjoy your meal.; Wie bitte? – Pardon?; Das war lecker. – That was delicious.; Wie geht's? – How are you?; Gut, danke. – Fine/Well, thanks.; Auf Wiedersehen. – Goodbye.; Sprechen Sie Englisch? – Do you speak English?; Entschuldigung! – Sorry!; Bis bald. – Bye for now. / See you soon.; Danke sehr. – Many thanks. / Thanks a lot; Tschüs. – Bye.; Bitte sehr. – You're welcome.; Hallo. – Hello/Hi.; Gute Nacht. – Goodnight.

p. 4

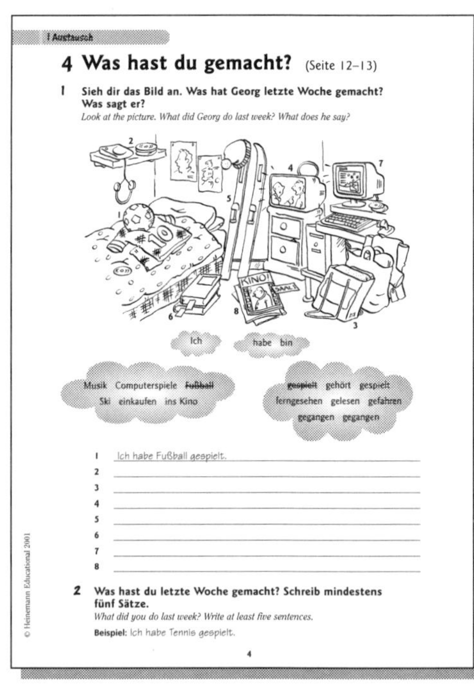

1 (AT4 Level 3)
1 Ich habe Fußball gespielt. **2** Ich habe Musik gehört. **3** Ich bin einkaufen gegangen. **4** Ich habe ferngesehen. **5** Ich bin Ski gefahren. **6** Ich habe gelesen. **7** Ich habe Computerspiele gespielt. **8** Ich bin ins Kino gegangen.
2 (AT4 Levels 4–5)
individual answers

p. 5

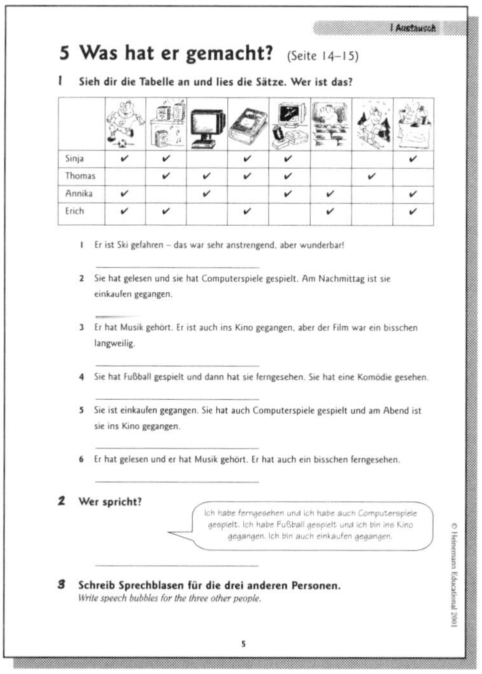

I Austausch

5 Was hat er gemacht? (Seite 14–15)

1 Sieh dir die Tabelle an und lies die Sätze. Wer ist das?

Sinja	✔	✔		✔	✔			✔
Thomas		✔	✔	✔	✔		✔	
Annika	✔		✔		✔	✔		✔
Erich	✔	✔		✔		✔		✔

1 Er ist Ski gefahren – das war sehr anstrengend, aber wunderbar!

2 Sie hat gelesen und sie hat Computerspiele gespielt. Am Nachmittag ist sie einkaufen gegangen.

3 Er hat Musik gehört. Er ist auch ins Kino gegangen, aber der Film war ein bisschen langweilig.

4 Sie hat Fußball gespielt und dann hat sie ferngesehen. Sie hat eine Komödie gesehen.

5 Sie ist einkaufen gegangen. Sie hat auch Computerspiele gespielt und am Abend ist sie ins Kino gegangen.

6 Er hat gelesen und er hat Musik gehört. Er hat auch ein bisschen ferngesehen.

2 Wer spricht?

Ich habe ferngesehen und ich habe auch Computerspiele gespielt. Ich habe Fußball gespielt und ich bin ins Kino gegangen. Ich bin auch einkaufen gegangen.

3 Schreib Sprechblasen für die drei anderen Personen.
Write speech bubbles for the three other people.

© Heinemann Educational 2001

5

1 (AT3 Level 3)
1 Thomas, **2** Sinja, **3** Erich, **4** Annika, **5** Annika, **6** Thomas
2 (AT3 Level 4)
Annika
3 (AT4 Level 4)
individual answers

p. 6

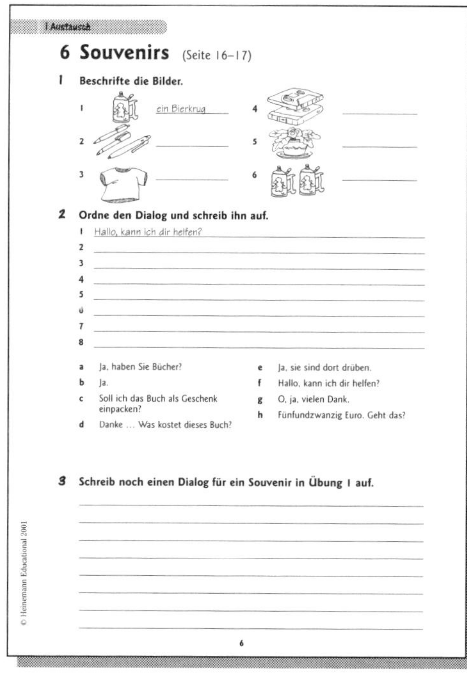

I Austausch

6 Souvenirs (Seite 16–17)

1 Beschrifte die Bilder.

1 ein Bierkrug
2
3
4
5
6

2 Ordne den Dialog und schreib ihn auf.

1 Hallo, kann ich dir helfen?
2
3
4
5
6
7
8

a Ja, haben Sie Bücher?
b Ja.
c Soll ich das Buch als Geschenk einpacken?
d Danke ... Was kostet dieses Buch?
e Ja, sie sind dort drüben.
f Hallo, kann ich dir helfen?
g O, ja, vielen Dank.
h Fünfundzwanzig Euro. Geht das?

3 Schreib noch einen Dialog für ein Souvenir in Übung 1 auf.

© Heinemann Educational 2001

6

1 (AT4 Level 1)
1 ein Bierkrug, **2** drei Kulis, **3** ein T-Shirt, **4** zwei Kassetten, **5** eine Pflanze, **6** zwei Bierkrüge
2 (AT4 Level 2)
f, a, e, d, h, b, c, g
3 (AT4 Level 3)
individual answers

p. 7

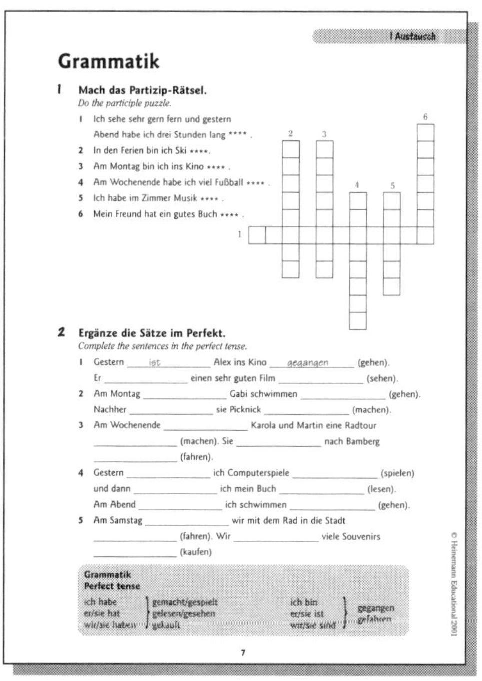

I Austausch

Grammatik

1 Mach das Partizip-Rätsel.
Do the participle puzzle.

1 Ich sehe sehr gern fern und gestern Abend habe ich drei Stunden lang **** .
2 In den Ferien bin ich Ski **** .
3 Am Montag bin ich ins Kino **** .
4 Am Wochenende habe ich viel Fußball **** .
5 Ich habe im Zimmer Musik **** .
6 Mein Freund hat ein gutes Buch **** .

2 Ergänze die Sätze im Perfekt.
Complete the sentences in the perfect tense.

1 Gestern ist Alex ins Kino gegangen (gehen). Er ______ einen sehr guten Film ______ (sehen).
2 Am Montag ______ Gabi schwimmen ______ (gehen). Nachher ______ sie Picknick ______ (machen).
3 Am Wochenende ______ Karola und Martin eine Radtour ______ (machen). Sie ______ nach Bamberg ______ (fahren).
4 Gestern ______ ich Computerspiele ______ (spielen) und dann ______ ich mein Buch ______ (lesen). Am Abend ______ ich schwimmen ______ (gehen).
5 Am Samstag ______ wir mit dem Rad in die Stadt ______ (fahren). Wir ______ viele Souvenirs ______ (kaufen).

Grammatik
Perfect tense
ich habe / er/sie hat / wir/sie haben } gemacht/gespielt / gelesen/gesehen / gekauft
ich bin / er/sie ist / wir/sie sind } gegangen / gefahren

© Heinemann Educational 2001

7

1 **1** ferngesehen, **2** gefahren, **3** gegangen, **4** gespielt, **5** gehört, **6** gelesen
2 **1** ist gegangen, hat gesehen, **2** ist gegangen, hat gemacht, **3** haben gemacht, sind gefahren, **4** habe gespielt, habe gelesen, bin gegangen, **5** sind gefahren, haben gekauft

p. 8

I Austausch

Wiederholung

Paulas Austausch

traurig	*sad*
kaputt	here: *exhausted*

Samstag: Heute bin ich mit dem Zug nach München gefahren. Meine Austauschpartnerin, Karina, war am Bahnhof. Sie wohnt in München, aber sie kommt aus Leipzig.
Sonntag: Heute sind wir zu Hause geblieben. Ich habe ein bisschen gelesen und ferngesehen. Um neun Uhr bin ich ins Bett gegangen.
Montag: Ich habe Fußball gespielt! Das war super und ich war den ganzen Tag im Park. Ich spiele sehr gern Fußball.
Dienstag: Heute war es langweilig und ich habe nur Computerspiele gespielt. Es hat den ganzen Tag geregnet.
Mittwoch: Heute sind wir nach Österreich gefahren und wir sind dort Ski gefahren. Das war wunderbar, aber sehr anstrengend. Am Abend war ich kaputt!
Donnerstag: Heute sind wir einkaufen gegangen und ich habe Souvenirs gekauft. Ich habe einen Bierkrug für meinen Bruder, eine Kassette für meine Schwester und ein T-Shirt für meine Mutter gekauft.
Freitag: Am Abend bin ich mit Karina und ihrem Freund ins Kino gegangen. Der Film war O.K. Karinas Freund ist Italiener und sehr nett.
Samstag: Heute bin ich wieder nach Hause gefahren. Ich war ein bisschen traurig. Karina hat mir «Gute Reise» gewünscht.

1 Lies das Tagebuch. An welchem Tag war das?

1 am Dienstag
2
3
4
5
6
7
8
9
10

© Heinemann Educational 2001

8

1 (AT3 Level 5)
1 am Dienstag, **2** am Montag, **3** am Sonntag, **4** am Mittwoch, **5** am Freitag, **6** am Donnerstag, **7** am Samstag, **8** am Sonntag, **9** am Sonntag, **10** am Samstag

p. 9

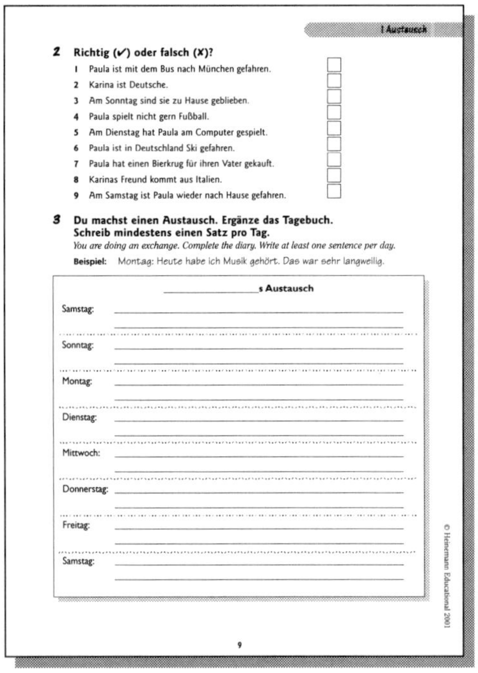

1 Austausch

2 Richtig (✓) oder falsch (✗)?

1 Paula ist mit dem Bus nach München gefahren.
2 Karina ist Deutsche.
3 Am Sonntag sind sie zu Hause geblieben.
4 Paula spielt nicht gern Fußball.
5 Am Dienstag hat Paula am Computer gespielt.
6 Paula ist in Deutschland Ski gefahren.
7 Paula hat einen Bierkrug für ihren Vater gekauft.
8 Karinas Freund kommt aus Italien.
9 Am Samstag ist Paula wieder nach Hause gefahren.

3 Du machst einen Austausch. Ergänze das Tagebuch. Schreib mindestens einen Satz pro Tag.
You are doing an exchange. Complete the diary. Write at least one sentence per day.
Beispiel: Montag: Heute habe ich Musik gehört. Das war sehr langweilig.

______s Austausch

Samstag:
Sonntag:
Montag:
Dienstag:
Mittwoch:
Donnerstag:
Freitag:
Samstag:

© Heinemann Educational 2001

9

p. 10

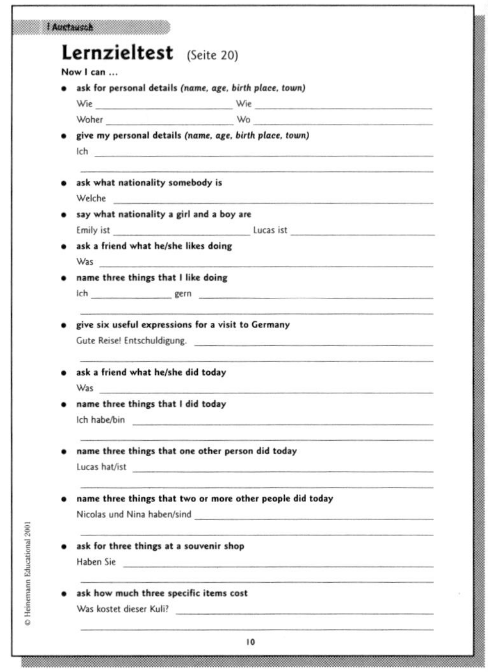

1 Austausch

Lernzieltest (Seite 20)

Now I can ...

- **ask for personal details *(name, age, birth place, town)***
  Wie ______ Wie ______
  Woher ______ Wo ______
- **give my personal details *(name, age, birth place, town)***
  Ich ______
- **ask what nationality somebody is**
  Welche ______
- **say what nationality a girl and a boy are**
  Emily ist ______ Lucas ist ______
- **ask a friend what he/she likes doing**
  Was ______
- **name three things that I like doing**
  Ich ______ gern ______
- **give six useful expressions for a visit to Germany**
  Gute Reise! Entschuldigung. ______
- **ask a friend what he/she did today**
  Was ______
- **name three things that I did today**
  Ich habe/bin ______
- **name three things that one other person did today**
  Lucas hat/ist ______
- **name three things that two or more other people did today**
  Nicolas und Nina haben/sind ______
- **ask for three things at a souvenir shop**
  Haben Sie ______
- **ask how much three specific items cost**
  Was kostet dieser Kuli? ______

© Heinemann Educational 2001

10

2 (AT3 Level 5)
1 ✗, 2 ✓, 3 ✓, 4 ✗, 5 ✓, 6 ✗, 7 ✗, 8 ✓, 9 ✓
3 (AT4 Level 5)
individual answers

individual answers

Resource & Assessment File

Arbeitsblatt 1
p. 4

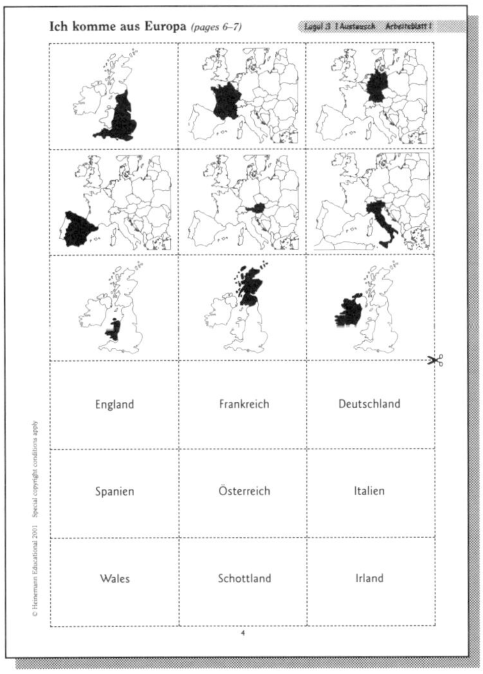

Ich komme aus Europa *(pages 6–7)*

Logo! 3 1 Austausch Arbeitsblatt 1

England	Frankreich	Deutschland
Spanien	Österreich	Italien
Wales	Schottland	Irland

© Heinemann Educational 2001 Special copyright conditions apply

4

Visuals of *England, Frankreich, Deutschland, Spanien, Österreich, Italien, Wales, Schottland, Irland*

Arbeitsblatt 2
p. 5

Ich bin Deutscher *(pages 8–9)*

Logo! 3 1 Austausch Arbeitsblatt 2

Ich spiele (nicht) gern Fußball.	Ich höre (nicht) gern Musik.	Ich lese (nicht) gern.
Ich sehe (nicht) gern fern.	Ich spiele (nicht) gern Computerspiele.	Ich gehe (nicht) gern ins Kino.
Ich fahre (nicht) gern Ski.	Ich gehe (nicht) gern einkaufen.	gern
	nicht gern	

© Heinemann Educational 2001 Special copyright conditions apply

5

Visuals of *Ich spiele (nicht) gern Fußball. Ich höre (nicht) gern Musik. Ich lese (nicht) gern. Ich sehe (nicht) gern fern. Ich spiele (nicht) gern Computerspiele. Ich gehe (nicht) gern ins Kino. Ich fahre (nicht) gern Ski. Ich gehe (nicht) gern einkaufen.*

Arbeitsblatt 3
p. 6

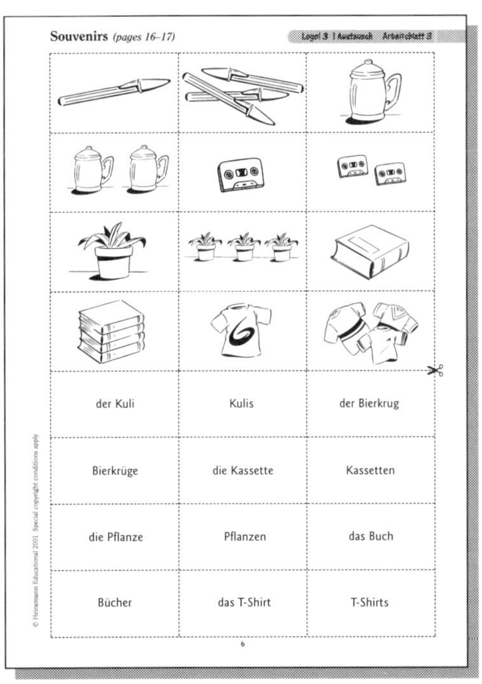

Souvenirs *(pages 16–17)*

Logo! 3 1 Austausch Arbeitsblatt 3

der Kuli	Kulis	der Bierkrug
Bierkrüge	die Kassette	Kassetten
die Pflanze	Pflanzen	das Buch
Bücher	das T-Shirt	T-Shirts

© Heinemann Educational 2001 Special copyright conditions apply

6

Visuals of *der Kuli, Kulis, der Bierkrug, Bierkrüge, die Kassette, Kassetten, die Pflanze, Pflanzen, das Buch, Bücher, das T-Shirt, T-Shirts*

Arbeitsblatt 4
p. 7

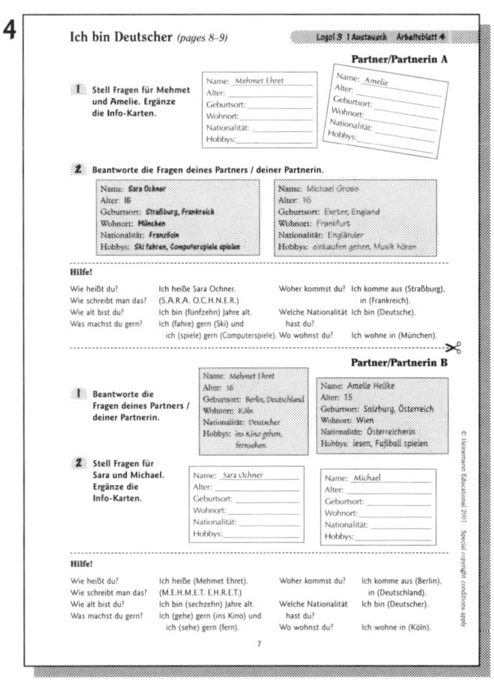

Ich bin Deutscher *(pages 8–9)*

Logo! 3 1 Austausch Arbeitsblatt 4

Partner/Partnerin A

1 Stell Fragen für Mehmet und Amelie. Ergänze die Info-Karten.

Name: *Mehmet Ehret*
Alter:
Geburtsort:
Wohnort:
Nationalität:
Hobbys:

Name: *Amelie*
Alter:
Geburtsort:
Wohnort:
Nationalität:
Hobbys:

2 Beantworte die Fragen deines Partners / deiner Partnerin.

Name: Sara Ochner
Alter: 15
Geburtsort: Straßburg, Frankreich
Wohnort: München
Nationalität: Französin
Hobbys: Ski fahren, Computerspiele spielen

Name: Michael Grose
Alter: 16
Geburtsort: Exeter, England
Wohnort: Frankfurt
Nationalität: Engländer
Hobbys: einkaufen gehen, Musik hören

Hilfe!

Wie heißt du?	Ich heiße Sara Ochner.	Woher kommst du?	Ich komme aus (Straßburg), in (Frankreich).
Wie schreibt man das?	(S.A.R.A. O.C.H.N.E.R.)		
Wie alt bist du?	Ich bin (fünfzehn) Jahre alt.	Welche Nationalität hast du?	Ich bin (Deutsche).
Was machst du gern?	Ich (fahre) gern (Ski) und ich (spiele) gern (Computerspiele).	Wo wohnst du?	Ich wohne in (München).

Partner/Partnerin B

1 Beantworte die Fragen deines Partners / deiner Partnerin.

Name: Mehmet Ehret
Alter: 16
Geburtsort: Berlin, Deutschland
Wohnort: Köln
Nationalität: Deutscher
Hobbys: ins Kino gehen, fernsehen

Name: Amelie Heilke
Alter: 15
Geburtsort: Salzburg, Österreich
Wohnort: Wien
Nationalität: Österreicherin
Hobbys: lesen, Fußball spielen

2 Stell Fragen für Sara und Michael. Ergänze die Info-Karten.

Name: *Sara Ochner*
Alter:
Geburtsort:
Wohnort:
Nationalität:
Hobbys:

Name: *Michael*
Alter:
Geburtsort:
Wohnort:
Nationalität:
Hobbys:

Hilfe!

Wie heißt du?	Ich heiße (Mehmet Ehret).	Woher kommst du?	Ich komme aus (Berlin), in (Deutschland).
Wie schreibt man das?	(M.E.H.M.E.T. E.H.R.E.T.)		
Wie alt bist du?	Ich bin (sechzehn) Jahre alt.	Welche Nationalität hast du?	Ich bin (Deutscher).
Was machst du gern?	Ich (gehe) gern (ins Kino) und ich (sehe) gern (fern).	Wo wohnst du?	Ich wohne in (Köln).

© Heinemann Educational 2001 Special copyright conditions apply

7

Information-gap activity on name, age, place of birth, place of residence, nationality and hobbies.

1 AT2 Level 4

2 AT2 Level 4

Arbeitsblatt 5
p. 8

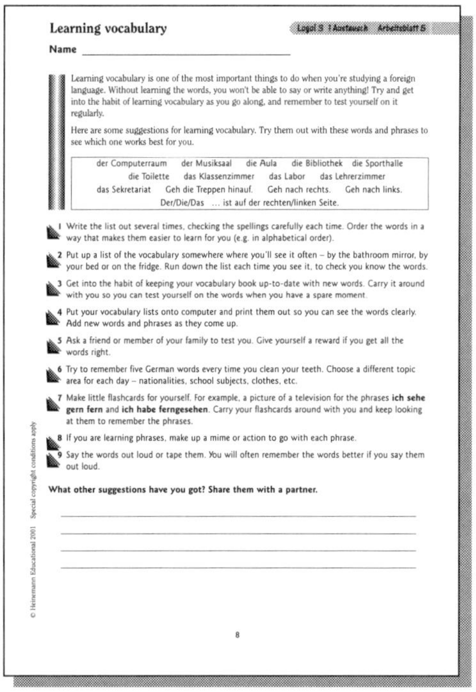

Learning vocabulary

Logo! 3 1 Austausch Arbeitsblatt 5

Name ____________

Learning vocabulary is one of the most important things to do when you're studying a foreign language. Without learning the words, you won't be able to say or write anything! Try and get into the habit of learning vocabulary as you go along, and remember to test yourself on it regularly.

Here are some suggestions for learning vocabulary. Try them out with these words and phrases to see which one works best for you.

der Computerraum der Musiksaal die Aula die Bibliothek die Sporthalle die Toilette das Klassenzimmer das Labor das Lehrerzimmer das Sekretariat Geh die Treppen hinauf. Geh nach rechts. Geh nach links. Der/Die/Das … ist auf der rechten/linken Seite.

1 Write the list out several times, checking the spellings carefully each time. Order the words in a way that makes them easier to learn for you (e.g. in alphabetical order).

2 Put up a list of the vocabulary somewhere where you'll see it often – by the bathroom mirror, by your bed or on the fridge. Run down the list each time you see it, to check you know the words.

3 Get into the habit of keeping your vocabulary book up-to-date with new words. Carry it around with you so you can test yourself on the words when you have a spare moment.

4 Put your vocabulary lists onto computer and print them out so you can see the words clearly. Add new words and phrases as they come up.

5 Ask a friend or member of your family to test you. Give yourself a reward if you get all the words right.

6 Try to remember five German words every time you clean your teeth. Choose a different topic area for each day – nationalities, school subjects, clothes, etc.

7 Make little flashcards for yourself. For example, a picture of a television for the phrases **ich sehe gern fern** and **ich habe ferngesehen**. Carry your flashcards around with you and keep looking at them to remember the phrases.

8 If you are learning phrases, make up a mime or action to go with each phrase.

9 Say the words out loud or tape them. You will often remember the words better if you say them out loud.

What other suggestions have you got? Share them with a partner.

Advice on learning vocabulary.

Grammatik 1
p. 9

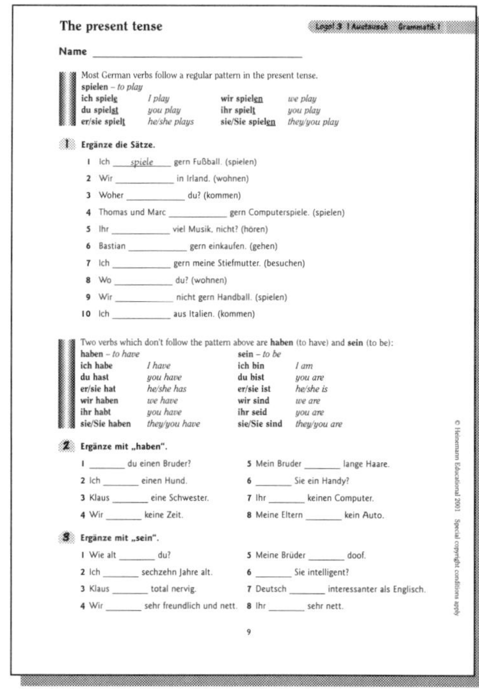

The present tense

Logo! 3 1 Austausch Grammatik 1

Name ____________

Most German verbs follow a regular pattern in the present tense.

spielen – *to play*

ich spiele	*I play*	**wir spielen**	*we play*
du spielst	*you play*	**ihr spielt**	*you play*
er/sie spielt	*he/she plays*	**sie/Sie spielen**	*they/you play*

1 Ergänze die Sätze.

1 Ich *spiele* gern Fußball. (spielen)
2 Wir ______ in Irland. (wohnen)
3 Woher ______ du? (kommen)
4 Thomas und Marc ______ gern Computerspiele. (spielen)
5 Ihr ______ viel Musik, nicht? (hören)
6 Bastian ______ gern einkaufen. (gehen)
7 Ich ______ gern meine Stiefmutter. (besuchen)
8 Wo ______ du? (wohnen)
9 Wir ______ nicht gern Handball. (spielen)
10 Ich ______ aus Italien. (kommen)

Two verbs which don't follow the pattern above are **haben** (to have) and **sein** (to be):

haben – *to have*		**sein** – *to be*	
ich habe	*I have*	**ich bin**	*I am*
du hast	*you have*	**du bist**	*you are*
er/sie hat	*he/she has*	**er/sie ist**	*he/she is*
wir haben	*we have*	**wir sind**	*we are*
ihr habt	*you have*	**ihr seid**	*you are*
sie/Sie haben	*they/you have*	**sie/Sie sind**	*they/you are*

2 Ergänze mit „haben".

1 ______ du einen Bruder?
2 Ich ______ einen Hund.
3 Klaus ______ eine Schwester.
4 Wir ______ keine Zeit.
5 Mein Bruder ______ lange Haare.
6 ______ Sie ein Handy?
7 Ihr ______ keinen Computer.
8 Meine Eltern ______ kein Auto.

3 Ergänze mit „sein".

1 Wie alt ______ du?
2 Ich ______ sechzehn Jahre alt.
3 Klaus ______ total nervig.
4 Wir ______ sehr freundlich und nett.
5 Meine Brüder ______ doof.
6 ______ Sie intelligent?
7 Deutsch ______ interessanter als Englisch.
8 Ihr ______ sehr nett.

Practice of the present tense.

1 **1** spiele, **2** wohnen, **3** kommst, **4** spielen, **5** hört, **6** geht, **7** besuche, **8** wohnst, **9** spielen, **10** komme

2 **1** Hast, **2** habe, **3** hat, **4** haben, **5** hat, **6** Haben, **7** habt, **8** haben

3 **1** bist, **2** bin, **3** ist, **4** sind, **5** sind, **6** Sind, **7** ist, **8** seid

Grammatik 2
p. 10

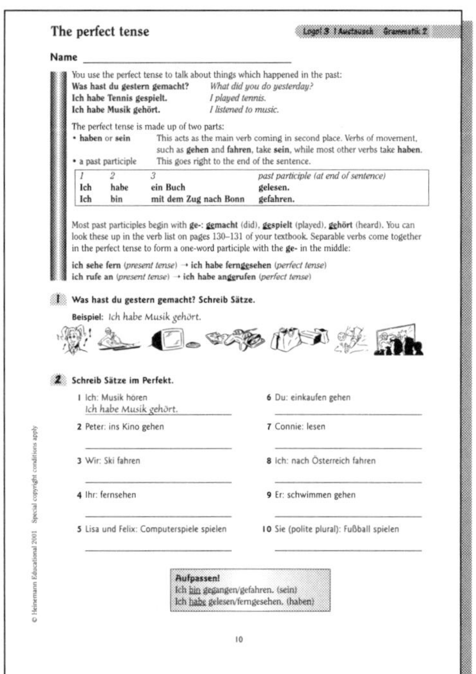

The perfect tense

Logo! 3 1 Austausch Grammatik 2

Name ____________

You use the perfect tense to talk about things which happened in the past:

Was hast du gestern gemacht? *What did you do yesterday?*
Ich habe Tennis gespielt. *I played tennis.*
Ich habe Musik gehört. *I listened to music.*

The perfect tense is made up of two parts:

- **haben** or **sein** – This acts as the main verb coming in second place. Verbs of movement, such as **gehen** and **fahren**, take **sein**, while most other verbs take **haben**.
- a past participle – This goes right to the end of the sentence.

1	*2*	*3*	*past participle (at end of sentence)*
Ich	**habe**	**ein Buch**	**gelesen.**
Ich	**bin**	**mit dem Zug nach Bonn**	**gefahren.**

Most past participles begin with **ge-**: **gemacht** (did), **gespielt** (played), **gehört** (heard). You can look these up in the verb list on pages 130–131 of your textbook. Separable verbs come together in the perfect tense to form a one-word participle with the **ge-** in the middle:

ich sehe fern (*present tense*) → **ich habe ferngesehen** (*perfect tense*)
ich rufe an (*present tense*) → **ich habe angerufen** (*perfect tense*)

1 Was hast du gestern gemacht? Schreib Sätze.

Beispiel: *Ich habe Musik gehört.*

2 Schreib Sätze im Perfekt.

1 Ich: Musik hören – *Ich habe Musik gehört.*
2 Peter: ins Kino gehen
3 Wir: Ski fahren
4 Ihr: fernsehen
5 Lisa und Felix: Computerspiele spielen
6 Du: einkaufen gehen
7 Connie: lesen
8 Ich: nach Österreich fahren
9 Er: schwimmen gehen
10 Sie (polite plural): Fußball spielen

Aufpassen!
Ich bin gegangen/gefahren. (sein)
Ich habe gelesen/ferngesehen. (haben)

Practice of the perfect tense.

2 **1** Ich habe Musik gehört. **2** Peter ist ins Kino gegangen. **3** Wir sind Ski gefahren. **4** Ihr habt ferngesehen. **5** Lisa und Felix haben Computerspiele gespielt. **6** Du bist einkaufen gegangen. **7** Connie hat gelesen. **8** Ich bin nach Österreich gefahren. **9** Er ist schwimmen gegangen. **10** Sie haben Fußball gespielt.

Grammatik 3
p. 11

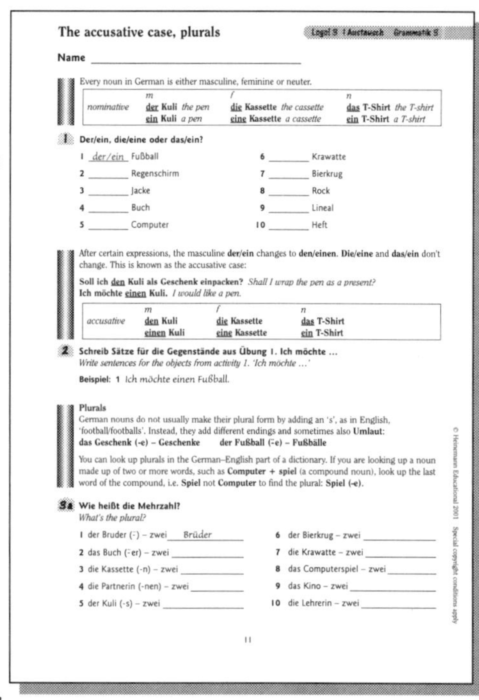

The accusative case, plurals

Logo! 3 1 Austausch Grammatik 3

Name ____________

Every noun in German is either masculine, feminine or neuter.

	m	*f*	*n*
nominative	**der Kuli** *the pen*	**die Kassette** *the cassette*	**das T-Shirt** *the T-shirt*
	ein Kuli *a pen*	**eine Kassette** *a cassette*	**ein T-Shirt** *a T-shirt*

1 Der/ein, die/eine oder das/ein?

1 *der/ein* Fußball
2 ______ Regenschirm
3 ______ Jacke
4 ______ Buch
5 ______ Computer
6 ______ Krawatte
7 ______ Bierkrug
8 ______ Rock
9 ______ Lineal
10 ______ Heft

After certain expressions, the masculine **der/ein** changes to **den/einen**. **Die/eine** and **das/ein** don't change. This is known as the accusative case:

Soll ich den Kuli als Geschenk einpacken? *Shall I wrap the pen as a present?*
Ich möchte einen Kuli. *I would like a pen.*

	m	*f*	*n*
accusative	**den Kuli**	**die Kassette**	**das T-Shirt**
	einen Kuli	**eine Kassette**	**ein T-Shirt**

2 Schreib Sätze für die Gegenstände aus Übung 1. Ich möchte …
Write sentences for the objects from activity 1. 'Ich möchte …'

Beispiel: 1 *Ich möchte einen Fußball.*

Plurals
German nouns do not usually make their plural form by adding an 's', as in English, 'football/footballs'. Instead, they add different endings and sometimes also **Umlaut**:
das Geschenk (-e) – Geschenke **der Fußball (¨-e) – Fußbälle**

You can look up plurals in the German–English part of a dictionary. If you are looking up a noun made up of two or more words, such as **Computer + spiel** (a compound noun), look up the last word of the compound, i.e. **Spiel** not **Computer** to find the plural: **Spiel (-e)**.

3a Wie heißt die Mehrzahl?
What's the plural?

1 der Bruder (¨) – zwei *Brüder*
2 das Buch (¨er) – zwei ______
3 die Kassette (-n) – zwei ______
4 die Partnerin (-nen) – zwei ______
5 der Kuli (-s) – zwei ______
6 der Bierkrug – zwei ______
7 die Krawatte – zwei ______
8 das Computerspiel – zwei ______
9 das Kino – zwei ______
10 die Lehrerin – zwei ______

Practice of the nominative and accusative cases and of plurals.

1 **1** der/ein Fußball, **2** der/ ein Regenschirm, **3** die/eine Jacke, **4** das/ ein Buch, **5** der/ein Computer, **6** die/eine Krawatte, **7** der/ein Bierkrug, **8** der/ein Rock, **9** das/ein Lineal, **10** das/ein Heft

2 **1** einen Fußball, **2** einen Regenschirm, **3** eine Jacke, **4** ein Buch, **5** einen Computer, **6** eine Krawatte, **7** einen Bierkrug, **8** einen Rock, **9** ein Lineal, **10** ein Heft

3a **1** Brüder, **2** Bücher, **3** Kassetten, **4** Partnerinnen, **5** Kulis

3b **1** Bierkrüge, **2** Krawatten, **3** Computerspiele, **4** Kinos, **5** Lehrerinnen

Wortschatz pp. 12–13 and Lernzieltest p. 14
These sheets are for revision at the end of the chapter. The *Wortschatz* sheet provides a list of all the key words and phrases from the chapter and the *Lernzieltest* gives a checklist of the areas covered, which pupils can check off as they revise.

2 Bei uns – bei euch (Pupil's Book pp. 24–41)

Topic area	Key language	Skills	Grammar	PoS
2.1 Schulfächer (pp. 24–25) Say why you like/dislike some subjects	*Magst du Religion, Deutsch, Erdkunde, Geschichte, Englisch, Französisch, Mathe, Physik-Chemie, Biologie, Sport, Musik, Kunst? Ja, ich mag* [subject] / *Nein, ich mag* [subject] *nicht, weil es interessant, nützlich, einfach, schwierig, langweilig, anstrengend, lustig ist.*	German-English dictionary	Word order after *weil* – verb to end	4c, 5c
2.2 Deutsch ist interessanter als Englisch (pp. 26–27) Compare your school subjects	*X ist interessanter, nützlicher, einfacher, schwieriger, langweiliger, anstrengender, lustiger, besser als Y, nicht? Ja, das stimmt. Nein, das stimmt nicht. X ist das interessanteste, nützlichste einfachste, schwierigste, langweiligste, anstrengendeste, lustigste, beste Fach, nicht?*	Pronunciation: umlauts	Comparatives and superlatives	1a, 2b, 5c
2.3 Die Hausordnung (pp. 28–29) Say what you are not allowed to do at school	*Was darf man in der Schule nicht machen? Man darf nicht rauchen, skaten, im Gang rennen, im Klassenzimmer kauen, spät zur Schule kommen. Man darf das Schulgelände nicht verlassen. Man darf niemanden hänseln oder ärgern, kein Zungenpiercing haben, keine Drogen mit in die Schule bringen, keinen Alkohol mit in die Schule bringen.*	Scanning text for key words	*dürfen* + infinitive to the end	2g, 2h, 3b, 5d
2.4 Nächstes Trimester (pp. 30–31) Talk about your plans for next term	*Was wirst du nächstes Trimester machen? Ich werde pünktlich zur Schule kommen, rechtzeitig Hausaufgaben machen, bessere Noten bekommen, viel Sport treiben, mit dem Rad zur Schule fahren, ein Instrument lernen, viel am Computer arbeiten, niemanden ärgern.*	Listening and repeating for intonation English-German dictionary for new words	Future tense	1b, 1c, 3d
2.5 Unsere Schule, eure Schule (pp. 32–33) Compare your school with a German school	*Wir stehen sehr / nicht so früh auf. Wir fahren oft mit dem Rad/ Auto/Bus zur Schule. Wir tragen keine/eine Uniform. Wir essen zu Hause / in der Kantine zu Mittag. Wir bleiben meistens/nicht im selben Klassenzimmer. Wir haben einige/viele AGs in der Schule. Wir haben manchmal/nie samstags Schule. Unsere Schule beginnt um acht/neun Uhr / endet gegen Mittag / drei Uhr. Am Nachmittag haben wir frei / bleiben wir in der Schule.*			4c, 4d
2.6 Wo ist die Bibliothek? (pp. 34–35) Direct someone around your school	*Entschuldigung, wo ist die Toilette, das Lehrerzimmer, der Musiksaal, das Klassenzimmer, das Labor, die Bibliothek, das Sekretariat, der Computerraum, die Aula, der Schulhof, die Sporthalle Der/Die/Das ... ist im ersten Stock / Erdgeschoss. Geh durch den Haupteingang. Geh die Treppen hinauf. Geh nach rechts/links. Der/Die/Das ... ist auf der rechten/linken Seite.*			2a, 3c, 5a
2.7 Lehrerzeugnis (pp. 36–37)		Extended reading		5b, 5f
Lernzieltest und Wiederholung (pp. 38–39)	Revision			5a, 5d
Wörter (pp. 40–41)	Word list			
Extra (pp. 112–113)	Differentiated reading and writing			3e

1 Schulfächer (pp. 24–25)

Pupils will learn how to:
- talk about why they like/dislike some subjects

Key language
Magst du ... ?
Religion
Deutsch
Erdkunde
Geschichte
Englisch
Französisch
Mathe
Physik-Chemie
Biologie
Sport
Musik
Kunst
Ja, ich mag ..., weil es ... ist.
Nein, ich mag ... nicht, weil es ... ist.
interessant
nützlich
einfach
schwierig
langweilig
anstrengend
lustig

Grammar focus
- word order after *weil* – verb to end

Skill focus
- German-English dictionary

Resources
- Cassette A, Side B
- Workbook pp. 11, 17
- R & A File: Arbeitsblatt 1 (p. 25), Grammatik 3 (p. 33)

This chapter explores various aspects of school life through the internet pages of the Thomas-Mann-Gymnasium, Freiburg.

This unit revises school subjects from Logo! 1 and introduces likes and dislikes through the use of *weil* clauses. Introduce the vocabulary orally first, using the visuals on Arbeitsblatt 1 (R & A File p. 25) copied onto an OHT to present the school subjects.

For further oral practice of school subjects, give each pair of pupils two copied sets of the visuals for them to cut up and place face-down on the desk. One pupil then turns over two visuals and gives the names of both subjects depicted. If a pupil turns over a matching pair, he/she can keep the cards. If the pair don't match, the pupil turns them back over and the other pupil has a go. The winner is the pupil with most pairs of cards.

1 Hör zu. Wie oft hat man das Fach am Thomas-Mann-Gymnasium? (1–12) (AT1 Level 1)

Pupils listen out for the subject mentioned each time and then find it on the timetable and note down how often the pupils have it each week.

Answers

1 fünfmal, **2** zweimal, **3** zweimal, **4** einmal, **5** dreimal, **6** viermal, **7** zweimal, **8** viermal, **9** zweimal, **10** zweimal, **11** fünfmal, **12** einmal

1 – Mathe
2 – Erdkunde
3 – Physik-Chemie
4 – Religion
5 – Sport
6 – Deutsch
7 – Kunst
8 – Französisch
9 – Geschichte
10 – Musik
11 – Englisch
12 – Biologie

2 Richtig oder falsch? (AT3 Level 2)

Pupils answer nine true/false statements about the frequency of subjects each week. Point out the meaning of *öfter als* (more often than) and practise further true/false statements orally in the class.

Answers

1 falsch, **2** richtig, **3** falsch, **4** richtig, **5** richtig, **6** falsch, **7** richtig, **8** richtig, **9** falsch

3 Mach eine Liste von 1 (dem besten Fach) bis 12 aus den Fächern oben. (AT4 Level 1)

Pupils list the school subjects in their personal order of preference.

4a Was bedeuten die unterstrichenen Adjektive auf Seite 25? Rate mal und überprüfe es dann im Wörterbuch. (AT3 Level 3)

Pupils read the text on p. 25 and try to work out what the adjectives mean. Any adjectives they cannot guess/remember can be looked up in a dictionary.

Answers

nützlich – useful, einfach – easy, interessant – interesting, lustig – funny (fun), anstrengend – tiring, schwierig – difficult, langweilig – boring

Ludwig: German–English dictionary

Point out Ludwig's advice and remind pupils that they can use a dictionary if they get stuck on a word. However, encourage pupils to try to guess or deduce words before they reach for a dictionary, and to see how many in the text on p. 25 can actually be guessed because they look like English, or because the context provides clues.

4b Hör zu. Wer spricht? (1–7) (AT1 Level 3)

Pupils listen and identify which of the teenagers from the website is talking each time.

Answers

1 Kathi, **2** Brigitte, **3** Nils, **4** Hasad, **5** Alex, **6** Lukas, **7** Lotte

1 – Ich mag Erdkunde, weil es lustig ist.
2 – Ich mag Französisch nicht, weil es schwierig ist.
3 – Ich mag Biologie nicht, weil es langweilig ist.
4 – Ich mag Englisch, weil es nützlich ist.
5 – Ich mag Deutsch, weil es einfach ist.
6 – Ich mag Sport nicht, weil es anstrengend ist.
7 – Ich mag Kunst, weil es interessant ist.

5 Hör zu. Wie finden sie die Fächer? Mach Notizen. (1–7) (AT1 Levels 3–4)

Pupils listen and note down seven teenagers' opinions of school subjects. They note down the subject and the adjective used to describe it.

Answers

1 Geschichte – langweilig, **2** Erdkunde – interessant, **3** Physik-Chemie – schwierig, **4** Musik – einfach, **5** Religion – lustig, **6** Französisch – nützlich, **7** Sport – anstrengend

1 – Magst du Geschichte?
– Nein, ich mag Geschichte nicht, weil es so langweilig ist. Der Lehrer ist total langweilig.
2 – Magst du Erdkunde?
– Erdkunde? Tja ... ja, ich mag Erdkunde, weil es interessant ist. Ich interessiere mich sehr für andere Länder.
3 – Magst du Physik-Chemie?
– Nein.
– Warum nicht?
– Weil es so schwierig ist. Dort verstehe ich fast kein Wort.
4 – Magst du Musik?
– Ja, ich mag Musik, weil es einfach ist! Ich spiele auch sehr gern Trompete.
5 – Und Religion? Magst du Religion?
– Ja, ich mag Religion, weil es lustig ist!
– Lustig?
– Ja, der Lehrer ist echt klasse und bringt uns alle zum Lachen.
6 – Magst du Französisch?
– Ja, ich mag Französisch, weil es nützlich ist. In den Ferien besuche ich meinen Austauschpartner in Paris.
7 – Magst du Sport?
– Nein, ich mag Sport nicht, weil es so anstrengend ist. Nach dem Sportunterricht bin ich immer kaputt!

6 Partnerarbeit. Schreib ein Adjektiv für jedes Fach für deinen Partner / deine Partnerin. Hast du richtig geraten? (AT2 Levels 3–4)

Pupils now guess what their partner thinks of each school subject, drawing up a list of subjects and adjectives. They then discuss their lists and see how accurate they were.

Grammatik: Word order after *weil* – verb to the end

Point out the grammar box to pupils and explain how *weil* joins two clauses to make a longer sentence. Stress the use of the comma before *weil* and the fact that the verb goes to the end of the sentence. Brainstorm as a class possible sentences using *weil*, and write them up on the board/OHT. Encourage pupils to use *weil* clauses wherever possible to make their writing and speaking more interesting.

R Refer to p. 133 of the Pupil's Book for further information. More practice of this grammar point is also provided on Grammatik 3 (R & A File p. 33) and on p. 17 of the Workbook.

7 Was schreibst du beim Schule-Chat? Schreib deine Meinung über deine Fächer auf. (AT4 Levels 3–4)

Pupils write their opinions about school subjects, following the style of the website at the top of the page.

2 Deutsch ist interessanter als Englisch (pp. 26–27)

Pupils will learn how to:
- compare their school subjects

Key language
X ist … als Y, nicht?
interessanter
nützlicher
einfacher
schwieriger
langweiliger
anstrengender
lustiger
besser
Ja, das stimmt.
Nein, das stimmt nicht.
X ist das … Fach, nicht?
interessanteste
nützlichste
einfachste
schwierigste
langweiligste
anstrengendeste
lustigste
beste

Grammar focus
- comparatives
- superlatives

Skill focus
- pronunciation: umlauts

Resources
- Cassette A, Side B
- Workbook p. 12
- R & A File: Grammatik 2, (p. 32)

This unit introduces comparatives and superlatives in the context of school subjects.

1a Hör zu. Sind sie derselben Meinung wie im Schul-Web? (1–8) (AT1 Levels 3–4)

Pupils listen and decide whether the statements they hear are the same as those they read on the web page.

Answers

1 nein, **2** ja, **3** ja, **4** ja, **5** ja, **6** nein, **7** nein, **8** nein

1 – Also, „Deutsch ist interessanter als Englisch." Findest du das richtig?
– Ach, nein. Englisch ist viel interessanter. Deutsch ist langweilig.
2 – O.K., „Biologie ist schwieriger als Sport." Stimmt das?
– Ja, das stimmt. Biologie ist sehr schwierig, finde ich.
3 – Und findest du Musik lustiger als Physik-Chemie?
– Ja, ich finde alles lustiger als Physik-Chemie!
4 – Und Sport? Findest du Sport anstrengender als Kunst?
– Ja, klar. Kunst ist gar nicht anstrengend.
5 – Und was meinst du hier? „Französisch ist nützlicher als Religion."
– Ja, das stimmt. Französisch ist sehr nützlich – mein Brieffreund ist Franzose!
6 – Jetzt bist du dran. Findest du Erdkunde einfacher als Geschichte?
– Tja, das weiß ich nicht so genau. Nein, ich finde Geschichte einfacher als Erdkunde.
7 – O.K., aber findest du Englisch langweiliger als Physik-Chemie?
– Nein, ich finde Physik-Chemie langweiliger – die Lehrerin ist super langweilig!
8 – Und was findest du besser – Sport oder Kunst?
– Ach, Kunst ist viel besser als Sport.

1b Bist du derselben Meinung wie im Schul-Web? Schreib deine Meinung auf. (AT4 Level 3)

Pupils read the statements and either agree or disagree with them.

1c Partnerarbeit. (AT2 Levels 3–4)

Pupils make comparisons of school subjects and see how far they agree with each other.

Grammatik: Comparing two things

Point out that the German comparative is similar to the English: both add *-er* to the end of the adjective. (Although there is no German equivalent of the English 'more …' comparative.) As in English, there are some irregular forms; the most common are listed for pupils to note. Do some whole-class practice to reinforce the endings: say an adjective and elicit the comparative form from a pupil.

R Refer to p. 136 in the Pupil's Book for further information. More practice of this grammar point is also provided on Grammatik 2 (R & A File p. 32).

2 Wähl die richtige Antwort aus. (AT3 Level 2)

Pupils read four statements comparing items and decide which comparative form best suits each.

Answers

1 kleiner, **2** kürzer, **3** größer, **4** größer

3 Hör zu. Wie viele Prozent meinen das? (1–8) (AT3 Level 3, AT1 Level 3)

Pupils now meet the superlative form of the adjective in some survey results. They listen and note down the subject each speaker mentions. They then look for the appropriate percentage listed in the survey on p. 27.

Answers

1 67%, **2** 53%, **3** 72%, **4** 58%, **5** 54%, **6** 78%, **7** 76%, **8** 72%

1 – Was ist das interessanteste Fach?
– Tja … also, Geschichte finde ich interessant. Ja, Geschichte ist das interessanteste Fach.
2 – Was ist das lustigste Fach?
– Ein lustiges Fach? Gibt es so was? Na ja, vielleicht Sport. Das ist ziemlich lustig.
3 – Und was ist das einfachste Fach?
– Das einfachste Fach ist Kunst – das ist immer sehr locker.
4 – Was ist das nützlichste Fach?
– Also, das nützlichste Fach? Das muss Englisch sein. Englisch ist in der ganzen Welt nützlich.
5 – Und was ist das langweiligste Fach?
– Das ist Religion. Religion finde ich stinklangweilig!

6 – Stimmt. Aber was ist das anstrengendste Fach?
– Ich finde Sport sehr anstrengend – man muss richtig fit sein!
7 – Und das schwierigste Fach? Was ist das?
– Das schwierigste Fach? Das ist wahrscheinlich Mathe – ich finde es irrsinnig schwierig.
8 – Also, was ist das beste Fach für dich?
– Das beste Fach muss Kunst sein – das finde ich so einfach!

4a Deine Meinung. Schreib für jedes unterstrichene Adjektiv oben einen Satz. (AT4 Levels 3–4)

Pupils re-write the sentences from activity 3 with their own choice of subject for each superlative form.

4b Partnerarbeit. Vergleicht eure Listen. (AT2 Levels 3–4)

Pupils compare their lists to see how similar/dissimilar they are.

Grammatik: The most ...

Go through the grammar box with pupils, showing them how the superlative is formed. Ask some questions around the class such as: *Wer ist der beste Lehrer? Was ist das interessanteste Fach? Was ist das langweiligste Buch?*

R Refer to p. 136 in the Pupil's Book for further information. More practice of this grammar point is also provided on Grammatik 2 (R & A File p. 32).

E Pupils carry out their own survey on school subjects in the class. To do this, each pupil could choose a different adjective for his/her question: *Was ist das ...ste Fach?* Pupils could then come together to compile their results.

5 Hör zu und wiederhole. So spricht man ä, ö und ü aus.

Pupils listen and repeat to practise the vowels with umlauts.

ä, ä, ä, ... ö, ö, ö, ... ü, ü, ü! So wie länger und Engländerin, größer und Österreicher, kürzer und nützlicher ... ä, ö, ü, ... ä, ö, ü, ... ä, ö, ü! Immer Umlaute üben!

Ludwig: Pronunciation: vowels with umlauts

Ludwig reminds pupils of the pronunciation of *ä, ö* and *ü*. Let pupils listen to the recording and repeat the sounds they hear. Say some words, either with or without an umlaut, and ask pupils to identify which words had an umlaut in them. Ask pupils to think of other words they know with umlauts and see if they can pronounce them accurately.

R Further practice of this unit's language is to be found on p. 112 of the Pupil's Book, activity 1.

E Further practice of this unit's language is to be found on p. 113 of the Pupil's Book, activity 1.

3 Die Hausordnung (pp. 28–29)

Pupils will learn how to:

- talk about what they are not allowed to do at school

Key language
Was darf man in der Schule nicht machen?
Man darf …
nicht rauchen
nicht skaten
nicht im Gang rennen
nicht im Klassenzimmer kauen
nicht zu spät zur Schule kommen
das Schulgelände nicht verlassen
niemanden hänseln oder ärgern
kein Zungenpiercing haben
keine Drogen mit in die Schule bringen
keinen Alkohol mit in die Schule bringen

Grammar focus
- *dürfen* + verb to the end

Skill focus
- scan text for key words

Resources
- Cassette A, Side B
- Workbook pp. 13, 17
- R & A File: Arbeitsblatt 2 (p. 26), 7 (p. 95), Grammatik 2 (p. 74)

This unit discusses school rules. Before you introduce the new language, ask pupils to predict in English ten rules for a school and write them on the board/OHT. Then copy the visuals on Arbeitsblatt 2 (R & A File p. 26) onto an OHT to introduce the new language orally and compare these rules with those predicted by the pupils. Once pupils are familiar with the vocabulary, show them a visual and start sentences for pupils to complete: *Man darf …* .

For further oral practice, give each pair of pupils a set of the visuals. One pupil asks: *Was darf man in der Schule nicht machen?* and points to a visual. The other pupil gives the correct reply, using *Man darf …* .

1a Hör zu und lies. (AT1 Level 3, AT3 Level 3)

Pupils listen to and read the set of school rules.

1 – Man darf nicht rauchen.
2 – Man darf nicht skaten.
3 – Man darf nicht im Gang rennen.
4 – Man darf nicht im Klassenzimmer kauen.
5 – Man darf kein Zungenpiercing haben.
6 – Man darf niemanden hänseln oder ärgern.
7 – Man darf nicht zu spät zur Schule kommen.
8 – Man darf das Schulgelände nicht verlassen.
9 – Man darf keine Drogen mit in die Schule bringen.
10 – Man darf keinen Alkohol mit in die Schule bringen.

1b Hör zu. Welche Punkte aus der Hausordnung nennen sie? (1–2) (AT1 Level 5)

Pupils listen to two teenagers talking about their school rules. They note down which of the rules in the pictures are mentioned.

Answers

1 2, 6, 9, 1, 5, 7; **2** 1, 3, 6, 7, 10, 4, 8, 2

1 – Hallo. Wie ist deine Hausordnung? Was darf man an deiner Schule nicht machen?
– Tja, also, man darf nicht skaten. Das weiß ich, weil ich das letzte Woche gemacht habe, und ich habe Ärger bekommen!
– O.K., man darf nicht skaten. Und was noch?
– Moment mal … was noch … ach, ja, man darf niemanden hänseln oder ärgern. Das finde ich sehr gut und auch total wichtig.
– Ja, sehr gut.
– Und man darf keine Drogen mit in die Schule bringen. Das ist klar – Drogen sind doof und auch illegal.
– Ganz richtig. Wahrscheinlich darf man auch nicht rauchen, oder?
– Doch, wenn man in der elften Klasse ist, darf man schon rauchen.
– Wirklich?
– Ja.
– Und darf man ein Zungenpiercing haben?
– Nee, Zungenpiercing ist verboten.
– Also, ist das alles?
– Ja, ich glaube schon. Ach, nein, man darf auch nicht zu spät zur Schule kommen.
– Ja, das ist normal, oder?
– Ja, aber jetzt ist es schon halb acht und ich komme zu spät! Tschüs!

2 – Hallo. Was darf man an deiner Schule nicht machen?
– Tja, vieles! Man darf nicht rauchen und man darf nicht im Gang rennen.
– Also, man darf nicht rauchen und man darf nicht im Gang rennen. Ja, das ist normal, glaube ich.
– Ja und man darf auch niemanden hänseln oder ärgern.
– Sehr gut. Und sonst noch was?
– Man darf nicht zu spät zur Schule kommen und man darf keinen Alkohol mit in die Schule bringen.
– Findest du das gut?
– Ja, klar. Alkohol in der Schule ist doof!
– O.K., gibt es sonst noch was?
– Ja, man darf nicht im Klassenzimmer kauen. Das weiß ich, weil ich das gestern in der Biologiestunde gemacht habe, und es gab Krach!
– O.K., ist das alles?
– Äh, nein, man darf das Schulgelände nicht verlassen und man darf nicht skaten. Das ist alles, glaube ich!

2a Welche Punkte oben findest du am wichtigsten? Schreib deine eigene Liste von eins (dem wichtigsten Punkt) bis zehn auf. (AT4 Level 2)

Pupils list the school rules in their own personal order of importance.

2b Partnerarbeit. Vergleicht eure Listen. (AT2 Levels 3–4)
Pupils compare their lists to see if they have the same priorities or not.

Grammatik: Talking about what you are not allowed to do
Point out the grammar box to pupils and explain that *man* is used a lot in Germany to express 'one'/'you'. Ask pupils if they can think of any other verbs which work like *darf* to send the verb to the end of the sentence (*muss* and *kann* are two examples from Logo! 2).

R Refer to pp. 127–128 in the Pupil's Book for further information. More practice of this grammar point is also provided on Grammatik 2 (R & A File p. 74) and p. 17 of the Workbook.

E Pupils make a poster describing their school rules.

▶ **3 Was ist deine ideale Hausordnung? (AT4 Level 4)**
Pupils write a text about what their ideal school rules would be. Encourage pupils to use their imagination and come up with some original ideas. Compare their ideas afterwards in a class session or display their ideas on the wall for other pupils to look at.

4a Lies die E-Mail und ordne die Bilder. (AT3 Levels 5–6)
Pupils read an e-mail from Christopher, who had some trouble keeping to the school rules last week. Pupils put the pictures in the order in which they are mentioned in the e-mail.

Answers
e, f, a, c, d, b

Ludwig: Scan text for key words
Go through Ludwig's advice with the class and ask pupils to select what they think to be important words in the e-mail. Then go through the pictures a–f and ask pupils to scan the text to find the relevant word for each picture.

R Further practice on coping with reading activities is provided on Arbeitsblatt 7 (R & A File p. 95).

4b Beantworte folgende Fragen.
Pupils answer ten comprehension questions in German on the e-mail. There is no need for them to write full sentences.

Answers
1 Beatrix, **2** um acht Uhr, **3** am Montagnachmittag, **4** ferngesehen, **5** mit dem Skateboard, **6** Herr Volpp, **7** Frau Keil, **8** Kunst, **9** Englisch, **10** in die Stadt

E Pupils look at the school rules on p. 28 of the Pupil's Book and identify which of them Christopher had a problem with last week.

5 Letzte Woche hattest du Probleme mit der Hausordnung! Schreib eine E-Mail wie oben und beschreib die Probleme, die du jeden Tag hattest. (AT4 Levels 5–6)
Pupils imagine that they had problems keeping to the school rules last week: they write a text in the perfect tense to describe what happened each day. Remind pupils that they can reuse some of the expressions from the text on p. 29 in their work.

MINI-TEST
At the end of the third unit in every chapter, there is a *Mini-Test*. This is intended as a half-way checkpoint for pupils to check that they are familiar with the key language of the chapter so far. Pupils could revise the language with a partner in class or for homework.

4 Nächstes Trimester (pp. 30–31)

Pupils will learn how to:
- talk about their plans for next term

Key language	**Grammar focus**
Was wirst du nächstes Trimester machen? Ich werde ... pünktlich zur Schule kommen rechtzeitig Hausaufgaben machen bessere Noten bekommen viel Sport treiben mit dem Rad zur Schule fahren ein Instrument lernen viel am Computer arbeiten niemanden ärgern	• future tense **Skill focus** • listening and repeating to improve intonation • English-German dictionary for new words **Resources** • Cassette A, Side B • Workbook p. 14 • R & A File: Arbeitsblatt 3 (p. 27), 5 (p. 29), Grammatik 1 (p. 31)

This unit discusses resolutions pupils might make for self-improvement next term. It also introduces the use of the future tense. Introduce the new language orally, using the visuals on Arbeitsblatt 3 (R & A File p. 27) copied onto an OHT. As you point at each one, ask pupils whether they think it is a good idea or not. Arrange the visuals in order of importance, according to the pupils' ideas.

For further oral practice, give each pair of pupils a set of the visuals. Pupils cut them up and place them face down on the table in a pile. Both pupils then guess what the next visual will be, giving the appropriate sentence in German. They turn the visual over: if a pupil is right, he/she keeps the visual. If both pupils are wrong, that visual goes to the bottom of the pile.

1a Hör zu und wiederhole. (AT1 Level 3)

Pupils listen to and repeat the resolutions of four German teenagers.

– Nächstes Trimester werde ich pünktlich zur Schule kommen. Ich werde auch rechtzeitig Hausaufgaben machen.
– Ich werde bessere Noten bekommen. Ich werde auch viel Sport treiben.
– Nächstes Trimester werde ich mit dem Rad zur Schule fahren. Ich werde auch ein Instrument lernen.
– Ich werde viel am Computer arbeiten. Ich werde auch niemanden ärgern.

Ludwig: Listening and repeating to improve intonation

Go through Ludwig's advice with the class, pointing out that it is important to try to imitate German intonation when speaking. Listening to the recordings is one way of improving. Play the recording in short stages and ask pupils to repeat what they hear. They could work in pairs and give each other marks out of ten as to how German they sound.

1b Wer wird das nächstes Trimester machen? (AT3 Level 3)

Pupils look at eight pictures and identify which teenager has made that resolution.

Answers

a Franziska, **b** Angela, **c** Christopher, **d** Sven, **e** Franziska, **f** Christopher, **g** Sven, **h** Angela

1c Partnerarbeit. Person A macht das Buch zu. (AT2 Levels 3–4)

Pupils spend a few minutes studying the speech bubbles at the top of the page, then partner A closes his/her textbook and asks partner B what he/she is planning to do next term. Partner B replies with one of the resolutions from the speech bubbles. Partner A should then be able to identify which teenager partner B is playing.

2a Hör zu. Was werden sie nächstes Trimester machen? Mach Notizen. (1–4) (AT1 Levels 5–6)

Pupils listen and note down the plans four teenagers have for next term. Remind pupils they need to jot down abbreviated notes rather than try to copy full sentences from the recording.

Answers

1 Computer, bessere Noten, pünktlich; **2** bessere Noten, Rad; **3** niemanden ärgern, Hausaufgaben; **4** Instrument, Sport

1 – Was wirst du nächstes Trimester machen?
– Ich werde viel am Computer arbeiten.
– Warum?
– Weil ich dann bessere Noten bekommen werde!
– Und was wirst du sonst noch machen?
– Tja, ich werde immer pünktlich zur Schule kommen. Das schaffe ich im Moment nur dreimal in der Woche!

2 – Und du? Wirst du auch pünktlich zur Schule kommen?
– Ja, aber das mache ich sowieso schon! Aber ich werde bessere Noten bekommen.
– Und wie schaffst du das?
– Ich werde in der Schule fleißiger arbeiten.
– Prima. Und hast du auch andere Ideen für das nächste Trimester?
– Ja, ich werde mit dem Rad zur Schule fahren, weil das viel gesünder als das Auto ist.
– Das ist eine gute Idee.

3 – Und du? Was sind deine Pläne für nächstes Trimester?
– Also, nächstes Trimester werde ich niemanden ärgern, weil ich das dieses Trimester zu oft gemacht habe, und jetzt habe ich fast keine Freunde mehr.
– Ja, das kann ich glauben. Und was wirst du sonst machen?
– Ich werde immer rechtzeitig Hausaufgaben machen.
– Warum?
– Ja, also, dieses Trimester war ich sehr faul und ich habe fast nie rechtzeitig Hausaufgaben gemacht und deshalb habe ich oft Ärger gekriegt. Das mag ich nicht.

4 – Und wirst du auch rechtzeitig Hausaufgaben machen?
– Äh ... vielleicht ... und ich werde auch ein Instrument lernen.
– Ja, was denn?
– Ach, ich bin nicht so sicher. Vielleicht Saxophon oder Trompete.
– Sehr gut. Und was wirst du sonst machen?
– Also, dieses Trimester habe ich fast keinen Sport getrieben, also nächstes Trimester werde ich viel Sport treiben – mindestens dreimal in der Woche.

2b Was haben sie gesagt? Schreib Sätze auf. (AT4 Level 3)

Pupils now write full sentences from the notes they jotted down in activity 2a.

Answers

1 Ich werde viel am Computer arbeiten. Ich werde bessere Noten bekommen. Ich werde pünktlich zur Schule kommen. **2** Ich werde bessere Noten bekommen. Ich werde mit dem Rad zur Schule fahren. **3** Ich werde niemanden ärgern. Ich werde Hausaufgaben immer rechtzeitig machen. **4** Ich werde auch ein Instrument lernen. Ich werde viel Sport treiben.

3 Lies den Artikel und beantworte die Fragen. (AT3 Level 5)

Pupils read the article written by a German class about their ideas for a school of the future. They then answer eight comprehension questions in German.

Answers

1 Die Klasse 8R hat die Ideen gehabt. **2** Man wird alles zu Hause lernen. **3** Man wird einen Computer im Zimmer haben. **4** Der Englischlehrer wird in England sein. **5** Der Französischlehrer wird in Frankreich sein. **6** Man wird ein Fitnessvideo brauchen. **7** In Erdkunde wird man Weltreisen machen. **8** Für den Deutschunterricht wird es viele Texte und Übungen am Computer geben.

Grammatik: Talking about the future

The grammar box shows pupils how the future tense is formed in the singular. Point out the similarity to the *man darf* construction, in which the main verb is sent to the end of the sentence. The form of *werden* always comes as the second idea in the sentence.

R Refer to p. 132 of the Pupil's Book for further information. More practice of this grammar point is also provided on Grammatik 1 (R & A File p. 31).

4a Was sind deine Ideen für eine Schule der Zukunft? Schreib eine Präsentation. (AT4 Levels 4–6)

Pupils write an article about their own ideas for a school of the future. Remind them to look back at the text in activity 3 for useful phrases to re-use.

Ludwig: English-German dictionary for new words

Encourage pupils to use an English-German dictionary if they want to write about something for which they do not know the vocabulary. Tell pupils it is a good idea to double-check the word they have found in the German-English section to avoid any misunderstandings.

4b Lies deine Präsentation in der Klasse vor und vergleiche sie mit deinen Mitschülern. (AT2 Levels 4–6)

Pupils give a presentation of their ideas to the class. Other pupils can then give their comments on the content of the ideas and the pronunciation of the text.

R The pairwork activity on Arbeitsblatt 5 (R & A File p. 29) provides further oral practice of the language of the unit.

5 Unsere Schule, eure Schule

(pp. 32–33)

Pupils will learn how to:
- compare their school with a German school

Key language

Wir stehen sehr / nicht so früh auf.
Wir fahren oft mit dem Rad/Auto/Bus zur Schule.
Wir tragen keine/eine Uniform.
Wir essen zu Hause / in der Kantine zu Mittag.
Wir bleiben meistens/nicht im selben Klassenzimmer.
WIr haben einige/viele AGs in der Schule.
Wir haben manchmal/nie samstags Schule.
Unsere Schule beginnt um acht/neun Uhr.
Unsere Schule endet gegen Mittag / drei Uhr.
Am Nachmittag haben wir frei / bleiben wir in der Schule.

Resources

- Cassette A, Side B
- Workbook p. 15

This unit … ol day with that of …

Brain… …s might have abou… …eir ideas on the boa… …mns to compare the pupi… …an counterparts. If any pupils have be… …hange visit to a German school, they could ta… …t their experiences.

1a Hör zu und wiederhole. Welcher Satz ist das? (1–10) (AT1 Level 3)

Pupils listen to and repeat some sentences about a school day and identify them in the list provided.

Answers

1 f, **2** j, **3** i, **4** c, **5** a, **6** h, **7** e, **8** b, **9** d, **10** g

1 – W…
2 – Wi…
3 – Am…
4 – Wi…
5 – Wi…
6 – Wi…
7 – Uns…
8 – Wir…
9 – Uns…
10 – Wir … …lben Klassenzimmer.

1b Was passt zusammen? (AT3 Level 3)

Pupils match the pictures to the statements describing a typical German school day.

Answers

1 d, **2** j, **3** c, **4** a, **5** f, **6** e, **7** g, **8** b, **9** h, **10** i

2 Hör zu. Gehen sie auf eine britische (B) oder eine deutsche (D) Schule? (1–12) (AT1 Level 3)

Pupils listen and decide whether the statements describe a typical British or German school day. A few of the statements could apply to either system, as not all British schools follow the 'typical' pattern, so pupils' answers can differ from those suggested below.

Answers

1 D, **2** B, **3** B, **4** D, **5** B, **6** B, **7** D/B, **8** B, **9** B, **10** B, **11** B, **12** D

1 – Man…
2 – Wir…
3 – Uns…
4 – Wir…
5 – Wir…
6 – Am…
7 – Wir…
8 – Wir…
9 – Uns…
10 – Am Samstag gehen wir nie zur Schule.
11 – Wir fahren oft mit dem Bus zur Schule.
12 – Wir bleiben meistens im selben Klassenzimmer.

3 Wie ist deine Schule? Mach eine Tabelle. (AT4 Levels 3–4)

Pupils adapt the statements from the top of the page to describe their typical school day. Some suggestions are given in clouds, but pupils might need further help to customise the sentences for their own situation. Remind pupils that they need to use the plural form of each verb with *wir* to describe what their school is like for everyone – this form is identical to the infinitive.

4 Partnerarbeit. A ist Deutscher/Deutsche und B ist Engländer/in. (AT2 Levels 4–6)

Pupils take on the role of a German and a British pupil and discuss their school day.

5a Lies den Text und beantworte die Fragen. (AT3 Level 5)

Pupils read about Mira's school – a drama school in Bremen – and answer eight comprehension questions in German on it. There is no need for them to write complete sentences.

Answers

1 fünfzehn Jahre alt, **2** eine Theaterschule, **3** gegen fünf Uhr, **4** in der Kantine, **5** von Montag bis Mittwoch, **6** nein, **7** Theaterunterricht, **8** weil sie die beste Schule der Welt ist

5b Was ist deine ideale Schule? Eine Fußballschule? Eine Kochschule? Beschreib sie. (AT4 Levels 4–5)

Pupils imagine they are at their ideal school and describe a typical day there. If necessary, brainstorm some ideas first and remind pupils that they can use phrases from the text in activity 5a to help them.

R Further practice of this unit's language is to be found on p. 112 of the Pupil's Book, activity 2.

E Further practice of this unit's language is to be found on p. 113 of the Pupil's Book, activity 2.

6 Wo ist die Bibliothek?

(pp. 34–35)

Pupils will learn how to:
- direct somebody around their school

Key language
Entschuldigung, wo ist ... ?
die Toilette
das Lehrerzimmer
der Musiksaal
das Klassenzimmer
das Labor
die Bibliothek
das Sekretariat
der Computerraum
die Aula
die Sporthalle

Der/Die/Das ... ist im ersten Stock/Erdgeschoss.
Geh durch den Haupteingang.
Geh die Treppen hinauf.
Geh nach rechts/links.
Der/Die/Das ... ist auf der rechten/linken Seite.

Resources
- Cassette A, Side B
- Workbook p. 16
- R & A File: Arbeitsblatt 4 (p. 28)

This unit introduces pupils to the rooms at school as well as giving directions around the school. Introduce the rooms first, presenting the visuals on Arbeitsblatt 4 (R & A File p. 28) on an OHT. Encourage pupils to use the correct form of the definite article as they name each visual you point to.

For further oral practice, give each pair of pupils a set of the visuals to cut up. The visuals are then placed face-up on the table and one pupil looks away. The other pupil removes two or three visuals and the first pupil looks at the remaining visuals and tries to identify the missing ones. Pupils can then swap roles.

1a Sieh dir den Plan an. Was passt zusammen? Hör dann zu und überprüfe es. (AT3 Level 1)

Pupils match the names of school rooms to their locations on the map. They then listen to check their answers.

Answers

1 g, **2** k, **3** b, **4** e/f, **5** d, **6** h, **7** j, **8** c, **9** i, **10** a

– Die Aula: Das ist g.
– Das Lehrerzimmer: Das ist k.
– Der Musiksaal: Das ist b. Das ist im ersten Stock.
– Das Klassenzimmer: Das ist e und f.
– Das Labor: Das ist d.
– Die Bibliothek: Das ist h. Das ist im Erdgeschoss.
– Das Sekretariat: Das ist j.
– Der Computerraum: Das ist c. Das ist im erstenstock.
– Die Toilette: Das ist i.
– Die Sporthalle: Das ist a. Das ist im erstenstock.

1b Partnerarbeit. (AT2 Level 2)

Pupils practise the names and genders of the school rooms by saying which floor each one is on.

Introduce the vocabulary for directions by drawing simple directions on the board/OHT and describing each one. You could then do some simple directing of pupils around the classroom to reinforce the phrases.

2a Was passt zusammen? (AT3 Level 2)

Pupils match the directions to the symbols.

Answers

1 g, **2** f, **3** e, **4** d, **5** a, **6** b, **7** c, **8** h

2b Hör zu. Welches Bild ist das? (1–8) (AT1 Level 2)

Pupils listen and decide which picture on p. 34 is being described each time.

Answers

1 c, **2** e, **3** d, **4** f, **5** g, **6** b, **7** a, **8** h

1 – Das ist auf der linken Seite.
2 – Geh die Treppen hinauf.
3 – Geh nach rechts.
4 – Das ist auf der rechten Seite.
5 – Geh nach links.
6 – Geh durch den Haupteingang.
7 – Das ist im ersten Stock.
8 – Geh geradeaus.

3a Sieh dir den Plan auf Seite 34 an. Was hat man gefragt? (AT3 Level 3)

Pupils read the directions and look at the map on p. 34 to work out which room must have been asked for.

Answers

1 Entschuldigung, wo ist das Klassenzimmer 8T? **2** Entschuldigung, wo ist die Aula? **3** Entschuldigung, wo ist der Musiksaal? **4** Entschuldigung, wo ist die Toilette?

3b Beantworte die Fragen. (AT4 Levels 3–4)

Pupils write directions in answer to the questions posed.

Answers

1 Geh durch den Haupteingang. Das Sekretariat ist im Erdgeschoss auf der linken Seite. **2** Der Computerraum ist im ersten Stock. Geh durch den Haupteingang und geh die Treppen hinauf. Geh dann nach links und geh geradeaus. Der Computerraum ist auf der rechten Seite neben dem Musiksaal. **3** Die Sporthalle ist im ersten Stock. Geh durch den Haupteingang und geh die Treppen hinauf. Geh dann nach links und geh geradeaus. Geh dann nach rechts. Die Sporthalle ist auf der linken Seite. **4** Der Musiksaal ist im ersten Stock. Geh durch den Haupteingang und geh die Treppen hinauf. Geh dann nach links und geh geradeaus. Der Musiksaal ist auf der rechten Seite neben dem Computerraum.

4 Hör zu. Welches Zimmer ist das? Folge den Anweisungen auf dem Plan. Sind sie immer richtig? (1–6) (AT1 Levels 3–4)

Pupils listen and follow the directions to identify whether they were correct.

Answers

1 das Lehrerzimmer ✓, **2** der Computerraum ✗, **3** das Klassenzimmer 8R ✓, **4** die Toilette ✗, **5** die Bibliothek ✗, **6** das Labor ✓

1 – Entschuldigung, wo ist das Lehrerzimmer?
– Das Lehrerzimmer? Also, geh durch den Haupteingang. Das Lehrerzimmer ist auf der rechten Seite.

2 – Entschuldigung, wo ist der Computerraum?
– Ach, das ist im ersten Stock. Geh durch den Haupteingang und geh die Treppen hinauf. Geh dann nach rechts. Der Computerraum ist gleich dort auf der rechten Seite.

3 – Entschuldigung, wo ist das Klassenzimmer 8R?
– Das ist im ersten Stock. Geh durch den Haupteingang und geh die Treppen hinauf. Geh dann nach rechts. Dort ist das Klassenzimmer 8R.

4 – Entschuldigung, wo ist die Toilette?
– Geh durch den Haupteingang und geh dann nach rechts. Die Toilette ist auf der rechten Seite.

5 – Entschuldigung, wo ist die Bibliothek?
– Die Bibliothek? Moment mal … ja, geh durch den Haupteingang und geh dann nach links. Geh geradeaus. Die Bibliothek ist auf der rechten Seite.

6 – Entschuldigung, wo ist das Labor?
– Das Labor ist im ersten Stock, also geh durch den Haupteingang und geh die Treppen hinauf. Geh dann nach links. Das Labor ist auf der rechten Seite.

5 Partnerarbeit. (AT2 Levels 3–4)

Pupils work in pairs to direct each other around the map of the school.

6 Wie ist deine Schule? Beschreib sie für einen Besucher. (AT4 Level 4)

Pupils write a description of their school for a visitor. They could also record their description on cassette for German visitors to the school.

7 Lehrerzeugnis (pp. 36–37)

Resources
- Cassette A, Side B

The *MEHR* unit is intended as extension material for more able pupils. Pupils will be more challenged by the longer reading texts and by exercises which draw together all the language of the chapter.

The context of this unit is a school report written by the pupils about their teachers.

1a Lies das Zeugnis. Wer hat etwas Positives im Zeugnis? (AT3 Levels 5–6)

Pupils read the report and identify which teachers received some praise for their work.

Answers

Herr Thomas, Frau Stribel, Frau Roth

1b Such dir Wörter und Sätze aus dem Zeugnis zu folgenden Stichpunkten aus. (AT3 Level 5)

Pupils go through the report and copy out the sentences which are positive and negative. They also copy out any orders given in the reports and any suggestions offered.

Answers

Suggested answers:

Negatives: Dieses Trimester war **Herr Thomas** sehr langweilig. Seine Stunden waren langweiliger als letztes Trimester und seine Klassen haben nicht genug gelernt. Herr Thomas war auch sehr unpünktlich und ist oft zehn oder fünfzehn Minuten zu spät zum Unterricht gekommen. **Frau White** hat ein furchtbares Trimester gehabt. Ihr Hauptfehler war, sie hat die Hausaufgaben fast nie rechtzeitig zurückgegeben. Das ärgert die Schüler/innen … . Ihre Stunden waren … nicht sehr nützlich. Sie (**Frau Adib**) kann nicht Fußball spielen, sie findet Leichtathletik sehr anstrengend und dieses Trimester war sie fast nie in der Sporthalle. Frau Adib raucht auch zu viel … . Dieses Trimester ist **Frau Stribel** immer zu spät ins Labor gekommen. … ihre Klassen haben schlechtere Noten bekommen. Frau Stribel hat dreimal Alkohol in die Schule mitgebracht … . Leider ist **Herr Weizmann** nicht sehr musikalisch. Im Musiksaal hat es dieses Trimester zu oft Krach gegeben. (**Frau Roth**) Ihre Stunden waren leider zu schwierig und sie ist oft im Gang gerannt, weil sie zu spät war.

Positives: **Herr Thomas** hat immer sehr ordentlich ausgesehen. Bravo, Herr Thomas! (**Frau White**) Ihre Stunden waren interessanter als letztes Trimester … . **Frau Stribel** kann sehr gut singen und sie hat im Schulchor mitgesungen – das finden wir sehr gut. Die Schüler/innen haben **Frau Roth** sehr lustig gefunden … . Frau Roth war meistens sehr hilfsbereit und hat vielen Schülern bei ihren Problemen geholfen.

Befehle: (**Herr Thomas**) Das kann natürlich nicht so weitergehen. … (**Frau White**) so kann es nicht weitergehen. … (**Frau Stribel**) das darf man nicht machen. (**Frau Roth**) Das darf man in der Schule nicht machen.

Vorschläge: (**Herr Thomas**) Nächstes Trimester müssen seine Stunden interessanter werden und er muss immer pünktlich im Klassenzimmer sein. (**Frau White**) Nächstes Trimester wird sie hoffentlich nicht so viel Zeit im Lehrerzimmer verbringen. (**Frau Adib**) … hoffentlich wird sich das nächstes Trimester ändern. Frau Adib muss jetzt versuchen, fit zu werden und mehr Sport zu treiben. Nächstes Trimester wird **Herr Weizmann** hoffentlich ein Instrument lernen und in den Stunden richtig unterrichten.

1c Beantworte die Fragen. (AT3 Level 5)

Pupils answer eight comprehension questions on the report in German.

Answers

1 Frau Adib, **2** Frau Stribel, **3** Mathe, **4** Sie hat die Hausaufgaben fast nie rechtzeitig zurückgegeben. **5** Er hat das Schulgelände verlassen. **6** Frau Stribel, **7** Sie hat vielen Schülern bei ihren Problemen geholfen. **8** Sie hat dreimal Alkohol in die Schule mitgebracht.

2 Hör zu und beantworte die Fragen über Frau Adibs Schultag. (AT1 Levels 5–6)

Pupils listen to an interview with Frau Adib in which she describes her life and routine as a teacher.

Answers

1 zehn vor acht, **2** Brot mit Wurst und drei Tassen Kaffee, **3** mit dem Auto, **4** um halb neun, **5** Sie haben Fußball und Hockey gespielt und Leichtathletik gemacht. **6** Sie konnte einen Kaffee und eine Zigarette haben. **7** sechs Stunden, **8** um fünf nach eins, **9** Hamburger und Pommes, **10** Sie hat einen tollen Film im Fernsehen gesehen. **11** Sie hat Computerspiele gespielt.

– Frau Adib, Sie sind Sportlehrerin, nicht?
– Ja, ich unterrichte Sport an der Hausmann-Hauptschule.
– Können Sie uns ein bisschen über Ihren Alltag erzählen? Zum Beispiel, was haben Sie gestern gemacht?
– Also, gestern? Ja, das war ein sehr typischer Tag! Um zehn vor acht bin ich aufgestanden und dann habe ich gefrühstückt. Ich habe Brot mit Wurst gegessen und ich habe drei Tassen Kaffee getrunken. Sehr stark, natürlich! Um Viertel nach acht bin ich mit dem Auto zur Schule gefahren. Die Fahrt dauert ungefähr zehn Minuten und dann beginnt die Schule um halb neun. Gestern waren die Klassen sehr brav und sie haben sehr gut Fußball und Hockey gespielt. Sie haben auch ein bisschen Leichtathletik gemacht. Gestern hatte ich leider Kopfschmerzen, also war ich sehr froh, als die Pause war und ich im Klassenzimmer mal einen Kaffee und eine Zigarette haben konnte. Ich unterrichte sechs Stunden pro Tag und das finde ich immer sehr

anstrengend. Um ein Uhr ist die Schule aus und gestern bin ich wie immer um fünf nach eins nach Hause gefahren. Gott sei Dank hatte ich keine Hausaufgaben zu korrigieren! Als ich wieder zu Hause war, habe ich zu Mittag gegessen – Hamburger und Pommes – und dann habe ich einen tollen Film im Fernsehen gesehen.

- Und was haben Sie danach gemacht? Haben Sie am Abend dann Training?
- Training? Nein, was denken Sie! Am Abend bin ich zu Hause geblieben und habe Computerspiele gespielt. Das Leben einer Sportlehrerin ist ganz schön anstrengend, wissen Sie!

3 Partnerarbeit. Person A ist Direktor/in, Person B ist ein Lehrer / eine Lehrerin von Seite 36. Diskutiert das Zeugnis. (AT2 Levels 5–6)

Pupil A assumes the role of headteacher and pupil B is a teacher from p. 36. They discuss what was written in the report and any suggestions for improvement.

4 Wie sind deine Lehrer/innen? Schreib ein Lehrerzeugnis für sie wie auf Seite 36. (AT4 Levels 4–6)

Pupils write a school report on their own teachers. Encourage them to give some positive feedback as well as the inevitable chastisement.

Lernzieltest and Wiederholung (pp. 38–39)

Resources	Wortschatz pp. 34–35
• Cassette, A, Side B	Lernzieltest p. 36
• Workbook pp. 18–20	Kontrolle 2 pp. 37–46
• R & A File:	(including teacher's notes)

At the end of each chapter there is a revision unit for pupils to use before the assessment materials. The unit begins with a *Lernzieltest* (like the *Mini-Test*) for pupils to test themselves on key language from the chapter. This is also provided as a checklist for pupils to write on (R & A File p. 36) and some related gapped sentences are also provided on p. 20 of the Workbook.

If pupils are unsure of any of the language, they should be encouraged to revise the relevant unit in the chapter. A complete wordlist containing key words and phrases from the whole chapter is provided on the *Wortschatz* sheets (R &A File pp. 34–35).

Wiederholung provides pupils with revision exercises in the four skills. The listening exercises should be done in class, but the other exercises could be done either in class or for homework. Further revision exercises are provided on pp. 18–19 of the Workbook.

Wiederholung

Hören

1 Hör zu. Was werden sie nächstes Trimester machen? (1–4) (AT1 Level 5)

Pupils listen to four teenagers talking about their resolutions for next term and make notes about them.

Answers

1 mehr Sport treiben, ein Instrument lernen, **2** niemanden ärgern, pünktlich zur Schule kommen, **3** Hausaufgaben rechtzeitig machen, mit dem Rad zur Schule fahren, **4** bessere Noten bekommen, viel am Computer arbeiten

1 – Nächstes Trimester werde ich einiges machen – und zwar erstens werde ich mehr Sport treiben. Im Moment bin ich total unfit und das finde ich nicht sehr gut. Ich werde wahrscheinlich auch mal versuchen, ein Instrument zu lernen. Vielleicht werde ich Klavier oder Trompete lernen. Ich bin nicht so sicher. Wahrscheinlich werde ich aber keine besseren Noten bekommen – das kann ich einfach nicht!

2 – Dieses Trimester habe ich viele Probleme in der Schule gehabt, also werde ich nächstes Trimester niemanden ärgern, weil ich das im Moment zu oft mache, und ich finde es nicht gut. Ich werde pünktlich zur Schule kommen, so dass ich dann weniger Ärger von den Lehrern bekommen werde.

3 – Ich habe oft Hausarrest, weil ich meine Hausaufgaben nie rechtzeitig mache, also werde ich nächstes Trimester versuchen, die Hausaufgaben rechtzeitig zu machen. Ob ich das schaffe, weiß ich nicht! Zum Geburtstag werde ich ein neues Rad bekommen, also werde ich jeden Tag mit dem Rad zur Schule fahren. Wenn es nicht regnet!

4 – Nächstes Trimester werde ich fleißiger in der Schule sein und so werde ich bessere Noten kriegen. Mein Bruder hat immer bessere Noten als ich, aber nächstes Trimester wird sich das ändern! Hoffentlich bekomme ich einen neuen Computer zu Weihnachten, also werde ich dann viel am Computer arbeiten. Ich werde meine Hausaufgaben am Computer machen und ich werde auch vom Internet viel lernen.

Sprechen

2 Partnerarbeit. Beschreibt eure Schule. (AT2 Levels 3–4)

Pupils ask each other how to get to certain school rooms and then give directions.

3 Bereite eine Präsentation über deinen Tag gestern in der Schule vor. (AT2 Levels 4–6)

Pupils prepare and give a presentation about what they did yesterday at school.

Lesen

4a Ist das in der E-Mail? Ja oder nein? (AT3 Levels 4–5)

Pupils read an e-mail from Judith and decide whether the activities depicted are mentioned in the e-mail or not.

Answers

a nein, **b** ja, **c** ja, **d** nein, **e** ja, **f** ja

4b Lies die E-Mail und beantworte die Fragen. (AT3 Level 4)

Pupils answer eight comprehension questions on the e-mail in German. There is no requirement for them to answer in full sentences, although full sentence answers are provided below.

Answers

1 Sie ist in der achten Klasse. **2** Sie findet Physik-Chemie schwierig. **3** Die Schule beginnt um Viertel vor acht. **4** Die Schule endet um halb eins. **5** Nein, sie trägt keine Uniform. **6** Sie isst (meistens) zu Hause. **7** Sie fährt mit dem Rad. **8** Sie macht Hausaufgaben.

Schreiben

5 Schreib eine E-Mail an Judith. Beantworte ihre Fragen. (AT4 Levels 4–6)

Pupils write a reply to Judith, answering the questions she poses at the end of her e-mail.

► EXTRA

The EXTRA pages at the back of the Pupil's Book are intended to provide consolidation/reinforcement activities (EXTRA A) and more challenging / extension activities (EXTRA B). The exercises concentrate on the skills of reading and writing only. They could be used for differentiated work in class or at home. The best place to use each activity is clearly indicated in these notes, just above the exercise rubric, e. g. [after pp. 26–27].

EXTRA A (p. 112)

[after pp. 26–27]

1a Welches Fach ist das? Du darfst die Vokabelliste auf Seite 40 benutzen. (AT4 Levels 1–2)

Pupils use the vocabulary list on p. 40 to help them label the symbols for school subjects.

Answers

a Sport, **b** Mathe, **c** Deutsch, **d** Englisch, **e** Religion, **f** Biologie, **g** Physik-Chemie, **h** Französisch, **i** Musik, **j** Kunst, **k** Geschichte, **l** Erdkunde

1b Wie findest du die Fächer oben? Schreib Sätze. (AT4 Level 3)

Pupils give their opinion of each of the school subjects, using *weil* clauses.

1c Beantworte die Fragen. (AT4 Levels 2–3)

Pupils give their opinion of various school subjects, using the comparative.

[after pp. 32–33]

2 Verbinde die Satzhälften und mach zwei Listen. (AT4 Levels 2–3)

Pupils put sentence halves together and then decide whether the completed sentences refer to a typical British or German school day.

Answers

deutsche Schule: 1f, 3i, 4h, 8b;
britische Schule: 2g, 5d, 6c, 7j, 9a, 10e

E Pupils write sentences to describe their school day. (AT4 Level 4)

EXTRA B (p. 113)

[after pp. 26–27]

1a Sieh dir Übung 1 auf Seite 112 an. Wie findest du die Fächer? Schreib Sätze. (AT4 Levels 3–4)

Pupils give their opinion of each of the school subjects on p. 112, using *weil* clauses.

1b Ergänze die Sätze. (AT4 Level 3)

Pupils complete sentences, using the comparative form of each adjective.

Answers

Individual answers, using these comparatives:
1 besser, **2** nützlicher, **3** anstrengender, **4** lustiger, **5** langweiliger, **6** interessanter

[after pp. 32–33]

2a Lies den Text über Roberts Schultag und ergänze die Tabelle mit den Verben. (AT3 Levels 5–6)

Pupils read a text about Robert's school day and complete a table with the present, perfect and future tense expressions.

Answers

Präsens: heiße, bin, ist, fahre, komme an, beginnt, habe, mache, spiele
Perfekt: habe geraucht/bekommen/gesehen/gemacht; bin gekommen/gegangen
Zukunft: werde kommen/ankommen/bekommen/haben

2b Richtig, falsch oder nicht im Text?

Pupils decide whether statements about Robert's school day are true, false or not mentioned in the text.

Answers

1 nicht im Text, **2** falsch, **3** falsch, **4** richtig, **5** falsch, **6** nicht im Text, **7** richtig, **8** richtig, **9** falsch, **10** falsch, **11** richtig, **12** falsch

2c Schreib einen Text über deinen Schultag. Benutz Verben im Präsens, im Perfekt und in der Zukunft. (AT4 Levels 5–6)

Pupils write a text about their school day, making sure they use the present, perfect and future tenses.

Workbook

p. 11

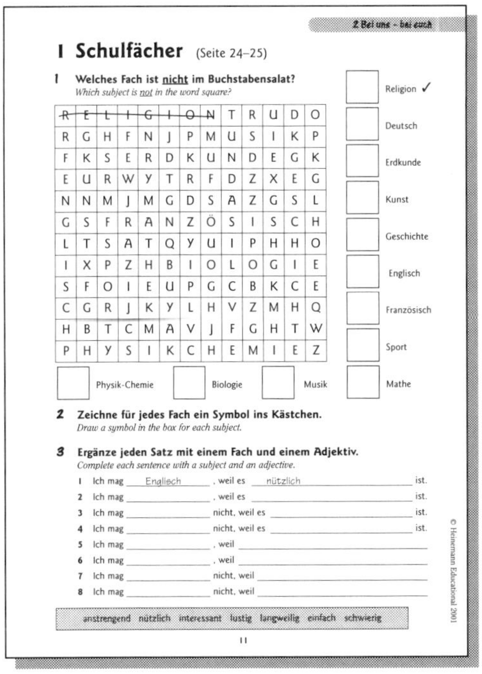

1 (AT3 Level 1)
Deutsch
2 (AT4 Level 2)
individual answers
3 (AT4 Levels 1–2)
individual answers

p. 12

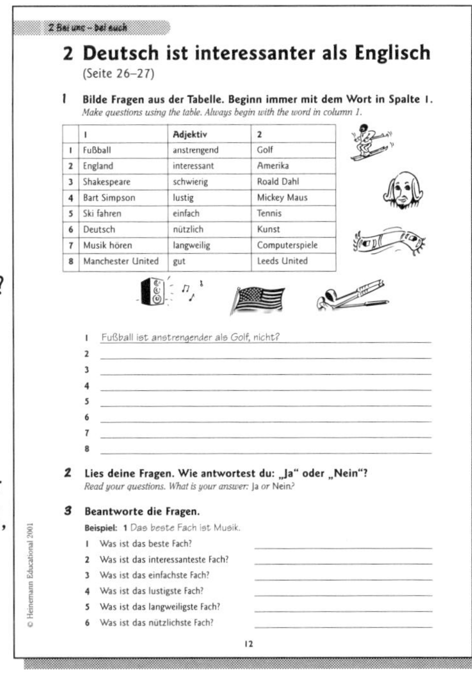

1 (AT4 Level 3)
1 Fußball ist anstrengender als Golf, nicht? **2** England ist interessanter als Amerika, nicht? **3** Shakespeare ist schwieriger als Roald Dahl, nicht? **4** Bart Simpson ist lustiger als Mickey Maus, nicht? **5** Skifahren ist einfacher als Tennis, nicht? **6** Deutsch ist nützlicher als Kunst, nicht? **7** Musik hören ist langweiliger als Computerspiele, nicht? **8** Manchester United ist besser als Leeds United, nicht?
2 (AT3 Level 3)
individual answers
3 (AT4 Level 3)
individual answers

p. 13

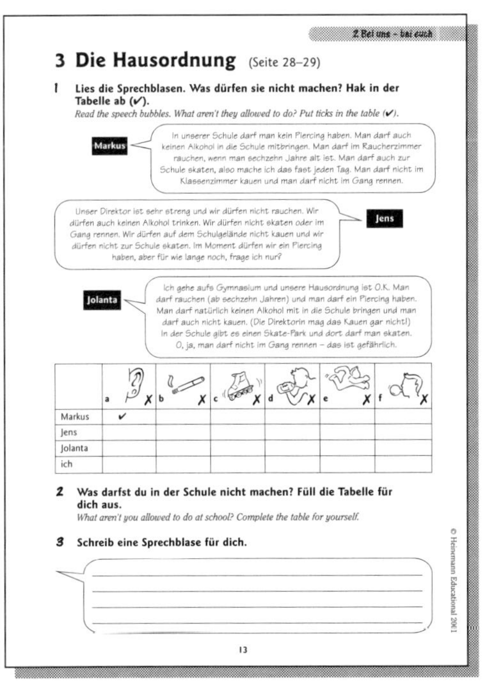

1 (AT3 Level 4)
Markus: a, d, e, f; **Jens:** b, c, d, e, f; **Jolanta:** d, e, f
3 (AT4 Level 4)
individual answers

p. 14

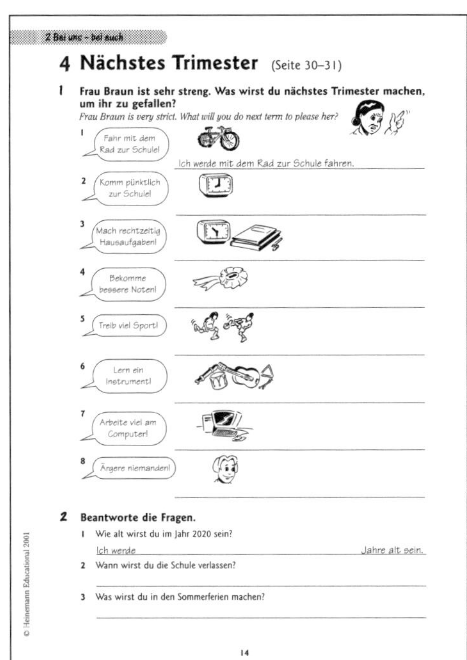

1 (AT4 Levels 3–4)
1 Ich werde mit dem Rad zur Schule fahren. **2** Ich werde pünktlich zur Schule kommen. **3** Ich werde rechtzeitig Hausaufgaben machen. **4** Ich werde bessere Noten bekommen. **5** Ich werde viel Sport treiben. **6** Ich werde ein Instrument lernen. **7** Ich werde viel am Computer arbeiten. **8** Ich werde niemanden ärgern.
2 (AT4 Levels 4–5)
individual answers

p. 15

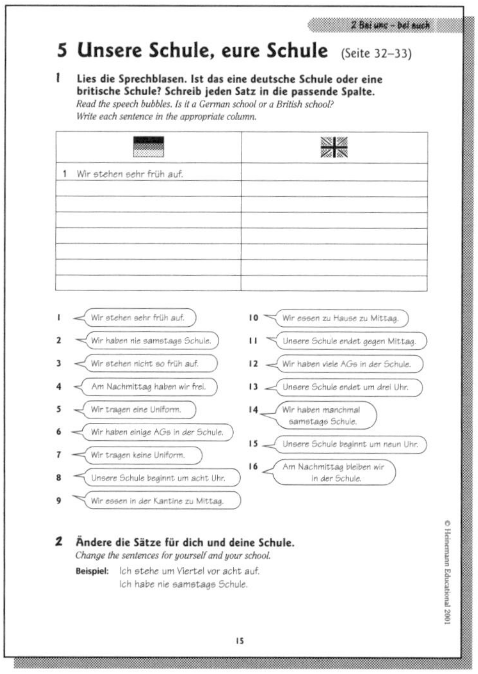

2 Bei uns – bei euch

5 Unsere Schule, eure Schule (Seite 32–33)

1 Lies die Sprechblasen. Ist das eine deutsche Schule oder eine britische Schule? Schreib jeden Satz in die passende Spalte.
Read the speech bubbles. Is it a German school or a British school? Write each sentence in the appropriate column.

(German flag)	(British flag)
1 Wir stehen sehr früh auf.	

1 Wir stehen sehr früh auf.
2 Wir haben nie samstags Schule.
3 Wir stehen nicht so früh auf.
4 Am Nachmittag haben wir frei.
5 Wir tragen eine Uniform.
6 Wir haben einige AGs in der Schule.
7 Wir tragen keine Uniform.
8 Unsere Schule beginnt um acht Uhr.
9 Wir essen in der Kantine zu Mittag.
10 Wir essen zu Hause zu Mittag.
11 Unsere Schule endet gegen Mittag.
12 Wir haben viele AGs in der Schule.
13 Unsere Schule endet um drei Uhr.
14 Wir haben manchmal samstags Schule.
15 Unsere Schule beginnt um neun Uhr.
16 Am Nachmittag bleiben wir in der Schule.

2 Ändere die Sätze für dich und deine Schule.
Change the sentences for yourself and your school.
Beispiel: Ich stehe um Viertel vor acht auf.
Ich habe nie samstags Schule.

© Heinemann Educational 2001

15

1 (AT3 Level 3)
Suggestions only:
eine deutsche Schule: 1, 4, 7, 10, 12, 14
eine britische Schule: 2, 3, 6, 15, 16
2 (AT4 Level 4)
individual answers

p. 16

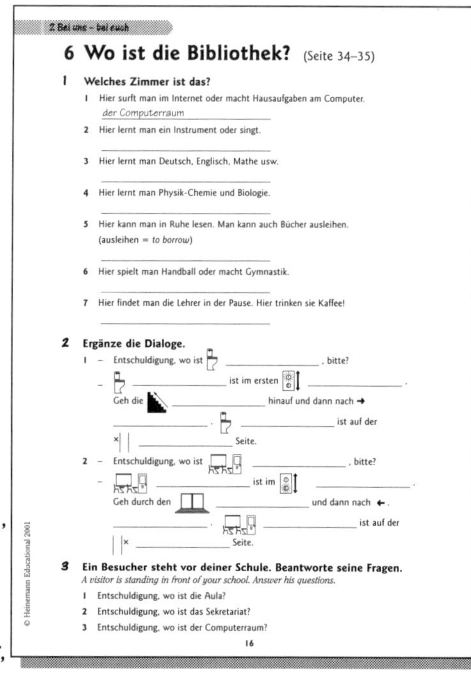

2 Bei uns – bei euch

6 Wo ist die Bibliothek? (Seite 34–35)

1 Welches Zimmer ist das?
1 Hier surft man im Internet oder macht Hausaufgaben am Computer. der Computerraum
2 Hier lernt man ein Instrument oder singt.
3 Hier lernt man Deutsch, Englisch, Mathe usw.
4 Hier lernt man Physik-Chemie und Biologie.
5 Hier kann man in Ruhe lesen. Man kann auch Bücher ausleihen. (ausleihen = *to borrow*)
6 Hier spielt man Handball oder macht Gymnastik.
7 Hier findet man die Lehrer in der Pause. Hier trinken sie Kaffee!

2 Ergänze die Dialoge.
1 – Entschuldigung, wo ist ______ , bitte?
– ______ ist im ersten ______ .
Geh die ______ hinauf und dann nach →
______ . ______ ist auf der ______ Seite.
2 – Entschuldigung, wo ist ______ , bitte?
– ______ ist im ______ .
Geh durch den ______ und dann nach ← .
______ . ______ ist auf der ______ Seite.

3 Ein Besucher steht vor deiner Schule. Beantworte seine Fragen.
A visitor is standing in front of your school. Answer his questions.
1 Entschuldigung, wo ist die Aula?
2 Entschuldigung, wo ist das Sekretariat?
3 Entschuldigung, wo ist der Computerraum?

© Heinemann Educational 2001

16

1 (AT3 Level 3)
1 der Computerraum, **2** der Musiksaal, **3** das Klassenzimmer, **4** das Labor, **5** die Bibliothek, **6** die Sporthalle, **7** das Lehrerzimmer
2 (AT4 Level 3)
1 die Toilette, die Toilette, Stock, Treppen, rechts, die Toilette, linken; **2** das Klassenzimmer 9, das Klassenzimmer 9, Erdgeschoss, Haupteingang, links, das Klassenzimmer 9, rechten
3 (AT4 Level 4)
individual answers

p. 17

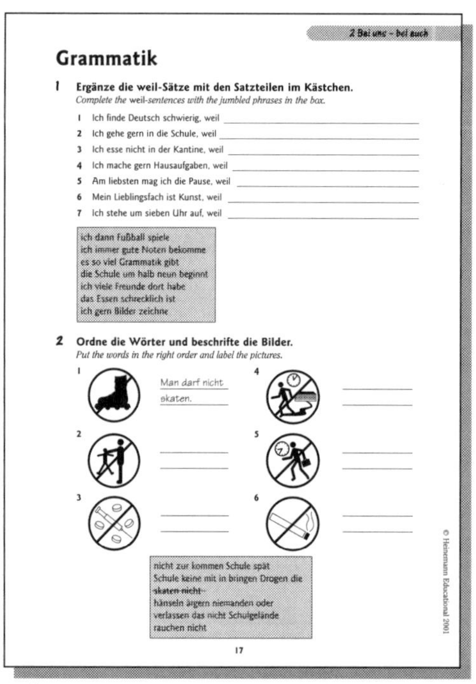

2 Bei uns – bei euch

Grammatik

1 Ergänze die weil-Sätze mit den Satzteilen im Kästchen.
Complete the weil-sentences with the jumbled phrases in the box.
1 Ich finde Deutsch schwierig, weil
2 Ich gehe gern in die Schule, weil
3 Ich esse nicht in der Kantine, weil
4 Ich mache gern Hausaufgaben, weil
5 Am liebsten mag ich die Pause, weil
6 Mein Lieblingsfach ist Kunst, weil
7 Ich stehe um sieben Uhr auf, weil

ich dann Fußball spiele
ich immer gute Noten bekomme
es so viel Grammatik gibt
die Schule um halb neun beginnt
ich viele Freunde dort habe
das Essen schrecklich ist
ich gern Bilder zeichne

2 Ordne die Wörter und beschrifte die Bilder.
Put the words in the right order and label the pictures.
1 Man darf nicht skaten.

nicht zur kommen Schule spät
Schule keine mit in bringen Drogen die
~~skaten nicht~~
hänseln ärgern niemanden oder
verlassen das nicht Schulgelände
rauchen nicht

© Heinemann Educational 2001

17

1 **1** Ich finde Deutsch schwierig, weil es so viel Grammatik gibt. **2** Ich gehe gern in die Schule, weil ich viele Freunde dort habe. **3** Ich esse nicht in der Kantine, weil das Essen schrecklich ist. **4** Ich mache gern Hausaufgaben, weil ich immer gute Noten bekomme. **5** Am liebsten mag ich die Pause, weil ich dann Fußball spiele. **6** Mein Lieblingsfach ist Kunst, weil ich gern Bilder zeichne. **7** Ich stehe um sieben Uhr auf, weil die Schule um halb neun beginnt.
2 **1** Man darf nicht skaten. **2** Man darf niemanden hänseln oder ärgern. **3** Man darf keine Drogen mit in die Schule bringen. **4** Man darf das Schulgelände nicht verlassen.
5 Man darf nicht spät zur Schule kommen. **6** Man darf nicht rauchen.

p. 18

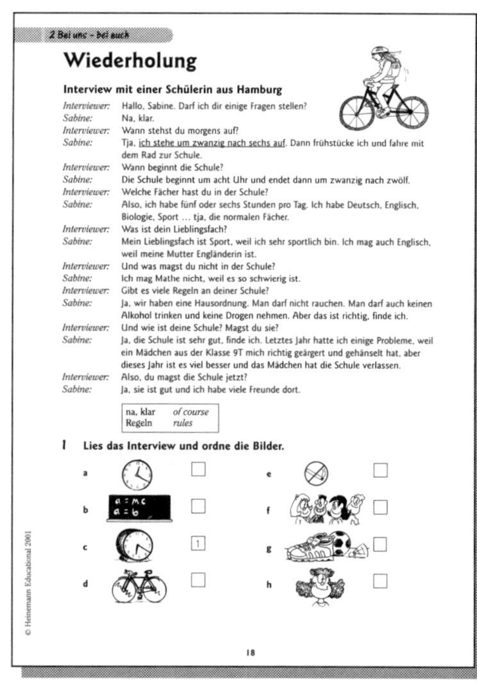

2 Bei uns – bei euch

Wiederholung

Interview mit einer Schülerin aus Hamburg

Interviewer: Hallo, Sabine. Darf ich dir einige Fragen stellen?
Sabine: Na, klar.
Interviewer: Wann stehst du morgens auf?
Sabine: Tja, ich stehe um zwanzig nach sechs auf. Dann frühstücke ich und fahre mit dem Rad zur Schule.
Interviewer: Wann beginnt die Schule?
Sabine: Die Schule beginnt um acht Uhr und endet dann um zwanzig nach zwölf.
Interviewer: Welche Fächer hast du in der Schule?
Sabine: Also, ich habe fünf oder sechs Stunden pro Tag. Ich habe Deutsch, Englisch, Biologie, Sport … tja, die normalen Fächer.
Interviewer: Was ist dein Lieblingsfach?
Sabine: Mein Lieblingsfach ist Sport, weil ich sehr sportlich bin. Ich mag auch Englisch, weil meine Mutter Engländerin ist.
Interviewer: Und was magst du nicht in der Schule?
Sabine: Ich mag Mathe nicht, weil es so schwierig ist.
Interviewer: Gibt es viele Regeln an deiner Schule?
Sabine: Ja, wir haben eine Hausordnung. Man darf nicht rauchen. Man darf auch keinen Alkohol trinken und keine Drogen nehmen. Aber das ist richtig, finde ich.
Interviewer: Und wie ist deine Schule? Magst du sie?
Sabine: Ja, die Schule ist sehr gut, finde ich. Letztes Jahr hatte ich einige Probleme, weil ein Mädchen aus der Klasse 9T mich richtig geärgert und gehänselt hat, aber dieses Jahr ist es viel besser und das Mädchen hat die Schule verlassen.
Interviewer: Also, du magst die Schule jetzt?
Sabine: Ja, sie ist gut und ich habe viele Freunde dort.

na, klar	*of course*
Regeln	*rules*

1 Lies das Interview und ordne die Bilder.
a b c 1 d e f g h

© Heinemann Educational 2001

18

1 (AT3 Level 5)
c, d, a, g, h, b, e, f

p. 19

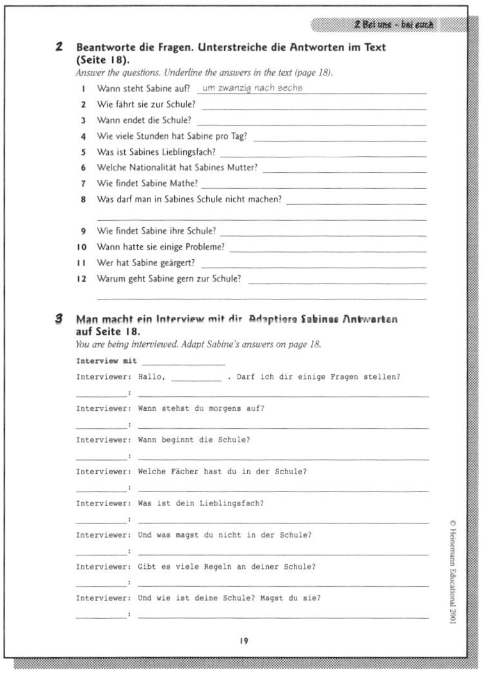

2 Bei uns – bei euch

2 Beantworte die Fragen. Unterstreiche die Antworten im Text (Seite 18).
Answer the questions. Underline the answers in the text (page 18).

1 Wann steht Sabine auf? um zwanzig nach sechs
2 Wie fährt sie zur Schule? ______
3 Wann endet die Schule? ______
4 Wie viele Stunden hat Sabine pro Tag? ______
5 Was ist Sabines Lieblingsfach? ______
6 Welche Nationalität hat Sabines Mutter? ______
7 Wie findet Sabine Mathe? ______
8 Was darf man in Sabines Schule nicht machen? ______
9 Wie findet Sabine ihre Schule? ______
10 Wann hatte sie einige Probleme? ______
11 Wer hat Sabine geärgert? ______
12 Warum geht Sabine gern zur Schule? ______

3 Man macht ein Interview mit dir. Adaptiere Sabines Antworten auf Seite 18.
You are being interviewed. Adapt Sabine's answers on page 18.

Interview mit ______
Interviewer: Hallo, ______ . Darf ich dir einige Fragen stellen?
______: ______
Interviewer: Wann stehst du morgens auf?
______: ______
Interviewer: Wann beginnt die Schule?
______: ______
Interviewer: Welche Fächer hast du in der Schule?
______: ______
Interviewer: Was ist dein Lieblingsfach?
______: ______
Interviewer: Und was magst du nicht in der Schule?
______: ______
Interviewer: Gibt es viele Regeln an deiner Schule?
______: ______
Interviewer: Und wie ist deine Schule? Magst du sie?
______: ______

19

p. 20

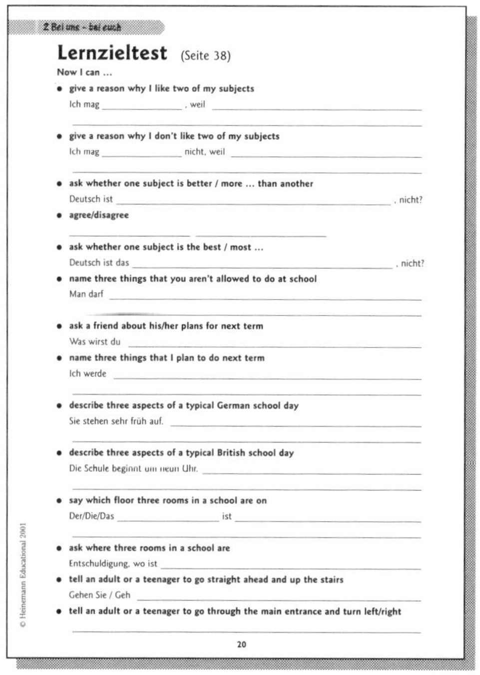

2 Bei uns – bei euch

Lernzieltest (Seite 38)

Now I can ...

- **give a reason why I like two of my subjects**
  Ich mag ______ , weil ______
- **give a reason why I don't like two of my subjects**
  Ich mag ______ nicht, weil ______
- **ask whether one subject is better / more ... than another**
  Deutsch ist ______ , nicht?
- **agree/disagree**
  ______ ______
- **ask whether one subject is the best / most ...**
  Deutsch ist das ______ , nicht?
- **name three things that you aren't allowed to do at school**
  Man darf ______
- **ask a friend about his/her plans for next term**
  Was wirst du ______
- **name three things that I plan to do next term**
  Ich werde ______
- **describe three aspects of a typical German school day**
  Sie stehen sehr früh auf. ______
- **describe three aspects of a typical British school day**
  Die Schule beginnt um neun Uhr. ______
- **say which floor three rooms in a school are on**
  Der/Die/Das ______ ist ______
- **ask where three rooms in a school are**
  Entschuldigung, wo ist ______
- **tell an adult or a teenager to go straight ahead and up the stairs**
  Gehen Sie / Geh ______
- **tell an adult or a teenager to go through the main entrance and turn left/right**
  ______

20

***2* (AT3 Level 5)**
1 um zwanzig nach sechs, **2** mit dem Rad, **3** um zwanzig nach zwölf, **4** fünf oder sechs, **5** Sport, **6** Engländerin, **7** schwierig, **8** rauchen, Alkohol trinken, Drogen nehmen, **9** sehr gut, **10** letztes Jahr, **11** ein Mädchen, **12** weil sie viele Freunde dort hat

***3* (AT4 Levels 4–5)**
individual answers

individual answers

Resource & Assessment File

Arbeitsblatt 1
p. 25

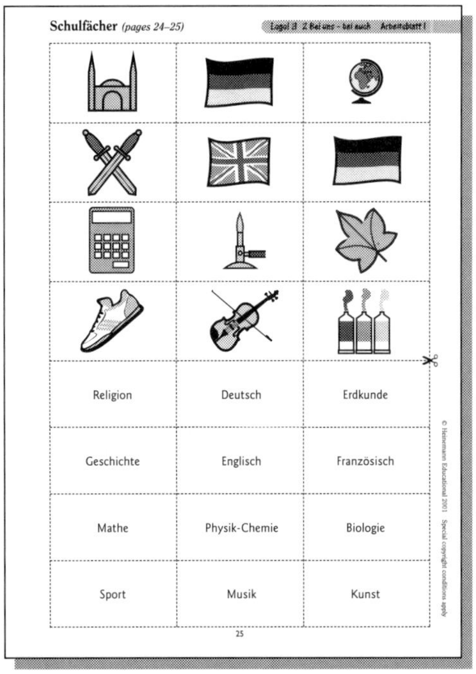

Schulfächer *(pages 24–25)* Logo! 3 2 Bei uns – bei euch Arbeitsblatt 1

Religion	Deutsch	Erdkunde
Geschichte	Englisch	Französisch
Mathe	Physik-Chemie	Biologie
Sport	Musik	Kunst

25

Visuals of *Religion, Deutsch, Erdkunde, Geschichte, Englisch, Französisch, Mathe, Physik-Chemie, Biologie, Sport, Musik, Kunst*

Arbeitsblatt 2
p. 26

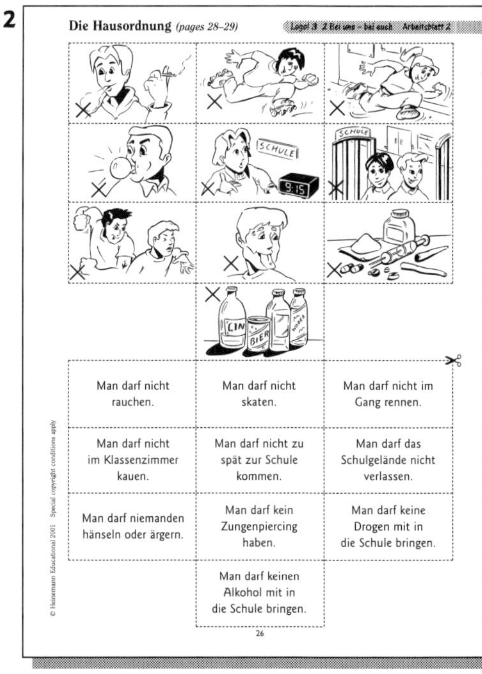

Die Hausordnung *(pages 28–29)* Logo! 3 2 Bei uns – bei euch Arbeitsblatt 2

Man darf nicht rauchen.	Man darf nicht skaten.	Man darf nicht im Gang rennen.
Man darf nicht im Klassenzimmer kauen.	Man darf nicht zu spät zur Schule kommen.	Man darf das Schulgelände nicht verlassen.
Man darf niemanden hänseln oder ärgern.	Man darf kein Zungenpiercing haben.	Man darf keine Drogen mit in die Schule bringen.
	Man darf keinen Alkohol mit in die Schule bringen.	

26

Visuals of *Man darf nicht rauchen. Man darf nicht skaten. Man darf nicht im Gang rennen. Man darf nicht im Klassenzimmer kauen. Man darf nicht zu spät zur Schule kommen. Man darf das Schulgelände nicht verlassen. Man darf niemanden hänseln oder ärgern. Man darf kein Zungenpiercing haben. Man darf keine Drogen mit in die Schule bringen. Man darf keinen Alkohol mit in die Schule bringen.*

Arbeitsblatt 3
p. 27

Nächstes Trimester *(pages 30–31)* Logo! 3 2 Bei uns – bei euch Arbeitsblatt 3

Ich werde pünktlich zur Schule kommen.	Ich werde rechtzeitig Hausaufgaben machen.	Ich werde bessere Noten bekommen.
Ich werde viel Sport treiben.	Ich werde mit dem Rad zur Schule fahren.	Ich werde ein Instrument lernen.
Ich werde viel am Computer arbeiten.	Ich werde niemanden ärgern.	

27

Visuals of *Ich werde pünktlich zur Schule kommen. Ich werde rechtzeitig Hausaufgaben machen. Ich werde bessere Noten bekommen. Ich werde viel Sport treiben. Ich werde mit dem Rad zur Schule fahren. Ich werde ein Instrument lernen. Ich werde viel am Computer arbeiten. Ich werde niemanden ärgern.*

Arbeitsblatt 4
p. 28

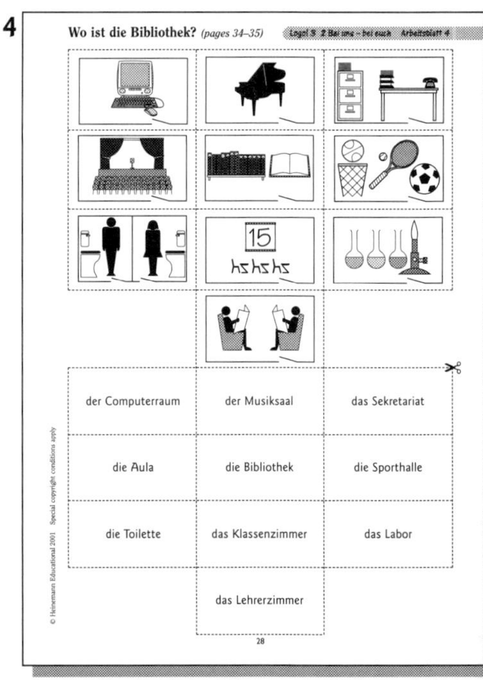

Wo ist die Bibliothek? *(pages 34–35)* Logo! 3 2 Bei uns – bei euch Arbeitsblatt 4

der Computerraum	der Musiksaal	das Sekretariat
die Aula	die Bibliothek	die Sporthalle
die Toilette	das Klassenzimmer	das Labor
	das Lehrerzimmer	

28

Visuals of *der Computerraum, der Musiksaal, das Sekretariat, die Aula, die Bibliothek, die Sporthalle, die Toilette, das Klassenzimmer, das Labor, das Lehrerzimmer*

Arbeitsblatt 5
p. 29

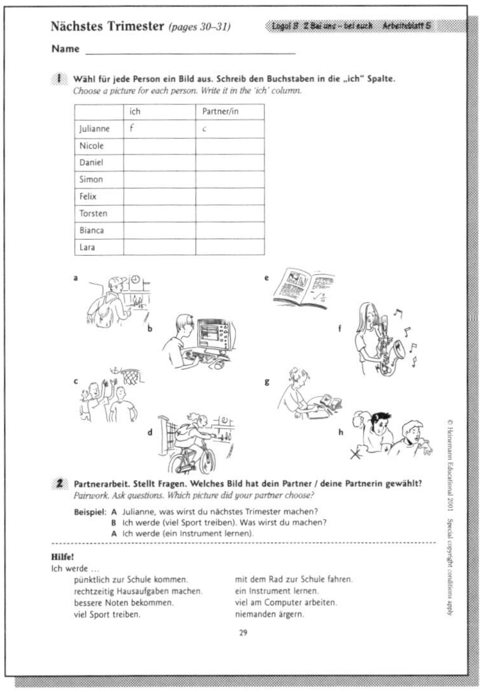

Nächstes Trimester *(pages 30–31)*

Name

1 Wähl für jede Person ein Bild aus. Schreib den Buchstaben in die „ich" Spalte. *Choose a picture for each person. Write it in the 'ich' column.*

	ich	Partner/in
Julianne	f	c
Nicole		
Daniel		
Simon		
Felix		
Torsten		
Bianca		
Lara		

2 Partnerarbeit. Stellt Fragen. Welches Bild hat dein Partner / deine Partnerin gewählt? *Pairwork. Ask questions. Which picture did your partner choose?*

Beispiel: A Julianne, was wirst du nächstes Trimester machen?
B Ich werde (viel Sport treiben). Was wirst du machen?
A Ich werde (ein Instrument lernen).

Hilfe!
Ich werde …
pünktlich zur Schule kommen. / mit dem Rad zur Schule fahren.
rechtzeitig Hausaufgaben machen. / ein Instrument lernen.
bessere Noten bekommen. / viel am Computer arbeiten.
viel Sport treiben. / niemanden ärgern.

29

Pairwork activity on plans for next term.
1 (AT2 Level 4)
2 (AT2 Level 4)

Arbeitsblatt 6
p. 30

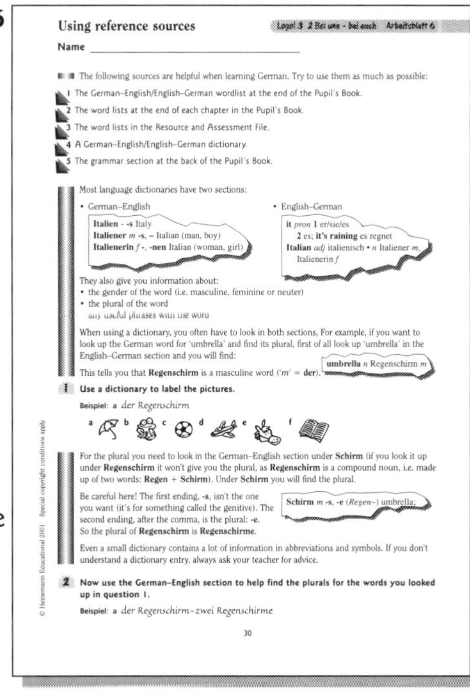

Using reference sources

Name

The following sources are helpful when learning German. Try to use them as much as possible:
1 The German–English/English–German wordlist at the end of the Pupil's Book.
2 The word lists at the end of each chapter in the Pupil's Book.
3 The word lists in the Resource and Assessment File.
4 A German–English/English–German dictionary.
5 The grammar section at the back of the Pupil's Book.

Most language dictionaries have two sections:
• German–English • English–German

They also give you information about:
• the gender of the word (i.e. masculine, feminine or neuter)
• the plural of the word
• any useful phrases with the word

1 Use a dictionary to label the pictures.
Beispiel: a *der Regenschirm*

2 Now use the German–English section to help find the plurals for the words you looked up in question 1.
Beispiel: a *der Regenschirm – zwei Regenschirme*

30

Advice on using reference sources.
1 a der Regenschirm **b** der Frosch **c** der Fußball **d** das Flugzeug **e** das Pferd **f** das Buch
2 a der Regenschirm – zwei Regenschirme **b** der Frosch – zwei Frösche **c** der Fußball – zwei Fußbälle **d** das Flugzeug – zwei Flugzeuge **e** das Pferd – zwei Pferde **f** das Buch – zwei Bücher

Grammatik 1
p. 31

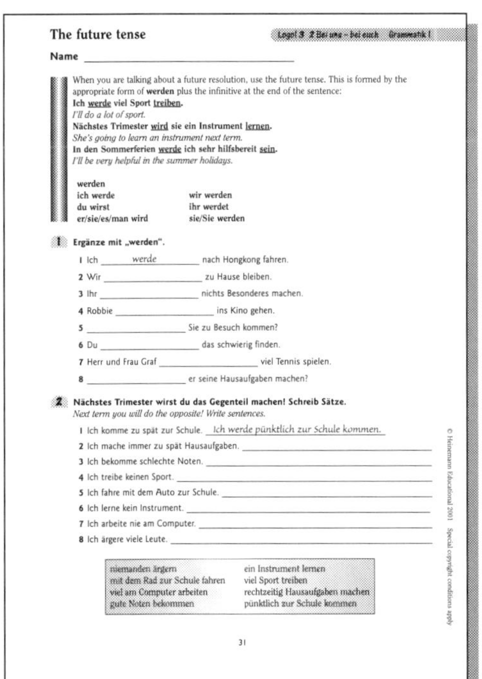

The future tense

Name

When you are talking about a future resolution, use the future tense. This is formed by the appropriate form of **werden** plus the infinitive at the end of the sentence:
Ich werde viel Sport treiben. *I'll do a lot of sport.*
Nächstes Trimester wird sie ein Instrument lernen. *She's going to learn an instrument next term.*
In den Sommerferien werde ich sehr hilfsbereit sein. *I'll be very helpful in the summer holidays.*

1 Ergänze mit „werden".

2 Nächstes Trimester wirst du das Gegenteil machen! Schreib Sätze. *Next term you will do the opposite! Write sentences.*

31

Practice of the future tense.
1 1 werde, **2** werden, **3** werdet, **4** wird, **5** Werden, **6** wirst, **7** werden, **8** wird,
2 1 Ich werde pünktlich zur Schule kommen. **2** Ich werde immer rechtzeitig Hausaufgaben machen. **3** Ich werde gute Noten bekommen. **4** Ich werde viel Sport treiben. **5** Ich werde mit dem Rad zur Schule fahren. **6** Ich werde ein Instrument lernen. **7** Ich werde viel am Computer arbeiten. **8** Ich werde niemanden ärgern.

Grammatik 2
p. 32

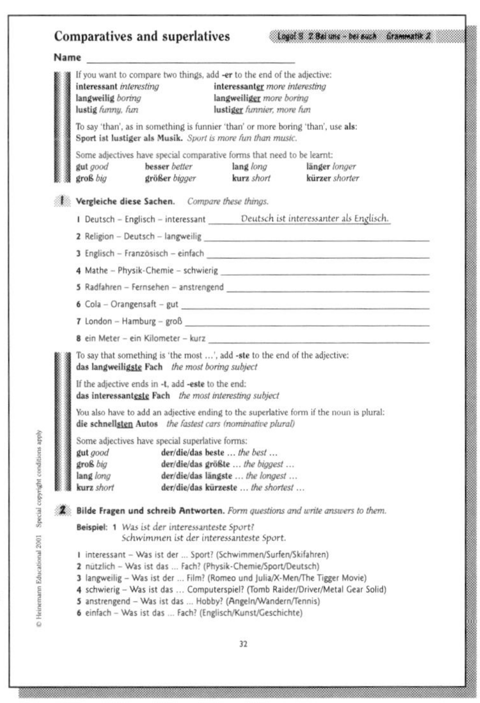

Comparatives and superlatives

Name

1 Vergleiche diese Sachen. *Compare these things.*

2 Bilde Fragen und schreib Antworten. *Form questions and write answers to them.*

32

Practice of comparatives and superlatives.
1 1 Deutsch ist interessanter als Englisch. **2** Religion ist langweiliger als Deutsch. **3** Englisch ist einfacher als Französisch. **4** Mathe ist schwieriger als Physik-Chemie. **5** Radfahren ist anstrengender als Fernsehen. **6** Cola ist besser als Orangensaft. **7** London ist größer als Hamburg. **8** Ein Meter ist kürzer als ein Kilometer.
2 1 interessanteste, **2** nützlichste, **3** langweiligste, **4** schwierigste, **5** anstrengendste, **6** einfachste

Grammatik 3 p. 33

Practice of *weil* + subordinate clause word order.

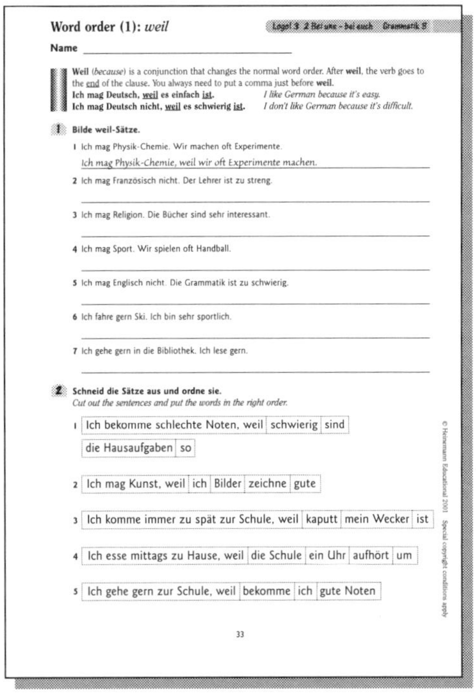

Word order (1): *weil*

Logo! 3 2 Bei uns – bei euch Grammatik 3

Name ______________________

Weil (*because*) is a conjunction that changes the normal word order. After **weil**, the verb goes to the end of the clause. You always need to put a comma just before **weil**.
Ich mag Deutsch, weil es einfach ist. *I like German because it's easy.*
Ich mag Deutsch nicht, weil es schwierig ist. *I don't like German because it's difficult.*

1 Bilde weil-Sätze.

1 Ich mag Physik-Chemie. Wir machen oft Experimente.
Ich mag Physik-Chemie, weil wir oft Experimente machen.
2 Ich mag Französisch nicht. Der Lehrer ist zu streng.
3 Ich mag Religion. Die Bücher sind sehr interessant.
4 Ich mag Sport. Wir spielen oft Handball.
5 Ich mag Englisch nicht. Die Grammatik ist zu schwierig.
6 Ich fahre gern Ski. Ich bin sehr sportlich.
7 Ich gehe gern in die Bibliothek. Ich lese gern.

2 Schneid die Sätze aus und ordne sie.
Cut out the sentences and put the words in the right order.

1 Ich bekomme schlechte Noten, weil | schwierig | sind | die Hausaufgaben | so
2 Ich mag Kunst, weil | ich | Bilder | zeichne | gute
3 Ich komme immer zu spät zur Schule, weil | kaputt | mein Wecker | ist
4 Ich esse mittags zu Hause, weil | die Schule | ein Uhr | aufhört | um
5 Ich gehe gern zur Schule, weil | bekomme | ich | gute Noten

33

1 **1** Ich mag Physik-Chemie, weil wir oft Experimente machen. **2** Ich mag Französisch nicht, weil der Lehrer zu streng ist. **3** Ich mag Religion, weil die Bücher sehr interessant sind. **4** Ich mag Sport, weil wir oft Handball spielen. **5** Ich mag Englisch nicht, weil die Grammatik zu schwierig ist. **6** Ich fahre gern Ski, weil ich sehr sportlich bin. **7** Ich gehe gern in die Bibliothek, weil ich gern lese.

2 **1** Ich bekomme schlechte Noten, weil die Hausaufgaben so schwierig sind. **2** Ich mag Kunst, weil ich gute Bilder zeichne. **3** Ich komme immer zu spät zur Schule, weil mein Wecker kaputt ist. **4** Ich esse mittags zu Hause , weil die Schule um ein Uhr aufhört. **5** Ich gehe gern zur Schule, weil ich gute Noten bekomme.

Wortschatz pp. 34–35 and Lernzieltest p. 36

These sheets are for revision at the end of the chapter. The *Wortschatz* sheet provides a list of all the key words and phrases from the chapter and the *Lernzieltest* gives a checklist of the areas covered, which pupils can check off as they revise.

3 Österreich und die Umwelt (Pupil's Book pp. 42–59)

Topic area	Key language	Skills	Grammar	PoS
3.2 Österreich für alle (pp. 42–43) Say why people visit Austria	*Warum fährst du nach Österreich? Ich fahre dahin, um Ski zu fahren, Wassersport zu treiben, wandern zu gehen, Salzburg zu besichtigen, Deutsch zu lernen, im See zu baden, die frische Luft zu genießen, Freunde zu besuchen.*	Using the grammar reference section Adapting a text / redrafting on computer	*um ... zu* Present tense of *fahren* (all forms)	2j, 3d, 4c
3.2 Österreich bei jedem Wetter (pp. 44–45) Say what you can do in all weathers	*Was machst du, wenn es heiß/schön ist, regnet, schneit? Wenn es heiß/kalt ist, schneit, regnet, fahre ich Ski, bleibe ich zu Hause, gehe ich Eis laufen / wandern / ins Kino / ins Hallenbad / einkaufen, bade ich im See, faulenze ich draußen, spiele ich Fußball/Tennis.*	Taking notes while listening	*wenn* + verb to the end	1b, 2i, 5e
3.3 Eine Woche in Salzburg (pp. 46–47) Say what people did on a visit	*Was haben sie am* [day] *gemacht? Am* [day] *haben sie eine Stadtrundfahrt gemacht / die Festung besichtigt, sind sie mit dem Zug nach München / mit dem Rad zum Hallenbad / in die Berge gefahren / einkaufen / ins Museum gegangen.*		Word order (inversion in perfect tense; time, manner, place)	1c, 2a
3.4 Stadt oder Dorf? (pp. 48–49) Talk about where you live	*Wo wohnst du? Ich wohne in Wien, in einem Dorf, in den Bergen, auf dem Land. Gefällt es dir dort? Ja, es gefällt mir hier / Nein, es gefällt mir nicht, weil die Luft so sauber/verschmutzt ist, viel/nichts los ist, ich viele/keine Freunde hier habe, es keine/schlechte Verkehrsverbindungen/Sportmöglichkeiten gibt, es viele/keine Cafés, Geschäfte und Kinos gibt.*	Preparing a short presentation on computer and cassette (Teacher's Guide only)	*weil* + verb to the end (revision) *gefallen* (revision)	5c, 5e
3.5 Umwelt-Aktionen (pp. 50–51) Talk about what you should do and what you do to help the environment	*Was sollte man für die Umwelt tun? Man sollte Wasser/Energie sparen, mit dem Rad fahren, Müll trennen, umweltfreundliche Produkte kaufen, alles Mögliche kompostieren, Was machst du für die Umwelt? Ich spare ..., kaufe ..., kompostiere ..., trenne ..., fahre ... .*		*man sollte* + infinitive to the end Present tense all forms (revision)	1b, 3c, 5a
3.6 Sehr geehrte Damen und Herren (pp. 52–53) Write a letter to a tourist office	*Teddington, den 4. Februar, Sehr geehrte Damen und Herren, ich möchte meinen Urlaub gern in ... verbringen und suche eine Ferienwohnung / ein Hotel für die Zeit vom ... bis ... Wir sind drei/ vier in der Gruppe – ein Erwachsener / zwei Erwachsene und ein Kind / zwei Kinder (12 und 16 Jahre alt). Ich interessiere mich auch für Informationen über Geschäfte/Kinos/Skifahren/ Radfahren/Wandern in der Region/Stadt. Mit vielem Dank im Voraus für Ihre Mühe. Mit freundlichen Grüßen*	Learning set phrases to re-use Adapting/Redrafting a letter on computer		2e, 3a
3.7 http://austria-tourism.at (pp. 54–55)		Groupwork		4a, 5e, 5g
Lernzieltest und Wiederholung (pp. 56–57)	Revision			5d
Wörter (pp. 58–59)	Word list			
Extra (pp. 114–115)	Differentiated reading and writing			3e

1 Österreich für alle (pp. 42–43)

Pupils will learn how to:

- talk about why people visit Austria

Key language
Warum fährst du nach Österreich?
Ich fahre dahin, um …
Ski zu fahren
Wassersport zu treiben
wandern zu gehen
Salzburg zu besichtigen
Deutsch zu lernen
im See zu baden
die frische Luft zu genießen
Freunde zu besuchen

Grammar focus
- *um … zu*
- present tense of *fahren* (all forms)

Skill focus
- using the grammar reference section
- adapting a text / redrafting on computer

Resources
- Cassette B, Side A
- Workbook p. 21
- R & A File: Arbeitsblatt 1 (p. 47), 4 (p. 115), Grammatik 1 (p. 52)

This chapter focuses on aspects of Austria, including environmental issues. Make sure that pupils are aware of Austria's location in Europe and encourage them to find out some basic facts about the country from the internet for homework.

This unit focuses on people's reasons for visiting Austria. Brainstorm ideas with the class first, then introduce the vocabulary orally using a copy of the visuals on Arbeitsblatt 1 (R & A File p. 47) on an OHT. Stress the word order used with *um … zu* constructions and familiarise pupils with the new sentence structure.

For further oral practice of the language, give each pair of pupils a set of the visuals. One pupil asks: *Warum fährst du nach Österreich?* and points to a visual. The other pupil gives the appropriate reply.

1a Hör zu. Welches Bild ist das? (1–8) (AT1 Level 2)

Pupils listen and decide which activity is mentioned each time.

Answers

1 g, **2** e, **3** a, **4** c, **5** d, **6** h, **7** f, **8** b

1 – Ich fahre dahin, um im See zu baden.
2 – Ich fahre dahin, um Deutsch zu lernen.
3 – Ich fahre dahin, um Ski zu fahren.
4 – Ich fahre dahin, um wandern zu gehen.
5 – Ich fahre dahin, um Salzburg zu besichtigen.
6 – Ich fahre dahin, um die frische Luft zu genießen.
7 – Ich fahre dahin, um Freunde zu besuchen.
8 – Ich fahre dahin, um Wassersport zu treiben.

1b Partnerarbeit. Ergänzt eure Sätze. (AT2 Levels 2–3)

Pupils build *um … zu* sentences themselves by completing the sentences started by their partner.

2a Hör zu. Schreib die Tabelle ab und füll sie aus. (1–6) (AT1 Level 3)

Pupils listen and write down where in Austria the people are going to and what they are going there for.

Answers

	Wohin?	Warum?
1	Gmunden	Wassersport
2	Innsbruck	Ski fahren
3	Zell am See	wandern gehen
4	Graz	Deutsch lernen
5	Wien	Wien besichtigen
6	Villach	im See baden, die frische Luft genießen

1 – Wo fahren Sie hin?
– Ich fahre nach Gmunden.
– Nach Gmunden? Sehr schön. Warum fahren Sie dahin?
– Tja, ich fahre nach Gmunden, um Wassersport zu treiben.
2 – Entschuldigung, wo fährst du hin?
– Ich fahre nach Innsbruck.
– Innsbruck … Ach, das ist schön. Warum fährst du denn nach Innsbruck?
– Um Ski zu fahren, natürlich.
3 – Und Sie? Wo fahren Sie hin?
– Ich fahre nach Zell am See.
– Also, Z.E.L.L. A.M. S.E.E. Super! Ich liebe Zell am See. Warum fahren Sie dahin?
– Tja, ich fahre dahin, um wandern zu gehen.
4 – Fahren Sie auch nach Zell am See?
– Nein, ich fahre nach Graz.
– Also, G.R.A.Z. Graz. O.K. Aber warum denn Graz?
– Also, ich fahre dahin, um Deutsch zu lernen.
5 – Entschuldigung, wo fährst du hin?
– Ich fahre nach Österreich, um Wien zu besichtigen.
– Ach, Wien ist die schönste Stadt in Europa. Gute Reise!
6 – Wo fahren Sie hin?
– Ich fahre nach Österreich.
– Ja, aber wohin genau?
– Tja, ich fahre nach Villach.
– V.I.L.L.A.C.H. O.K. Das habe ich. Warum denn Villach?
– Ich fahre dahin, um im See zu baden und um die frische Luft zu genießen.

2b Schreib Sätze über die Leute aus Übung 2a. (AT4 Level 3)

Pupils write up their findings from activity 2a in *um … zu* sentences.

Answers

Person 1 fährt nach Gmunden, um Wassersport zu treiben. **Person 2** fährt nach Innsbruck, um Ski zu fahren. **Person 3** fährt nach Zell am See, um wandern zu gehen. **Person 4** fährt nach Graz, um Deutsch zu lernen. **Person 5** fährt nach Wien, um Wien zu besichtigen. **Person 6** fährt nach Villach, um im See zu baden und die frische Luft zu genießen.

Grammatik: *um ... zu* – in order to
This grammar box shows pupils how to form the *um ... zu* sentences. Point out the use of the comma before *um* and that the infinitive is sent to the end after *zu*.

Refer to p. 133 of the Pupil's Book for further information. More practice of this grammar point is also provided on Grammatik 1 (R & A File p. 52).

Ludwig: Using the grammar reference section
Ludwig reminds pupils that the grammar section at the back of the Pupil's Book is there to support them whenever they encounter new grammar. Encourage pupils to read the explanations and do the activities each time they encounter a new item of grammar, and to go back over the activities as revision as they progress through the course.

3a Gruppenarbeit. Wähl einen Grund auf Seite 42 aus. Wer hat denselben Grund wie du? (AT2 Levels 3–4)
Pupils each select a reason for going to Austria and then circulate in the class to see how many other pupils have chosen the same reason. They should note down everybody's reasons for the next part of the task. Instead of taking a reason from p. 42, pupils may prefer to make up their own reasons.

3b Schreib deine Resultate auf. (AT4 Levels 3–4)
Pupils write up the results of their questioning, taking care to use the correct part of the verb *fahren* to do so.

Grammatik: The present tense of *fahren*
This grammar box shows pupils the present tense conjugation of *fahren*. Point out the irregular *du* and *er/sie* forms, which add an umlaut to the *a*.

4a Lies den Text. Richtig oder falsch? (AT3 Level 4)
Pupils read a text written by an Austrian boy and answer eight true/false statements on it.

Answers
1 richtig, **2** richtig, **3** falsch, **4** falsch, **5** falsch, **6** falsch, **7** richtig, **8** falsch

4b Schreib Ricos Text am Computer. Ändere dann die unterstrichenen Wörter für dich. Ist dein Land wie Österreich? (AT4 Levels 4–5)
Pupils change the underlined parts in Rico's text to write about themselves and their country.

Ludwig: Adapting a text / redrafting on computer
If pupils have access to a computer, they should follow Ludwig's advice and prepare this written work on it. This makes subsequent corrections and refinements much easier to do and pupils end up with a neat and accurate piece of written work. Warn pupils against spending too much time formatting and adding graphics to their text. For this type of activity, they should just treat the computer as a useful tool for writing.

R Further practice in coping with writing activities is provided on Arbeitsblatt 4 (R & A File p. 115).

2 Österreich bei jedem Wetter (pp. 44–45)

Pupils will learn how to:
- talk about what they can do in all weathers

Key language
Was machst du,
wenn es ... ?
heiß/schön ist
regnet/schneit
Wenn es ... , ...
fahre ich Ski
bleibe ich zu Hause
gehe ich Eis laufen / wandern / einkaufen
gehe ich ins Kino/Hallenbad
bade ich im See
faulenze ich draußen
spiele ich Fußball/Tennis

Grammar focus
- *wenn* + subordinate clause word order

Skill focus
- taking notes while listening

Resources
- Cassette B, Side A
- Workbook pp. 22, 27
- R & A File: Arbeitsblatt 2 (p. 48), Grammatik 2 (p. 53)

This unit introduces *wenn* clauses in the context of suitable activities for different weather conditions. Introduce the new language by presenting the visuals on Arbeitsblatt 2 (R & A File p. 48) on an OHT and familiarising pupils with the word order of the *wenn* clause. Point to a weather visual and an activity visual and build the sentence up. Once pupils are familiar with the language, get them to complete the activity part of the sentence when you have supplied the *wenn* clause, e.g.: *Wenn es heiß ist,* ... . Finally, get pupils to make up both parts of the sentence.

For further oral practice, give each pair of pupils a set of the visuals on Arbeitsblatt 2 to cut up and put into two groups face-down on the desk: weather and activities. One pupil then turns over a visual from the weather pile and starts the sentence: *Wenn es heiß ist,* ... . The other pupil turns over an activity visual and completes the sentence: *fahre ich Ski.* If the sentence makes sense, then the pupil who said the second part of it gets a point. If not, he/she loses a point.

1a Wer sagt das? (AT3 Level 2)

Pupils look at the table and read the statements 1–12. They decide who said each statement.

Answers

1 Jana, **2** Rico, **3** Jana, **4** Annabel, **5** Annabel, **6** Rico, **7** Rico, **8** Jana, **9** Annabel, **10** Jana, **11** Annabel, **12** Rico

1b Hör zu. Wer spricht? (1–12) (AT1 Levels 2–3)

Pupils listen to the recording and look at the table in activity 1a to work out who is speaking.

Answers

1 Annabel, **2** Rico, **3** Jana, **4** Jana, **5** Jana, **6** Annabel, **7** Rico, **8** Rico, **9** Rico, **10** Jana, **11** Annabel, **12** Annabel

1 – Wenn es regnet, gehe ich ins Hallenbad. Schwimmen ist mein Lieblingshobby.
2 – Wenn es regnet, gehe ich ins Kino. Ich liebe Horrorfilme.
3 – Wenn es heiß ist, spiele ich Fußball.
4 – Wenn es regnet, gehe ich einkaufen. Ich gehe so gern einkaufen.
5 – Wenn es schneit, gehe ich Eis laufen.
6 – Wenn es schneit, bleibe ich zu Hause. Dann lese ich oder ich sehe fern.
7 – Wenn es heiß ist, bade ich im See. Das finde ich wunderbar.
8 – Wenn es schneit, fahre ich Ski. Das mache ich sehr gern.
9 – Wenn es schön ist, spiele ich Tennis. Ich kann sehr gut Tennis spielen.
10 – Wenn es schön ist, gehe ich wandern. Das finde ich ein bisschen anstrengend.
11 – Wenn es heiß ist, faulenze ich draußen. Fantastisch!
12 – Wenn es schön ist, mache ich eine Radtour. Das mache ich oft mit meiner Familie.

1c Partnerarbeit. (AT2 Level 3)

Pupils produce the *wenn* clauses for themselves now, based on the table in activity 1a.

2 Wähl die richtige Antwort aus. (AT3 Level 2)

Pupils choose the appropriate end for each *wenn* sentence.

Answers

1 Wenn es kalt ist, trägt man <u>einen Pulli</u>. **2** Wenn es regnet, braucht man <u>einen Regenschirm</u>. **3** Wenn es sonnig ist, braucht man <u>eine Sonnenbrille</u>. **4** Wenn es heiß ist, geht man <u>baden</u>. **5** Wenn es schneit, fährt man <u>Ski</u>. **6** Wenn es windig ist, geht man <u>windsurfen</u>. **7** Wenn man sehr hungrig ist, isst man <u>Hamburger mit Pommes</u>. **8** Wenn man nach Österreich fährt, spricht man <u>Deutsch</u>.

Grammatik: *Wenn* – 'when/if' + verb to the end

This grammar box shows pupils the structure of a *wenn* sentence, emphasising the verb–comma–verb structure, which needs to be learned. Brainstorm other activities which pupils do in different weather conditions, to practise *wenn* sentences further.

Refer to p. 133 of the Pupil's Book for further information. More practice of this grammar point is also provided on Grammatik 2 (R & A File p. 53) and on p. 27 of the Workbook.

3 Hör zu und mach Notizen. (1–4) (AT1 Level 4)

Pupils listen and make notes about four teenagers' activities in various weather conditions.

Answers

1 kalt: zu Hause, langweilig; **2** sonnig: Radtour, sehr gern; schneit: Eis laufen, super; **3** regnet: wandern, liebe Regen; windig: Kino, Wind schrecklich; **4** schön: faulenze, bade im See, das beste Wetter; kalt: zu Hause, O.K.

1 – Was machst du, wenn es kalt ist?
– Tja, wenn es kalt ist, bleibe ich zu Hause.
– Und wie findest du das?
– Ach, ich finde das total langweilig.
2 – Was machst du, wenn es sonnig ist?
– Wenn es sonnig ist, mache ich eine Radtour.
– Ach, du machst eine Radtour? Sehr schön.
– Ja, das mache ich sehr gern.
– Und wenn es schneit? Was machst du dann?
– Wenn es schneit, gehe ich Eis laufen.
– Ach, Eislaufen kann ich nicht ausstehen.
– Doch, das finde ich super.
3 – Was machst du, wenn es regnet?
– Tja, wenn es regnet, gehe ich wandern.
– Wandern? Magst du das?
– Ja, ich nehme einen Regenschirm mit – ich liebe den Regen!
– Und was machst du, wenn es windig ist?
– Wenn es windig ist, gehe ich ins Kino.
– Das ist eine gute Idee. Ich hasse den Wind.
– Ja, ich auch. Den Wind finde ich schrecklich.
4 – Was machst du, wenn es schön ist?
– Wenn es schön ist, faulenze ich draußen oder ich bade im See.
– Und das gefällt dir gut, oder?
– Ja, schönes Wetter ist das beste Wetter!
– Und was machst du, wenn es kalt ist?
– Ach, wenn es kalt ist, bleibe ich meistens zu Hause.
– Gefällt dir das?
– Ja, das ist O.K.

Ludwig: Taking notes while listening

Ludwig reminds pupils that they must just write notes while they listen. Writing full sentences is time-consuming and unnecessary.

4 Was sagen diese Leute? Schreib Sätze. (AT4 Levels 3–4)

Pupils look at the pictures and write *wenn* sentences to describe what the people do in different types of weather.

Answers

a Wenn es heiß ist, bleibe ich zu Hause. **b** Wenn es schneit, gehe ich ins Kino. **c** Wenn es regnet, spiele ich Fußball. **d** Wenn es schön ist, gehe ich Eis laufen. **e** Wenn es regnet, gehe ich einkaufen. **f** Wenn es schneit, gehe ich ins Hallenbad.

► 5 Schreib Unsinnsätze. (AT4 Levels 3–4)

Pupils make up nonsense sentences for what they do in different types of weather. You could have a class session afterwards to see who has come up with the craziest ideas!

R Further practice of this unit's language is to be found on p. 114 of the Pupil's Book, activity 1.

E Further practice of this unit's language is to be found on p. 115 of the Pupil's Book, activity 1.

3 Eine Woche in Salzburg
(pp. 46–47)

Pupils will learn how to:
- talk about what people did on a visit

Key language	Grammar focus
Was haben sie am Montag gemacht? Am Montag haben sie ... eine Stadtrundfahrt gemacht die Festung besichtigt Am Montag sind sie ... mit dem Zug nach München gefahren mit dem Rad zum Hallenbad gefahren in die Berge gefahren einkaufen gegangen ins Museum gegangen	• word order (inversion in perfect tense; time, manner, place) **Resources** • Cassette B, Side A • Workbook pp. 23, 27 • R & A File: Arbeitsblatt 4 (p. 50), Grammatik 3 (p. 54)

This unit focuses on Rico's visit to Annabel in Salzburg and provides practice of the plural of the perfect tense. Most of the vocabulary should be familiar to pupils, so familiarise them with the inverted word order by starting sentences and inviting them to supply the past participle: *Am Dienstag haben sie die Festung ...* . Next, just give the day: *Am Samstag ...* . Sketch a quick symbol on the board/OHT to depict the activity.

1a Hör zu und lies. (AT1 Level 4, AT3 Level 4)
Pupils listen to the recording and read the photo diary of Annabel's and Rico's week in Salzburg. Show pupils the location of Salzburg on the map of Austria at the front of the Pupil's Book and find out whether any class members have visited the city or know anything about it.

- Letzte Woche waren Rico und Annabel in Salzburg. Sie haben vieles gemacht ...
- Am Montag haben sie eine Stadtrundfahrt gemacht.
- Am Dienstag haben sie die Festung besichtigt.
- Am Mittwoch sind sie einkaufen gegangen.
- Am Donnerstag sind sie mit dem Zug nach München gefahren.
- Am Freitag sind sie in die Berge gefahren.
- Am Samstag hat es geregnet und sie sind ins Museum gegangen.
- Am Sonntag sind sie mit dem Rad zum Hallenbad gefahren.

1b Partnerarbeit: Frage und Antwort. Person B macht das Buch zu. (AT2 Level 5)
Pupils question each other about what Annabel and Rico did in Salzburg.

Grammatik: Word order
Remind pupils of the basic German word order rules. The verb always comes in second place. If the sentence contains adverbial expressions – information about 'when?' (time), 'how?' (manner) or 'where?' (place) – time expressions always come first, then manner and finally place. Remind pupils that it is common to invert sentences by beginning with a time expression rather than the subject.

R Refer to pp. 133–34 of the Pupil's Book for further information. More practice of this grammar point is also provided on Grammatik 3 (R & A File p. 54) and p. 27 of the Workbook.

2 Hör zu. Was haben Otto und seine Freunde letzte Woche gemacht? Korrigiere die Sätze. (AT1 Level 5)
Pupils listen to Otto's account of what he and his friends did last week and they correct the six statements to reflect what they hear.

Answers

1 Am Montag sind sie Ski gefahren und es war anstrengend. **2** Am Mittwoch haben sie die Festung besichtigt und es war O.K./langweilig. **3** Am Sonntag sind sie in die Berge gefahren und das war toll. **4** Am Donnerstag sind sie einkaufen gegangen, und es war gut. **5** Am Dienstag sind sie mit dem Bus nach Innsbruck gefahren. **6** Am Freitag sind sie ins Museum gegangen. Das war sehr interessant.

- Hallo, Otto. Was habt ihr am Montag gemacht?
- Ach, wir sind Ski gefahren.
- Und wie habt ihr das gefunden?
- Es war sehr anstrengend.
- Und was habt ihr am Mittwoch gemacht?
- Am Mittwoch? Also, am Mittwoch haben wir die Festung besichtigt.
- Schön! Wie war das?
- O.K. ... aber ich habe es ein bisschen langweilig gefunden.
- Und am Sonntag? Was habt ihr dann gemacht?
- Am Sonntag sind wir in die Berge gefahren.
- Sehr gut.
- Ja, das war super – die Berge sind toll.
- Und was habt ihr am Donnerstag gemacht?
- Am Donnerstag sind wir einkaufen gegangen.
- Ach ja. Und was hast du gekauft?
- Ich habe ein Geschenk für meine Mutter gekauft. Das war gut.
- Und was habt ihr am Dienstag gemacht?
- Am Dienstag sind wir mit dem Bus nach Innsbruck gefahren.
- War das schön?
- Nein, es war sehr kalt und es hat geregnet.
- Und was habt ihr am Freitag gemacht?
- Am Freitag sind wir ins Museum gegangen. Das war sehr interessant. Ich habe viel über Österreich gelernt.

3a Lies Janas Tagebuch. An welchem Tag war das? (AT3 Level 5)

Pupils read Jana's diary account of a school trip and decide on which day she did each of the activities depicted.
Erratum: teachers using the first printing (April 2001) of the Pupil's Book, please note that the pictures in question **3a** (p. 47) should be as follows: **a** shopping, **b** mountains, **c** disco, **d** bus to Graz, **e** looking at the city through the bus window, **f** train home. The item showing Jana and Peter on bikes should be omitted.

Answers

a am Mittwoch, **b** am Dienstag, **c** am Freitag, **d** am Montag, **e** am Donnerstag, **f** am Samstag

3b Beantworte die Fragen.

Pupils answer six comprehension questions in German about Jana's diary. There is no need for them to answer in full sentences.

Answers

1 am Dienstag, **2** sehr nett, **3** ein Geschenk für seine Schwester, **4** in die Disco, **5** sie war krank, **6** seine Freundin

4 Du hast eine Woche in Salzburg verbracht. Beschreib die Woche. (AT4 Levels 5–6)

Pupils write a diary for a week's visit to Salzburg, using the information in this unit. They can also include any other activities in their diary which they might have been able to do while in Salzburg, i. e. go skiing, enjoy coffee and cakes, go ice skating etc.

Pupils compare their diaries in pairs to find out whether they did the same things, and to discuss who had the more interesting week.

The pairwork activity on Arbeitsblatt 4 (R & A File p. 50) provides further oral practice of the language of the unit.

MINI-TEST

At the end of the third unit in every chapter there is a *Mini-Test*. This is intended as a half-way checkpoint for pupils to check that they are familiar with the key language of the chapter so far. Pupils could revise the language with a partner in class or for homework.

4 Stadt oder Dorf? (pp. 48–49)

Pupils will learn how to:
- talk about where they live

<table>
<tr><td>

Key language
Wo wohnst du?
Ich wohne ...
in Wien
in einem Dorf
in den Bergen
auf dem Land
Gefällt es dir dort?
Ja, es gefällt mir hier, weil ...
Nein, es gefällt mir nicht, weil ...
die Luft so sauber/verschmutzt ist
viel/nichts los ist
ich viele/keine Freunde hier habe
es gute/keine/schlechte Verkehrsverbindungen gibt
es gute/keine Sportmöglichkeiten gibt
es viele/keine Cafés, Geschäfte und Kinos gibt

</td><td>

Grammar focus
- *weil* + subordinate clause word order (revision)
- *gefallen* (revision)

Skill focus
- prepare a short presentation on computer and cassette (Teacher's Guide only)

Resources
- Cassette B, Side A
- Workbook p. 24

</td></tr>
</table>

This unit focuses on the environment in which you live and your opinion of it. The three characters from this chapter, Jana, Rico and Annabel, explain where they live and give their opinions. Read through the speech bubbles with the class and make two lists on the board/OHT for positive and negative opinions given.

1a Hör zu und lies. Welches Foto gehört wem? (AT1 Level 4, AT3 Level 4)

Pupils read the speech bubbles and identify each character's home location.

Answers
a Jana, **b** Annabel, **c** Rico

- Hallo! Ich heiße Jana und ich wohne in einem Dorf in den Bergen. Es gefällt mir hier, weil die Luft so sauber ist. Ich habe viele Freunde hier und im Winter fahre ich Ski.
- Grüß dich! Ich heiße Annabel und ich wohne in Salzburg. Es gefällt mir hier sehr, weil viel los ist. Es gefällt mir auch, weil es gute Verkehrsverbindungen gibt.
- Servus! Ich bin Rico und ich wohne auf dem Land. Es gefällt mir hier nicht, weil nichts los ist. Es gibt keine Cafés, keine Kinos, keine Geschäfte und keine Sportmöglichkeiten. Die Verkehrsverbindungen sind auch furchtbar.

1b Ist das Jana, Annabel oder Rico? (AT3 Level 4)

Pupils read the statements and look at the speech bubbles to identify whose home location is being described.

Answers
1 Rico, **2** Jana, **3** Jana, **4** Annabel, **5** Rico, **6** Annabel, **7** Rico

2a Was passt zusammen? (AT3 Level 3)

Pupils decide which of six *weil* clauses go with *Es gefällt mir hier* and which go with *Es gefällt mir hier nicht.*

Answers
Es gefällt mir hier: 1, 3; Es gefällt mir hier nicht: 2, 4, 5, 6

2b Wie ist dein Wohnort? Hast du noch weitere Ideen? (AT4 Level 4)

Pupils write about where they live, using the language just presented and offering any further ideas specific to their home location.

3 Hör zu. Schreib die Tabelle ab und füll sie aus. (1–4) (AT1 Levels 4–5)

Pupils listen to four Austrian teenagers talking about where they live. Pupils note down where they live, whether they like it or not and also any reasons they give.

Answers

Wohnort	☺	☹	Warum?
1 Graz	✓		viel los, Geschäfte
2 Wien		✓	verschmutzt, keine Freunde
3 Dorf	✓		viele Freunde, Ski fahren, frische Luft, fast kein Verkehr
4 Land		✓	langweilig, keine Sportmöglichkeiten, Verkehrsverbindungen sind schlecht, hat nur einen kleinen Supermarkt

1 – Hallo. Wo wohnst du?
– Ich wohne in Graz.
– Ach, das ist eine schöne Stadt, nicht?
– Ja, ich mag Graz sehr.
– Warum denn?
– Tja, weil dort so viel los ist.
– Ja, das ist gut.
– Und ich mag es auch, weil die Geschäfte toll sind.
2 – Hallo, wo wohnst du?
– Ich wohne in Wien.
– Ach, die schöne Hauptstadt. Wie findest du Wien?
– Also, Wien gefällt mir nicht.
– Wien gefällt dir nicht? Das kann ich nicht glauben!
– Doch, die Luft ist sehr verschmutzt – es gibt so viel

Verkehr in der Stadt und das finde ich schrecklich.
- Ach, ja, das kann ich verstehen. Aber gibt's sonst noch Gründe?
- Ja, ich habe keine Freunde hier.
- Wie bitte?
- Ich habe keine Freunde hier.
- O, das ist schade. Wie lange wohnst du jetzt in Wien?
- Erst drei Monate.
- Ach, du wirst bald Freunde kennen lernen.

3 – Hallo, wo wohnst du?
- Ich wohne in einem Dorf.
- Ach, schön! Wie gefällt es dir dort?
- Ach, es geht. Ich habe viele Freunde dort, weil ich schon zehn Jahre lang dort wohne.
- Schön. Ist das ein Dorf in den Bergen?
- Ja, also im Winter fahren wir Ski. Das ist wunderbar.
- Ski fahren! Ja, das muss ganz toll sein.
- Ja, ich mag das Dorf auch sehr, weil die Luft so frisch ist. Wir haben fast keinen Verkehr und man kann draußen auf der Straße spielen.
- Na, so was.

4 – Hallo, wo wohnst du?
- Ich wohne auf dem Land.
- Schön. Wie gefällt es dir dort?
- Ach, ich finde das Landleben sehr langweilig.
- Wirklich? Warum denn?
- Tja, weil es keine Sportmöglichkeiten gibt und die Verkehrsverbindungen sehr schlecht sind.
- Also, keine Sportmöglichkeiten und schlechte Verkehrsverbindungen. Ja, das ist schade. Aber gibt es nichts für junge Leute? Gibt es keine Geschäfte oder Cafés?
- Nee! Hier gibt es nur einen kleinen Supermarkt. Sonst nichts!
- Aber kannst du nicht mal Ski fahren?
- Nee, hier gibt es keine Berge!

4 Partnerarbeit. (AT2 Levels 4–6)
Pupils conduct interviews about where people live and what they think of it, based on question prompts and language grid provided.

Pupils circulate in the class and interview people to find out about where they live and what they think of it.

5 Schreib am Computer eine Präsentation über deinen Wohnort. (AT4 Levels 4–6)
Pupils write a detailed presentation on computer about where they live, providing as much detail as possible. Remind pupils to print their work and correct / add to it and then print a finalised version.

Pupils record their presentation on a cassette to help them to memorise it for presenting to the class later on. If they want to make subsequent changes, they can do so quite readily on the computer and then print another version to record and memorise.

5 Umwelt-Aktionen (pp. 50–51)

Pupils will learn how to:

- talk about what you should do and what they do to help the environment

Key language

Was sollte man für die Umwelt tun?

Man sollte …

- Wasser/Energie sparen
- mit dem Rad fahren
- Müll trennen
- umweltfreundliche Produkte kaufen
- alles Mögliche kompostieren

Was tust du für die Umwelt?

Ich spare Wasser/Energie.

Ich fahre mit dem Rad.

Ich trenne Müll.

Ich kaufe umweltfreundliche Produkte.

Ich kompostiere alles Mögliche.

Grammar focus

- *man sollte* + infinitive to the end
- present tense all forms (revision)

Resources

- Cassette B, Side A
- Workbook p. 25
- R & A File: Arbeitsblatt 3 (p. 49), Grammatik 2 (p. 74)

This unit focuses on things everybody can do to help the environment. Austria, like Germany, is very aware of environmental issues and pupils might be able to research the topic on the internet, starting with www.greenpeace.at or using an Austrian search engine, such as www.a-site.at or www.austronaut.at or www.softsurf.com to find relevant information.

Have a class brainstorming session to gather some initial ideas on the board/OHT. Then introduce the new language orally, using the visuals on Arbeitsblatt 3 (R & A File p. 49) copied onto an OHT. Discuss how far the ideas of the class match those on the OHT.

For further oral practice, give each pair of pupils two sets of the visuals and text from Arbeitsblatt 3 above: they cut up the visuals and each keeps a copy of the text. Pupils take turns turning over a visual and saying the appropriate sentence. If they say it correctly, they place the visual on the matching text. If they say it incorrectly or they already have that visual, they replace it face-down on the desk. The winner is the first pupil to have collected a complete set of visuals.

1a Hör zu und wiederhole. Welches Bild ist das? (1–6) (AT1 Level 3)

Pupils listen to the recording and repeat the six sentences, identifying which picture matches each statement.

Answers

1 c, **2** e, **3** a, **4** f, **5** d, **6** b

1 – Man sollte mit dem Rad fahren.
2 – Man sollte umweltfreundliche Produkte kaufen.
3 – Man sollte Wasser sparen.
4 – Man sollte alles Mögliche kompostieren.
5 – Man sollte Müll trennen.
6 – Man sollte Energie sparen.

1b Partnerarbeit. (AT2 Levels 3–4)

Pupils question each other about the pictures at the top of the page to reinforce the new structure with *sollte*.

Grammatik: Talking about what you should do

Remind pupils that *man sollte* works in the same way as *man darf*, sending the infinitive to the end of the sentence.

R Refer to p. 127 of the Pupil's Book for further information. More practice of word order with modals is provided on Grammatik 2 (R & A File p. 74).

2 Mach ein Umweltposter. (AT4 Level 3)

Pupils make an environmental poster, giving ideas for helping the environment. Some of the ideas from the class brainstorming session could be included here.

3a Lies den Artikel. Wer ist nicht sehr umweltfreundlich? (AT3 Levels 4–5)

Pupils read the texts and decide who is the least environmentally friendly person.

Answers

Annabel

3b Was tun Jana, Annabel und Rico für die Umwelt? Schreib Sätze. (AT4 Level 4)

Pupils summarise what the three teenagers do to help the environment.

Answers

Jana und Rico kaufen umweltfreundliche Produkte. Jana hat einen Komposthaufen im Garten. Jana, Annabel und Rico trennen Müll. Rico fährt immer mit dem Rad. Rico spart Wasser und Energie.

Wiederholung: The present tense

This grammar revision box reminds pupils of the present tense forms of the five key verbs in this unit. Go through the paradigms with pupils, pointing out the different endings and reminding them to use them accurately in their work.

4 Hör zu und mach Notizen. Wer ist die umweltfreundlichste Person? (1–4) (AT1 Levels 5–6)

Pupils listen to four teenagers talking about what they do to help the environment. Pupils make notes and then decide which person does the most for the environment.

Answers

1 Müll trennen, Energie sparen; **2** Müll trennen, mit dem Rad/Bus fahren, umweltfreundliche Produkte kaufen; **3** Energie und Wasser sparen, Müll trennen, recyclen, mit dem Rad fahren; **4** Müll trennen, mit dem Rad fahren
Number 3 is the most environmentally friendly person.

1 – Also, ich interessiere mich nicht so sehr für die Umwelt, aber ich tue schon was dafür. Zum Beispiel trenne ich Müll. Das finde ich wichtig, weil wir alle zu viel Müll haben. Und ich spare auch Energie. Es geht mir total auf die Nerven, wenn die Leute dauernd die Tür und die Fenster aufhaben und die Heizung auch an ist. Das ist schrecklich.

2 Also, ich versuche mal, der Umwelt zu helfen, indem ich Müll trenne. Ich fahre auch oft mit dem Rad zur Schule, und wenn ich in die Stadt fahre, fahre ich immer mit dem Bus – nie mit dem Auto. Im Supermarkt kaufe ich meistens umweltfreundliche Produkte, zum Beispiel Schreibpapier, Lebensmittel und Kleidung. Das finde ich wichtig, aber es kann auch ziemlich teuer sein.

3 – Die Umwelt ist sehr wichtig und ich versuche, möglichst viel dafür zu tun. Erstens spare ich Energie und Wasser. Das finde ich sehr wichtig und gar nicht schwierig. Ich trenne auch immer Müll, weil das jetzt ein Teil vom Alltag geworden ist, und ich recycle das, was ich nicht wegwerfen kann. Auch fahre ich so oft wie möglich mit dem Rad – das heißt, wenn das Wetter nicht zu schrecklich ist.

4 – Tja, die Umwelt ist ein wichtiges Thema, das weiß ich, aber ich kann mich nicht dafür interessieren. Ich weiß, das wir zu viel Müll produzieren, aber was kann ich tun? Also, ich trenne Müll, weil man das machen muss. Ich fahre auch oft mit dem Rad, aber das mache ich, weil ich das mag, nicht weil es umweltfreundlich ist! Meine Mutter kauft immer umweltfreundliche Produkte, aber sie gefallen mir nicht, also schreibe ich auf normalem Papier!

5 Gruppenarbeit. Wie umweltfreundlich ist eure Klasse? Macht eine Umfrage. (AT2 Levels 4–5)

Pupils do a survey in the class to see how environmentally friendly its members are.

Pupils write their results up to show what they found out, e.g. *Eine Person trennt Müll. Fünf Personen fahren mit dem Rad.*

6 Was machst du für die Umwelt? Schreib einen kurzen Text. (AT4 Levels 4–5)

Pupils write a text about what they do for the environment. Encourage them to use some of the structures they have learned so far in Logo! 3, such as *weil, um ... zu* and *wenn* clauses and modal verbs.

6 Sehr geehrte Damen und Herren (pp. 52–53)

Pupils will learn how to:
- write a letter to a tourist office

Key language
Teddington, den 4. Februar,
Sehr geehrte Damen und Herren,
Ich möchte meinen Urlaub gern in … verbringen.
Ich suche eine Ferienwohnung/ein Hotel.
für die Zeit vom … bis …
Wir sind drei/vier in der Gruppe.
ein Erwachsener/zwei Erwachsene und ein Kind/zwei Kinder
Ich interessiere mich auch für Informationen über … in der Region/Stadt.
Geschäfte
Kinos
Skifahren
Radfahren
Wandern
Mit vielem Dank im Voraus für Ihre Mühe.
Mit freundlichen Grüßen

Skill focus
- learn set phrases to re-use
- adapt/redraft a letter on computer

Resources
- Cassette B, Side A
- Workbook p. 26

This unit shows pupils how to write a formal letter to a tourist office, requesting information for a visit. Introduce the letter by copying the red phrases onto the board/OHT and discussing possible alternatives for each one, e.g. *Gmunden* could be *Salzburg*, *Villach* or *Wien; eine Ferienwohnung* could be *ein Hotel* or *einen Campingplatz.*

Gmunden is a picturesque lake-side resort, not far from Salzburg. Further information can be found on its website at www.tiscover.com/gmunden.

1a Lies den Brief. Welche Familie möchte nach Gmunden fahren? (AT3 Level 4)
Pupils read the letter and decide which of the families wants to travel to Gmunden.

Answers
Familie b

1b Verbinde die Satzhälften.
Pupils connect the sentence halves according to the information in the letter.

Answers
1 f, **2** c, **3** e, **4** b, **5** a, **6** d

2a Was passt zusammen? (AT3 Level 4)
Pupils match German sentences taken from letters to their English equivalents.

Answers
1 f, **2** e, **3** b, **4** a, **5** d, **6** c

2b Welche Sätze oben schreibt man in einem Brief ans Verkehrsamt?
Pupils decide which of the sentences would be found in a formal letter to a tourist office.

Answers
1, 4, 5

Ludwig: Learn set phrases to re-use
Encourage pupils to learn the extracts from the formal letter so they can then re-use them in future letters on other subjects.

3a Hör zu. Schreib die Tabelle ab und füll sie aus. (1–4) (AT1 Levels 4–5)
Pupils listen to the recording and note down the holiday booking requirements of four tourists.

Answers

	Wo?	Wann?	Unterkunft?	Erwachsene/ Kinder?	Sonstiges?
1	Wien	2. – 10. Sep.	Hotel	2/1 (12 J.)	Theater/ Kinos
2	Graz	20.– 30. Juli	Ferienwohnung	1/3 (10, 15, 17 J.)	Eis laufen
3	Salzburg	13.–16. Februar	Hotel	2/0	Ski fahren
4	Linz	4.–16. Mai	Hotel	1/0	Liste von Restaurants

1 – Hallo, Verkehrsamt Wien. Kann ich Ihnen helfen?
– Ja, ich möchte im September nach Wien fahren.
– Sehr gut. Wann im September wäre das?
– Also, vom zweiten bis zehnten September.
– Alles klar. Suchen Sie ein Hotel?
– Ja, ich brauche ein Hotel.
– Und wie viele Leute sind das in der Gruppe?
– Also, wir sind zwei Erwachsene und ein Kind.
– Zwei Erwachsene und ein Kind. Wie alt ist das Kind?
– Ach .. äh … zwölf Jahre alt. Und wir suchen auch Informationen über Theater und Kinos in Wien. Haben Sie so was?
– Ja, Moment mal, bitte …
2 – Hallo, Verkehrsamt Graz. Kann ich Ihnen helfen?
– Ja, ich möchte im Juli nach Graz fahren.
– Ja. Was sind die Daten?
– Also, ich möchte vom 20. bis 30. Juli Urlaub machen.
– Aha. Suchen Sie ein Hotel oder eine Ferienwohnung?
– Eine Ferienwohnung, bitte.

- Und wie viele Leute kommen?
- Vier. Ein Erwachsener und drei Kinder. Die Kinder sind 10, 15 und 17 Jahre alt.
- Also, 10, 15 und 17 Jahre alt. ... O.K. Und brauchen Sie sonst noch etwas?
- Ja, wir interessieren uns für Eis laufen. Gibt es eine Eishalle in der Stadt?
- Ja, klar. Also, ich schaue schnell auf dem Computer nach. Moment mal ...

3
- Hallo, Verkehrsamt Salzburg. Kann ich Ihnen helfen?
- Ja, ich möchte im Februar nach Salzburg kommen.
- Ja. Wann wäre das genau?
- Also, vom 13. bis 16. Februar.
- O.K. Suchen Sie ein Hotel oder eine Ferienwohnung?
- Ein Hotel, bitte.
- Und wie viele Leute kommen?
- Zwei. Nur zwei Erwachsene. Wir wollen Ski fahren, also brauchen wir ein Hotel mit Busverbindung zu den Bergen. Gibt es so was?
- Moment mal ... ich schaue mal nach ....

4
- Hallo, Verkehrsamt Linz. Kann ich Ihnen helfen?
- Ja, ich möchte im Mai nach Linz kommen.
  Im Mai. Wann genau möchten Sie kommen?
- Am 4. und ich bleibe dann bis 16. Mai.
- O, also vom 4. bis 16. Mai. Und Sie suchen ein Hotel oder eine Ferienwohnung?
- Ein Hotel, bitte.
- Und für wie viele Leute wäre das?
- Eine Person. Das ist nur für mich. Ein Erwachsener. Ich komme für eine Konferenz. Haben Sie auch eine Liste von Restaurants?
- Ja. Bleiben Sie bitte am Apparat ...

3b Beate ruft das Verkehrsamt an. Ergänze den Dialog. Du darfst die Dialoge zu Übung 3a noch einmal anhören. (AT4 Level 4)

Pupils complete a holiday booking dialogue, based on what they have just heard. Pupils might need to listen to activity 3a again to complete this task. The clouds and pictures indicate the details to be included.

Answers

1 Hallo, Verkehrsamt Kirchdorf. Kann ich Ihnen helfen? **2** Ja, ich möchte im Oktober nach Kirchdorf fahren. **3** Sehr gut. Wann wäre das genau? **4** Also, vom vierzehnten bis achtzehnten Oktober. **5** O.K. Suchen Sie ein Hotel oder eine Ferienwohnung? **6** Ja, ich suche ein Hotel. **7** Und wie viele Leute sind das in der Gruppe? **8** Also, wir sind zwei Erwachsene und ein Kind. **9** Prima. Moment mal, bitte ...

4a Partnerarbeit. Übt Dialoge im Verkehrsamt. (AT2 Levels 4–5)

Pupils practise conversations in a tourist office, with one pupil taking the role of the tourism officer and the other pupil requesting the information on one of the cue cards.

4b Schreib für Frau Bauer aus Berlin oder Herrn Roos aus Rostock einen Brief an das Verkehrsamt. Der Brief auf Seite 52 hilft dir dabei. Du kannst die roten Wörter ändern. (AT4 Levels 4–5)

Pupils write a formal letter to a tourist office, using the example provided on p. 52 and customising the coloured phrases.

R Further practice of this unit's language is to be found on p. 114 of the Pupil's Book, activity 2.

E Further practice of this unit's language is to be found on p. 115 of the Pupil's Book, activity 2.

► 7 http://austria-tourism.at
(pp. 54–55)

Skill focus	Resources
• Groupwork	• Cassette B, Side A

The *MEHR* unit is intended as extension material for more able pupils. Pupils will be more challenged by the longer reading text and by exercises which draw together all the language of the chapter.

The context of this unit is the Austrian tourist board's website, providing general information about the country.

1a Lies den Text. Welcher Titel passt zu welchem Absatz? (AT3 Levels 6–7)
Pupils read the web page and allocate each heading to the appropriate piece of text.

Answers

a 2, **b** 4, **c** 5, **d** 1, **e** 6, **f** 3

1b Such dir mindestens drei Wörter zu folgenden Themen aus dem Text aus. (AT3 Level 3)
Pupils find at least three words to do with five different categories from the text.

1c Beantworte folgende Fragen. (AT3 Levels 6–7)
Pupils answer ten comprehension questions on the text in German. There is no requirement for them to answer in full sentences, although full sentence answers are provided below.

Answers

1 Sie fahren gern dorthin, weil immer etwas los ist. **2** Es gibt einen ganzen Spielwagen. **3** Man kann auf guten Wanderwegen schön wandern gehen. **4** Man findet die Fauna und Flora des Berges. **5** Sie heißt die Kärntner Straße. **6** Er kommt aus Salzburg. **7** Es gibt das Arts-Electronica-Center. **8** Die „klassischen" Sportarten sind Tennis, Golf, Reiten, Fischen, Schwimmen, Segeln und Wasserskifahren. **9** Viele Österreicher machen Inline-Skating. **10** Die Flüsse und Wasserfälle sind für Kanu- und Rafting-Freunde ideal.

E Pupils choose the paragraph they find most interesting and translate it into English.

2 Hör zu. Warum sind sie in Österreich? Welcher Absatz auf Seite 54 ist das? (1–6) (AT1 Level 5)
Pupils listen to six people talking about their reasons for visiting Austria and decide which paragraph is most relevant for each person.

Answers

1 Absatz 6, **2** Absatz 3, **3** Absatz 5, **4** Absatz 1, **5** Absatz 4, **6** Absatz 2

1 – Einen schönen guten Tag. Ich habe eine Frage. Können Sie mir sagen, warum Sie nach Österreich gekommen sind?
– Ja, ähm, wissen Sie, ich bin hier, weil ... weil die österreichische Küche so ... so lecker ist! Also, ganz besonders mag ich ja Wiener Schnitzel und den Apfelstrudel.

2 – Hallo, junge Dame. Was machst du in Österreich?
– Ja, also, ich mag die Natur besonders und ich genieße vor allem auch die ruhigen Spaziergänge in der Natur. Ich habe auch schon tolle Wanderungen gemacht im Nationalpark Hohe Tauern und ganz tolle und außergewöhnliche Pflanzen habe ich dort entdeckt. Es macht riesig Spaß!

3 – Hallo, du Sportskanone! Was treibt dich nach Österreich?
– He! Ja, Mann, sieht man das nicht? Ich bin hier, um zu skaten. Und echt cool Spaß, Mann. Es gibt viele Skate-Parks hier in Österreich und ich bin ein totaler Skate-Fan. Hab' auch echt schon viele Leute getroffen – es ist echt cool!

4 – Guten Tag. Eine kurze Frage: Warum haben Sie gerade Österreich für Ihren Urlaub gewählt?
– Ähm, ja, also ... ich fahre schon seit Jahren her. Ich habe drei Kinder und Österreich ist einfach ideal. Also, die Schwimmbäder sind super schön und die Leute sind sehr sehr nett und hilfsbereit. Also, ich finde Österreich einfach toll für die Familie!

5 – Sagen Sie mir bitte: Was machen Sie in Österreich?
– Wissen Sie, seit ich zwölf bin, bin ich Fan von klassischer Musik. Und ich meine, wer die Klassik liebt, der liebt auch Österreich. Na ja, und jetzt habe ich mir endlich diesen Traum erfüllt. Diese Woche sind wir in Salzburg gewesen und haben Mozarts Geburtshaus besichtigt. Das war ein Erlebnis, sage ich Ihnen. Und nächste Woche, da fahren wir weiter nach Wien und gehen in die Oper!

6 – Hallo, junger Mann. Was machst du hier in Österreich?
– Na ja, ich wollte meine Ruhe haben. Ich bin hier zum Wandern. Ich wollte so weg aus der Großstadt und bin jetzt so für eine Woche hier, um jeden Tag wandern zu gehen. Das macht mir am meisten Spaß und ich genieße die Ruhe.

3 Welche Spezialität ist das? Such Informationen im Internet.
Pupils search on the internet for information about some Austrian specialities in order to identify the pictures.

Answers

a Strudel, **b** Wiener Schnitzel, **c** Knödel, **d** Salzburger Nockerln

4 Gruppenarbeit. Bereitet für eine Tourismusseite im Web kurze Texte über euer Land vor. Jeder wählt eine Kategorie aus und schreibt einen Text. Lest dann eure Präsentation vor. (AT2 Level 4–7)

Pupils work in a group to prepare a web page about their own country. Each pupil chooses a category to work on (shown by the clouds). Once this task is completed, pupils work as a group on the texts to improve and correct them.

Ludwig: Groupwork

Ludwig emphasises the usefulness of groupwork and encourages pupils to work as a group to achieve their task.

Pupils look up the Austrian tourist board's website at http://austria-tourism.at to find up-to-the-minute information about Austria and find links for further research.

Lernzieltest and Wiederholung (pp. 56–57)

Resources
- Cassette, A, Side B
- Workbook pp. 28–30
- R & A File: Wortschatz pp. 55–56

Lernzieltest p. 57
Kontrolle 3 pp. 58–67 (including teacher's notes)

At the end of each chapter there is a revision unit for pupils to use before the assessment materials. The unit begins with a *Lernzieltest* (like the *Mini-Test*) for pupils to test themselves on key language from the chapter. This is also provided as a checklist for pupils to write on (R & A File p. 57) and some related gapped sentences are also provided on p. 30 of the Workbook.

If pupils are unsure of any of the language, they should be encouraged to revise the relevant unit in the chapter. A complete wordlist containing key words and phrases from the whole chapter is provided on the *Wortschatz* sheets (R &A File pp. 55–56).

Wiederholung provides pupils with revision exercises in the four skills. The listening exercises should be done in class, but the other exercises could be done either in class or for homework. Further revision exercises are provided on pp. 28–29 of the Workbook.

Wiederholung

Hören

1 Hör zu und beantworte die Fragen. (1–4) (AT1 Levels 4–5)

Pupils listen to four teenagers talking about their home environment and then answer four questions about each teenager. Pupils should answer in note form, rather than writing complete sentences.

Answers

1 a in den Bergen, **b** nein, **c** nichts los, keine Freunde, langweilig, **d** es schneit: zu Hause bleiben, fernsehen; schön: wandern
2 a in einem Dorf, **b** ja, **c** ziemlich viel los, Jugendclub mit Disco, gute Sportmöglichkeiten, **d** schlechtes Wetter: im Café treffen; kalt: Eis laufen
3 a auf dem Land, **b** ja, **c** Luft sauber, fast kein Verkehr / ruhig, viele Freunde,
d schön: Fußball spielen; es regnet: nach Salzburg fahren, ins Kino gehen, zu McDonalds gehen
4 a Linz, **b** ja, **c** viele Cafés, Geschäfte, Kinos, verschmutzt, zu viel Verkehr, **d** heiß: in die Berge fahren; es regnet: ins Kino gehen, Freunde im Café treffen

1 – Also, ich heiße Stefan und komme aus Österreich. Jetzt wohne ich in den Bergen und das gefällt mir gar nicht. Vorher habe ich in Salzburg gewohnt und das war super. In den Bergen ist nichts los und ich habe keine Freunde hier. Ich langweile mich die ganze Zeit. Das Wetter ist auch ganz schlimm, und wenn es schneit, kann man nicht ausgehen. Dann bleibe ich zu Hause und sehe fern. Im Sommer ist es besser, und wenn es schön ist, gehe ich wandern. Das finde ich O.K.

2 – Mein Name ist Rebecca und ich wohne in einem Dorf in Niederösterreich. Ich habe immer hier gewohnt und es gefällt mir hier sehr, weil ziemlich viel los ist. Zum Beispiel haben wir einen Jugendclub und es gibt jedes Wochenende eine Disco. Wir haben auch gute Sportmöglichkeiten im Dorf – einen tollen Spielplatz und viele Tennisplätze. Wenn das Wetter schlecht ist, treffen wir uns im Café, und das finde ich immer lustig. Im Winter ist es auch toll, und wenn es kalt ist, gehen wir Eis laufen. Das liebe ich!

3 – Mein Name ist Hannes und ich wohne auf dem Land im Salzburger Land. Es gefällt mir hier sehr gut, weil die Luft so sauber ist. Wir haben fast keinen Verkehr und es ist sehr ruhig. Ich habe auch viele Freunde hier und wir treffen uns oft. Wenn das Wetter schön ist, spielen wir auf der Wiese Fußball. Das finde ich toll, aber wenn es regnet, fahren wir mit dem Zug nach Salzburg und gehen ins Kino oder wir gehen zu McDonalds.

4 – Ich heiße Lisa und ich wohne in Linz. Das ist eine schöne Stadt in Österreich. Es gefällt mir hier, weil es viele Cafés, Geschäfte und Kinos gibt. Das Leben in Linz ist nie langweilig. Aber es ärgert mich auch, weil die Luft so verschmutzt ist. Es gibt zu viel Verkehr und das finde ich schlimm. Wenn das Wetter heiß ist, ist die Verschmutzung schrecklich, also fahre ich in die Berge und übernachte bei meiner Großmutter. Wenn es regnet, kann man ins Kino gehen oder man kann im Café Freunde treffen. Das mache ich sehr gern.

Sprechen

2 Partnerarbeit. Seht euch die Bilder auf Seite 57 an. Was haben sie auf der Klassenfahrt gemacht? (AT2 Levels 5–6)

Pupils look at the picture diary on p. 57 and ask each other questions in the perfect tense plural about what a group did on a school trip.

Lesen

3 Lies den Brief. Richtig oder falsch? (AT3 Level 4)

Pupils read the letter and answer ten true/false statements on it.

Answers

1 falsch, **2** falsch, **3** richtig, **4** richtig, **5** falsch, **6** falsch, **7** falsch, **8** richtig, **9** falsch, **10** falsch

Schreiben

4 Sieh dir die Info-Karte an und schreib einen Brief an das St. Johanner Verkehrsamt. (AT4 Level 4)

Pupils use the details on the cue card to write a letter to the St. Johann tourist office requesting information for a stay there.

5 Du bist in den Ferien nach Österreich gefahren. Beschreib deine Reise und nimm die Beschreibung auf Kassette auf. (AT4 Levels 5–6, AT2 Levels 5–6)

Pupils describe a recent (imaginary) trip to Austria and then record it on cassette.

▶ EXTRA

The EXTRA pages at the back of the Pupil's Book are intended to provide consolidation/reinforcement activities (EXTRA A) and more challenging / extension activities (EXTRA B). The exercises concentrate on the skills of reading and writing only. They could be used for differentiated work in class or at home. The best place to use each activity is clearly indicated in these notes, just above the exercise rubric, e. g. [after pp. 44–45].

EXTRA A (p. 114)

[after pp. 44–45]

1a Sieh dir die Grafik an. Richtig oder falsch? (AT3 Levels 2–3)

Pupils look at a pie chart showing what people do in different weather conditions and decide whether the sentences are true or false.

Answers

1 falsch, **2** falsch, **3** richtig, **4** richtig, **5** falsch, **6** richtig, **7** richtig, **8** richtig **9** falsch, **10** falsch

1b Ergänze die Sätze für dich. (AT4 Level 3)

Pupils complete sentences to state what they do in different weather conditions. A help box is provided to give them some ideas.

[after pp. 52–53]

2a Sieh dir diese Sätze an. Welche findest du in einem Brief an das Verkehrsamt? (AT3 Level 3)

Pupils read some torn up extracts from letters and decide which pieces come from a letter sent to a tourist office.

Answers

b, c, d, e, g, h, j, k, m, p, q

2b Ordne die Sätze und schreib den Brief ab. (AT4 Level 3)

Pupils write out the letter by copying the torn up extracts in the correct order.

Answers

g, p, h, m, b, j, e, k, c, q, d

EXTRA B (p. 115)

[after pp. 44–45]

1a Beschrifte die Grafik. (AT4 Level 3)

Pupils write *wenn* sentences to describe what people do in different weather conditions.

Answers

Wenn es sonnig ist, spiele ich Tennis. Wenn es regnet, gehe ich ins Kino. Wenn es schneit, fahre ich Ski. Wenn es windig ist, bleibe ich zu Hause. Wenn es heiß ist, bade ich im See. Wenn es kalt ist, gehe ich Eis laufen.

1b Beantworte folgende Fragen. (AT4 Levels 3–4)

Pupils answer questions, using *wenn* sentences, about what they do in different circumstances.

[after pp. 52–53]

2a Sieh dir den Brief an und ergänze die Sätze. (AT3 Level 4)

Pupils read a letter to a tourist information office and complete the gapped sentences.

Answers

1 März, **2** Villach, **3** Mai, **4** am siebzehnten, **5** vier, **6** drei, **7** einkaufen, wandern, **8** Thomas

2b Adaptiere jetzt den Brief für Frau Goldmann und ihre Familie. (AT4 Level 4)

Pupils adapt the letter with details of Mrs Goldmann's holiday requirements.

Answers

Salzburg, den 6. April

Sehr geehrte Damen und Herren,

ich möchte meinen Urlaub gern in Zell am See verbringen und suche eine Ferienwohnung für die Zeit vom dreiundzwanzigsten Juni bis vierten Juli. Wir sind fünf in der Gruppe – zwei Erwachsene und drei Kinder (8, 11 und 15 Jahre alt). Ich interessiere mich auch für Informationen über Wandermöglichkeiten und Radtouren in der Region.

Mit vielem Dank im Voraus für Ihre Mühe.

Mit freundlichen Grüßen
Birgit Goldmann

Workbook

p. 21

1 (AT4 Level 3)

1 Ich fahre dahin, um die frische Luft zu genießen. **2** Ich fahre dahin, um Wassersport zu treiben. **3** Ich fahre dahin, um wandern zu gehen. **4** Ich fahre dahin, um Salzburg zu besichtigen. **5** Ich fahre dahin, um Deutsch zu lernen. **6** Ich fahre dahin, um im See zu baden. **7** Ich fahre dahin, um Ski zu fahren. **8** Ich fahre dahin, um Freunde zu besuchen.

2 (AT4 Level 4)

individual answers

3 Österreich und die Umwelt

1 Österreich für alle (Seite 42–43)

1 Warum fahren diese Leute nach Österreich? Was sagen sie?

1 Ich fahre dahin, um die frische Luft zu genießen.
2
3
4
5
6
7
8

Ski fahren / Deutsch lernen / ~~die frische Luft genießen~~ / im See baden / wandern gehen / Salzburg besichtigen / Wassersport treiben / Freunde besuchen

1 2 3 4 5 6 7 8

2 Schreib Sätze über fünf andere Länder.
Beispiel: Ich fahre nach Italien, um Rom zu besichtigen.
Ich fahre nach Holland, um eine Radtour zu machen.

21

© Heinemann Educational 2001

p. 22

1 (AT3 Level 4)

	David	Stefanie	Karima
hot	lake	tennis	hiking
rain	house	shopping	indoor pool
snow	skis	house	house
cold	cinema	ice-skating	hiking

2 (AT4 Levels 4–5)

individual answers

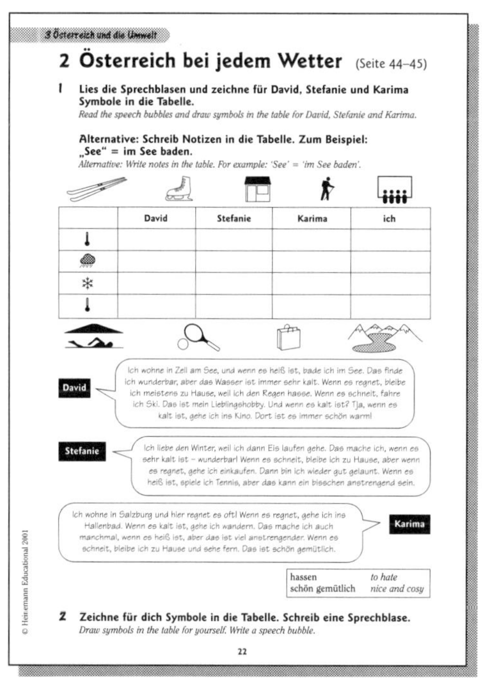

3 Österreich und die Umwelt

2 Österreich bei jedem Wetter (Seite 44–45)

1 Lies die Sprechblasen und zeichne für David, Stefanie und Karima Symbole in die Tabelle.
Read the speech bubbles and draw symbols in the table for David, Stefanie and Karima.

Alternative: Schreib Notizen in die Tabelle. Zum Beispiel: „See" = im See baden.
Alternative: Write notes in the table. For example: 'See' = 'im See baden'.

	David	Stefanie	Karima	ich

David: Ich wohne in Zell am See, und wenn es heiß ist, bade ich im See. Das finde ich wunderbar, aber das Wasser ist immer sehr kalt. Wenn es regnet, bleibe ich meistens zu Hause, weil ich den Regen hasse. Wenn es schneit, fahre ich Ski. Das ist mein Lieblingshobby. Und wenn es kalt ist? Tja, wenn es kalt ist, gehe ich ins Kino. Dort ist es immer schön warm!

Stefanie: Ich liebe den Winter, weil ich dann Eis laufen gehe. Das mache ich, wenn es sehr kalt ist – wunderbar! Wenn es schneit, bleibe ich zu Hause, aber wenn es regnet, gehe ich einkaufen. Dann bin ich wieder gut gelaunt. Wenn es heiß ist, spiele ich Tennis, aber das kann ein bisschen anstrengend sein.

Karima: Ich wohne in Salzburg und hier regnet es oft! Wenn es regnet, gehe ich ins Hallenbad. Wenn es kalt ist, gehe ich wandern. Das mache ich auch manchmal, wenn es heiß ist, aber das ist viel anstrengender. Wenn es schneit, bleibe ich zu Hause und sehe fern. Das ist schön gemütlich.

hassen	*to hate*
schön gemütlich	*nice and cosy*

2 Zeichne für dich Symbole in die Tabelle. Schreib eine Sprechblase.
Draw symbols in the table for yourself. Write a speech bubble.

22

© Heinemann Educational 2001

p. 23

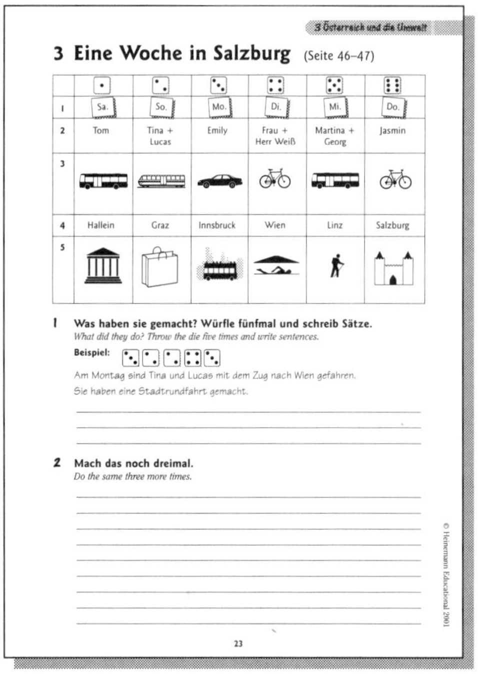

1 (AT4 Level 5)
individual answers
2 (AT4 Level 5)
individual answers

p. 24

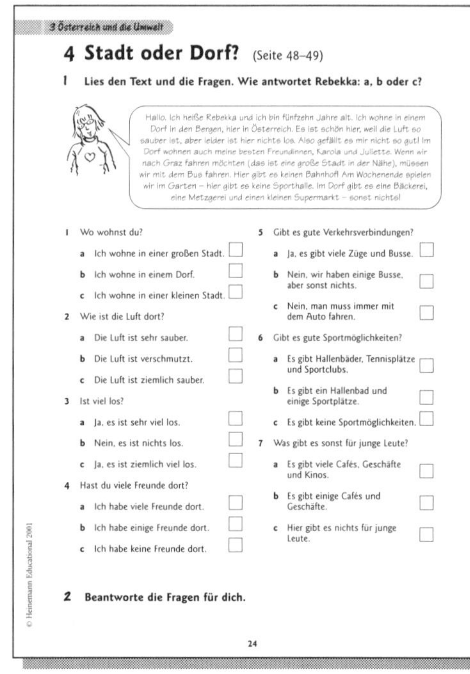

1 (AT3 Levels 4–5)
1 b, **2** a, **3** b, **4** b, **5** b, **6** c, **7** c
2 (AT3 Level 4)
individual answers

p. 25

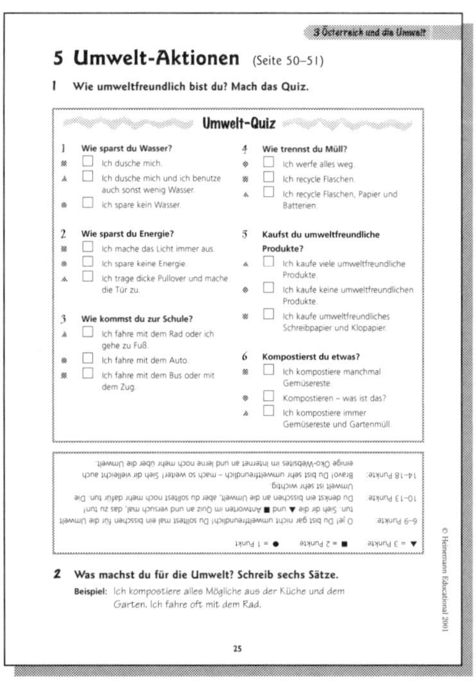

1 (AT 3 Levels 4–5)
individual answers
2 (AT 4 Levels 4–5)
individual answers

p. 26

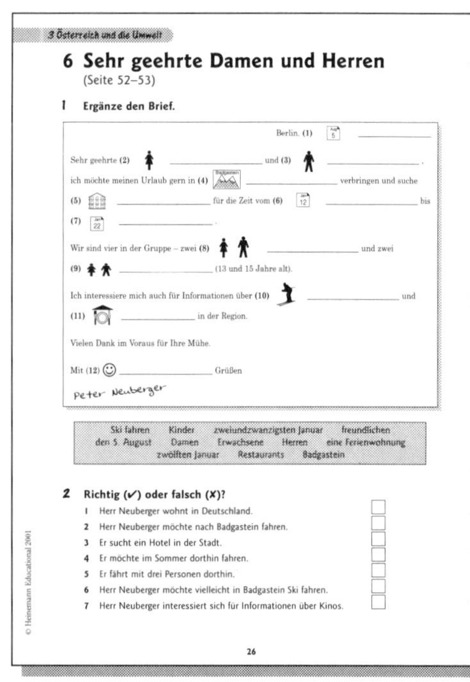

1 (AT4 Level 4)
1 den 5. August, **2** Damen, **3** Herren, **4** Badgastein, **5** eine Ferienwohnung, **6** zwölften Januar, **7** zweiundzwanzigsten Januar, **8** Erwachsene, **9** Kinder, **10** Ski fahren, **11** Restaurants, **12** freundlichen
2 (AT3 Level 4)
1 ✓, **2** ✓, **3** ✗, **4** ✗, **5** ✓, **6** ✓, **7** ✗

p. 27

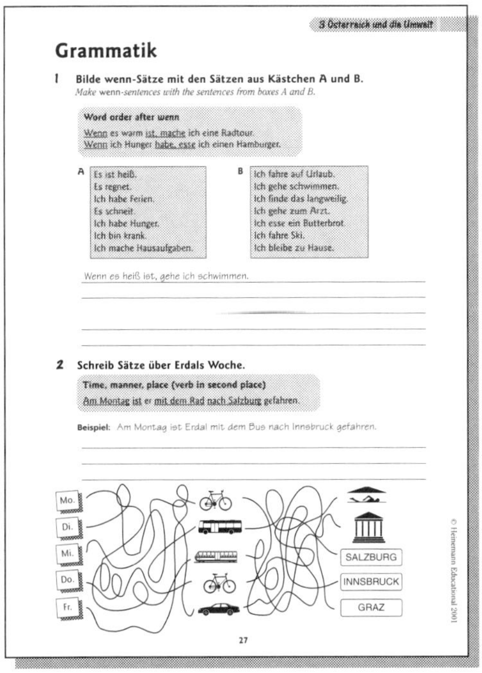
3 Österreich und die Umwelt

Grammatik

1 Bilde wenn-Sätze mit den Sätzen aus Kästchen A und B.
Make wenn-sentences with the sentences from boxes A and B.

Word order after wenn
Wenn es warm ist, mache ich eine Radtour.
Wenn ich Hunger habe, esse ich einen Hamburger.

A
Es ist heiß.
Es regnet.
Ich habe Ferien.
Es schneit.
Ich habe Hunger.
Ich bin krank.
Ich mache Hausaufgaben.

B
Ich fahre auf Urlaub.
Ich gehe schwimmen.
Ich finde das langweilig.
Ich gehe zum Arzt.
Ich esse ein Butterbrot.
Ich fahre Ski.
Ich bleibe zu Hause.

Wenn es heiß ist, gehe ich schwimmen.

2 Schreib Sätze über Erdals Woche.

Time, manner, place (verb in second place)
Am Montag ist er mit dem Rad nach Salzburg gefahren.

Beispiel: Am Montag ist Erdal mit dem Bus nach Innsbruck gefahren.

© Heinemann Educational 2001

27

1 Wenn es heiß ist, gehe ich schwimmen. Wenn es regnet, bleibe ich zu Hause. Wenn ich Ferien habe, fahre ich auf Urlaub. Wenn es schneit, fahre ich Ski. Wenn ich Hunger habe, esse ich ein Butterbrot. Wenn ich krank bin, gehe ich zum Arzt. Wenn ich Hausaufgaben mache, finde ich das langweilig.

2 Am Montag ist Erdal mit dem Bus nach Innsbruck gefahren. Am Dienstag ist Erdal mit dem Zug nach Salzburg gefahren. Am Mittwoch ist Erdal mit dem Rad zum Hallenbad gefahren. Am Donnerstag ist Erdal mit dem Rad zum Museum gefahren. Am Freitag ist Erdal mit dem Auto nach Graz gefahren.

p. 28

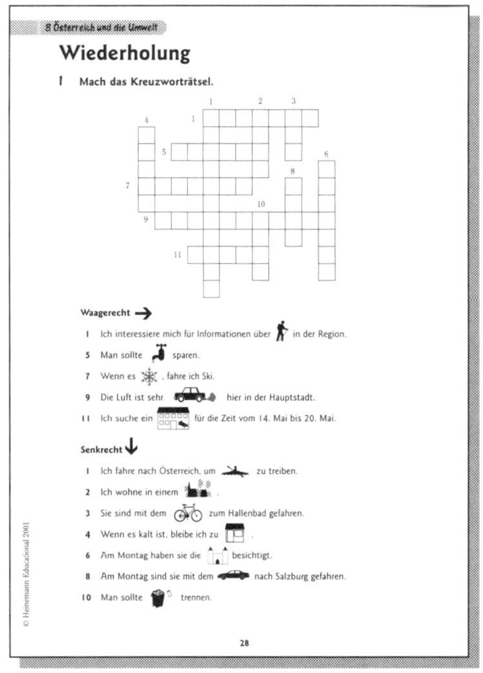
3 Österreich und die Umwelt

Wiederholung

1 Mach das Kreuzworträtsel.

Waagerecht →
1 Ich interessiere mich für Informationen über [picture] in der Region.
5 Man sollte [picture] sparen.
7 Wenn es [picture], fahre ich Ski.
9 Die Luft ist sehr [picture] hier in der Hauptstadt.
11 Ich suche ein [picture] für die Zeit vom 14. Mai bis 20. Mai.

Senkrecht ↓
1 Ich fahre nach Österreich, um [picture] zu treiben.
2 Ich wohne in einem [picture].
3 Sie sind mit dem [picture] zum Hallenbad gefahren.
4 Wenn es kalt ist, bleibe ich zu [picture].
6 Am Montag haben sie die [picture] besichtigt.
8 Am Montag sind sie mit dem [picture] nach Salzburg gefahren.
10 Man sollte [picture] trennen.

© Heinemann Educational 2001

28

1 (AT3 Level 3, AT4 Level 2)
Waagerecht: **1** Wandern, **5** Wasser, **7** schneit, **9** verschmutzt, **11** Hotel
Senkrecht: **1** Wassersport, **2** Dorf, **3** Rad, **4** Hause, **6** Festung, **8** Auto, **10** Müll

p. 29

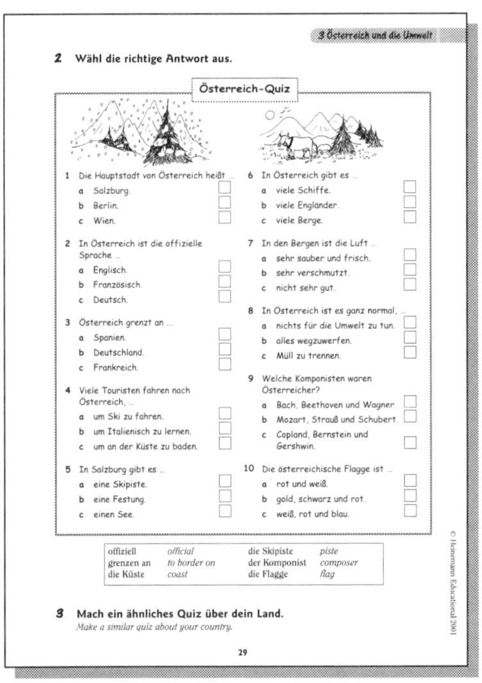
3 Österreich und die Umwelt

2 Wähl die richtige Antwort aus.

Österreich-Quiz

1 Die Hauptstadt von Österreich heißt …
a Salzburg.
b Berlin.
c Wien.

2 In Österreich ist die offizielle Sprache …
a Englisch.
b Französisch.
c Deutsch.

3 Österreich grenzt an …
a Spanien.
b Deutschland.
c Frankreich.

4 Viele Touristen fahren nach Österreich, …
a um Ski zu fahren.
b um Italienisch zu lernen.
c um an der Küste zu baden.

5 In Salzburg gibt es …
a eine Skipiste.
b eine Festung.
c einen See.

6 In Österreich gibt es …
a viele Schiffe.
b viele Engländer.
c viele Berge.

7 In den Bergen ist die Luft …
a sehr sauber und frisch.
b sehr verschmutzt.
c nicht sehr gut.

8 In Österreich ist es ganz normal, …
a nichts für die Umwelt zu tun.
b alles wegzuwerfen.
c Müll zu trennen.

9 Welche Komponisten waren Österreicher?
a Bach, Beethoven und Wagner
b Mozart, Strauß und Schubert
c Copland, Bernstein und Gershwin

10 Die österreichische Flagge ist …
a rot und weiß.
b gold, schwarz und rot.
c weiß, rot und blau.

offiziell	*official*	die Skipiste	*piste*
grenzen an	*to border on*	der Komponist	*composer*
die Küste	*coast*	die Flagge	*flag*

3 Mach ein ähnliches Quiz über dein Land.
Make a similar quiz about your country.

© Heinemann Educational 2001

29

2 (AT3 Level 4)
1 c, **2** c, **3** b, **4** a, **5** b, **6** c, **7** a, **8** c, **9** b, **10** a
3 (AT4 Level 4)
individual answers

p. 30

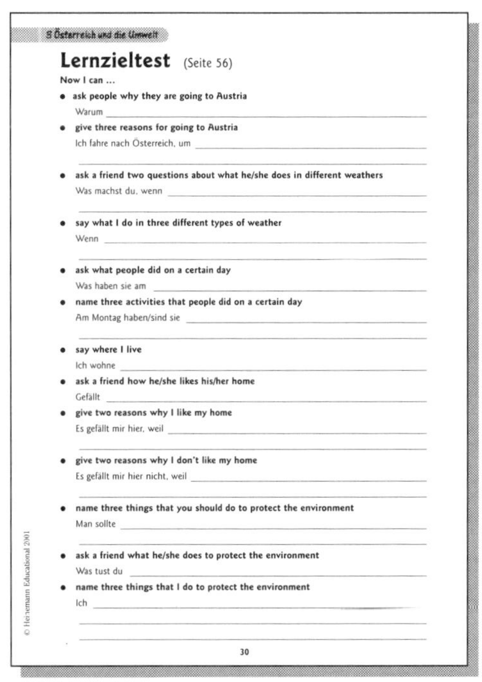
3 Österreich und die Umwelt

Lernzieltest (Seite 56)

Now I can …
- ask people why they are going to Austria
Warum
- give three reasons for going to Austria
Ich fahre nach Österreich, um
- ask a friend two questions about what he/she does in different weathers
Was machst du, wenn
- say what I do in three different types of weather
Wenn
- ask what people did on a certain day
Was haben sie am
- name three activities that people did on a certain day
Am Montag haben/sind sie
- say where I live
Ich wohne
- ask a friend how he/she likes his/her home
Gefällt
- give two reasons why I like my home
Es gefällt mir hier, weil
- give two reasons why I don't like my home
Es gefällt mir hier nicht, weil
- name three things that you should do to protect the environment
Man sollte
- ask a friend what he/she does to protect the environment
Was tust du
- name three things that I do to protect the environment
Ich

© Heinemann Educational 2001

30

individual answers

Arbeitsblatt 1
p. 47

Österreich für alle *(pages 42–43)* — Logo! 3 3 Österreich und die Umwelt Arbeitsblatt 1

um Ski zu fahren	um Wassersport zu treiben	um wandern zu gehen
um Salzburg zu besichtigen	um Deutsch zu lernen	um im See zu baden
um die frische Luft zu genießen	um Freunde zu besuchen	

47

Visuals of *um Ski zu fahren, um Wassersport zu treiben, um wandern zu gehen, um Salzburg zu besichtigen, um Deutsch zu lernen, um im See zu baden, um die frische Luft zu genießen, um Freunde zu besuchen*

Arbeitsblatt 2
p. 48

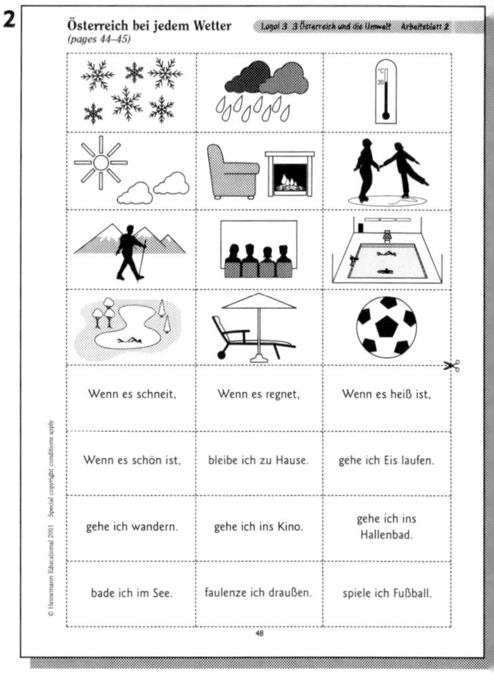

Österreich bei jedem Wetter *(pages 44–45)* — Logo! 3 3 Österreich und die Umwelt Arbeitsblatt 2

Wenn es schneit,	Wenn es regnet,	Wenn es heiß ist,
Wenn es schön ist,	bleibe ich zu Hause.	gehe ich Eis laufen.
gehe ich wandern.	gehe ich ins Kino.	gehe ich ins Hallenbad.
bade ich im See.	faulenze ich draußen.	spiele ich Fußball.

48

Visuals of *Wenn es schneit, Wenn es regnet, Wenn es heiß ist, Wenn es schön ist, bleibe ich zu Hause, gehe ich Eis laufen, gehe ich wandern, gehe ich ins Kino, gehe ich ins Hallenbad, bade ich im See, faulenze ich draußen, spiele ich Fußball*

Arbeitsblatt 3
p. 49

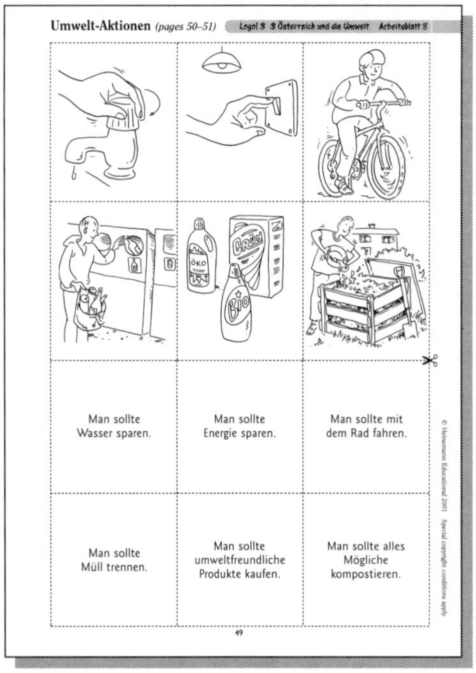

Umwelt-Aktionen *(pages 50–51)* — Logo! 3 3 Österreich und die Umwelt Arbeitsblatt 3

Man sollte Wasser sparen.	Man sollte Energie sparen.	Man sollte mit dem Rad fahren.
Man sollte Müll trennen.	Man sollte umweltfreundliche Produkte kaufen.	Man sollte alles Mögliche kompostieren.

49

Visuals of *Man sollte Wasser sparen. Man sollte Energie sparen. Man sollte mit dem Rad fahren. Man sollte Müll trennen. Man sollte umweltfreundliche Produkte kaufen. Man sollte alles Mögliche kompostieren.*

Arbeitsblatt 4
p. 50

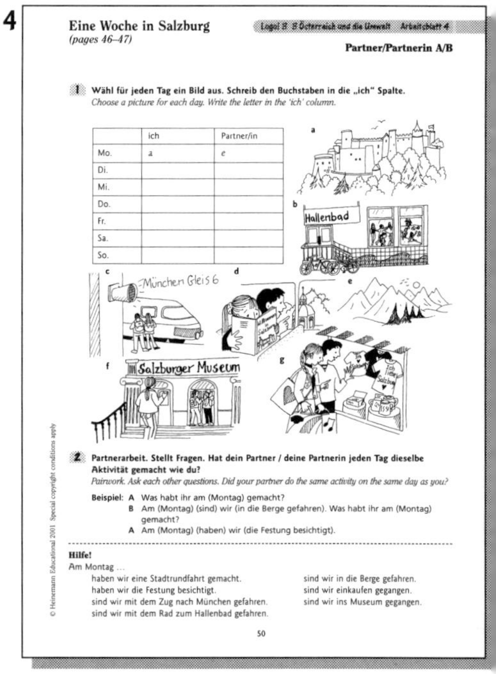

Eine Woche in Salzburg *(pages 46–47)* — Logo! 3 3 Österreich und die Umwelt Arbeitsblatt 4

Partner/Partnerin A/B

1 **Wähl für jeden Tag ein Bild aus. Schreib den Buchstaben in die „ich" Spalte.**
Choose a picture for each day. Write the letter in the 'ich' column.

	ich	Partner/in
Mo.	a	e
Di.		
Mi.		
Do.		
Fr.		
Sa.		
So.		

2 **Partnerarbeit. Stellt Fragen. Hat dein Partner / deine Partnerin jeden Tag dieselbe Aktivität gemacht wie du?**
Pairwork. Ask each other questions. Did your partner do the same activity on the same day as you?

Beispiel: A Was habt ihr am (Montag) gemacht?
B Am (Montag) (sind) wir (in die Berge gefahren). Was habt ihr am (Montag) gemacht?
A Am (Montag) (haben) wir (die Festung besichtigt).

Hilfe!
Am Montag …
haben wir eine Stadtrundfahrt gemacht.
haben wir die Festung besichtigt.
sind wir mit dem Zug nach München gefahren.
sind wir mit dem Rad zum Hallenbad gefahren.
sind wir in die Berge gefahren.
sind wir einkaufen gegangen.
sind wir ins Museum gegangen.

50

Pairwork activity on what you did last week (plural).
1 AT2 Levels 4–5

Arbeitsblatt 5 p. 51
Advice on speaking activities.

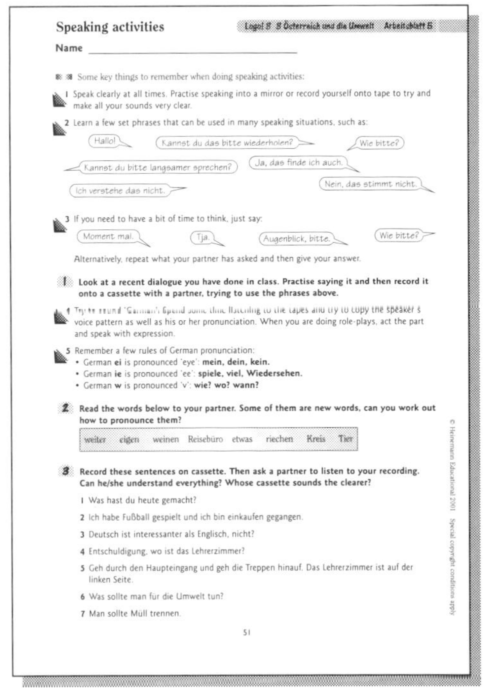

Speaking activities

Name ______________________________

Some key things to remember when doing speaking activities:

1 Speak clearly at all times. Practise speaking into a mirror or record yourself onto tape to try and make all your sounds very clear.

2 Learn a few set phrases that can be used in many speaking situations, such as:

3 If you need to have a bit of time to think, just say:

Alternatively, repeat what your partner has asked and then give your answer.

1 Look at a recent dialogue you have done in class. Practise saying it and then record it onto a cassette with a partner, trying to use the phrases above.

4 Try to sound 'German'. Spend some time listening to the tapes and try to copy the speaker's voice pattern as well as his or her pronunciation. When you are doing role-plays, act the part and speak with expression.

5 Remember a few rules of German pronunciation:
- German **ei** is pronounced 'eye': **mein, dein, kein.**
- German **ie** is pronounced 'ee': **spiele, viel, Wiedersehen.**
- German **w** is pronounced 'v': **wie? wo? wann?**

2 Read the words below to your partner. Some of them are new words, can you work out how to pronounce them?

weiter eigen weinen Reisebüro etwas riechen Kreis Tier

3 Record these sentences on cassette. Then ask a partner to listen to your recording. Can he/she understand everything? Whose cassette sounds the clearer?

1 Was hast du heute gemacht?
2 Ich habe Fußball gespielt und ich bin einkaufen gegangen.
3 Deutsch ist interessanter als Englisch, nicht?
4 Entschuldigung, wo ist das Lehrerzimmer?
5 Geh durch den Haupteingang und geh die Treppen hinauf. Das Lehrerzimmer ist auf der linken Seite.
6 Was sollte man für die Umwelt tun?
7 Man sollte Müll trennen.

Grammatik 1 p. 52
Practice of *um ... zu.*

1 **1** Man geht ins Kino, um einen Film zu sehen. **2** Man trägt eine Jacke, um warm zu bleiben. **3** Man spielt Fußball, um fit zu bleiben. **4** Man geht in die Bibliothek, um Bücher zu lesen. **5** Man geht in die Bäckerei, um Brot zu kaufen. **6** Man geht in die Schule, um vieles zu lernen. **7** Man surft im Internet, um viele Websites zu finden. **8** Man fährt nach Frankreich, um Französisch zu sprechen. **9** Man geht in den Musikladen, um CDs zu kaufen. **10** Man kompostiert alles Mögliche, um umweltfreundlich zu sein.

2 **1** Wir fahren nach Berlin, um einen Kurs zu machen. **2** Ich gehe in die Stadt, um eine Jacke zu kaufen. **3** Ich habe einen Job, um Geld zu verdienen. **4** Ich gehe in die Schule, um meine Freunde zu sehen. **5** Meine Eltern gehen joggen, um fit zu bleiben. **6** Mein Bruder fährt nach Spanien, um Spanisch zu lernen. **7** Ich surfe im Internet, um Informationen zu suchen. **8** Meine Schwester fährt nach Italien, um viel Eis zu essen.

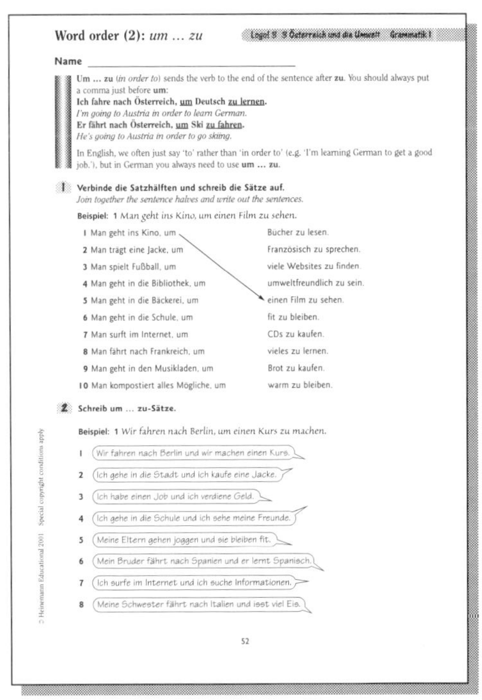

Word order (2): ***um ... zu***

Name ______________________________

Um ... zu (*in order to*) sends the verb to the end of the sentence after **zu**. You should always put a comma just before **um**:
Ich fahre nach Österreich, um Deutsch zu lernen.
I'm going to Austria in order to learn German.
Er fährt nach Österreich, um Ski zu fahren.
He's going to Austria in order to go skiing.

In English, we often just say 'to' rather than 'in order to' (e.g. 'I'm learning German to get a good job.'), but in German you always need to use **um ... zu**.

1 Verbinde die Satzhälften und schreib die Sätze auf.
Join together the sentence halves and write out the sentences.

Beispiel: 1 *Man geht ins Kino, um einen Film zu sehen.*

1 Man geht ins Kino, um	Bücher zu lesen.
2 Man trägt eine Jacke, um	Französisch zu sprechen.
3 Man spielt Fußball, um	viele Websites zu finden.
4 Man geht in die Bibliothek, um	umweltfreundlich zu sein.
5 Man geht in die Bäckerei, um	einen Film zu sehen.
6 Man geht in die Schule, um	fit zu bleiben.
7 Man surft im Internet, um	CDs zu kaufen.
8 Man fährt nach Frankreich, um	vieles zu lernen.
9 Man geht in den Musikladen, um	Brot zu kaufen.
10 Man kompostiert alles Mögliche, um	warm zu bleiben.

2 Schreib um ... zu-Sätze.

Beispiel: 1 *Wir fahren nach Berlin, um einen Kurs zu machen.*

Grammatik 2 p. 53

Practice of *wenn.*

1 **1** Was machst du, wenn es heiß ist? **2** Was machst du, wenn es kalt ist? **3** Was machst du, wenn es regnet? **4** Was machst du, wenn es schneit? **5** Was machst du, wenn du Hunger hast? **6** Was machst du, wenn du Kopfschmerzen hast? **7** Was machst du, wenn du kein Geld hast? **8** Was machst du, wenn du Durst hast? **9** Was machst du, wenn du schlechte Noten bekommst? **10** Was machst du, wenn du viele Geschenke bekommst?

2 **1** Wenn es heiß ist, faulenze ich draußen. **2** Wenn es kalt ist, bleibe ich zu Hause. **3** Wenn es regnet, gehe ich ins Kino. **4** Wenn es schneit, fahre ich Ski. **5** Wenn ich Hunger habe, esse ich Pommes. **6** Wenn ich Kopfschmerzen habe, gehe ich ins Bett. **7** Wenn ich kein Geld habe, gehe ich zur Bank. **8** Wenn ich Durst habe, trinke ich Wasser. **9** Wenn ich schlechte Noten bekomme, spreche ich mit dem Lehrer. **10** Wenn ich viele Geschenke bekomme, schreib ich viele Briefe.

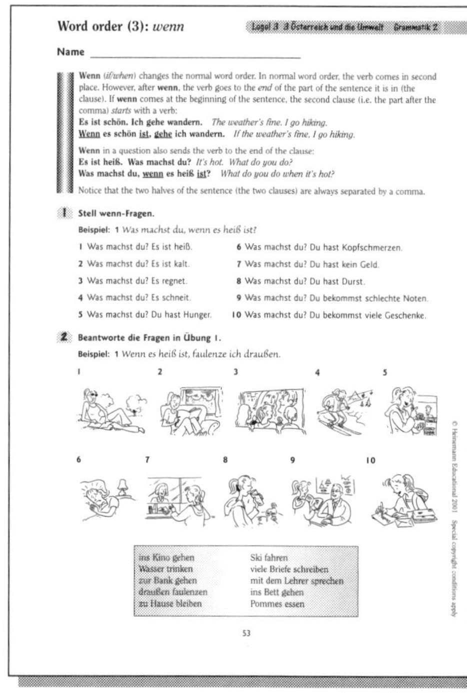

Word order (3): *wenn*

Logo! 3 3 Österreich und die Umwelt Grammatik 2

Name ______________________

Wenn (*if/when*) changes the normal word order. In normal word order, the verb comes in second place. However, after **wenn**, the verb goes to the *end* of the part of the sentence it is in (the clause). If **wenn** comes at the beginning of the sentence, the second clause (i.e. the part after the comma) *starts* with a verb:

Es ist schön. Ich gehe wandern. *The weather's fine. I go hiking.*

Wenn es schön ist, gehe ich wandern. *If the weather's fine, I go hiking.*

Wenn in a question also sends the verb to the end of the clause:

Es ist heiß. Was machst du? *It's hot. What do you do?*

Was machst du, wenn es heiß ist? *What do you do when it's hot?*

Notice that the two halves of the sentence (the two clauses) are always separated by a comma.

1 **Stell wenn-Fragen.**

Beispiel: 1 *Was machst du, wenn es heiß ist?*

1 Was machst du? Es ist heiß.
2 Was machst du? Es ist kalt.
3 Was machst du? Es regnet.
4 Was machst du? Es schneit.
5 Was machst du? Du hast Hunger.
6 Was machst du? Du hast Kopfschmerzen.
7 Was machst du? Du hast kein Geld.
8 Was machst du? Du hast Durst.
9 Was machst du? Du bekommst schlechte Noten.
10 Was machst du? Du bekommst viele Geschenke.

2 **Beantworte die Fragen in Übung 1.**

Beispiel: 1 *Wenn es heiß ist, faulenze ich draußen.*

1 2 3 4 5 6 7 8 9 10

ins Kino gehen	Ski fahren
Wasser trinken	viele Briefe schreiben
zur Bank gehen	mit dem Lehrer sprechen
draußen faulenzen	ins Bett gehen
zu Hause bleiben	Pommes essen

53

Grammatik 3 p. 54

Practice of word order.

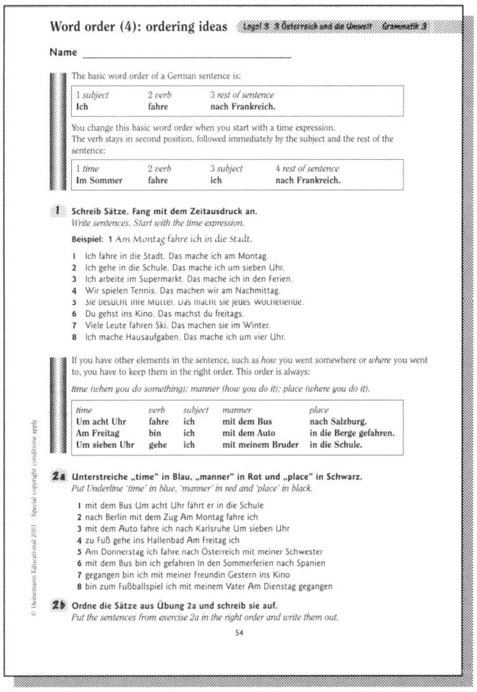

Word order (4): ordering ideas Logo! 3 3 Österreich und die Umwelt Grammatik 3

Name ______________________

The basic word order of a German sentence is:

1 *subject*	2 *verb*	3 *rest of sentence*
Ich	**fahre**	**nach Frankreich.**

You change this basic word order when you start with a time expression.
The verb stays in second position, followed immediately by the subject and the rest of the sentence:

1 *time*	2 *verb*	3 *subject*	4 *rest of sentence*
Im Sommer	**fahre**	**ich**	**nach Frankreich.**

1 Schreib Sätze. Fang mit dem Zeitausdruck an.
Write sentences. Start with the time expression.

Beispiel: 1 Am Montag fahre ich in die Stadt.

1 Ich fahre in die Stadt. Das mache ich am Montag.
2 Ich gehe in die Schule. Das mache ich um sieben Uhr.
3 Ich arbeite im Supermarkt. Das mache ich in den Ferien.
4 Wir spielen Tennis. Das machen wir am Nachmittag.
5 Sie besucht ihre Mutter. Das macht sie jedes Wochenende.
6 Du gehst ins Kino. Das machst du freitags.
7 Viele Leute fahren Ski. Das machen sie im Winter.
8 Ich mache Hausaufgaben. Das mache ich um vier Uhr.

If you have other elements in the sentence, such as *how* you went somewhere or *where* you went to, you have to keep them in the right order. This order is always:

time (when you do something); manner (how you do it); place (where you do it).

time	*verb*	*subject*	*manner*	*place*
Um acht Uhr	**fahre**	**ich**	**mit dem Bus**	**nach Salzburg.**
Am Freitag	**bin**	**ich**	**mit dem Auto**	**in die Berge gefahren.**
Um sieben Uhr	**gehe**	**ich**	**mit meinem Bruder**	**in die Schule.**

2a Unterstreiche „time" in Blau, „manner" in Rot und „place" in Schwarz.
Put Underline 'time' in blue, 'manner' in red and 'place' in black.

1 mit dem Bus Um acht Uhr fährt er in die Schule
2 nach Berlin mit dem Zug Am Montag fahre ich
3 mit dem Auto fahre ich nach Karlsruhe Um sieben Uhr
4 zu Fuß gehe ins Hallenbad Am Freitag ich
5 Am Donnerstag ich fahre nach Österreich mit meiner Schwester
6 mit dem Bus bin ich gefahren In den Sommerferien nach Spanien
7 gegangen bin ich mit meiner Freundin Gestern ins Kino
8 bin zum Fußballspiel ich mit meinem Vater Am Dienstag gegangen

2b Ordne die Sätze aus Übung 2a und schreib sie auf.
Put the sentences from exercise 2a in the right order and write them out.

54

1 **1** Am Montag fahre ich in die Stadt. **2** Um sieben Uhr gehe ich in die Schule. **3** In den Ferien arbeite ich im Supermarkt. **4** Am Nachmittag spielen wir Tennis. **5** Jedes Wochenende besucht sie ihre Mutter. **6** Freitags gehst du ins Kino. **7** Im Winter fahren viele Leute Ski. **8** Um vier Uhr mache ich Hausaufgaben.

2a 1 [manner:] <u>mit dem Bus</u> [time:] <u>Um acht Uhr</u> [place:] <u>in die Schule</u>
2 [place:] <u>nach Berlin</u> [manner:] <u>mit dem Zug</u> [time:] <u>Am Montag</u>
3 [manner:] <u>mit dem Auto</u> [place:] <u>nach Karlsruhe</u> [time:] <u>Um sieben Uhr</u>
4 [manner:] <u>zu Fuß</u> [place:] <u>ins Hallenbad</u> [time:] <u>Am Freitag</u>
5 [time:] <u>Am Donnerstag</u> [place:] <u>nach Österreich</u> [manner:] <u>mit meiner Schwester</u>
6 [manner:] <u>mit dem Bus</u> [time:] <u>In den Sommerferien</u> [place:] <u>nach Spanien</u>
7 [manner:] <u>mit meiner Freundin</u> [time:] <u>Gestern</u> [place:] <u>ins Kino</u>
8 [place:] <u>zum Fußballspiel</u> [manner:] <u>mit meinem Vater</u> [time:] <u>Am Dienstag</u>

2b 1 Um acht Uhr fährt er mit dem Bus zur Schule. **2** Am Montag fahre ich mit dem Zug nach Berlin. **3** Um sieben Uhr fahre ich mit dem Auto nach Karlsruhe. **4** Am Freitag gehe ich zu Fuß ins Hallenbad. **5** Am Donnerstag fahre ich mit meiner Schwester nach Österreich. **6** In den Sommerferien bin ich mit dem Bus nach Spanien gefahren. **7** Gestern bin ich mit meiner Freundin ins Kino gegangen. **8** Am Dienstag bin ich mit meinem Vater zum Fußballspiel gegangen.

Wortschatz pp. 55–56 and Lernzieltest p. 57

These sheets are for revision at the end of the chapter. The *Wortschatz* sheet provides a list of all the key words and phrases from the chapter and the *Lernzieltest* gives a checklist of the areas covered, which pupils can check off as they revise.

4 Medien (Pupil's Book pp. 60–77)

Topic area	Key language	Skills	Grammar	PoS
4.1 Gefallen dir Horrorfilme? (pp. 60–61) Talk about films	*Gefallen dir Liebesfilme, Science-Fiction-Filme, Actionfilme, Horrorfilme, Krimis, Zeichentrickfilme, Komödien? Ja, sie gefallen mir gut. Nein, sie gefallen mir nicht. Was für Filme gefallen dir am besten / gar nicht? Warum? Weil sie ziemlich/so/total/sehr lustig, unterhaltsam, spannend, romantisch, schrecklich, gruselig, langweilig, blöd sind.*		*weil* + verb to the end (revision) *gefallen* (revision)	2i, 3c, 5c
4.2 Möchtest du ins Kino gehen? (pp. 62–63) Phone a friend to invite him/her to the cinema	*Hallo, Katja. Hier spricht Ronny. Sag mal, Katja, hast du am Samstagabend frei? Möchtest du mit mir ins Kino gehen? Was gibt's im Kino? Er soll sehr spannend ... sein. Was für ein Film ist das? Das ist ein Actionfilm ... Kommst du mit? Ja, klar!*	Using fillers (*tja, ach, so*, etc.) to gain time when speaking		2g, 5f, 5b, 5h
4.3 Hörst du gern Popmusik? (pp. 64–65) Talk about music Talk about what you did in the past	*Wie viele CDs/Musikvideos hast du letzten Monat gekauft? Letzten Monat habe ich keine CDs/Musikvideos eine CD / ein Musikvideo gekauft. Wie oft bist du dieses Jahr ins Konzert gegangen? Dieses Jahr bin ich nicht/einmal ... ins Konzert gegangen. Wie viele Musiksendungen hast du letzte Woche gesehen? Letzte Woche habe ich keine Musiksendungen / eine Musiksendung gesehen. Wer ist dein/e Lieblingssänger/in? Was ist deine Lieblingsgruppe?*	Asking questions Pronunciation: cognates	Perfect tense with inversion (revision)	2b, 2c
4.4 Leseratten (pp. 66–67) Talk about your reading habits	*Was für Bücher liest du gern? Ich lese gern Fantasy, Sportbücher, Comics, Zeitschriften, Jugendbücher, Pferdebücher, Liebesromane, Sachbücher. Was ist dein Lieblingsbuch? Mein Lieblingsbuch ist ... Warum? Weil es gut geschrieben, interessant, lustig, unterhaltsam, spannend ist. Wie viele Bücher hast du letztes Jahr gelesen? Letztes Jahr habe ich ungefähr zwei, drei ... Bücher gelesen.*	Compounds Listening: predicting what you might hear	*weil* + verb to the end (revision)	2a, 3b
4.5 Wir surfen (pp. 68–69) Talk about what you can do on a computer Talk about what you have done on a computer recently	*Was kann man am Computer machen? Man kann Computerspiele spielen, Musik hören, E-Mails schreiben/lesen, Produkte kaufen, Programme schreiben, Bilder zeichnen, Hausaufgaben machen, im Internet surfen. Was hat ... letzte Woche gemacht? Letzte Woche hat ... Computerspiele gespielt, Musik gehört, ein Buch / eine CD gekauft, E-Mails geschrieben/gelesen, Programme geschrieben, Bilder gezeichnet, Hausaufgaben gemacht. Letzte Woche ist ... im Internet gesurft.*	Using a computer to redraft written work and find information	*können* + infinitive to the end (revision) Perfect tense singular (revision)	1b, 2f, 2j, 5e
4.6 Wie war es? (pp. 70–71) Talk about a project week	*Wo warst du am ...? Am ... war ich im Kino/Computerraum, in der Bibliothek/Stadt, zu Hause. Was hast du dort gemacht? Ich habe gelesen, einen Film gesehen. Ich bin im Internet gesurft, einkaufen gegangen. Ich hatte eine Party. Es war sehr, total, echt, besonders, so, ein bisschen, ziemlich, gar nicht ...*	Useful short words for writing	*war/hatte* *in* + dative (no movement) (revision)	1c, 2d
4.7 Online-Soaps (pp. 72–73)		Extended reading		4a, 5d, 5g
Lernzieltest und Wiederholung (pp. 74–75)	Revision			2a. 5d
Wörter (pp. 76–77)	Word list			

1 Gefallen dir Horrorfilme?
(pp. 60–61)

Pupils will learn how to:
- talk about films

Key language
Gefallen dir ... ?
Liebesfilme
Science-Fiction-Filme
Actionfilme
Horrorfilme
Krimis
Zeichentrickfilme
Komödien
Ja, sie gefallen mir gut.
Nein, sie gefallen mir nicht.
Was für Filme gefallen dir am besten / gar nicht?
Warum?
Weil sie ziemlich/so/total/sehr ... sind.
lustig
unterhaltsam
spannend
romantisch
schrecklich
gruselig
langweilig
blöd

Grammar focus
- revision of *gefallen*
- revision of *weil*

Resources
- Cassette B, Side B
- Workbook p. 31
- R & A File: Arbeitsblatt 1 (p. 68)

This chapter has media as its topic and covers a range of ideas and pupils' opinions. The three main teenagers in this chapter are Mesut, Katja and Ronny, who help steer pupils through the various aspects of the topic.

This unit focuses on film types and going to the cinema. Introduce the vocabulary orally first, using the visuals on Arbeitsblatt 1 (R & A File p. 68) copied onto an OHT. Then name some films currently showing in cinemas and ask pupils to say which types of film they are. Alternatively, name a category of film and ask pupils to name a film to fit it.

For further oral practice, give each pair of pupils a set of the visuals to cut up and place face down on the desk. They will also need two counters or pieces of card to represent a negative and a positive opinion. Pupil A turns over a visual while pupil B holds the two counters or pieces of card behind his/her back. Pupil B asks about the type of film on the visual, for example: *Gefallen dir Liebesfilme?* Pupil A chooses a counter/piece of card and accordingly responds to the question using either a negative or a positive adjective. Pupils should aim not to repeat any adjective.

1 Hör zu. Was für Filme gefallen ihnen? Was sind die beliebtesten und die unbeliebtesten Filme? (1–7) (AT1 Levels 3–4)

Pupils listen to seven teenagers talking about which film categories they like. They then work out which type of film is the most popular and which is the least popular.

Answers

1 e, d, c; **2** f, c; **3** d, g; **4** g, c; **5** c; **6** a, g, f; **7** b, e
most popular: c (liked by four people); least popular: a, b (liked by one person)

1 – Was für Filme gefallen dir?
– Tja, Krimis gefallen mir sehr. Sie sind so spannend. Ich mag auch Horrorfilme und Actionfilme.
– Magst du auch Science-Fiction-Filme?
– Nein, die finde ich total langweilig.

2 – Und du? Was für Filme gefallen dir?
– Ach, ich mag Zeichentrickfilme. Sie sind immer so lustig.
– Ist das alles?
– Tja, ich mag auch manche Actionfilme.

3 – Gefallen dir auch Actionfilme?
– Nein, sie sind langweilig. Horrorfilme gefallen mir gut.
– Ach, so. Horrorfilme. Und sonst noch etwas?
– Ja, ich mag auch Komödien.

4 – Und du? Was sind deine Lieblingsfilme?
– Ähm ... ich weiß nicht ... vielleicht Komödien. Ja, ich lache sehr gern!
– Und wie steht's mit Actionfilmen? Magst du sie?
– Ja, Actionfilme sind ziemlich gut.

5 – Und was für Filme gefallen dir?
– Ach, Actionfilme gefallen mir – sie sind immer laut und lustig!
– Und magst du auch Science-Fiction-Filme oder Horrorfilme?
– Nee, die beiden finde ich blöd.

6 – Und du? Magst du auch Actionfilme?
– Ach, nein, sie sind blöd. Ich mag Liebesfilme. Je romantischer, desto besser!
– Liebesfilme. Sehr gut. Und was gefällt dir sonst?
– Ach, ich mag Komödien und Zeichentrickfilme.

7 – Was für Filme gefallen dir?
– Science-Fiction-Filme gefallen mir am besten.
– Ach, ja? Und was noch?
– Also ... Zeichentrickfilme gefallen mir nicht, aber Krimis gefallen mir ziemlich gut.

2 Wie gefallen deinem Partner / deiner Partnerin die Filme? Mach eine Liste von 1 bis 7. Partnerarbeit. Hast du richtig geraten? (AT2 Level 4)

Pupils guess in which order their partner would categorise the films and they write a list from one (the best type of film) to seven. They then question each other to find out whether they were right or wrong.

3 Lies die Auszüge. Was für ein Film ist das? (AT3 Level 3)

Pupils read the extracts about four films and identify which category each film belongs to.

Answers

1 ein Science-Fiction-Film, **2** ein Liebesfilm,
3 ein Zeichentrickfilm, **4** ein Krimi

4a Lies die Auszüge und schreib die Adjektive auf. Wie heißen sie auf Englisch? Du darfst ein Wörterbuch benutzen. (AT3 Levels 3–4)
Pupils read the film reviews and note down the adjectives with their English meanings. They can use a dictionary if necessary to help them in this activity, but they should first of all try to work out as many of the adjectives as possible.

Answers
spannend – exciting, unterhaltsam – entertaining, gruselig – scary, schrecklich – terrible, romantisch – romantic, langweilig – boring, blöd – stupid, lustig – funny

4b Wie sollte ein guter Film sein? Mach eine Liste aus den Adjektiven von oben.
Pupils rank the adjectives in their own personal order of importance. They could also add their own ideas by looking up further adjectives in a dictionary and writing them on the board/OHT for the rest of the class to use.

5a Mesut, Katja und Ronny diskutieren Filme. Notiere die Adjektive. (AT1 Level 4)
Pupils listen and note down what Mesut, Katja and Ronny say about the four film categories listed.

Answers
1 romantisch, total blöd, **2** spannend, langweilig, unterhaltsam, **3** lustig, schrecklich, **4** gruselig

- Hallo, Katja, hast du den Film gestern Abend im Fernsehen gesehen?
- Ja, er war sehr romantisch, nicht?
- Romantisch? Nein, er war total blöd!
- Ach, Ronny. Gefallen dir denn Liebesfilme nicht?
- Nein, ich mag spannende Actionfilme.
- Actionfilme? Nein, die finde ich langweilig. Du auch, Mesut?
- Ach, nein, manchmal sind sie unterhaltsam.
- Siehst du!
- O.K. Aber am liebsten sehe ich Zeichentrickfilme. Sie sind meistens sehr lustig.
- Ja, du hast Recht. Was meinst du, Ronny?
- Zeichentrickfilme? Sie sind schrecklich!
- Also, was für Filme gefallen dir, Ronny?
- Horrorfilme!
- Warum?
- Weil sie so gruselig sind!

5b Bist du derselben Meinung? Schreib Sätze. (AT4 Level 3)
Pupils then give their own opinions on the films, using *weil* clauses. Remind pupils of the *weil* construction, and if necessary go back over their work from chapter 2.

6a Gruppenarbeit. Frag sechs Personen in der Klasse. (AT2 Level 4)
Pupils ask six people in the class what their favourite film category is. They should answer using a *weil* clause.

6b Schreib die Resultate auf. (AT4 Level 4)
Pupils write up the results of the survey.

R Further practice of this unit's language is to be found on p. 116 of the Pupil's Book, activity 1.

E Further practice of this unit's language is to be found on p. 117 of the Pupil's Book, activity 1.

2 Möchtest du ins Kino gehen? (pp. 62–63)

Pupils will learn how to:
- phone a friend to invite him/her to the cinema

Key language
Hallo, Katja. Hier spricht Ronny.
Sag mal, Katja, …
Hast du am Samstagabend frei?
Möchtest du mit mir ins Kino gehen?
Was gibt's im Kino?
Er soll sehr spannend sein.
Was für ein Film ist das?
Das ist ein Actionfilm.
Kommst du mit?
Ja, klar!
Nein, danke!

Skill focus
- Using fillers (*tja, ach, so,* etc.) to gain time when speaking

Resources
- Cassette B, Side B
- Workbook p. 32
- R & A File: Arbeitsblatt 4 (p. 71)

This unit features a dialogue for inviting a friend out to the cinema. Most of the vocabulary should be familiar to pupils.

1a Hör zu und lies. (AT1 Level 4)

Pupils listen to and read a dialogue in which Ronny invites Katja out to the cinema. Ask pupils to pick out any useful phrases in the dialogue which they might be able to use on other occasions, such as *Grüß dich* and *Wie bitte*?

– Hallo.
– Hallo, Katja. Hier spricht Ronny.
– Grüß dich, Ronny. Wie geht's?
– Gut, danke. Sag mal, Katja, hast du am Samstagabend frei?
– Samstagabend … Samstagabend … Warum denn?
– Ja … möchtest du mit mir ins Kino gehen?
– Ins Kino gehen? Tja … was gibt's denn im Kino?
– *Tankmann*.
– Wie bitte?
– *Tankmann*. Er soll sehr spannend sein.
– *Tankmann*? Ach, ja. Was für ein Film ist das, Ronny?
– Das ist ein Actionfilm.
– Na so was.
– Also, kommst du mit?
– Ja, klar!

1b Beantworte die Fragen. (AT3 Level 4)

Pupils answer five comprehension questions in German on the dialogue.

Answers

1 Samstagabend, **2** *Tankmann*, **3** sehr spannend, **4** ein Actionfilm, **5** ja

2 Hör zu. Schreib die Tabelle ab und füll sie aus. (1–4) (AT1 Level 4)

Pupils listen and note down the details of four conversations in which people invite friends to the cinema.

Answers

	Wann?	Film?	Wie soll er sein?	Filmsorte?
1	Mittwochabend	*Das Fahrrad*	gruselig	Horrorfilm
2	Montagabend	*Ein Kind und zwei Hunde*	lustig	Komödie
3	Sonntagabend	*Die Italienerin*	romantisch	Liebesfilm
4	Samstagabend	*Sommer in Wien*	spannend	Krimi

1 – Hallo.
– Hallo, Kai. Hier spricht Ruth.
– Grüß dich, Ruth. Wie geht's?
– Nicht schlecht, danke. Sag mal, Kai, hast du am Mittwochabend frei?
– Äh … Mittwochabend … Mittwochabend … Warum denn?
– Ja … möchtest du mit mir ins Kino gehen?
– Ins Kino gehen? Tja … was gibt's im Kino?
– *Das Fahrrad*. Er soll sehr gruselig sein.
– Wie bitte?
– *Das Fahrrad*. Er soll sehr gruselig sein.
– *Das Fahrrad*? Ach, ja. Was für ein Film ist das, Ruth?
– Das ist ein Horrorfilm.
– Ach, so.
– Also, kommst du mit?
– Ja, klar!

2 – Hallo.
– Hallo, Marie. Hier spricht Georg.
– Grüß dich, Georg. Wie geht's?
– O.K., danke. Sag mal, Marie, hast du am Montagabend frei?
– Montagabend … Montagabend … Warum denn?
– Ja … möchtest du mit mir ins Kino gehen?
– Ins Kino gehen? Tja … was gibt's im Kino?
– *Ein Kind und zwei Hunde*.
– Wie bitte?
– *Ein Kind und zwei Hunde*. Er soll sehr lustig sein.
– Lustig, ja? Ach, ja. Ist das eine Komödie?
– Genau. Das ist die neue Komödie mit Hans Flinker.
– Ach, so. Äh … Moment mal …

3 – Hallo.
– Hallo, Tina. Hier spricht Wolfgang.
– Grüß dich, Wolfgang. Wie geht's?
– Prima, danke. Sag mal, Tina, hast du am Sonntagabend frei?
– Sonntagabend? Äh … Warum denn?
– Ja … möchtest du mit mir ins Kino gehen?
– Ins Kino gehen? Tja … was gibt's im Kino?
– *Die Italienerin*.
– Wie bitte?
– *Die Italienerin*.
– Ach, ist das ein lustiger Film?
– Nein, aber er soll sehr romantisch sein.
– Romantisch? Na so was.
– Ja, ein Liebesfilm ist das.
– Prima!

4 – Hallo.
– Hallo, Ingo. Hier spricht Annette.
– Grüß dich, Annette. Wie geht's?
– Gut, danke. Sag mal, Ingo, hast du am Samstagabend frei?
– Samstagabend? Warum denn?
– Also, möchtest du mit mir ins Kino gehen?
– Ins Kino gehen? Na so was! Was gibt's im Kino?
– *Sommer in Wien*.
– Wie bitte?
– *Sommer in Wien*. Er soll sehr spannend sein.
– Ach, ja. Sag mal, was für ein Film ist das?
– Das ist ein Krimi.
– Ach, so.
– Also, kommst du mit?
– Ja, klar!

3 Hör zu und wiederhole. So gewinnt man Zeit!
Pupils listen to and repeat some phrases from the dialogue which enable them to slow down a conversation in order to gain some thinking time. You could play the recording for activity 2 again and ask pupils to identify where these phrases occur.

– Ach, ja.
– Ach, so.
– Tja.
– Wie bitte?
– Äh …
– Moment mal.
– Sag mal, …
– Na so was.

Ludwig: Using fillers (*tja, ach, so,* etc.) to gain time when speaking
Go through Ludwig's advice with the pupils and encourage them to note down the given expressions for use at a later date. Also, ask whether pupils have other time-gaining strategies which they could share with the class.

4a Partnerarbeit. Übt Dialoge. (AT2 Levels 4–5)
Pupils practise phone conversations, based on the dialogue on p. 62. Encourage pupils to act out their dialogues in a lively manner and make sure they use some of the expressions for gaining thinking time.

4b Schreib für diese Details einen Dialog auf. Der Dialog in Übung 4a hilft dir dabei. (AT4 Levels 4–5)
Pupils write a dialogue based on the information provided. They could then practise it with a partner. The best ones could be performed for the whole class.

R The pairwork activity on Arbeitsblatt 4 (R & A File p. 71) provides further oral practice of the language of the unit.

3 Hörst du gern Popmusik?
(pp. 64–65)

Pupils will learn how to:
- talk about music
- talk about what they did in the past

Key language
Wie viele CDs/Musikvideos hast du letzten Monat gekauft?
Letzten Monat habe ich … gekauft.
keine CDs/ Musikvideos
eine CD / ein Musikvideo
Wie oft bist du dieses Jahr ins Konzert gegangen?
Dieses Jahr bin ich nicht / einmal … ins Konzert gegangen.
Wie viele Musiksendungen hast du letzte Woche gesehen?
Letzte Woche habe ich keine Musiksendungen / eine Musiksendung gesehen.
Wer ist dein/e Lieblingssänger/in?
Was ist deine Lieblingsgruppe?

Grammar focus
- perfect tense with inversion (revision)

Skill focus
- asking questions
- pronunciation: cognates

Resources
- Cassette B, Side B
- Workbook pp. 33, 37
- R & A File: Grammatik 1 (p. 73)

This unit covers the topic of pop music and pupils' musical preferences. You could introduce this topic by telling the class about your musical preferences (either real or outlandish) and telling them about the CDs you have recently bought and concerts you have been to. The class could then share their musical tastes with you.

Practice of giving opinions is provided on Grammatik 1 (R & A File p. 73).

1a Hör zu und notiere Katjas Antworten zum Musikquiz. (AT1 Levels 4–5, AT3 Level 4)
Pupils listen to the recording and note down which answers Katja gives to the music quiz.

Answers
1 c (vier), **2** a, **3** b, **4** c (drei), **5** Craig David, **6** Britney Spears, **7** „Backstreet Boys"

Mesut: Also, Katja, die erste Frage: Wie viele CDs hast du letzten Monat gekauft?
Katja: CDs? Moment mal … also letzten Monat habe ich vier CDs gekauft.
Mesut: Vier CDs … sehr gut. Und wie viele Musikvideos hast du letzten Monat gekauft?
Katja: Musikvideos? Also, letzten Monat habe ich keine Musikvideos gekauft.
Mesut: Wow, keine Musikvideos? Wirklich?
Katja: Ja, aber nächsten Monat kaufe ich eins.
Mesut: O.K. Dritte Frage: Wie viele Musiksendungen hast du letzte Woche gesehen?
Katja: Letzte Woche? Ach, Moment mal … also letzte Woche habe ich nur eine Musiksendung am Wochenende gesehen.
Mesut: O.K. Vierte Frage: Wie oft bist du dieses Jahr ins Konzert gegangen?
Katja: Ach, dieses Jahr bin ich oft ins Konzert gegangen. Ende Mai habe ich Robbie Williams gesehen, dann habe ich die Spice Girls auf Tournee gesehen und letzten Monat habe ich eine neue Band, Die Wildkatzen, gehört – die waren schrecklich!
Mesut: O.K. Fünfte Frage: Wer ist dein Lieblingssänger, Katja?
Katja: Mein Lieblingssänger? Das ist Craig David.
Mesut: Ach ja, den finde ich auch toll. Und deine Lieblingssängerin?
Katja: Das ist Britney Spears.
Mesut: Und was ist deine Lieblingsgruppe?
Katja: Meine Lieblingsgruppe sind die Backstreet Boys.

Ludwig: Asking questions
Check that pupils know what the question words in the quiz mean and ask them to give you any further question words they know, such as *wo? wann?* and *warum*? You could do some whole class work, putting the questions to the class and eliciting a few answers before pupils work in pairs.

1b Partnerarbeit. Macht das Musikquiz. (AT2 Level 4)
Pupils do the music quiz in pairs, comparing their answers.

1c Schreib deine Antworten zum Musikquiz auf. (AT4 Level 3)
Pupils write up their answers to the music quiz.

E Pupils write up their partner's results as well, using the *er/sie* forms of the verbs.

Wiederholung: The perfect tense – inversion
This grammar revision box reminds pupils of the frequent use of inversion in German sentences. Here the time expression is at the start of every sentence.

R An exercise on the perfect tense is provided on p. 37 of the Workbook.

2a Hast du meistens (a), (b) oder (c) ausgewählt? Lies die Antworten unten. (AT3 Level 5)
Pupils do the music quiz and read the answer key to see which category they fit into.

2b Ist das (a), (b) oder (c)? (AT 3 Level 4)
Pupils identify which text each of the nine pictures refers to.

Answers

1 b, **2** a, **3** c, **4** b, **5** c, **6** a, **7** c, **8** a, **9** a

2c Bist du ein Musikfan oder nicht? Adaptiere die Texte aus Übung 2a für dich. (AT4 Level 4)
Pupils write a text about their musical preferences, using the texts in activity 2a.

3 Wie spricht man das aus? Hör dann zu und überprüfe die Aussprache. (AT2 Level 2)
Pupils listen to and repeat some cognates to improve their pronunciation.

- Musik ... Ich höre gern Musik.
- Musikvideo ... Ich habe ein Musikvideo gekauft.
- CD ... Ich habe eine CD gekauft.
- Kassette ... Ich habe eine Kassette gekauft.
- Konzert ... Ich gehe gern ins Konzert.
- Popmusik ... Ich liebe Popmusik.

Ludwig: Pronunciation of cognates
Encourage pupils to improve their German pronunciation by listening to as much German as possible. If they have a German penfriend, they could ask him/her to send a taped letter for them to copy the pronunciation. Ask pupils if they know any other German words which look like their English equivalents. Write them on the board/OHT and discuss how the pronunciation differs from English.

MINI-TEST
At the end of the third unit in every chapter, there is a *Mini-Test*. This is intended as a half-way checkpoint for pupils to check that they are familiar with the key language of the chapter so far. Pupils could revise the language with a partner in class or for homework.

4 Leseratten (pp. 66–67)

Pupils will learn how to:
- talk about their reading habits

Key language
Was für Bücher liest du gern?
Ich lese gern ...
 Fantasy
 Sportbücher
 Comics
 Zeitschriften
 Jugendbücher
 Pferdebücher
 Liebesromane
 Sachbücher
Was ist dein Lieblingsbuch?
Mein Lieblingsbuch ist X.
Warum?
Weil es ... ist.
 gut geschrieben
 interessant
 lustig
 unterhaltsam
 spannend
Wie viele Bücher hast du letztes Jahr gelesen?
Letztes Jahr habe ich ungefähr zwei Bücher gelesen.

Grammar focus
- *weil* + subordinate clause word order (revision)

Skill focus
- compounds
- listening: predicting what you might hear

Resources
- Cassette B, Side B
- Workbook p. 34
- R & A File: Arbeitsblatt 2 (p. 69)

This unit focuses on book types and pupils' reading habits. Introduce the book vocabulary by copying the visuals on Arbeitsblatt 2 (R & A File p. 69) onto an OHT and asking questions: *Gefallen dir Pferdebücher oder Sachbücher? Welche Bücher gefallen dir am besten?* Try to bring in a few teenage books for pupils to categorise.

For further oral practice of the language, give each pair of pupils a set of the visuals. One pupils throws a coin or die onto the sheet and gives the appropriate sentence for whichever visual it lands on, e.g.: *Ich lese gern Sachbücher.* The next pupil then does the same and adds the new category, e.g.: *Ich lese gern Sachbücher und Jugendbücher.* If the coin lands on a category already mentioned, pupils just repeat the existing list. The game continues until all categories are in the list.

1a Wer ist das: Katja, Mesut oder Ronny? (AT3 Level 4)

Pupils read three texts written by Katja, Mesut and Ronny about their reading habits and identify to whom the seven statements refer.

Answers
1 Mesut, **2** Katja, **3** Ronny, **4** Mesut, **5** Ronny, **6** Mesut, **7** Mesut

► 1b Mach eine deutsch-englische Liste von Büchern.

Pupils pick the book types out of the three texts and then make a German–English list of them.

Answers
Pferdebücher – horse books, Liebesromane – love stories, Fantasy – fantasy, Sportbücher – sports books, Jugendbücher – teenage fiction, Sachbücher – non-fiction, Comics – comics, Zeitschriften – magazines

Ludwig: Compounds

Point out to pupils that many long German nouns are compounds made up of several smaller words. Encourage them to break down long German words into their component parts when they come across them: this might help them to work out the meaning, as in Ludwig's example. Give a few examples of other compound words from this chapter for pupils to break down into their component parts: *Lieblingssänger, Horrorfilme, Liebesfilme, Samstagabend, Musiksendung.* Pupils could then look through Logo! 3 for further examples of compounds.

Ludwig: Listening – predicting what you might hear

Go through Ludwig's advice with the pupils before they do activity 2. Tell them that a table like this provides useful clues about the content of the recording they are going to hear.

2 Hör zu. Schreib die Tabelle ab und füll sie aus. (1–4) (AT1 Levels 4–5)

Pupils listen to the recording and note down what four teenagers say about themselves and their reading habits.

	Alter	Hobbys	Lieblingsbücher	Lieblingsbuch	Warum?
1	15	lesen, tanzen	Comics, Fantasy	*Superman*	spannend
2	16	lesen, Tennis	Sportbücher	*Fußball in Deutschland*	interessant
3	16	Ski fahren, Musik	Liebesromane Zeitschriften	*Popmusik*	unterhaltsam
4	15	lesen, fernsehen	Fantasy, Jugendbücher	*Neunzehn*	spannend, gruselig, gut geschrieben

1 – Hallo, Iris. Wie alt bist du?
– Ich bin 15 Jahre alt.
– Und was sind deine Hobbys?
– Also, ich lese gern und ich tanze gern.
– Prima! Hast du ein Lieblingsbuch?
– Äh ... Moment mal ... ja, das ist wahrscheinlich *Superman*.
– O, liest du denn gern Comics?
– Ja, ich lese sehr gern Comics und ich mag auch Fantasy.

- Fantasy und Comics? Sehr gut. Warum ist *Superman* dein Lieblingscomic?
- Weil es so spannend ist.

2 – Hallo, Hannes. Was sind deine Hobbys?
- Also, ich lese gern und ich spiele gern Tennis.
- Lesen und Tennis spielen. Prima! Wie alt bist du?
- Ich bin 16 Jahre alt.
- Sechzehn Jahre. Sag mal, Hannes, was für Bücher liest du gern?
- Tja, ich lese gern Sportbücher. Ja, Sportbücher mag ich sehr.
- Alles klar. Und was ist dein Lieblingsbuch?
- Mein Lieblingsbuch? Das ist wahrscheinlich *Fußball in Deutschland*.
- *Fußball in Deutschland*? Warum denn?
- Weil es so interessant ist.

3 – Hallo, Margit. Wie alt bist du?
- Ich bin 16 Jahre alt.
- Was für Bücher liest du gern?
- Ach, Liebesromane oder Zeitschriften.
- Liebesromane oder Zeitschriften? Toll. Und was ist dein Lieblingsbuch oder deine Lieblingszeitschrift?
- Das ist *Popmusik*.
- *Popmusik*? Ach, ja, warum denn?
- Weil sie so unterhaltsam ist.
- Und was sind deine Hobbys?
- Also, ich fahre gern Ski und ich höre gern Musik.

4 – Hallo, Christian. Wie alt bist du?
- Ich bin 15 Jahre alt.
- Und was machst du gern in deiner Freizeit?
- Also, ich lese gern und ich sehe gern fern.
- Lesen und fernsehen. Sehr gut. Hast du ein Lieblingsbuch?
- Ja, das lese ich gerade. Es heißt *Neunzehn*.
- *Neunzehn*? Warum ist das dein Lieblingsbuch?
- Weil es so spannend und gruselig ist und weil es so gut geschrieben ist.
- Was für Bücher liest du gern?
- Ach, Fantasy oder Jugendbücher.

3 Partnerarbeit. Ordne den Dialog und mach Interviews mit Katja, Mesut und Ronny. (AT2 Levels 4–5)

Pupils put the interview questions and Katja's answers in the correct order and then conduct further interviews with Mesut and Ronny, using the information on p. 66.

Answers

- Wie heißt du?
- Ich heiße Katja.
- Wie alt bist du?
- Ich bin fünfzehn Jahre alt.
- Was sind deine Hobbys?
- Ich lese gern, ich gehe gern schwimmen und ich höre gern Musik.
- Was für Bücher liest du gern?
- Ich lese gern Liebesromane und Pferdebücher.
- Was ist dein Lieblingsbuch?
- Mein Lieblingsbuch ist *Der Pferdeflüsterer*.
- Warum?
- Weil es gut geschrieben ist.
- Wie viele Bücher hast du letztes Jahr gelesen?
- Letztes Jahr habe ich ungefähr zwölf Bücher gelesen.

E Pupils interview each other using the same questions. They write up their findings in the third person singular.

4 Bereite eine kurze Präsentation wie die von Katja vor. Nimm sie auf Kassette auf. (AT4 Levels 4–6, AT2 Levels 4–6)

Pupils write a short presentation about themselves and their reading habits, using the texts on p. 66 to help them. If possible, they should prepare their work on computer so that they can redraft and refine it later. Pupils then record their presentation on cassette to help them memorise it for a class presentation.

R Further practice of this unit's language is to be found on p. 116 of the Pupil's Book, activity 2.

E Further practice of this unit's language is to be found on p. 117 of the Pupil's Book, activity 2.

5 Wir surfen (pp. 68–69)

Pupils will learn how to:
- talk about what you can do on a computer
- talk about what they have done on a computer recently

Key language
Was kann man am Computer machen?
Man kann ...
Computerspiele spielen.
Musik hören.
E-Mails schreiben/ lesen.
Produkte kaufen.
Programme schreiben.
Bilder zeichnen.
Hausaufgaben machen.
im Internet surfen.
Was hat X letzte Woche gemacht?
Letzte Woche hat X ...
Computerspiele gespielt.
Musik gehört.
E-Mails geschrieben/gelesen.
ein Buch / eine CD gekauft.
Programme geschrieben.
Bilder gezeichnet.
Hausaufgaben gemacht.
Letzte Woche ist X im Internet gesurft.

Grammar focus
- *können* + infinitive to end (revision)
- perfect tense singular (revision)

Skill focus
- Using a computer to redraft written work / find information

Resources
- Cassette B, Side B
- Workbook p. 35
- R & A File: Arbeitsblatt 3 (p. 70), Grammatik 2 (p. 74)

This unit focuses on computers and what pupils can use them for. Have a class brainstorming session first of all for ideas about what you use a computer for. Gather the ideas on the board/OHT. Then present the vocabulary by copying the visuals on Arbeitsblatt 3 (R & A File p. 70) onto an OHT and comparing them to the pupils' own list. Ask pupils which earlier structures the construction *man kann* ... reminds them of (*man darf/sollte* ...).

For further oral practice, give each pair of pupils a set of the visuals. One pupil points to a visual and asks: *Was kann man am Computer machen?* The other pupil gives the appropriate reply.

1a Was passt zusammen? (AT3 Level 2)

Pupils read the captions and match them to the appropriate computer screen.

Answers
1 g, **2** b, **3** a, **4** c, **5** e, **6** f, **7** h, **8** d

1b Hör zu und wiederhole. Welches Bild ist das? (1–8) (AT1 Level 2)

Pupils listen to and repeat the sentences and match them to the appropriate computer screen.

Answers
1 f, **2** c, **3** e, **4** a, **5** d, **6** h, **7** b, **8** g

1 – Was kann man am Computer machen?
– Man kann Bilder zeichnen.
2 – Man kann Computerspiele spielen.
3 – Man kann Musik hören.
4 – Man kann Hausaufgaben machen.
5 – Man kann Produkte kaufen.
6 – Man kann Programme schreiben.
7 – Man kann E-Mails schreiben und lesen.
8 – Man kann im Internet surfen.

1c Partnerarbeit. Memoryspiel. (AT2 Level 3)

Pupils play a memory game, adding on another computer function each time and repeating the ones already mentioned until all the functions have been mentioned. Pupils could close their textbooks to make the task more challenging.

Wiederholung: Talking about what you can do

This grammar revision box reinforces the structure of *man kann* + infinitive. Go through it with the pupils, starting some sentences for them to finish, e.g.: *Man kann E-Mails* ... and asking questions, e.g.: *Was kann man mit Musik am Computer machen?*

R Refer to p. 127 of the Pupil's Book for further information. More practice of this grammar point is also provided on Grammatik 2 (R & A File p. 74).

2 Hör zu. Was haben sie am Computer gemacht? Mach Notizen. (1–4) (AT1 Levels 4–5)

Pupils listen and make notes about what four teenagers have done recently on a computer.

Answers
1 E-Mails, Hausaufgaben, Musik; **2** Internet, Produkte; **3** Bilder, Computerspiele; **4** Computerspiele, Programme, E-Mails

1 – Was hast du letzte Woche am Computer gemacht?
– Tja, ich habe E-Mails geschrieben und gelesen.
– Ja, und sonst noch etwas?
– Also, äh ... ja, ich habe Hausaufgaben gemacht.
– Gut. War das alles? Hast du vielleicht etwas gekauft?
– Ach, nein, aber ich habe Musik gehört.
2 – Und du? Was hast du letzte Woche am Computer gemacht?
– Ich bin im Internet gesurft, weil das mein Lieblingshobby ist!

- Ach, schön. Kaufst du manchmal Produkte vom Internet?
- Ja, aber nur wenn meine Mutter dabei ist. Sonst darf ich das nicht machen. Letzte Woche habe ich eine tolle CD gekauft.
- Schreibst du auch Programme am Computer?
- Ja, das machen wir ab und zu in der Schule, aber ich finde es sehr langweilig.
- Also, letzte Woche hast du das nicht gemacht, oder?
- Nein.

3 – Was hast du letzte Woche am Computer gemacht?
- Also, letzte Woche war ich nicht viel am Computer. Am Wochenende habe ich einige Bilder gezeichnet, aber sie waren sehr blöd. Meine Schwester macht das viel besser als ich. Und sie ist erst acht Jahre alt!
- O, hast du dann sonst nichts am Computer gemacht?
- Nee, ich habe Computerspiele gespielt. Das ist mein Lieblingshobby, also das habe ich bestimmt gemacht.
- Computerspiele? Ja, das machen viele!

4 – Und du? Hast du auch Computerspiele gespielt?
- Was, letzte Woche? Ja, ich glaube schon. Aber ich habe meistens Programme geschrieben.
- Ach, findest du das interessant?
- Ja, das ist mein Hobby. Ich schreibe viele Programme.
- Und sind sie gut?
- Ja, sie sind ziemlich gut.
- Und hast du sonst noch etwas gemacht?
- Also, ich habe einige E-Mails geschrieben. Das war alles!

R Remind pupils of the formation of the perfect tense before they do activity 3a and 3b. Elicit the third person singular forms *er/sie hat* and *er/sie ist*, also the past participles of the key verbs in this unit: *gehört, geschrieben, gelesen, gekauft, gezeichnet, gemacht, gesurft.*

3a Was haben sie letzte Woche am Computer gemacht? Schreib Sätze. (AT4 Levels 3–4)

Pupils solve the spaghetti puzzle and write sentences in the perfect tense describing what people did on a computer last week. Pupils can refer to the key language box for support if needed.

Answers

Letzte Woche hat Katja Musik gehört. Letzte Woche hat Mesut Hausaufgaben gemacht. Letzte Woche hat Ronny E-Mails geschrieben und gelesen. Letzte Woche hat Lars Bilder gezeichnet. Letzte Woche hat Karl Computerspiele gespielt. Letzte Woche ist Steffi im Internet gesurft. Letzte Woche hat Detlef ein Buch gekauft. Letzte Woche hat Nils ein Programm geschrieben.

3b Partnerarbeit. (AT2 Levels 4–5)

Pupils question each other about the spaghetti puzzle in activity 3a.

4 Beantworte die Fragen. Kannst du noch weitere Details hinzufügen? (AT4 Levels 4–5)

Pupils answer questions about their recent computer experience and add as many details as possible. If they are working on a computer, they could firstly answer the questions one by one and then string them together with conjunctions to write a complete text.

Ludwig: Using a computer to redraft written work / find information

Go through Ludwig's advice with pupils, reminding them of the benefits of working on a computer both for redrafting and for presentational purposes. Also remind pupils that they can find out a wealth of information about Germany via the internet. Two useful starting points are www.yahoo.de and www.netscape.com/de, which are German search engines.

6 Wie war es? (pp. 70–71)

Pupils will learn how to:
• talk about a project week

Key language Wo warst du am Montag? Am Montag war Ich … im Kino/ Computerraum in der Bibliothek/Stadt zu Hause. Was hast du dort gemacht? Ich habe gelesen / einen Film gesehen. Ich bin im Internet gesurft. Ich bin einkaufen gegangen. Ich hatte eine Party. Es war sehr / total / echt/ besonders / so / ein bisschen / ziemlich / gar nicht …	**Grammar focus** • *war/hatte* • *in* + dative (no movement) (revision) **Skill focus** • useful short words for writing **Resources** • Cassette B, Side B • Workbook p. 36 • R & A File: Grammatik 3 (p. 75)

This unit focuses on Ronny's diary report about a media project week and uses the imperfect forms *war* and *hatte*. Once pupils have read the report, you could ask a few general questions, e.g.: *Ich war in der Bibliothek. Welcher Tag war das?* You could also ask pupils to pick out the German equivalents of phrases you give, such as 'we had a party'.

1a Lies Ronnys Tagebuch und beantworte die Fragen. (AT3 Levels 5–6)

Pupils read the diary report and answer ten comprehension questions in German about it. There is no need for them to write full sentences.

Answers

1 spannend, **2** blöd, **3** sehr interessant, **4** All Saints, **5** im Computerraum in der Schule, **6** Schottland, **7** in der Bibliothek, **8** einfach, **9** im Klassenzimmer, **10** eine Stereoanlage

1b Hör zu. Mesut hat die Projektwoche auch mitgemacht, aber er hat alles schon vergessen. Welche Fehler macht er? (AT1 Levels 5–6)

Pupils listen to Mesut describing the same media project week as Ronny, but he makes mistakes. Pupils compare his description with Ronny's and spot the mistakes.

Answers

Montag: im Kino = „in der Schule"; **Mittwoch**: E-Mails geschrieben = „Computerspiele gespielt", im Internet gesurft = „Hausaufgaben gemacht"; **Donnerstag**: in der Bibliothek = „im Klassenzimmer"; **Freitag**: CD = „Musikvideo", keine Stereoanlage = „keinen Fernseher"

– Also, Mesut. Du hast die Projektwoche mitgemacht, nicht?
– Ja, aber ich habe sie ein bisschen langweilig gefunden.
– Ach, schade. Was habt ihr am Montag gemacht?
– Montag … Montag … Moment mal. Ach, ja, am Montag waren wir **in der Schule**. Wir haben Videos angesehen.
– Und am Dienstag, was habt ihr da gemacht?
– Ach, Dienstag war besser, weil wir im Studio von Radio Pop waren.
– Super. Und was habt ihr dort gemacht?
– Äh … wir haben Musik gehört.
– Schön. Und was habt ihr am Mittwoch gemacht?
– Am Mittwoch … tja, ich weiß es nicht … Moment mal … ja, am Mittwoch waren wir im Computerraum.
– Und was habt ihr dort gemacht?
– Wir haben **Computerspiele gespielt**.
– Computerspiele gespielt? Echt wahr?
– Ja, und wir haben auch **Hausaufgaben gemacht**.
– O.K., und was habt ihr am Donnerstag gemacht?
– Am Donnerstag waren wir **im Klassenzimmer**. Wir haben ein Quiz gemacht, aber das war stinklangweilig.
– Und am Freitag? Was habt ihr da gemacht?
– Ach, am Freitag hatten wir eine Party.
– Schön. Wie war das?
– Ach, das war blöd. Jeder hat **ein Musikvideo** mitgenommen, aber es gab **keinen Fernseher** im Klassenzimmer.

Grammatik: 'was' and 'had'

Pupils have come across *war* and *hatte* receptively before; this grammar box shows the conjugation of the singular and plural to enable them to use these forms.

R Refer to pp. 131–132 of the Pupil's Book for further information. More practice of this grammar point is also provided on Grammatik 3 (R & A File p. 75).

Wiederholung: *in* + dative

Prepositions were dealt with in detail in Logo! 2, but this grammar revision box reminds pupils that when they use *in* with no movement they need to use the dative case.

2 Such die deutschen Wörter im Text auf Seite 70. (AT3 Level 3)

Pupils read the report on p. 70 to locate the qualifiers listed here.

Answers

1 sehr, **2** ein bisschen, **3** echt, **4** total, **5** besonders, **6** so, **7** gar nicht, **8** ziemlich

Ludwig: Useful short words for writing

Ludwig reminds pupils of the importance of qualifiers such as *total* and *echt* which make texts more interesting and lively. Encourage pupils to note these words in their vocabulary books and learn them. If pupils know of any more qualifiers, they could share them with the class.

3 Ordne die Sätze.

Pupils put the jumbled sentences in the right order, focusing on the position of the qualifier.

Answers

1 Der Film war sehr blöd. **2** Die Musiksendung war besonders laut. **3** Die Technomusik war so doof. **4** Der Horrorfilm war total gruselig. **5** Der Film war gar nicht romantisch. **6** Die CDs waren ein bisschen langweilig. **7** Die Zeitschriften waren ziemlich kindisch. **8** Also hatte ich eine Party – sie war echt klasse.

4 Hör zu und beantworte die Fragen. (1–6) (AT1 Level 5)

Pupils listen to the recording and answer four questions for each speaker about the day, location, what they did and what it was like. They should answer in note form.

Answers

1 a Montag, **b** zu Hause, **c** eine Party, **d** echt klasse; **2 a** Mittwoch, **b** in der Bibliothek, **c** Hausaufgaben, **d** ziemlich langweilig; **3 a** Donnerstag, **b** im Kino, **c** einen Actionfilm gesehen, **d** gar nicht spannend, **4 a** Samstag, **b** zu Hause, **c** viele Zeichentrickfilme gesehen, **d** total lustig; **5 a** Sonntag, **b** in der Stadt, **c** viele CDs gekauft, **d** ein bisschen anstrengend; **6 a** Dienstag, **b** im Computerraum, **c** im Internet gesurft, **d** sehr interessant

1 – Hallo, wo warst du am Montag?
– Am Montag? Tja, ich war zu Hause.
– Zu Hause? Schön. Was hast du gemacht?
– Ich hatte eine Party.
– Ach, ja? Wie war das?
– Ach, das war echt klasse.

2 – Hallo, wo warst du am Mittwoch?
– Am Mittwoch … am Mittwoch war ich in der Bibliothek.
– Ach, ja? Was hast du dort gemacht?
– O, ich habe Hausaufgaben gemacht. Es war ziemlich langweilig.

3 – Hallo, wo warst du am Donnerstag?
– Am Donnerstag war ich im Kino.
– Schön. Was hast du gesehen?
– Ach, es war ein Actionfilm, aber er war gar nicht spannend.

4 – Hallo, wo warst du am Samstag?
– Ach, ich war zu Hause.
– Und was hast du gemacht?
– Ich habe viele Zeichentrickfilme gesehen.
– O, ja. War das nicht langweilig?
– Nein, das war total lustig.

5 – Hallo, wo warst du am Sonntag?
– Also, am Sonntag … Moment mal … ja, am Sonntag war ich in der Stadt.
– Und was hast du dort gemacht?
– Ich habe viele CDs gekauft.
– Ach, wie schön!
– Ja, aber es war auch ein bisschen anstrengend.

6 – Hallo, wo warst du am Dienstag?
– Am Dienstag war ich im Computerraum.
– Im Computerraum? Was hast du dort gemacht?
– Ich bin im Internet gesurft.
– Ach, so. Wie war das?
– Das war sehr interessant.

5a Schreib die Tabelle ab und ergänze sie für Montag bis Freitag.

Pupils copy the table and note down what they did last week, using the language in the clouds and deciding whether they enjoyed the activity or not.

5b Partnerarbeit. Macht Interviews. (AT2 Levels 5–6)

Pupils interview each other, based on the notes they made from the writing activity 5a and using the phrases in the key language grid for support.

6 Schreib Details über die letzte Woche auf. (AT4 Levels 5–6)

Pupils write a diary report about what they did last week, focusing on the chapter's topic of media. They could copy the style of Ronny's diary report or use the information from activity 5a as a starting point for their own ideas.

7 Online-Soaps (pp. 72–73)

Resources
- Cassette B, Side B

The *MEHR* unit is intended as extension material for more able pupils. Pupils will be more challenged by the longer reading text and by exercises which draw together all the language of the chapter.
The context of this unit is an internet article about the increasing popularity of online soaps.

1a Lies den Artikel mit Hilfe eines Wörterbuches. (AT3 Levels 6–7)
Pupils read the article about online soaps with the help of a dictionary, if needed. Some words are provided in a vocabulary box at the bottom of the page. This article is adapted from a web page on Südwestrundfunk (www.swr3.de/Fun/Elchbox/Soaps).

1b Welcher Absatz ist das?
Pupils read sentences and identify which paragraph of the text each summarises.

Answers
1 d, **2** e, **3** b, **4** c, **5** a, **6** b, **7** d

1c Richtig oder falsch?
Pupils answer ten true/false statements on the article.

Answers
1 richtig, **2** richtig, **3** falsch, **4** falsch, **5** richtig, **6** richtig, **7** richtig, **8** falsch, **9** richtig, **10** richtig

2 *Heartbreak High* ist eine Soap über Schüler/innen. Hör zu. Wie sind die Hauptfiguren? Mach Notizen. (AT1 Levels 5–6)
Pupils listen to the characters in a reality soap being described and make notes on what they hear.

Answers
Kimberly – 17 J. , hübsch; **AC** – 16 J. , blonde Haare, seit 1 Jahr in der Schule; **Chae** – 17 J., braune Haare, in derselben Klasse wie AC; **Tygress** – 16 J. , seit kurzem bei den Girls; **Fyre** – 17 J. , Power-Frau, rote Haare, kurze Tops; **Tonia** – kleine Schwester von Spice, lieb, nervig; **Lee** – 15 J. , blonde Haare, blaue Augen, Power-Girl, gute Freundin, tanzt, singt, HipHop, rappt, Breakdance, andere Hobbys: einkaufen, telefonieren, abhängen, flirten; **Spice** (Melissa) – Power-Girl , 16 J. , blonde/braune Haare

- Kimberly ist die Leiterin der Girls. Sie ist 17 Jahre alt und eines der hübschesten Mädchen in der Schule.
- AC ist 16 Jahre alt und macht meist mit Spice die Choreografie. Sie hat blonde Haare und ist erst seit einem Jahr in der Schule.
- Chae ist 17 Jahre alt. Sie hat braune Haare und ist in derselben Klasse wie AC.
- Tygress ist 16 Jahre und erst seit kurzem bei den Girls.
- Fyre ist 17 Jahre und eine echte Power-Frau. Sie hat meist rote Haare und trägt kurze Tops.
- Tonia ist die kleine Schwester von Spice und geht noch ein Jahr auf die Junior High. Sie ist ein total liebes Mädchen, aber manchmal nervt sie auch.
- Lee ist 15 Jahre, hat blonde Haare und blaue Augen. Sie ist ein echtes Powergirl und eine echt gute Freundin. Sie tanzt und singt gern. Sie ist ein HipHop Fan, rappt und macht Breakdance. Ihre anderen Hobbys sind einkaufen, telefonieren mit Freunden, abhängen, flirten ...
- Spice (eigentlich Melissa) ist das Power-Girl und macht meist die Choreografie für die Nitro Girls. Sie ist 16 Jahre und hat mal blonde oder braune Haare.

E Pupils search for a German online soap on the internet.

3 Gruppenarbeit. Erfindet eine Online-Soap. (AT2 Levels 4–7, AT4 Levels 4–7)
Pupils work as a group to invent an online soap of their own. They should give the soap a name and decide which characters are in it and what they are like. Pupils should try to write a script for an episode of the soap.

Lernzieltest and Wiederholung (pp. 74–75)

Resources	
• Cassette, B, Side B • Workbook pp. 38–40 • R & A File: Wortschatz pp. 76–77	Lernzieltest p. 78 Kontrolle 4 pp. 79–88 (including teacher's notes)

At the end of each chapter there is a revision unit for pupils to use before the assessment materials. The unit begins with a *Lernzieltest* (like the *Mini-Test*) for pupils to test themselves on key language from the chapter. This is also provided as a checklist for pupils to write on (R & A File p. 78) and some related gapped sentences are also provided on p. 40 of the Workbook.

If pupils are unsure of any of the language, they should be encouraged to revise the relevant unit in the chapter. A complete wordlist containing key words and phrases from the whole chapter is provided on the *Wortschatz* sheet (R & A File p. 76–77).

Wiederholung provides pupils with revision exercises in the four skills. The listening exercises should be done in class, but the other exercises could be done either in class or for homework. Further revision exercises are provided on pp. 38–39 of the Workbook.

Wiederholung

Hören

1 Hör zu. Sieh dir Kais Pläne für das Wochenende an. Hat er das eigentlich gemacht? (AT1 Levels 5–6)

Pupils listen to Kai explaining what he did at the weekend and compare the conversation with his 'to-do list'. They then indicate which of the things on his list he actually did.

Answers

1 nein, **2** ja, **3** ja, **4** ja, **5** ja, **6** nein, **7** ja, **8** nein

– Wie war das Wochenende, Kai? War es gut oder langweilig?
– Tja, langweilig war es sicher nicht! Ich habe so viel gemacht, weißt du.
– Ja, was denn?
– Also, ich habe hauptsächlich Computerspiele gespielt. Das finde ich immer total spannend. Am Samstag bin ich mit meiner Mutter einkaufen gegangen und wir haben das neue Spiel von Megatod gekauft. Es ist total klasse.
– Ja, Mensch hast du Glück! Das ist total teuer, nicht?
– Ja, aber am Sonntag hatte ich Geburtstag, also war das ein Geschenk!
– Und was hast du dann zum Geburtstag gemacht?
– O, nichts Besonderes. Ich habe meine neuen CDs gehört und ich habe im Park Fußball gespielt, aber sonst war es ein normaler Tag. Ich habe auch eine sehr lustige E-Mail von meiner Freundin aus Berlin bekommen, aber leider hatte ich nicht genug Zeit, eine Antwort zu schreiben.
– Sie wird sicher traurig sein! He, sag mal, hast du die Informatikhausaufgaben gemacht?
– Ja, klar. Ich habe am Samstagvormittag alle meine Hausaufgaben gemacht. Das mache ich fast immer. Sie waren ganz schön schwierig, nicht?
– Ja, ich habe ein sehr doofes Programm geschrieben. Es funktioniert gar nicht!
– Ja, ich auch. Programme schreiben finde ich sehr kompliziert.
– Ich habe eine tolle Homepage von Bayern München gefunden. Man kann sogar mit den Spielern sprechen. Es ist total toll.
– Ach, ja. Vielleicht schaue ich sie mir mal an, aber im Moment darf ich nicht im Internet surfen, weil unsere Telefonrechnung letzten Monat irrsinnig teuer war.
– Ach, schade. Komm mal vorbei – du kannst sie dir bei mir anschauen.

Sprechen

2 Partnerarbeit. (AT2 Levels 4–5)

Pupils practise a dialogue for inviting a friend out to the cinema.

Lesen

3 Lies den Text und beantworte die Fragen. (AT3 Level 5)

Pupils read about Robert's weekend and answer ten comprehension questions in German about it. They should answer in full sentences.

Answers

1 Am Samstag ist Robert in die Stadt gefahren. **2** Er war drei Stunden im Musikladen. **3** Er hat drei CDs und ein Musikvideo gekauft. **4** Am Abend ist er ins Konzert gegangen. **5** Sie ist seine Freundin. **6** Für Robert war es echt klasse, aber das Konzert hat Tanja gar nicht gefallen. **7** Am Sonntag ist er zu Hause geblieben. **8** Am Sonntagabend ist er ins Kino gegangen. **9** Für Robert war der Film blöd. Für Tanja war der Film romantisch/prima. **10** Nein, sie mögen nicht die gleichen Sachen.

Schreiben

4 Beschreib einen Samstagabend aus Übung 2. Schreib mindestens siebzig Wörter. (AT4 Levels 4–6)

Pupils describe a trip to the cinema (at least 70 words).

EXTRA

The EXTRA pages at the back of the Pupil's Book are intended to provide consolidation/reinforcement activities (EXTRA A) and more challenging / extension activities (EXTRA B). The exercises concentrate on the skills of reading and writing only. They could be used for differentiated work in class or at home. The best place to use each activity is clearly indicated in these notes, just above the exercise rubric, e. g. [after pp. 60–61].

EXTRA A (p. 116)

[after pp. 60–61]

1a Was für Filme sind das? Beschrifte sie. (AT4 Level 1)

Pupils label the pictures of different film genres, using the help box if needed.

Answers

a Zeichentrickfilme, **b** Komödien, **c** Science-Fiction-Filme, **d** Horrorfilme, **e** Actionfilme, **f** Liebesfilme, **g** Krimis

1b Gefallen dir die Filme oben oder nicht? Schreib Sätze. (AT4 Levels 3–4)

Pupils write *weil* sentences to give their opinions of the films, using the help from the clouds.

[after pp. 66–67]

2a Sieh dir die Anzeigen an. Was für Bücher sind das? (AT3 Level 4)

Pupils read some adverts for books and decide which book genres are being advertised. The necessary vocabulary is provided in a help box.

Answers

1 Sportbuch, **2** Liebesroman, **3** Sachbuch, **4** Zeitschrift, **5** Pferdebuch

2b Schreib eine kurze Anzeige für dein Lieblingsbuch oder deine Lieblingszeitschrift. (AT4 Level 4)

Pupils write a short advert for their favourite book or magazine, using the prompts in the clouds.

EXTRA B (p. 117)

[after pp. 60–61]

1a Sieh dir die Filme auf Seite 116 an. Wie gefallen dir diese Filme? Schreib Sätze. (AT4 Levels 3–4)

Pupils look at the film genres on p. 116 and offer an opinion on each one.

1b Beantworte die Fragen. Vergleich deine Antworten mit einem Partner / einer Partnerin. (AT4 Levels 3–4)

Pupils answer questions about their favourite film and then compare what they have written with a partner.

[after pp. 66–67]

2a Lies die Buchempfehlung. Du darfst ein Wörterbuch benutzen. (AT3 Level 5)

Pupils read a book review of *Karotte, Maulwurf und die erste Liebe*, using a dictionary to help them with any unfamiliar vocabulary.

2b Beantworte folgende Fragen.

Pupils answer questions on the book review. There is no need for them to write full sentences.

Answers

1 Willem van Toorn, **2** sieben, **3** eine Karotten-Perücke, **4** Paolo, **5** Walter, **6** auf der Klassenfahrt, **7** Lindas Eltern, **8** in den Ferien, **9** sehr langweilig, **10** schön und sehr gut geschrieben, sehr spannend, ein bisschen langweilig

2c Was ist dein Lieblingsbuch? Schreib eine Empfehlung dafür wie oben. (AT4 Levels 4–5)

Pupils write a review of their favourite book, using the example given as support.

Workbook

p. 31

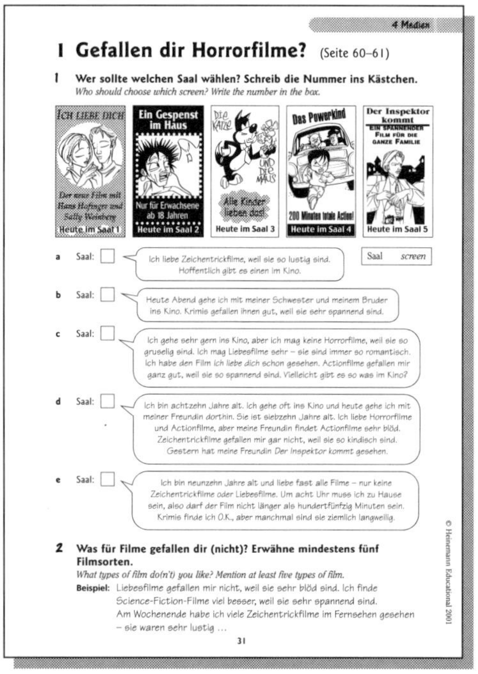
4 Medien

1 Gefallen dir Horrorfilme? (Seite 60–61)

1 Wer sollte welchen Saal wählen? Schreib die Nummer ins Kästchen.
Who should choose which screen? Write the number in the box.

Saal	*screen*

a Saal: ☐ Ich liebe Zeichentrickfilme, weil sie so lustig sind. Hoffentlich gibt es einen im Kino.

b Saal: ☐ Heute Abend gehe ich mit meiner Schwester und meinem Bruder ins Kino. Krimis gefallen ihnen gut, weil sie sehr spannend sind.

c Saal: ☐ Ich gehe sehr gern ins Kino, aber ich mag keine Horrorfilme, weil sie so gruselig sind. Ich mag Liebesfilme sehr – sie sind immer so romantisch. Ich habe den Film *Ich liebe dich* schon gesehen. Actionfilme gefallen mir ganz gut, weil sie so spannend sind. Vielleicht gibt es so was im Kino?

d Saal: ☐ Ich bin achtzehn Jahre alt. Ich gehe oft ins Kino und heute gehe ich mit meiner Freundin dorthin. Sie ist siebzehn Jahre alt. Ich liebe Horrorfilme und Actionfilme, aber meine Freundin findet Actionfilme sehr blöd. Zeichentrickfilme gefallen mir gar nicht, weil sie so kindisch sind. Gestern hat meine Freundin *Der Inspektor kommt* gesehen.

e Saal: ☐ Ich bin neunzehn Jahre alt und liebe fast alle Filme – nur keine Zeichentrickfilme oder Liebesfilme. Um acht Uhr muss ich zu Hause sein, also darf der Film nicht länger als hundertfünfzig Minuten sein. Krimis finde ich O.K., aber manchmal sind sie ziemlich langweilig.

2 Was für Filme gefallen dir (nicht)? Erwähne mindestens fünf Filmsorten.
What types of film do(n't) you like? Mention at least five types of film.
Beispiel: Liebesfilme gefallen mir nicht, weil sie sehr blöd sind. Ich finde Science-Fiction-Filme viel besser, weil sie sehr spannend sind. Am Wochenende habe ich viele Zeichentrickfilme im Fernsehen gesehen – sie waren sehr lustig …

31

p. 32

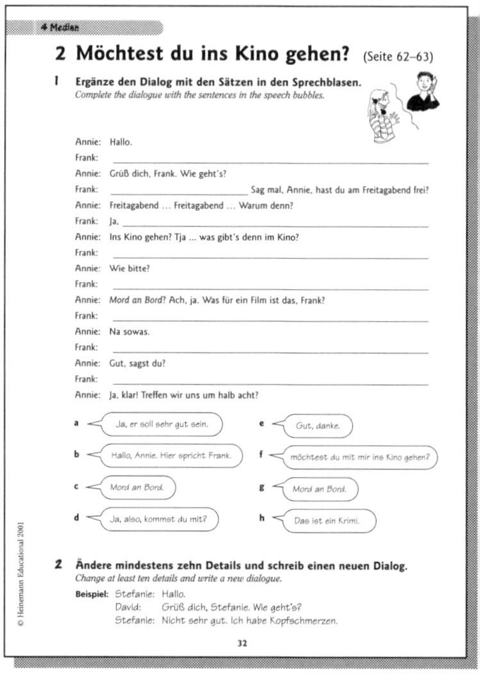
4 Medien

2 Möchtest du ins Kino gehen? (Seite 62–63)

1 Ergänze den Dialog mit den Sätzen in den Sprechblasen.
Complete the dialogue with the sentences in the speech bubbles.

Annie: Hallo.
Frank: ________
Annie: Grüß dich, Frank. Wie geht's?
Frank: ________ Sag mal, Annie, hast du am Freitagabend frei?
Annie: Freitagabend … Freitagabend … Warum denn?
Frank: Ja, ________
Annie: Ins Kino gehen? Tja ... was gibt's denn im Kino?
Frank: ________
Annie: Wie bitte?
Frank: ________
Annie: *Mord an Bord*? Ach, ja. Was für ein Film ist das, Frank?
Frank: ________
Annie: Na sowas.
Frank: ________
Annie: Gut, sagst du?
Frank: ________
Annie: Ja, klar! Treffen wir uns um halb acht?

a Ja, er soll sehr gut sein.
b Hallo, Annie. Hier spricht Frank.
c Mord an Bord.
d Ja, also, kommst du mit?
e Gut, danke.
f möchtest du mit mir ins Kino gehen?
g Mord an Bord.
h Das ist ein Krimi.

2 Ändere mindestens zehn Details und schreib einen neuen Dialog.
Change at least ten details and write a new dialogue.
Beispiel: Stefanie: Hallo.
David: Grüß dich, Stefanie. Wie geht's?
Stefanie: Nicht sehr gut. Ich habe Kopfschmerzen.

32

1 (AT3 Levels 4–5)
a Saal 3, **b** Saal 5, **c** Saal 4, **d** Saal 1, **e** Saal 2
2 (AT4 Level 4–6)
individual answers

1 (AT3 Level 4)
b, e, f, c/g, g/c, h, a, d
2 (AT4 Level 4)
individual answers

p. 33
1 (AT3 Level 5)
1 b Also, Phoenix, du warst schon immer sehr musikalisch, nicht? **2** c Und hast du auch Musikvideos gekauft? **3** e Und wann bist du zum ersten Mal ins Konzert gegangen? **4** d Hörst du viel Musik, zum Beispiel im Radio oder Fernsehen? **5** a Wer ist dein Lieblingssänger?
2 (AT3 Level 5)
Studio, Radio-Pop, Sänger, Folklore-Gruppe, Kassette, Musikvideos, Konzert, Rockband, Sänger, Konzert, Tournee, Live-Musik, Musik, Rock, Folklore, klassische Musik, Musiksendungen, Folksänger
3 (AT3 Level 5)
1 Er ist neunzehn Jahre alt. **2** Er war vier Jahre alt. **3** Er ist mit seinem Vater ins Konzert gegangen. **4** Er hat wenig Zeit, weil er immer auf Tournee ist. **5** Er hört Rock, Folklore oder klassische Musik. **6** Sein Lieblingssänger ist Bob Dylan.

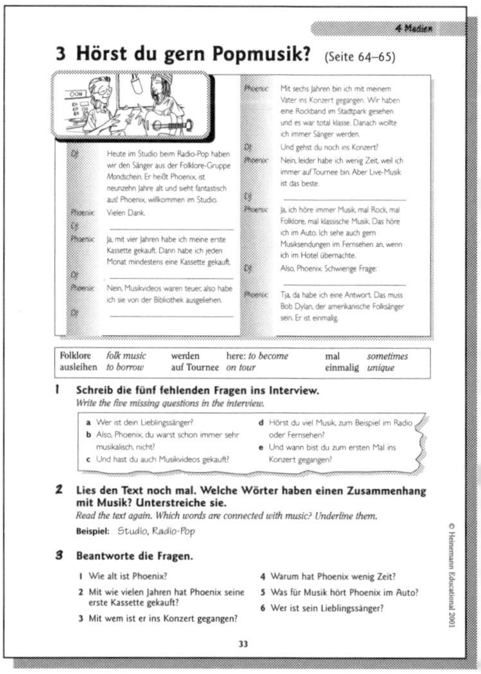
4 Medien

3 Hörst du gern Popmusik? (Seite 64–65)

DJ: Heute im Studio beim Radio-Pop haben wir den Sänger aus der Folklore-Gruppe *Mondschein*. Er heißt Phoenix, ist neunzehn Jahre alt und sieht fantastisch aus! Phoenix, willkommen im Studio.
Phoenix: Vielen Dank.
DJ: ________
Phoenix: Ja, mit vier Jahren habe ich meine erste Kassette gekauft. Dann habe ich jeden Monat mindestens eine Kassette gekauft.
DJ: ________
Phoenix: Nein, Musikvideos waren teuer, also habe ich sie von der Bibliothek ausgeliehen.
DJ: ________
Phoenix: Mit sechs Jahren bin ich mit meinem Vater ins Konzert gegangen. Wir haben eine Rockband im Stadtpark gesehen und es war total klasse. Danach wollte ich immer Sänger werden.
DJ: Und gehst du noch ins Konzert?
Phoenix: Nein, leider habe ich wenig Zeit, weil ich immer auf Tournee bin. Aber Live-Musik ist das beste.
DJ: ________
Phoenix: Ja, ich höre immer Musik, mal Rock, mal Folklore, mal klassische Musik. Das höre ich im Auto. Ich sehe auch gern Musiksendungen im Fernsehen an, wenn ich im Hotel übernachte.
DJ: Also, Phoenix. Schwierige Frage: ________
Phoenix: Tja, da habe ich eine Antwort. Das muss Bob Dylan, der amerikanische Folksänger sein. Er ist einmalig.

Folklore	*folk music*	werden	here: *to become*	mal	*sometimes*
ausleihen	*to borrow*	auf Tournee	*on tour*	einmalig	*unique*

1 Schreib die fünf fehlenden Fragen ins Interview.
Write the five missing questions in the interview.

a Wer ist dein Lieblingssänger?
b Also, Phoenix, du warst schon immer sehr musikalisch, nicht?
c Und hast du auch Musikvideos gekauft?
d Hörst du viel Musik, zum Beispiel im Radio oder Fernsehen?
e Und wann bist du zum ersten Mal ins Konzert gegangen?

2 Lies den Text noch mal. Welche Wörter haben einen Zusammenhang mit Musik? Unterstreiche sie.
Read the text again. Which words are connected with music? Underline them.
Beispiel: Studio, Radio-Pop

3 Beantworte die Fragen.
1 Wie alt ist Phoenix?
2 Mit wie vielen Jahren hat Phoenix seine erste Kassette gekauft?
3 Mit wem ist er ins Konzert gegangen?
4 Warum hat Phoenix wenig Zeit?
5 Was für Musik hört Phoenix im Auto?
6 Wer ist sein Lieblingssänger?

33

p. 34

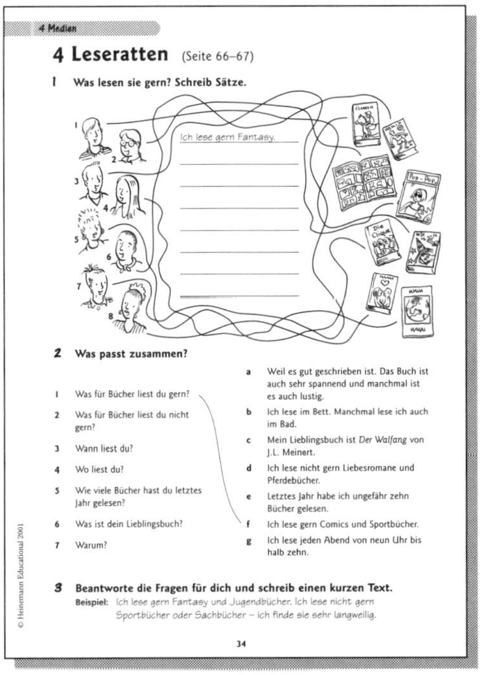

4 Medien

4 Leseratten (Seite 66–67)

1 Was lesen sie gern? Schreib Sätze.

Ich lese gern Fantasy.

2 Was passt zusammen?

1 Was für Bücher liest du gern?
2 Was für Bücher liest du nicht gern?
3 Wann liest du?
4 Wo liest du?
5 Wie viele Bücher hast du letztes Jahr gelesen?
6 Was ist dein Lieblingsbuch?
7 Warum?

a Weil es gut geschrieben ist. Das Buch ist auch sehr spannend und manchmal ist es auch lustig.
b Ich lese im Bett. Manchmal lese ich auch im Bad.
c Mein Lieblingsbuch ist *Der Walfang* von J.L. Meinert.
d Ich lese nicht gern Liebesromane und Pferdebücher.
e Letztes Jahr habe ich ungefähr zehn Bücher gelesen.
f Ich lese gern Comics und Sportbücher.
g Ich lese jeden Abend von neun Uhr bis halb zehn.

3 Beantworte die Fragen für dich und schreib einen kurzen Text.
Beispiel: Ich lese gern Fantasy und Jugendbücher. Ich lese nicht gern Sportbücher oder Sachbücher – ich finde sie sehr langweilig.

34

p. 35

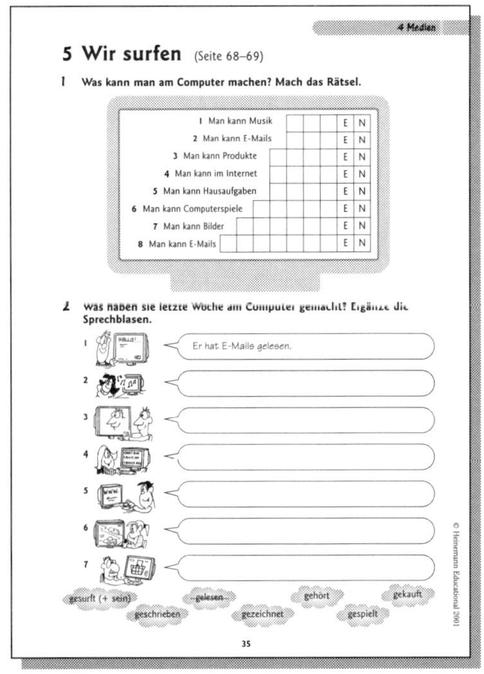

4 Medien

5 Wir surfen (Seite 68–69)

1 Was kann man am Computer machen? Mach das Rätsel.

1 Man kann Musik ... E N
2 Man kann E-Mails ... E N
3 Man kann Produkte ... E N
4 Man kann im Internet ... E N
5 Man kann Hausaufgaben ... E N
6 Man kann Computerspiele ... E N
7 Man kann Bilder ... E N
8 Man kann E-Mails ... E N

2 Was haben sie letzte Woche am Computer gemacht? Ergänze die Sprechblasen.

1 Er hat E-Mails gelesen.
2
3
4
5
6
7

gesurft (+ sein) ~~gelesen~~ gehört gekauft geschrieben gezeichnet gespielt

35

1 (AT4 Level 3)

1 Ich lese gern Fantasy. **2** Ich lese gern Comics. **3** Ich lese gern Zeitschriften. **4** Ich lese gern Sachbücher. **5** Ich lese gern Jugendbücher. **6** Ich lese gern Sportbücher. **7** Ich lese gern Pferdebücher. **8** Ich lese gern Liebesromane.

2 (AT3 Level 3)

1 f, **2** d, **3** g, **4** b, **5** e, **6** c, **7** a

3 (AT4 Level 4)

individual answers

1 (AT4 Level 2)

1 hören, **2** lesen, **3** kaufen, **4** surfen, **5** machen, **6** spielen, **7** zeichnen, **8** schreiben

2 (AT4 Level 5)

1 Er hat E-Mails gelesen. **2** Sie hat Musik gehört. **3** Er hat Bilder gezeichnet. **4** Sie hat Programme geschrieben. **5** Er ist im Internet gesurft. **6** Sie hat Computerspiele gespielt. **7** Er hat Produkte gekauft.

p. 36

1 (AT3 Level 5)

Tag?	Wo?	Was gemacht?	Wie war es?
Montag	Kino	eine Komödie gesehen	ganz toll
Dienstag	Stadt	das Fernseh-Museum besichtigt	sehr interessant
Mittwoch	Schule	im Internet gesurft (Computerraum)	ziemlich langweilig
Donnerstag	Stadt	einkaufen gegangen	besonders schön
Freitag	Jugendhaus	Party	echt klasse

2 (AT4 Level 5)

individual answers

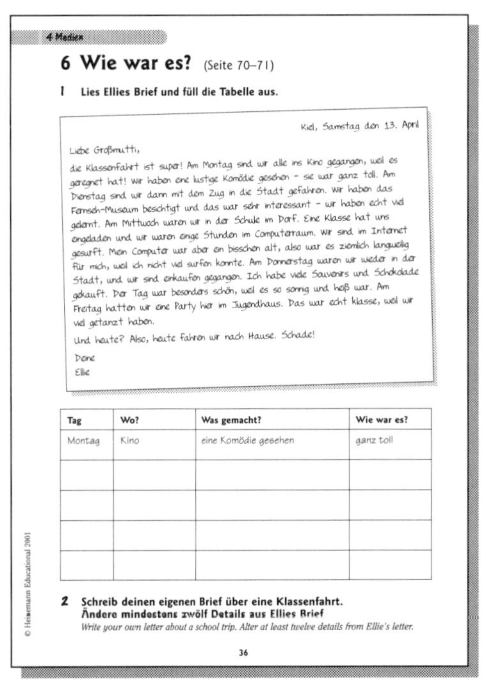

4 Medien

6 Wie war es? (Seite 70–71)

1 Lies Ellies Brief und füll die Tabelle aus.

Kiel, Samstag den 13. April

Liebe Großmutti,
die Klassenfahrt ist super! Am Montag sind wir alle ins Kino gegangen, weil es geregnet hat! Wir haben eine lustige Komödie gesehen – sie war ganz toll. Am Dienstag sind wir dann mit dem Zug in die Stadt gefahren. Wir haben das Fernseh-Museum besichtigt und das war sehr interessant – wir haben echt viel gelernt. Am Mittwoch waren wir in der Schule im Dorf. Eine Klasse hat uns eingeladen und wir waren einige Stunden im Computerraum. Wir sind im Internet gesurft. Mein Computer war aber ein bisschen alt, also war es ziemlich langweilig für mich, weil ich nicht viel surfen konnte. Am Donnerstag waren wir wieder in der Stadt, und wir sind einkaufen gegangen. Ich habe viele Souvenirs und Schokolade gekauft. Der Tag war besonders schön, weil es so sonnig und heiß war. Am Freitag hatten wir eine Party hier im Jugendhaus. Das war echt klasse, weil wir viel getanzt haben.
Und heute? Also, heute fahren wir nach Hause. Schade!
Deine
Ellie

Tag	Wo?	Was gemacht?	Wie war es?
Montag	Kino	eine Komödie gesehen	ganz toll

2 Schreib deinen eigenen Brief über eine Klassenfahrt. Ändere mindestens zwölf Details aus Ellies Brief
Write your own letter about a school trip. Alter at least twelve details from Ellie's letter.

36

p. 37

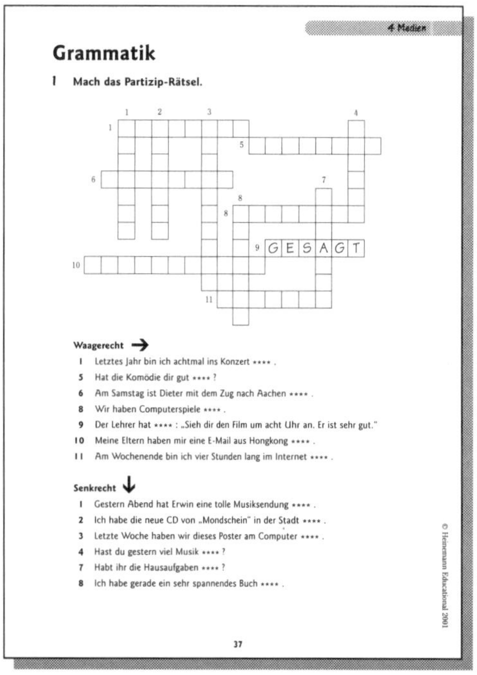

4 Medien

Grammatik

1 Mach das Partizip-Rätsel.

9 G E S A G T

Waagerecht →

1 Letztes Jahr bin ich achtmal ins Konzert **** .
5 Hat die Komödie dir gut **** ?
6 Am Samstag ist Dieter mit dem Zug nach Aachen **** .
8 Wir haben Computerspiele **** .
9 Der Lehrer hat **** : „Sieh dir den Film um acht Uhr an. Er ist sehr gut."
10 Meine Eltern haben mir eine E-Mail aus Hongkong **** .
11 Am Wochenende bin ich vier Stunden lang im Internet **** .

Senkrecht ↓

1 Gestern Abend hat Erwin eine tolle Musiksendung **** .
2 Ich habe die neue CD von „Mondschein" in der Stadt **** .
3 Letzte Woche haben wir dieses Poster am Computer **** .
4 Hast du gestern viel Musik **** ?
7 Habt ihr die Hausaufgaben **** ?
8 Ich habe gerade ein sehr spannendes Buch **** .

© Heinemann Educational 2001

37

1 **Waagerecht**: **1** gegangen, **5** gefallen, **6** gefahren, **8** gespielt, **9** gesagt, **10** geschrieben, **11** gesurft
Senkrecht: **1** gesehen, **2** gekauft, **3** gezeichnet, **4** gehört, **7** gemacht, **8** gelesen

p. 38

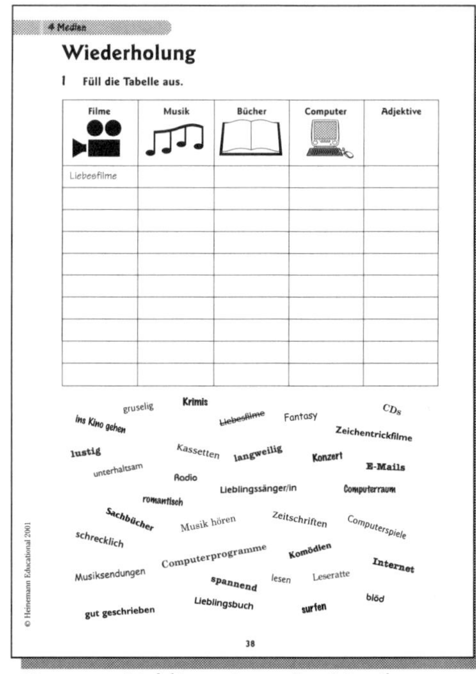

4 Medien

Wiederholung

1 Füll die Tabelle aus.

Filme	Musik	Bücher	Computer	Adjektive
Liebesfilme				

gruselig, Krimis, Liebesfilme, Fantasy, CDs, ins Kino gehen, Zeichentrickfilme, lustig, Kassetten, langweilig, Konzert, E-Mails, unterhaltsam, Radio, Lieblingssänger/in, Computerraum, romantisch, Sachbücher, Musik hören, Zeitschriften, Computerspiele, schrecklich, Computerprogramme, Komödien, Internet, Musiksendungen, spannend, lesen, Leseratte, blöd, gut geschrieben, Lieblingsbuch, surfen

© Heinemann Educational 2001

38

1 (AT 3 Level 2)
Filme: ins Kino gehen, Krimis, Liebesfilme, Komödien, Zeichentrickfilme,
Musik: Radio, Kassetten, CDs, Konzert, Lieblingssänger/in, Musik hören, Musiksendungen
Bücher: Fantasy, Zeitschriften, Sachbücher, lesen, Leseratte, Lieblingsbuch
Computer: E-Mails, Computerraum, Computerprogramme, Internet, Computerspiele, surfen
Adjektive: gruselig, lustig, spannend, langweilig, romantisch, unterhaltsam, blöd, schrecklich, gut geschrieben

p. 39

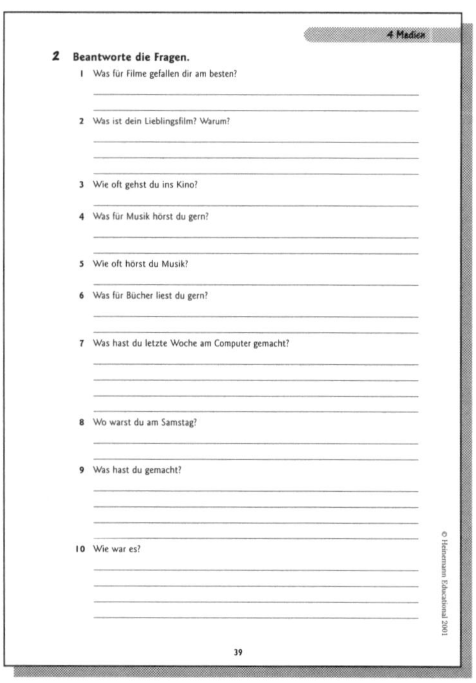

4 Medien

2 **Beantworte die Fragen.**

1 Was für Filme gefallen dir am besten?
2 Was ist dein Lieblingsfilm? Warum?
3 Wie oft gehst du ins Kino?
4 Was für Musik hörst du gern?
5 Wie oft hörst du Musik?
6 Was für Bücher liest du gern?
7 Was hast du letzte Woche am Computer gemacht?
8 Wo warst du am Samstag?
9 Was hast du gemacht?
10 Wie war es?

© Heinemann Educational 2001

39

2 (AT4 Levels 4–5)
individual answers

p. 40

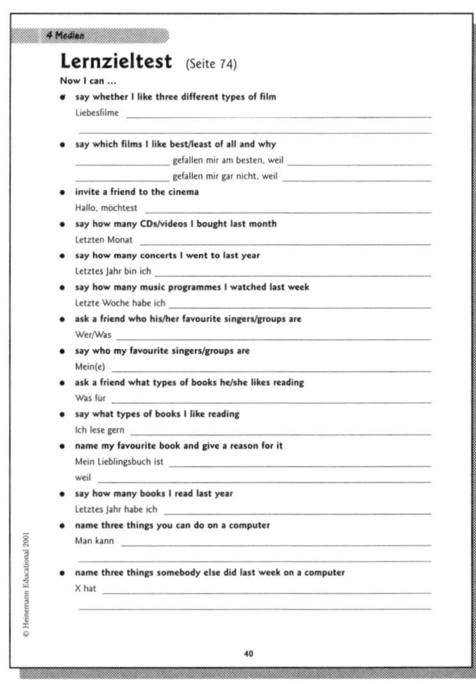

4 Medien

Lernzieltest (Seite 74)

Now I can ...

- **say whether I like three different types of film**
  Liebesfilme
- **say which films I like best/least of all and why**
  gefallen mir am besten, weil
  gefallen mir gar nicht, weil
- **invite a friend to the cinema**
  Hallo, möchtest
- **say how many CDs/videos I bought last month**
  Letzten Monat
- **say how many concerts I went to last year**
  Letztes Jahr bin ich
- **say how many music programmes I watched last week**
  Letzte Woche habe ich
- **ask a friend who his/her favourite singers/groups are**
  Wer/Was
- **say who my favourite singers/groups are**
  Mein(e)
- **ask a friend what types of books he/she likes reading**
  Was für
- **say what types of books I like reading**
  Ich lese gern
- **name my favourite book and give a reason for it**
  Mein Lieblingsbuch ist
  weil
- **say how many books I read last year**
  Letztes Jahr habe ich
- **name three things you can do on a computer**
  Man kann
- **name three things somebody else did last week on a computer**
  X hat

© Heinemann Educational 2001

40

individual answers

Resource & Assessment File

Arbeitsblatt 1
p. 68

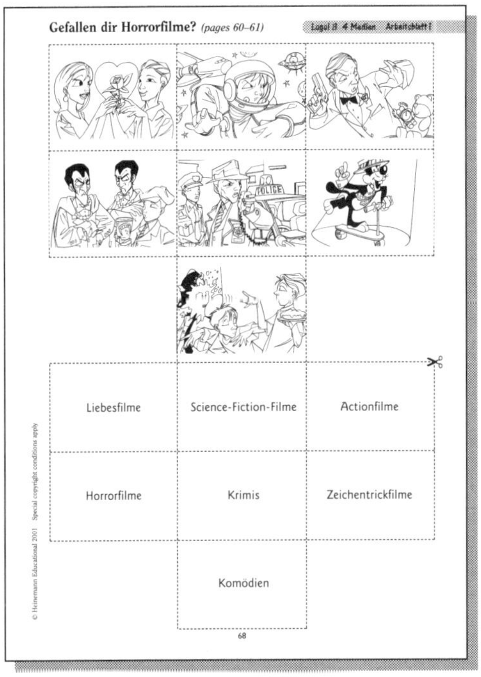
Gefallen dir Horrorfilme? *(pages 60–61)* Logo! 3 4 Medien Arbeitsblatt 1

Liebesfilme	Science-Fiction-Filme	Actionfilme
Horrorfilme	Krimis	Zeichentrickfilme
	Komödien	

© Heinemann Educational 2001 Special copyright conditions apply

68

Visuals of *Liebesfilme, Science-Fiction-Filme, Actionfilme, Horrorfilme, Krimis, Zeichentrickfilme, Komödien*

Arbeitsblatt 2
p. 69

Leseratten *(pages 66–67)* Logo! 3 4 Medien Arbeitsblatt 2

Fantasy	Sportbücher	Comics
Zeitschriften	Jugendbücher	Pferdebücher
Liebesromane	Sachbücher	

© Heinemann Educational 2001 Special copyright conditions apply

69

Visuals of *Fantasy, Sportbücher, Comics, Zeitschriften, Jugendbücher, Pferdebücher, Liebesromane, Sachbücher*

Arbeitsblatt 3
p. 70

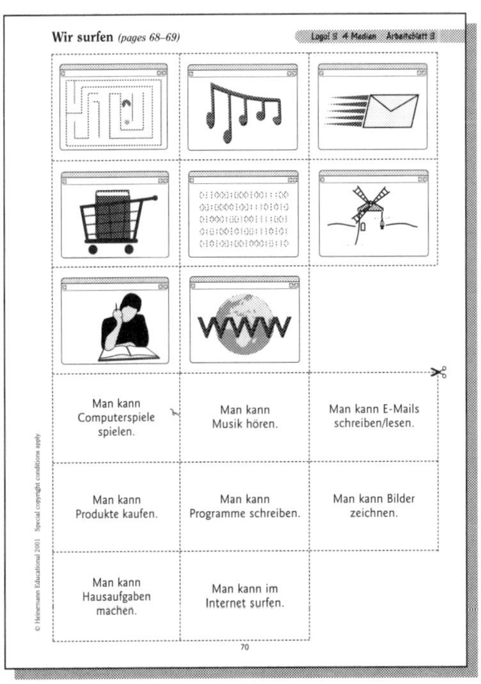
Wir surfen *(pages 68–69)* Logo! 3 4 Medien Arbeitsblatt 3

Man kann Computerspiele spielen.	Man kann Musik hören.	Man kann E-Mails schreiben/lesen.
Man kann Produkte kaufen.	Man kann Programme schreiben.	Man kann Bilder zeichnen.
Man kann Hausaufgaben machen.	Man kann im Internet surfen.	

© Heinemann Educational 2001 Special copyright conditions apply

70

Visuals of *Man kann Computerspiele spielen. Man kann Musik hören. Man kann E-Mails schreiben/lesen. Man kann Produkte kaufen. Man kann Programme schreiben. Man kann Bilder zeichnen. Man kann Hausaufgaben machen. Man kann im Internet surfen.*

Arbeitsblatt 4
p. 71

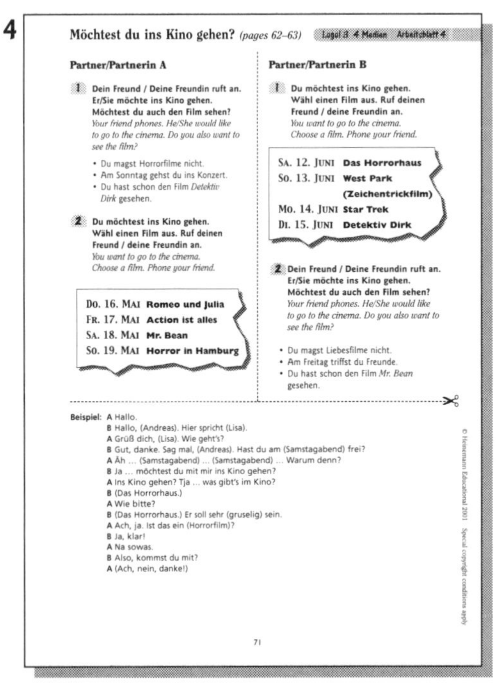
Möchtest du ins Kino gehen? *(pages 62–63)* Logo! 3 4 Medien Arbeitsblatt 4

Partner/Partnerin A

1 **Dein Freund / Deine Freundin ruft an. Er/Sie möchte ins Kino gehen. Möchtest du auch den Film sehen?**
Your friend phones. He/She would like to go to the cinema. Do you also want to see the film?

- Du magst Horrorfilme nicht.
- Am Sonntag gehst du ins Konzert.
- Du hast schon den Film *Detektiv Dirk* gesehen.

2 **Du möchtest ins Kino gehen. Wähl einen Film aus. Ruf deinen Freund / deine Freundin an.**
You want to go to the cinema. Choose a film. Phone your friend.

Do. 16. Mai **Romeo und Julia**
Fr. 17. Mai **Action ist alles**
Sa. 18. Mai **Mr. Bean**
So. 19. Mai **Horror in Hamburg**

Partner/Partnerin B

1 **Du möchtest ins Kino gehen. Wähl einen Film aus. Ruf deinen Freund / deine Freundin an.**
You want to go to the cinema. Choose a film. Phone your friend.

Sa. 12. Juni **Das Horrorhaus**
So. 13. Juni **West Park (Zeichentrickfilm)**
Mo. 14. Juni **Star Trek**
Di. 15. Juni **Detektiv Dirk**

2 **Dein Freund / Deine Freundin ruft an. Er/Sie möchte ins Kino gehen. Möchtest du auch den Film sehen?**
Your friend phones. He/She would like to go to the cinema. Do you also want to see the film?

- Du magst Liebesfilme nicht.
- Am Freitag triffst du Freunde.
- Du hast schon den Film *Mr. Bean* gesehen.

Beispiel: **A** Hallo.
B Hallo, (Andreas). Hier spricht (Lisa).
A Grüß dich, (Lisa). Wie geht's?
B Gut, danke. Sag mal, (Andreas). Hast du am (Samstagabend) frei?
A Äh … (Samstagabend) … (Samstagabend) … Warum denn?
B Ja … möchtest du mit mir ins Kino gehen?
A Ins Kino gehen? Tja … was gibt's im Kino?
B (Das Horrorhaus.)
A Wie bitte?
B (Das Horrorhaus.) Er soll sehr (gruselig) sein.
A Ach, ja. Ist das ein (Horrorfilm)?
B Ja, klar!
A Na sowas.
B Also, kommst du mit?
A (Ach, nein, danke!)

© Heinemann Educational 2001 Special copyright conditions apply

71

Pairwork practice of inviting a friend to the cinema.
1 AT2 Levels 4–5

Arbeitsblatt 5 p. 72
Advice on listening activities.

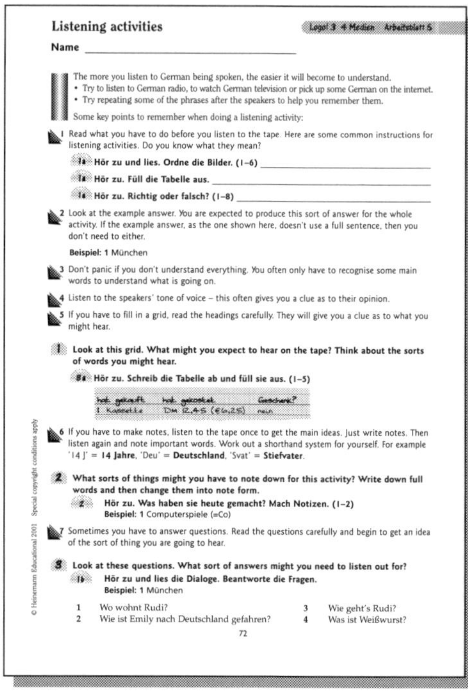

Listening activities

Logo! 3 4 Medien Arbeitsblatt 5

Name ______________________

The more you listen to German being spoken, the easier it will become to understand.
- Try to listen to German radio, to watch German television or pick up some German on the internet.
- Try repeating some of the phrases after the speakers to help you remember them.

Some key points to remember when doing a listening activity:

1 Read what you have to do before you listen to the tape. Here are some common instructions for listening activities. Do you know what they mean?

1a **Hör zu und lies. Ordne die Bilder. (1–6)** ______________________

1a **Hör zu. Füll die Tabelle aus.** ______________________

1a **Hör zu. Richtig oder falsch? (1–8)** ______________________

2 Look at the example answer. You are expected to produce this sort of answer for the whole activity. If the example answer, as the one shown here, doesn't use a full sentence, then you don't need to either.

Beispiel: 1 München

3 Don't panic if you don't understand everything. You often only have to recognise some main words to understand what is going on.

4 Listen to the speakers' tone of voice – this often gives you a clue as to their opinion.

5 If you have to fill in a grid, read the headings carefully. They will give you a clue as to what you might hear.

1 Look at this grid. What might you expect to hear on the tape? Think about the sorts of words you might hear.

8a **Hör zu. Schreib die Tabelle ab und füll sie aus. (1–5)**

hat gekauft	hat gekostet	Geschenk?
1 Kassette	DM 12,45 (€6,25)	nein

6 If you have to make notes, listen to the tape once to get the main ideas. Just write notes. Then listen again and note important words. Work out a shorthand system for yourself. For example '14 J' = **14 Jahre**, 'Deu' = **Deutschland**, 'Svat' = **Stiefvater**.

2 What sorts of things might you have to note down for this activity? Write down full words and then change them into note form.

2 **Hör zu. Was haben sie heute gemacht? Mach Notizen. (1–2)**
Beispiel: 1 Computerspiele (=Co)

7 Sometimes you have to answer questions. Read the questions carefully and begin to get an idea of the sort of thing you are going to hear.

3 Look at these questions. What sort of answers might you need to listen out for?

1b **Hör zu und lies die Dialoge. Beantworte die Fragen.**
Beispiel: 1 München

1 Wo wohnt Rudi?
2 Wie ist Emily nach Deutschland gefahren?
3 Wie geht's Rudi?
4 Was ist Weißwurst?

72

Grammatik 1 p. 73
Practice of expressing opinions (adjectives, *gern*, *gefallen*).

1 gut – good, spannend – exciting, klasse/toll – great, lustig – funny, einfach – easy, schrecklich – terrible, langweilig – boring, blöd/doof – stupid, anstrengend – tiring, schwierig – difficult
2 *individual answers*
3 **1** Ich höre gern Popmusik. **2** Ich lese nicht gern Sachbücher. **3** Peter schreibt gern E-Mails. **4** Wir schreiben gern Programme. **5** Ich kaufe nicht gern CDs. **6** Ihr macht nicht gern Hausaufgaben. **7** Erol surft nicht gern im Internet. **8** Wir fahren gern nach Italien.
4 **1** Gefallen dir Liebesfilme? **2** Gefällt dir Pokémon? **3** Gefallen dir Pferdebücher? **4** Gefällt dir der Film *Star Wars*? **5** Gefallen dir Horrorfilme? **6** Gefällt dir Popmusik? **7** Gefällt dir das Internet? **8** Gefallen dir Comics?

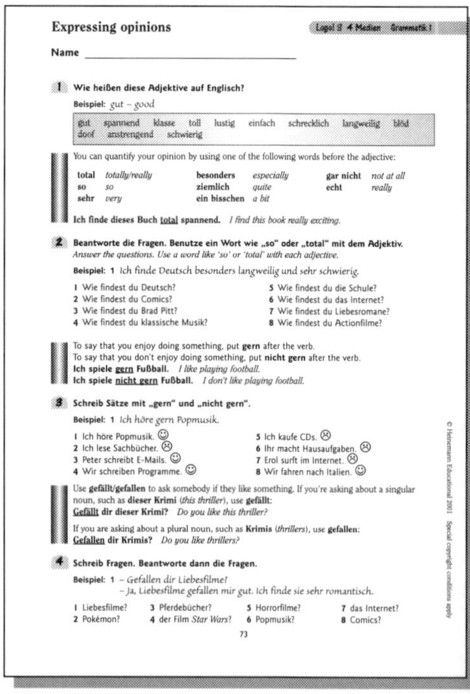

Expressing opinions

Logo! 3 4 Medien Grammatik 1

Name ______________________

1 Wie heißen diese Adjektive auf Englisch?

Beispiel: *gut – good*

gut spannend klasse toll lustig einfach schrecklich langweilig blöd doof anstrengend schwierig

You can quantify your opinion by using one of the following words before the adjective:

total	*totally/really*	**besonders**	*especially*	**gar nicht**	*not at all*
so	*so*	**ziemlich**	*quite*	**echt**	*really*
sehr	*very*	**ein bisschen**	*a bit*		

Ich finde dieses Buch total spannend. *I find this book really exciting.*

2 Beantworte die Fragen. Benutze ein Wort wie „so" oder „total" mit dem Adjektiv.
Answer the questions. Use a word like 'so' or 'total' with each adjective.

Beispiel: 1 *Ich finde Deutsch besonders langweilig und sehr schwierig.*

1 Wie findest du Deutsch?
2 Wie findest du Comics?
3 Wie findest du Brad Pitt?
4 Wie findest du klassische Musik?
5 Wie findest du die Schule?
6 Wie findest du das Internet?
7 Wie findest du Liebesromane?
8 Wie findest du Actionfilme?

To say that you enjoy doing something, put **gern** after the verb.
To say that you don't enjoy doing something, put **nicht gern** after the verb.
Ich spiele gern Fußball. *I like playing football.*
Ich spiele nicht gern Fußball. *I don't like playing football.*

3 Schreib Sätze mit „gern" und „nicht gern".

Beispiel: 1 *Ich höre gern Popmusik.*

1 Ich höre Popmusik. ☺
2 Ich lese Sachbücher. ☹
3 Peter schreibt E-Mails. ☺
4 Wir schreiben Programme. ☺
5 Ich kaufe CDs. ☹
6 Ihr macht Hausaufgaben. ☹
7 Erol surft im Internet. ☹
8 Wir fahren nach Italien. ☺

Use **gefällt/gefallen** to ask somebody if they like something. If you're asking about a singular noun, such as **dieser Krimi** (*this thriller*), use **gefällt**:
Gefällt dir dieser Krimi? *Do you like this thriller?*

If you are asking about a plural noun, such as **Krimis** (*thrillers*), use **gefallen**:
Gefallen dir Krimis? *Do you like thrillers?*

4 Schreib Fragen. Beantworte dann die Fragen.

Beispiel: 1 – *Gefallen dir Liebesfilme?*
– *Ja, Liebesfilme gefallen mir gut. Ich finde sie sehr romantisch.*

1 Liebesfilme? **2** Pokémon? **3** Pferdebücher? **4** der Film *Star Wars*? **5** Horrorfilme? **6** Popmusik? **7** das Internet? **8** Comics?

73

Grammatik 2 p. 74
Practice of modal verbs: *dürfen, können, sollen.*
1 **1** Man darf nicht skaten. **2** Man darf nicht rauchen. **3** Man darf keinen Alkohol trinken. **4** Man darf keine Sportschuhe tragen. **5** Man darf keine Handys in die Schule mitbringen. **6** Man darf nicht im Gang singen. **7** Man darf keine Süßigkeiten essen. **8** Man darf keine Baseballmützen tragen. **9** Man darf keine Computerspiele spielen. **10** Man darf keine Messer in die Schule mitbringen.
2 **1** Man kann im Internet surfen. **2** Man kann Zeitungen lesen. **3** Man kann Radio hören. **4** Man kann fernsehen. **5** Man kann Zeitschriften lesen. **6** Man kann mit Leuten sprechen.
3 **1** Man sollte gesund essen. **2** Man sollte alles Mögliche kompostieren. **3** Man sollte mit dem Rad fahren. **4** Man sollte keine Spraydosen benutzen. **5** Man sollte umweltfreundlich sein. **6** Man sollte viel Obst und Gemüse essen. **7** Man sollte keinen Alkohol trinken. **8** Man sollte sich über die Umwelt informieren. **9** Man sollte Wasser und Energie sparen. **10** Man sollte der Umwelt helfen.
4 *individual answers*

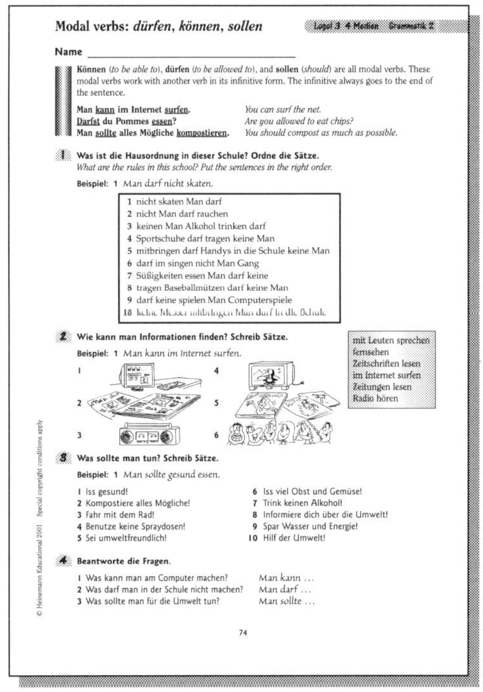
Modal verbs: *dürfen, können, sollen* — Logo! 3 4 Medien Grammatik 2

Name ______________________

Können (*to be able to*), **dürfen** (*to be allowed to*), and **sollen** (*should*) are all modal verbs. These modal verbs work with another verb in its infinitive form. The infinitive always goes to the end of the sentence.

Man kann im Internet surfen. *You can surf the net.*
Darfst du Pommes essen? *Are you allowed to eat chips?*
Man sollte alles Mögliche kompostieren. *You should compost as much as possible.*

1 Was ist die Hausordnung in dieser Schule? Ordne die Sätze.
What are the rules in this school? Put the sentences in the right order.
Beispiel: 1 Man darf nicht skaten.

1 nicht skaten Man darf
2 nicht Man darf rauchen
3 keinen Man Alkohol trinken darf
4 Sportschuhe darf tragen keine Man
5 mitbringen darf Handys in die Schule keine Man
6 darf im singen nicht Man Gang
7 Süßigkeiten essen Man darf keine
8 tragen Baseballmützen darf keine Man
9 darf keine spielen Man Computerspiele
10 keine Messer mitbringen Man darf in die Schule

2 Wie kann man Informationen finden? Schreib Sätze.
Beispiel: 1 Man kann im Internet surfen.
1 2 3 4 5 6

mit Leuten sprechen
fernsehen
Zeitschriften lesen
im Internet surfen
Zeitungen lesen
Radio hören

3 Was sollte man tun? Schreib Sätze.
Beispiel: 1 Man sollte gesund essen.
1 Iss gesund!
2 Kompostiere alles Mögliche!
3 Fahr mit dem Rad!
4 Benutze keine Spraydosen!
5 Sei umweltfreundlich!
6 Iss viel Obst und Gemüse!
7 Trink keinen Alkohol!
8 Informiere dich über die Umwelt!
9 Spar Wasser und Energie!
10 Hilf der Umwelt!

4 Beantworte die Fragen.
1 Was kann man am Computer machen? Man kann …
2 Was darf man in der Schule nicht machen? Man darf …
3 Was sollte man für die Umwelt tun? Man sollte …

© Heinemann Educational 2001 Special copyright conditions apply

74

Grammatik 3 p. 75
Practice of *war* and *hatte*.
1 **1** hatte, **2** war, **3** hattest, **4** war, **5** hatte, **6** warst, **7** hatten, **8** wart, **9** haben, **10** hatte
2 Am Montag war ich im Computerraum und ich habe E-Mails geschrieben. Am Dienstag war ich in der Bibliothek und ich habe Hausaufgaben gemacht. Am Mittwoch hatte ich Kopfschmerzen und ich bin zu Hause geblieben. Am Donnerstag war ich im Schwimmbad und ich bin schwimmen gegangen. Am Freitag hatte ich Ohrenschmerzen und ich bin zum Arzt gegangen. Am Samstag war ich zu Hause und ich hatte eine Party. Am Sonntag war ich im Zimmer und ich habe Musik gehört und ferngesehen.

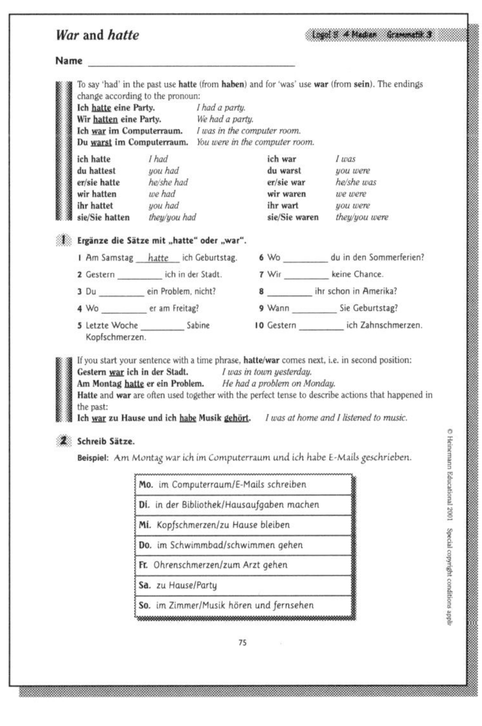
War* and *hatte — Logo! 3 4 Medien Grammatik 3

Name ______________________

To say 'had' in the past use **hatte** (from **haben**) and for 'was' use **war** (from **sein**). The endings change according to the pronoun:
Ich hatte eine Party. *I had a party.*
Wir hatten eine Party. *We had a party.*
Ich war im Computerraum. *I was in the computer room.*
Du warst im Computerraum. *You were in the computer room.*

ich hatte	*I had*	**ich war**	*I was*
du hattest	*you had*	**du warst**	*you were*
er/sie hatte	*he/she had*	**er/sie war**	*he/she was*
wir hatten	*we had*	**wir waren**	*we were*
ihr hattet	*you had*	**ihr wart**	*you were*
sie/Sie hatten	*they/you had*	**sie/Sie waren**	*they/you were*

1 Ergänze die Sätze mit „hatte" oder „war".
1 Am Samstag *hatte* ich Geburtstag.
2 Gestern ________ ich in der Stadt.
3 Du ________ ein Problem, nicht?
4 Wo ________ er am Freitag?
5 Letzte Woche ________ Sabine Kopfschmerzen.
6 Wo ________ du in den Sommerferien?
7 Wir ________ keine Chance.
8 ________ ihr schon in Amerika?
9 Wann ________ Sie Geburtstag?
10 Gestern ________ ich Zahnschmerzen.

If you start your sentence with a time phrase, **hatte/war** comes next, i.e. in second position:
Gestern war ich in der Stadt. *I was in town yesterday.*
Am Montag hatte er ein Problem. *He had a problem on Monday.*
Hatte and **war** are often used together with the perfect tense to describe actions that happened in the past:
Ich war zu Hause und ich habe Musik gehört. *I was at home and I listened to music.*

2 Schreib Sätze.
Beispiel: Am Montag war ich im Computerraum und ich habe E-Mails geschrieben.

Mo.	im Computerraum/E-Mails schreiben
Di.	in der Bibliothek/Hausaufgaben machen
Mi.	Kopfschmerzen/zu Hause bleiben
Do.	im Schwimmbad/schwimmen gehen
Fr.	Ohrenschmerzen/zum Arzt gehen
Sa.	zu Hause/Party
So.	im Zimmer/Musik hören und fernsehen

© Heinemann Educational 2001 Special copyright conditions apply

75

Wortschatz pp. 76–77 and Lernzieltest p. 78
These sheets are for revision at the end of the chapter. The *Wortschatz* sheets provide a list of all the key words and phrases from the chapter and the *Lernzieltest* gives a checklist of the areas covered, which pupils can check off as they revise.

5 Jobs und Geld (Pupil's Book pp. 78–95)

Topic area	Key language	Skills	Grammar	Pos
5.1 Ich habe einen Job (pp. 78–79) Talk about part-time work	*Hast du einen Job? Ja, ich arbeite im Supermarkt/Friseursalon/ Restaurant, trage Zeitungen aus, wasche das Auto, helfe zu Hause. mache Babysitting/Gartenarbeit. Wann machst du das? Das mache ich samstags/freitags / in den Ferien / jeden Tag. von ein/ zwei ... Uhr bis zwei/drei ... Uhr. Gefällt dir den Job? Er gefällt mir sehr gut/nicht. Er ist sehr/total/ziemlich/ein bisschen interessant, langweilig, klasse, anstrengend.*	Drafting/redrafting a text on computer	Present tense, singular (revision) *in* + dative *gefallen* (revision)	2j, 2h
5.2 Jobanzeigen (pp. 80–81) Talk about qualities required for certain jobs	*Bist du intelligent, vernünftig, sportlich, fleißig, höflich, pünktlich, hilfsbereit, gut gelaunt, geduldig, freundlich, computererfahren, ordentlich? Ja, ich bin sehr/ziemlich ... . Nein, ich bin gar nicht ... .*			2a, 5d
5.3 Worauf sparst du? (pp. 82–83) Talk about what you are saving for Count to 10,000	*1–10,000, Worauf sparst du? einen Computer, den Führerschein, eine Stereoanlage, ein Auto/Mofa/Fahrrad, die Ferien, Kleidung/ CDs/Videos/Computerspiele/Sportausrüstung. Was kostet dieser Computer/Fotoapparat, diese Stereoanlage/Jacke, dieses Fahrrad/ Mofa? ... Euro.*	Learning and revising vocabulary	*dieser/diese/dieses* (revision) *sparen auf* + acc.	1a, 3a
5.4 Im Second-Hand-Laden (pp. 84–85) Buy clothes	*Hallo, kann ich dir helfen? Ja, kann ich bitte diese Röcke/Hosen/ Jacken/T-Shirts/Schuhe anprobieren? Ja, natürlich. Die Kabine ist dort drüben. Danke. Na, welcher Rock, welche Hose/Jacke, welches T-Shirt passt dir am besten? welche Schuhe passen dir am besten? Der blaue/weiße Rock, Die karierte/gelbe Hose/Jacke, Das rote/grüne T-Shirt ist genau richtig, zu lang/groß/klein/kurz. Die schwarzen/braunen Schuhe sind genau richtig. O.K., der/die/ das ... kostet ... Euro, bitte. Die Schuhe kosten ... . Ach, das ist sehr preiswert. Vielen Dank.*	Understanding speech at normal pace	'the', 'this', 'which?' Adjective endings after *der, die, das* (revision)	2a, 5f
5.5 Eine 20. Jahrhundert-Party (pp. 86–87) Talk about clothes	*Wer trägt ... einen gelben Hut / großen Ohrring, eine rote Hose / schwarze Sonnenbrille / bunte Perlenschnur, ein enges T-Shirt / langes Kleid, braune Sandalen / dicke Stiefel / große Ohrringe? Wer hat wilde/lange Haare?*	Using picture clues to guess words	Adjective endings after *einen, eine, ein* and plural (revision)	2h, 3b, 5g
5.6 Das Geldspiel (pp. 88–89) Talk about what you'll do with your money Play a game	*Wie viel Geld hast du verdient/gespart? Was wirst du damit machen? Er/Sie wird / Ich werde einen Computer/Walkman, eine Sonnenbrille/Hose/Stereoanlage, ein Fahrrad/Kleid/Handy, Stiefel/ Sportschuhe/CDs/Kleidung kaufen, ins Kino / in die Disco gehen, nach Italien/Spanien fahren, es sparen.*	Using game vocabulary	Future tense (revision)	1b, 2g, 5b, 5h
5.7 Ein Job in Ehren (pp. 90–91)		Coping with new vocabulary in a text		3d, 4a, 4d
Lernzieltest und Wiederholung (pp. 92–93)	Revision			5a, 5d
Wörter (pp. 94–95)	Word list			

1 Ich habe einen Job (pp. 78–79)

Pupils will learn how to:
- talk about part-time work

Key language
Hast du einen Job?
Ich arbeite im ...
Supermarkt
Friseursalon
Restaurant
Ich trage Zeitungen aus.
Ich wasche das Auto.
Ich helfe zu Hause.
Ich mache Babysitting/Gartenarbeit.
Wann machst du das?
Das mache ich ...
samstags / in den Ferien / jeden Tag
von ein Uhr bis drei Uhr.
Gefällt dir der Job?
Er gefällt mir sehr gut / nicht.
Er ist sehr/total/echt/ziemlich/ ein bisschen ...
interessant
langweilig
anstrengend
Er ist (total/echt) klasse.

Grammar focus
- present tense, singular (revision)
- *in* + dative (revision)
- *gefallen* (revision)

Skill focus
- drafting and redrafting a text on computer

Resources
- Cassette C, Side A
- Workbook p. 41
- R & A File: Arbeitsblatt 1 (p. 89), 6 (p. 94)

This chapter deals with the topics of part-time work and money as reflected in the lives of five teenagers: Vicky, Aschi, Daniela, Guido and Nicole.

This unit looks at the topic of part-time work. Ask pupils whether they do any part-time work, and list the jobs on the board/OHT. Then introduce the new job vocabulary orally, using a copy of the visuals on Arbeitsblatt 1 (R & A File p. 89) on an OHT. Discuss whether the jobs on the Arbeitsblatt match those done by pupils.

For further oral practice, give each pair of pupils a copy of Arbeitsblatt 1. One pupil points to a picture and asks: *Hast du einen Job?* The other pupil gives the appropriate response.

1a Hör zu und lies. Wer ist das im Bild? (AT1 Level 4, AT3 Level 4)

Pupils read the article and listen to the recording to work out who is who in the pictures.

Answers

a Vicky, **b** Aschi, **c** Daniela, **d** Guido, **e** Nicole

- Guido ist siebzehn Jahre alt. Samstags arbeitet er im Supermarkt. Er arbeitet von neun Uhr bis fünf Uhr. Er findet den Job sehr interessant, aber ein bisschen anstrengend.
- Vicky ist sechzehn Jahre alt. Samstags arbeitet sie im Restaurant. Sie arbeitet von zwölf Uhr bis fünf Uhr und sie findet den Job ziemlich langweilig.
- Aschi ist fünfzehn Jahre alt. Jeden Tag trägt er Zeitungen aus. Er arbeitet von sechs Uhr bis halb acht. Der Job gefällt Aschi gar nicht, weil er anstrengend ist und weil es draußen oft sehr kalt ist.
- Daniela ist vierzehn Jahre alt. In den Ferien hilft sie viel zu Hause – sie wäscht das Auto, sie macht Gartenarbeit und sie macht Babysitting. Sie findet das sehr gut.
- Nicole ist sechzehn Jahre alt. In den Ferien arbeitet sie im Friseursalon. Sie arbeitet montags bis freitags von zehn Uhr bis fünf Uhr. Der Job gefällt Nicole sehr gut, weil sie ziemlich gut verdient.

1b Beantworte die Fragen. (AT3 Level 4)

Pupils answer ten *wer?* questions on the article. Some questions have more than one answer.

Answers

1 Vicky, Aschi, **2** Aschi, Daniela, **3** Daniela, **4** Daniela, Nicole, **5** Guido, **6** Aschi, **7** Vicky, **8** Guido, **9** Guido, Vicky, Aschi **10** Guido

2 Hör zu. Schreib die Tabelle ab und füll sie aus. (1–4) (AT1 Levels 4–5)

Pupils listen to four teenagers talking about their part-time work. They note down the details in a grid.

Answers

	Alter	Job	Wann?	Uhr	Meinung
1	16	Restaurant	sonntags	11–5	echt klasse
2	14	Zeitungen austragen	Montag bis Freitag	6–7	total anstrengend
3	15	Babysitting	samstags	10–12	total super
4	17	Friseursalon	donnerstags	3–7	sehr interessant

1 – Hallo, Iris. Du, sag mal, wie alt bist du?
– Ich bin sechzehn Jahre alt.
– Und hast du einen Job?
– Ja, ich arbeite in einem Restaurant in der Stadt, „Der große Tisch".
– Ach, „Der große Tisch" – da war ich letzten Samstagabend! Wann arbeitest du dort?
– Ach, ich arbeite nur sonntags von elf Uhr bis fünf Uhr.
– Ach, dann komme ich vielleicht noch mal vorbei!
– Ja, mach das.
– Gefällt dir der Job?
– Ach, ja, er ist echt klasse.

2 – Grüß dich, Latze, wie geht's?
– Prima, danke. Ich habe einen neuen Job gefunden!
– Mensch, hast du Glück! Was für ein Job ist das?
– Ach, ich trage Zeitungen aus.
– Du spinnst wohl! Du bist vierzehn Jahre alt und du trägst schon Zeitungen aus! Meine Güte. Ist das nicht anstrengend?
– Ja, klar. Ich muss jeden Tag sehr früh aufstehen.
– Was, jeden Tag machst du das?
– Also, nein, ich arbeite von Montag bis Freitag.
– Und wann musst du beginnen?
– Tja, ich arbeite von sechs Uhr bis sieben Uhr.
– Von sechs Uhr bis sieben Uhr?

- Ja, das finde ich total anstrengend.

3 – Julia, wie alt bist du eigentlich?
- Ich bin fünfzehn Jahre alt.
- Und hast du einen Job?
- Ja, ich mache Babysitting.
- Babysitting. Ach, gefällt dir das?
- Ja, das finde ich total super. Ich liebe Babys, weißt du?
- Ach, ja? Und wann machst du das Babysitting?
- Samstags.
- Samstags – am Abend, oder?
- Nein, ich mache das von zehn Uhr bis zwölf Uhr.
- Prima. Dann kannst du Samstagabend mit mir ins Kino gehen!

4 – Frank, herzlichen Glückwunsch zum Geburtstag!
- Danke sehr!
- Na, wie alt bist du heute?
- Siebzehn Jahre alt. Das ist schon alt, nicht?
- Nee. Und wie geht's mit dem Job? Arbeitest du noch im Friseursalon?
- Ja, klar. Aber jetzt arbeite ich nur donnerstags von drei Uhr bis sieben Uhr.
- Ach, das ist nicht viel. Gefällt dir der Job denn nicht so gut?
- Doch, er ist sehr interessant, aber ich muss für das Abi lernen. Ich habe wenig Zeit.

3a Partnerarbeit. Seht euch die Info-Karten an und übt Interviews mit Patrick, Fatima und Anke. (AT2 Levels 4–5)
Pupils conduct interviews using the information given on the cue cards.

3b Schreib Texte für Fatima und Anke oder schreib über einen Freund / eine Freundin. (AT4 Levels 4–5)
Pupils write up the details from activity 3a in text form. Encourage them to use conjunctions such as *weil* and *wenn* to add interest to their text.

Ludwig: Drafting and redrafting a text on computer
Discuss Ludwig's advice with pupils and gather some ideas about making texts more interesting on the board/OHT. This could include the use of qualifiers (e.g. *total, ein bisschen, ziemlich*), conjunctions (e.g. *dann, und, aber, weil*) and adjectives (e.g. *langweilig, blöd, einfach*). Once pupils have prepared a first draft of the activity, they could swap their print-outs with a partner to work on and improve.

Wiederholung: The present tense, singular
This grammar revision box reminds pupils of the present tense conjugation (single forms) of the key verbs from this unit. Go through the box, pointing out the irregular forms of *helfen, tragen, waschen* and *sein*.

E Pupils conduct further interviews around the class, finding out similar information about their classmates' part-time work. They then report their findings to the class.

R The pairwork activity on Arbeitsblatt 6 (R & A File p. 94) provides further oral practice of the language of the unit.

2 Jobanzeigen (pp. 80–81)

Pupils will learn how to:
- talk about qualities required for certain jobs

Key language
Bist du ... ?
intelligent
vernünftig
sportlich
fleißig
höflich
pünktlich
hilfsbereit
gut gelaunt
geduldig
freundlich
computererfahren
ordentlich
Ja, ich bin sehr/ ziemlich ...
Nein, ich bin gar nicht ...

Resources
- Cassette C, Side A
- Workbook p. 42

This unit focuses on job adverts and the personal qualities required for certain jobs.

1a Hör zu und lies den Dialog. (AT1 Levels 4–5, AT3 Levels 4–5)
Pupils listen to and read the dialogue between Vicky and Guido.

- Grüß dich, Vicky. Wie geht's?
- Ach, nicht sehr gut. Ich brauche einen neuen Job.
- Warum denn?
- Weil es im Restaurant so langweilig ist.
- Ach, sag mal, hast du diese Anzeigen gesehen?
- Nein.
- Guck mal. Hier ist ein Job im Friseursalon.
- Toll!
- Ach, Moment mal. Nein, das ist nichts für dich.
- Warum denn?
- Weil man freundlich, fleißig und gut gelaunt sein muss.
- Ach, fleißig bin ich nicht. Aber Babysitter. Das ist besser.
- Aber Vicky, du magst Babys nicht.
- Stimmt.
- Hier. Diese Anzeige ist besser. Bist du sportlich?
- Ja.
- Bist du höflich?
- Äh ... manchmal.
- Und bist du hilfsbereit?
- Ja, klar.
- Dann ist dieser Job im Hallenbad ideal für dich.
- Nein, Guido. Das ist gar nicht ideal.
- Warum denn?
- Ich kann nicht schwimmen!

1b Richtig oder falsch? (AT3 Level 4)
Pupils answer eight true/false statements on the dialogue.

Answers
1 falsch, **2** richtig, **3** richtig, **4** richtig, **5** falsch, **6** richtig, **7** falsch, **8** richtig

2a Schreib die Tabelle ab und füll sie mit den Adjektiven aus den Anzeigen auf Seite 80 aus.
Pupils copy the table and complete it with the adjectives taken from the job adverts on page 80. They could then compare their table with their partner's to see how similar/different they are.

2b Welche Charaktereigenschaft ist das? Such das Wort in den Anzeigen auf Seite 80. (AT3 Level 3)
Pupils find the appropriate adjective from page 80 to fit eight descriptions of people.

Answers
1 gut gelaunt, **2** fleißig/intelligent, **3** pünktlich, **4** hilfsbereit, **5** computererfahren, **6** ordentlich, **7** höflich, **8** sportlich

E Pupils write a list of their personal qualities, or prioritise the personal qualities from page 80 into their own order of importance.

3 Partnerarbeit. Wähl eine Anzeige für deinen Partner / deine Partnerin aus. (AT2 Level 4)
Pupils select a job advert from page 80 and then question their partner to see if he/she would be suitable for the job.

4 Hör zu und mach Notizen über die Jobs. Welcher Job gefällt dir am besten? (1–3) (AT1 Level 5)
Pupils listen to the recording and make notes about three different jobs. They then read through their notes and decide which job appeals to them most.

Answers
1 im Sportgeschäft – samstags, 9–1, sportlich, fleißig und hilfsbereit, muss auch freundlich sein, es ist immer was los, nie langweilig, Ferien auch montags und mittwochs
2 im Restaurant, am Wochenende und in den Ferien, anstrengend, muss immer freundlich und gut gelaunt sein, Tische abwischen, Getränke holen, am liebsten in der Küche, Leute dort lustig
3 im Büro, 18 J. , liebt den Job, jeden Tag 8–4, toll, trifft Freundinnen am Nachmittag, computererfahren, hilfsbereit, Job interessant, lernt immer was Neues, viel am Computer arbeiten, nächste Woche an der Rezeption

1 – Hallo, ich heiße Johannes und ich arbeite im Sportgeschäft. Das mache ich samstags von neun Uhr bis ein Uhr, und der Job gefällt mir sehr gut. Ich habe den Job bekommen, weil ich sportlich, fleißig und hilfsbereit bin. Das hilft viel bei der Arbeit. Ich muss auch freundlich sein, aber manchmal ist das schwierig, weil die Kunden sehr launisch sind. Der Job gefällt mir, weil immer was los ist und weil es im Geschäft nie langweilig ist. In den Ferien werde ich hoffentlich auch montags und mittwochs hier arbeiten.

2 – Hallo, ich heiße Martin und ich habe einen Job im Restaurant. Mein Vater ist Manager, also hat er mir den Job gegeben. Ich arbeite am Wochenende und in den Ferien dort, aber der Job gefällt mir nicht, weil er so anstrengend ist. Man muss immer freundlich und gut gelaunt sein, aber das finde ich sehr schwierig. Ich muss Tische abwischen und Getränke holen. Am liebsten arbeite ich in der Küche, weil die Leute dort echt lustig sind. Ich suche einen neuen Job – vielleicht etwas in einem Büro.

3 – Hallo, ich bin die Jasmin und ich arbeite im Büro. Ich bin achtzehn Jahre alt und ich liebe meinen Job. Ich arbeite jeden Tag von acht Uhr bis vier Uhr und das finde ich toll, weil ich am Nachmittag dann noch meine Freundinnen treffen kann. Ich bin computererfahren und hilfsbereit und den Job finde ich immer interessant, weil man immer was Neues lernt. Im Moment arbeite ich viel am Computer, aber nächste Woche werde ich an der Rezeption arbeiten. Ich freue mich sehr darauf.

5 Was ist dein idealer Job? Beschreib ihn. (AT4 Levels 4–6)

Pupils describe their ideal job, using ideas from this unit or including ideas of their own. You may need to brainstorm some ideas as a class before pupils work on their own.

6 Partnerarbeit. Lest den Dialog auf Seite 80 zu zweit vor. Adaptiert dann die Details und macht einen neuen Dialog. (AT2 Levels 4–6)

Pupils act out the dialogue on p. 80, and then alter details to create a new dialogue.

R Further practice of this unit's language is to be found on p. 118 of the Pupil's Book, activity 1.

E Further practice of this unit's language is to be found on p. 119 of the Pupil's Book, activity 1.

3 Worauf sparst du? (pp. 82–83)

Pupils will learn how to:
- talk about what they are saving for
- count to 10,000

Key language	Cardinal numbers
Key language Worauf sparst du? Ich spare auf ... einen Computer eine Stereoanlage ein Auto/Mofa/Fahrrad den Führerschein die Ferien Kleidung/Sportausrüstung CDs/Videos/Computerspiele Was kostet ... ? dieser Computer/Fotoapparat diese Stereoanlage/Jacke dieses Fahrrad/Mofa ... Euro.	*Cardinal numbers* *1–10,000* **Grammar focus** • *dieser/diese/dieses* (revision) • *sparen auf* + accusative **Skill focus** • Learning and revising vocabulary **Resources** • Cassette C, Side A • Workbook p. 43 • R & A File: Arbeitsblatt 2 (p. 90)

This unit practises numbers up 10,000 and looks at teenagers' saving habits. Introduce the new vocabulary orally first, copying the visuals on Arbeitsblatt 2 (R & A File p. 90) onto an OHT. First establish how many of the items pupils already know, and then introduce the unfamiliar items.

For further oral practice, give each pair of pupils a set of the visuals to cut up and place face-down on the table. One pupil asks: *Worauf sparst du?* The other pupil turns over a card and responds: *Ich spare auf ...* .

This unit introduces numbers in the context of money and shopping. Due to the introduction of the Euro as legal tender in 2002 (with the gradual disappearance of the Deutschmark) prices have generally been provided in both currencies. Listening material involving prices is provided in two versions. Version 1 uses Deutschmarks and Version 2 uses euros. Ensure that pupils are aware of the change in currency and indicate which set of prices you are referring to when focusing on a specific activity.

1 Sieh dir den Text an und beantworte die Fragen. (AT3 Levels 4–5)

Pupils read a text about teenagers' saving habits and then answer eight comprehension questions in German about it. There is no need for them to answer in full sentences.

Answers

1 drei, **2** zwei, **3** zwölf, **4** zehn, **5** eine Stereoanlage, einen CD-Player, **6** ein Auto, **7** Mädchen, **8** den Führerschein

2 Hör zu. Worauf sparen sie? Haben sie ein Sparkonto? (1–4) (AT1 Level 4)

Pupils listen and note down what each speaker is saving for and whether they have a savings account.

Answers

1 die Ferien, einen Computer, ja; **2** ein Fahrrad, nein; **3** CDs, ja; **4** den Führerschein, ja

1 – Entschuldigung, ich mache eine Umfrage über Sparen. Sparst du dein Geld?
– Ja, ich spare auf die Ferien.
– Und wirst du danach auf noch etwas Anderes sparen?
– Ja, ich werde dann auf einen neuen Computer sparen.
– Prima, du hast also ein Sparkonto, oder?
– Ja, ich habe ein Konto bei der Raiffeisenbank.

2 – Entschuldigung, ich mache eine Umfrage über Sparen. Hast du ein Sparkonto?
– Nein, so was habe ich nicht.
– Ach, du sparst also nichts?
– Doch, das habe ich nicht gesagt. Ich spare auf ein neues Fahrrad.
– Ach, toll. Und wie sparst du denn das Geld, wenn du kein Sparkonto hast?
– Ich spare es zu Hause. Das finde ich besser als die Bank.

3 – Und du? Sparst du dein Geld?
– Ja, ich habe zwei Sparkontos – eins bei der Bank und eins bei einer Internetbank.
– Toll, und worauf sparst du?
– Tja, letzten Monat habe ich einen CD-Player gekauft, also jetzt spare ich auf CDs!

4 – Entschuldigung, hast du ein Sparkonto?
– Ja, ich habe ziemlich viel Geld auf dem Sparkonto, weil ich einen Job habe.
– Und du sparst das Geld, nicht?
– Ja.
– Und sparst du auf etwas Bestimmtes?
– Ja, ich spare auf den Führerschein.
– Und danach wirst du auf ein Auto sparen, oder?
– Nee. Mein Vater wird ein Auto für mich kaufen.

3a Gruppenarbeit. Stellt Fragen und beantwortet sie. (AT2 Levels 3–4)

Pupils carry out a survey in the class about what people are saving for. Point out to pupils that *sparen auf* is always followed by the accusative case, so the masculine *der* and *ein* become *den* and *einen*.

▶ 3b Beschreib deine Resultate wie oben. (AT4 Levels 2–4)

Pupils write a report about their survey results. Do some oral practice of higher numbers at this point, revising numbers pupils already know and then moving on to the thousands.

4 Hör zu und wiederhole. Welche Zahl ist das? (1–10) (AT1 Level 2)
Pupils listen to and repeat the numbers given on the recording and then write them down as figures. They might need to listen to the numbers several times to complete the activity.

Answers
1 100, **2** 400, **3** 1000, **4** 200, **5** 3000, **6** 110, **7** 220, **8** 4000, **9** 810, **10** 999

1 – hundert
2 – vierhundert
3 – tausend
4 – zweihundert
5 – dreitausend
6 – hundertzehn
7 – zweihundertzwanzig
8 – viertausend
9 – achthundertzehn
10 – neunhundertneunundneunzig

5a Welche Zahl ist das?
Pupils read some numbers and then write them in figures. Draw pupils' attention to the fact that German numbers are always written as one continuous word.

Answers
1 134, **2** 1500, **3** 311, **4** 6213, **5** 8085, **6** 4090, **7** 703, **8** 2940

Ludwig: Learning and revising vocabulary
Ludwig reminds pupils of the need for constant learning and revising of vocabulary. Try to establish a regular pattern of revising language learned earlier, by setting a short test on it at regular intervals, so that it is not forgotten as pupils move on to new topics.

5b Gruppenarbeit. Das Zahlenspiel. Gebt immer die nächste Zahl an. (AT2 Level 2)
Pupils work in groups to play a counting game, saying the number in each cloud and giving the number which follows it.

E More challenging variants on the counting game include: counting backwards; missing every number with a five in it; counting in multiples of five.

6a Partnerarbeit. Ratet mal, was das kostet, und notiert die Preise. (AT2 Levels 3–4)
Pupils look at some pictures of articles for sale and estimate what they cost.

6b Hör zu. Was kostet das? Wer hat am besten geraten? (1–6) (AT1 Levels 3–4)
Pupils listen and find out the actual cost of the items so they can compare them with their own guesses.

Answers
1 Stereoanlage – €1555, **2** Jacke – €60, **3** CDs – €100,15, **4** Mofa – €2150, **5** Computer – €1200, **6** Fahrrad – €225

1 – Entschuldigung, was kostet diese Stereoanlage?
– Die Stereoanlage. Moment mal, bitte ... Ach, ja. Die Stereoanlage kostet €1555.
– €1555!
2 – Entschuldigung, ich interessiere mich für diese Jacke. Was kostet sie?
– Die Jacke? Tja, Moment mal, bitte. Also, die Jacke kostet €60.
– €60. Ach, das ist zu viel.
3 – Hallo, was kosten denn diese CDs?
– Also, wie viele sind es?
– Zehn Stück.
– Also, zehn CDs – das macht €100,15 bitte.
4 – Entschuldigung, was kostet das blaue Mofa?
– Das blaue Mofa? Ach, das kostet €2150.
– 2150, sagen Sie?
– Ja, 2150.
5 – Hallo, was kostet dieser Computer?
– Wie bitte?
– Dieser Computer. Was kostet er?
– Ach ... Moment mal ... ach, ja der Computer kostet €1200.
6 – Hallo, ich möchte dieses Fahrrad kaufen. Wie viel kostet es?
– Das Fahrrad kostet €225.
– €225?
– Ja, genau.

MINI-TEST
At the end of the third unit in every chapter, there is a *Mini-Test*. This is intended as a half-way checkpoint for pupils to check that they are familiar with the key language of the chapter so far. Pupils could revise the language with a partner in class or for homework.

4 Im Second-Hand-Laden
(pp. 84–85)

Pupils will learn how to:
- buy clothes

Key language
Kann ich dir helfen?
Kann ich bitte diese … anprobieren?
Röcke/Hosen/Jacken/ T-Shirts/Schuhe
Ja, natürlich.
Die Kabine ist dort drüben.
Welcher/Welche/Welches … passt dir am besten?
Rock/Hose/Jacke/ T-Shirt
Welche Schuhe passen dir am besten?
… ist/sind genau richtig / zu lang/groß/klein/kurz.
Der blaue/weiße Rock
Die karierte/gelbe Hose/Jacke
Das rote/grüne T-Shirt
Die schwarzen/ braunen Schuhe
Der/Die/Das/Die … kostet/kosten zehn Euro, bitte.
Das ist sehr preiswert.
Vielen Dank.

Grammar focus
- 'the', 'this/these', 'which?'
- adjective endings after *der, die, das* (revision)

Skill focus
- understanding speech at normal pace

Resources
- Cassette C, Side A
- Workbook pp. 44, 47
- R & A File: Arbeitsblatt 3 (p. 91), Grammatik 1, 2 (pp. 96–97)

This unit introduces and practises a dialogue for buying clothes in a secondhand shop. Introduce or revise the vocabulary for clothes using a copy of the visuals from Arbeitsblatt 3 (R & A File p. 91) on an OHT. Focus on both the singular and the plural forms.

For further oral practice, give each pair of pupils a set of the visuals to cut up and place face-down in a pile. One pupil takes a card and asks the question: *Kann ich bitte diese … anprobieren?* The other pupil then asks: *Welcher/Welche/Welches … passt dir am besten?* to which the first pupil can reply: *Der/Die/Das … ist genau richtig.* The level of language to be used can be dictated by the teacher, with prompts written on the board/OHT for support.

Ludwig: Getting used to speech delivered at a normal native-speaker pace
Go through Ludwig's advice with pupils, alerting them to the fact that they will hear the dialogue three times. After they have heard it at normal speed, ask pupils how much they could understand and what helped them understand as much as they did.

1 Hör zu und lies den Dialog. Dann hör noch einmal zu, ohne ins Buch zu schauen. Notiere fünf Details, die du verstehst. (AT1 Levels 3–4)
Pupils listen to and read the dialogue, before closing their books and just listening to the dialogue on the cassette. They will then hear the dialogue three times at increasing speeds, and note down five details which they understand.

– Hallo, kann ich dir helfen?
– Ja, kann ich bitte diese Hosen anprobieren?
– Ja, natürlich. Die Kabine ist dort drüben.
– Danke.
…
– Na, welche Hose passt dir am besten?
– Die gestreifte Hose ist genau richtig.
– O.K., die Hose kostet €7,50, bitte.
– Ach, das ist sehr preiswert. Vielen Dank.

Grammatik: 'the', 'this/these', 'which'
This grammar box shows *der, dieser* and *welcher* together to reinforce the similarities in the endings.

R Refer to p. 124 of the Pupil's Book for further information. More practice of this grammar point is also provided on Grammatik 1 (R & A File p. 96) and p. 47 of the Workbook.

2 Ergänze die Sätze.
Pupils complete the sentences, filling in the item of clothing each time.

Answers
1 Kann ich bitte diese Schuhe anprobieren? **2** Welches T-Shirt passt dir am besten? **3** Der gelbe Rock ist genau richtig. **4** Die Jacke kostet zehn Euro. **5** Diese Schuhe sind genau richtig. **6** Kann ich bitte diese Röcke anprobieren? **7** Welche Hose passt dir am besten?

3 Hör zu. Schreib die Tabelle ab und füll sie aus. (1–5) (AT1 Level 4)
Pupils listen to five shopping dialogues and note down the required details in a table.

Answers

	Was?	Farbe	€
1	T-Shirt	rot	6
2	Rock	gelbe	10,50
3	Schuhe	blau	15
4	Hose	braun	7
5	Jacke	grün	16,50

1 – Hallo, kann ich dir helfen?
– Ja, kann ich bitte diese T-Shirts anprobieren?
– Ja, natürlich. Die Kabine ist dort drüben.
– Danke.
…

- Na, welches T-Shirt passt dir am besten?
- Ach, das gelbe T-Shirt ist zu klein, aber das rote T-Shirt ist genau richtig.
- O.K., das rote T-Shirt kostet €6, bitte.
- Ach, das ist sehr preiswert. Vielen Dank.

2 – Hallo, kann ich dir helfen?
- Ja, kann ich bitte diese Röcke anprobieren?
- Ja, natürlich.

...
- Also, welcher Rock passt dir am besten?
- Ach, der karierte Rock ist ein bisschen zu lang, aber der gelbe Rock ist genau richtig.
- O.K., der gelbe Rock kostet € 10,50, bitte.
- Ach, super. Den kaufe ich für die Party am Samstag.

3 – Hallo, kann ich dir helfen?
- Ja, ich möchte diese Schuhe anprobieren, bitte.
- Ja, natürlich.

...
- Also, welche Schuhe passen dir am besten?
- Ach, die passen mir alle sehr gut, aber die blauen Schuhe finde ich fantastisch. Die nehme ich!
- O.K., die Schuhe kosten € 15, bitte.
- Ach, das ist sehr preiswert. Vielen Dank.

4 – Hallo, kann ich dir helfen?
- Ja, wo ist die Kabine? Ich möchte schnell diese Hosen anprobieren.
- Die Kabine ist dort drüben.
- Danke.

...
- Na, welche Hose passt dir am besten?
- Ach, die schwarze Hose ist sehr cool, aber leider ist sie zu kurz. Ich nehme lieber die braune Hose, bitte.
- O.K., die Hose kostet €7, bitte.
- Ach, das ist sehr preiswert. Vielen Dank.

5 – Hallo, kann ich dir helfen?
- Ja, kann ich bitte diese Jacken anprobieren?
- Ja, natürlich.
- Danke.

...
- Also, welche Jacke passt dir am besten?
- Ach, die rote Jacke ist zu groß, aber die grüne Jacke ist genau richtig. Was kostet sie?
- Moment mal ... Ja, die grüne Jacke kostet € 16,50, bitte.
- Ach, prima. Vielen Dank.

4 Partnerarbeit. Übt den Dialog im Second-Hand-Laden – mit Pfiff! (AT2 Level 4)

Pupils act out a shopping dialogue of their own, using as much expression and vivacity as possible. The dialogue and pictures on the page give them the details they need. Pupils could act out their dialogues to the whole class and be awarded points for their efforts.

Wiederholung: Adjective endings after *der, die, das*

This grammar revision box reminds pupils that in German an adjective needs an ending if it appears before a noun.

R Refer to p. 135 of the Pupil's Book for further information. More practice of this grammar point is also provided on Grammatik 2 (R & A File p. 97).

5 Schreib eine Radioanzeige für einen Second-Hand-Laden. Füg auch einen Dialog wie oben hinzu. (AT4 Levels 4–6)

Pupils prepare a radio advert for a secondhand shop and include a dialogue in their advert. Pupils could record their adverts on cassette, possibly with a jingle and/or background music, and then play it back to the class.

5 Eine 20. Jahrhundert-Party
(pp. 86–87)

Pupils will learn how to:
- talk about clothes

Key language	Grammar focus
Wer trägt ... ? einen gelben Hut einen großen Ohrring eine rote Hose eine schwarze Sonnenbrille eine bunte Perlenschnur ein enges T-Shirt ein langes Kleid braune Sandalen dicke Stiefel große Ohrringe Wer hat wilde/lange Haare?	• adjective endings after *einen, eine, ein* and in the plural (revision) **Skill focus** • using picture clues to guess words **Resources** • Cassette C, Side A • Workbook pp. 45, 47 • R & A File: Arbeitsblatt 4 (p. 92), Grammatik 2 (p. 97)

This unit continues the topic of clothes, featuring a fancy-dress party and associated outfits. Introduce the new vocabulary orally first, using the visuals on Arbeitsblatt 4 (R & A File p. 92) on an OHT. Alternatively, you could have a selection of clothes in a box at the front of the class and say their German names as you pull them out.

For further oral practice, give each pair of pupils a copy of the visuals to cut up. Pupils then place the visuals in two piles, labelled A and B (or given two names). One pupil starts the question-and-answer session by asking: *Wer trägt ... ?* naming the item on the top of pile A or B. The other pupil replies: *A/B trägt ...* . Alternatively, one pupil can ask: *Was trägt A?* and the other pupil must name the item of clothing on the top of the pile.

1a Hör zu und lies. Beschreib die Bilder a–k. (AT1 Levels 6–7, AT3 Levels 6–7)
Pupils listen to and read the account of a party last weekend. They then describe the items of clothing depicted.

Answers

a Vicky hat lange Haare. **b** Vicky trägt einen gelben Hut. **c** Vicky trägt eine bunte Perlenschnur. **d** Vicky trägt ein langes Kleid. **e** Vicky trägt braune Sandalen. **f** Guido hat wilde Haare / trägt eine wilde Perücke. **g** Guido trägt große Ohrringe. **h** Guido trägt eine schwarze Sonnenbrille. **i** Guido trägt ein enges schwarzes T-Shirt. **j** Guido trägt eine gestreifte Hose. **k** Guido trägt dicke Stiefel.

Letztes Wochenende sind Vicky und Guido auf eine Party aus dem 20. Jahrhundert gegangen.

Vicky ist als ein Hippie aus den sechziger Jahren gegangen. Sie hat einiges für die Party im Second-Hand-Laden gekauft und das Einkaufen hat irrsinnig viel Spaß gemacht. Zuerst hat sie aber ein tolles Kleid gefunden – es war sehr lang mit einem Blumenmuster darauf. Das hat sie in der Kommode ihrer Mutter gefunden! Dann hat sie braune Sandalen im Second-Hand-Laden gekauft. Sie waren nicht sehr bequem, aber sie waren wenigstens billig. Sie hat auch einen wunderbaren gelben Hut und eine bunte Perlenschnur gekauft. Vicky hat lange Haare. Als sie für die Party fertig war, sah sie genau wie eine Frau aus den sechziger Jahren aus!

Guido wollte als ein Punker aus den siebziger Jahren zur Party gehen. Zu Hause hatte er eine wilde Perücke, die perfekt für einen Punker war! Er ist auch in vier Second-Hand-Läden gegangen, weil es nicht so einfach war, das perfekte Outfit zu finden. Im ersten Laden hat er eine wunderbare schwarze Lederhose gefunden, aber leider war sie zu klein, also hat er eine bunte gestreifte Hose gekauft. Im nächsten Laden hat er ein enges schwarzes T-Shirt gekauft. Dicke Stiefel hat er in einem dritten Second-Hand-Laden gekauft und dann hat er eine schwarze Sonnenbrille und große Ohrringe in einem vierten kleinen Laden gefunden. Am Ende sah er sehr cool aus!

Als Vicky und Guido zur Party kamen, war sie schon in vollem Schwung. Aber die anderen Gäste trugen alle ganz normale Outfits. Warum denn das? Also, Vicky und Guido haben die falschen Einladungen bekommen. Die Party war eine Party für das 21. Jahrhundert, aber die ersten Einladungen hatten einen Druckfehler darauf. Statt „Eine 21.-Jahrhundert-Party am 20. Mai" stand: „Eine 20. Jahrhundert-Party am 20. Mai." O je!

Ludwig: Using picture clues to guess words
As this text has some unfamiliar vocabulary, Ludwig suggests that pupils look for clues in the pictures which accompany the text to help them with meanings. Other ideas could include: looking for cognates; breaking down compound nouns; using a dictionary; and just realising that you don't need to understand every word to do the activity.

Wiederholung: Adjective endings after *einen, eine, ein* and in the plural
This grammar revision box summarises the adjective endings pupils need to use in activity 1a.

R Refer to p. 136 of the Pupil's Book for further information. More practice of this grammar point is also provided on Grammatik 2 (R & A File p. 97) and on p. 47 of the Workbook.

1b Partnerarbeit. Stellt Fragen und beantwortet sie. (AT2 Level 4)
Pupils question each other about the clothes on page 86. Encourage them to pay particular attention to the adjective endings whenever they describe an item.

2 Hör zu. Was haben die anderen Gäste auf der Party getragen? Notiere das Outfit und den Preis. (1–4) (AT1 Levels 4–5)
Pupils listen and note down what other guests wore to the party.

Answers
1 schwarze Stiefel, enge Hose, weißes T-Shirt – €117; **2** eine karierte Hose, eine schwarze Jacke, Sportschuhe – €215; **3** ein langes Kleid, eine bunte Perlenschnur, eine Sonnenbrille – €10; **4** eine schwarze Hose, eine schwarze Jacke, dicke schwarze Stiefel – €400

1 – Nina, was hast du auf der Party getragen?
– Also, ich habe schwarze Stiefel und eine enge, gestreifte Hose getragen.
– Schwarze Stiefel und eine enge gestreifte Hose? Sehr schön!
– Ja, und ich habe auch ein weißes T-Shirt getragen.
– Und was hat das gekostet?
– Das hat €117 gekostet.

2 – Robert, was hast du auf der Party getragen?
– Tja, ich habe meine Lieblingshose getragen. Das ist eine karierte Hose und ich habe auch eine schwarze Jacke getragen.
– O.K., eine karierte Hose und eine schwarze Jacke. Sonst noch was?
– Ja, klar. Ich habe Sportschuhe getragen.
– Und was hat das gekostet?
– Ach, das hat €215 gekostet. Aber ich habe das nicht alles nur für die Party gekauft.

3 – Und Petra, was hast du auf der Party getragen?
– Ach, ich habe ein langes Kleid getragen. Es ist sehr schön.
– Ein langes Kleid. Toll.
– Ja, und ich habe auch eine bunte Perlenschnur und eine Sonnenbrille getragen.
– Prima. War das nicht teuer?
– Nee, ich habe alles von meiner Schwester geborgt – ich habe nur die Sonnenbrille gekauft, und sie hat €10 gekostet.

4 – Willi, was hast du auf der Party getragen?
– Ach, weißt du, ich trage immer eine schwarze Hose und eine schwarze Jacke auf Partys.
– Immer in Schwarz?
– Ja, und ich trage auch dicke, schwarze Stiefel dazu.
– Schön. Das ist billig, nicht, wenn du immer das Gleiche trägst?
– Na ja. Das Outfit hat ungefähr €400 gekostet, also kein Wunder, dass ich immer das Gleiche trage!

3 Was hat das im Second-Hand-Laden gekostet? Wie findest du das Outfit? (AT3 Level 4)
Pupils read the outfit descriptions and work out what each one cost at the secondhand shop. They also give their opinion of each item.

Answers
1 Der rote Hut hat vier Euro gekostet und das schwarze T-Shirt hat vier Euro fünfzig gekostet, also hat das ganze Outfit acht Euro fünfzig gekostet. **2** Die karierte Hose hat zwölf Euro fünfzig gekostet. Die schwarze Sonnenbrille hat fünf Euro gekostet, also hat das ganze Outfit siebzehn Euro. **3** Die weißen Sandalen haben acht Euro gekostet und das bunte Kleid hat siebzehn Euro gekostet, also hat das ganze Outfit fünfundzwanzig Euro gekostet. **4** Das schwarze T-Shirt hat vier Euro fünfzig gekostet und die schwarzen Stiefel haben einundzwanzig Euro fünfzig gekostet, also hat das ganze Outfit sechsundzwanzig Euro gekostet. **5** Die karierte Hose hat zwölf Euro fünfzig gekostet, die coole Sonnenbrille hat fünf Euro gekostet und das grüne T-Shirt hat sechs Euro gekostet, also hat das ganze Outfit dreiundzwanzig Euro fünfzig.

4 Was hast du zur Party getragen? Beschreib und zeichne dein Outfit für eine Party aus dem 20. Jahrhundert. Vergleich dann dein Outfit mit einem Partner / einer Partnerin. (AT4 Levels 4–6, AT2 Levels 4–6)
Pupils choose an outfit for themselves and describe and draw it, using as many adjectives as possible to give details. They then compare their outfit with a partner's.

E Pupils adapt the account of the party on page 86 to reach a higher level, or find a picture of an outfit to describe for extra practice.

R Further practice of this unit's language is to be found on p. 118 of the Pupil's Book, activity 2.

E Further practice of this unit's language is to be found on p. 119 of the Pupil's Book, activity 2.

6 Das Geldspiel (pp. 88–89)

Pupils will learn how to:
- talk about what they will do with their money
- play a game

Key language
Wie viel Geld hast du verdient/gespart?
Was wirst du damit machen?
Ich werde ... kaufen.
einen Computer/Walkman
eine Sonnenbrille/Hose/Stereoanlage
ein Fahrrad/Kleid/Handy
Stiefel/Sportschuhe/CDs/Kleidung
Ich werde ...
ins Kino / in die Disco gehen.
nach Italien/Spanien fahren.
es sparen.

Grammar focus
- future tense (revision)

Resources
- Cassette C, Side A
- Workbook p. 46
- R & A File: Arbeitsblatt 5 (p. 93)

This unit provides a game on the topic of money and also revises the future tense. Introduce the new vocabulary by using the visuals on Arbeitsblatt 5 (R & A File p. 93) on an OHT.

For further oral practice, copy the visuals on Arbeitsblatt 5 and distribute them around the class. Reinforce the structure of the future tense by asking questions, e.g.: *Jake wird einen Computer kaufen. Stimmt das? Wer wird eine Stereoanlage kaufen? Was wird Claire kaufen?* Pupils can then take over the questioning role.

1 Hör zu und lies. Wem gehört das? (AT1 Level 5, AT3 Level 5)

Pupils listen to and read the article about what the teenagers are planning to do with their money. They note down which picture relates to which teenager.

Answers
a Aschi, **b** Guido, **c** Vicky, **d** Nicole, **e** Daniela

– Seit zwei Jahren hat **Guido** sein Taschengeld gespart und jetzt hat er €200 auf dem Konto. Er wird das Geld bald abheben und ausgeben. Ende April wird er nach Spanien fahren.
– Vicky findet es gar nicht so einfach zu sparen, aber jetzt hat sie endlich mal €25 zusammengekriegt. Am Samstag wird sie in die Stadt fahren und einen Walkman kaufen.
– Aschi spart ziemlich gern. Diesen Monat hat er €45 gespart. Er wird damit neue Kleidung kaufen.
– Letzte Woche hat Daniela €20 zum Geburtstag bekommen. Sie wird ins Kino gehen und das Geld dort ausgeben.
– Nicole hat €150 im Friseursalon verdient und gespart. Sie wird damit ein Handy kaufen.

2 Hör zu und mach Notizen. Wer hat das meiste Geld auf dem Konto? (1–4) (AT1 Levels 4–5)

Pupils listen and make notes as to what people have bought, so they can then work out who has the most money left in his/her bank account.

Answers
1 €63 – Jacke kaufen €50 = €13 auf dem Konto
2 €50, 3 CDs kaufen 3 x €15 = €5 auf dem Konto
3 €100 auf dem Konto
4 Süßigkeiten, Kleidung, Kinokarten gekauft = €10 auf dem Konto
Person 3 hat das meiste Geld auf dem Konto.

1 – Hallo. Wie viel Geld hast du gespart?
– Ich habe €63 gespart.
– Toll. Was wirst du damit machen?
– Ich werde eine neue Jacke kaufen.
– Und wie viel wird das denn kosten?
– Ach, das wird ja ungefähr €50 kosten.
2 – Grüß dich, wie geht's mit dem Sparen?
– O.K., danke. Bis jetzt habe ich schon €50 gespart.
– Und was wirst du mit den €50 machen? Gibst du das aus?
– Ja, klar, ich werde CDs kaufen. Sie kosten nur €15 pro Stück, also kaufe ich drei Stück.
– Und dann ist dein Konto fast leer, nicht?
– Ja, aber dann werde ich weiter sparen!
3 – Hallo, wie geht's mit dem Job im Supermarkt?
– Ach, es ist ganz schön anstrengend, das kann ich schon sagen.
– Ja, aber du verdienst eine Menge Geld, nicht?
– Nee, ich habe nur €100 verdient.
– Und was wirst du mit dem Geld machen?
– Also, das liegt auf dem Sparkonto. Ich werde weiter sparen, bis ich €500 habe, und dann werde ich ein neues Fahrrad kaufen.
4 – Hast du viel Geld gespart?
– Nein, ich habe nur €10 auf dem Konto.
– Nur €10? Was hast du dann mit dem Rest gemacht?
– Ach, ich habe Süßigkeiten, Kleidung, Kinokarten usw. gekauft. Das Geld verschwindet einfach!
– Und was wirst du jetzt mit den €10 machen?
– Äh ... ich werde Comics kaufen.
– Und dann wirst du ein bisschen sparen?
– Nee, Geld ausgeben macht mehr Spaß als sparen!

3 „Geld ausgeben macht mehr Spaß als Geld sparen." Was meinst du? (AT4 Level 4)

Pupils write an article about money, discussing whether it is better to spend or save it.

► 4 Partnerarbeit. Das Geldspiel. (AT2 Levels 4–6)

Pupils play the money game, using the vocabulary provided and working their way around the board by throwing a die, starting at *Start* and ending at *Ziel.* If they land on a square with a choice of options, they decide what they want to buy or if they want to save the money. They make a note of their decision. If pupils make a mistake, they miss a turn; if they land on a !! square, they move two squares backwards.

E Pupils write a detailed account of what they earned, saved and spent during the game.

7 Ein Job in Ehren (pp. 90–91)

Skill focus	Resources
• Coping with new vocabulary in a text	• Cassette C, Side B

The *MEHR* unit is intended as extension material for more able pupils. Pupils will be more challenged by the longer reading text and by exercises which draw together all the language of the chapter.

The context of this unit is an article taken from *JUMA* on the internet (www.juma.de) about teenagers and their voluntary work.

1a Hör zu und mach das Buch zu. Wie viel kannst du verstehen? Mach Notizen. (AT1 Level 7)

Pupils listen to a recording of the article and see how much they can understand without referring to the text. They make notes on what they understand.

– Sie machen einen Job, aber bekommen kein Geld dafür. Trotzdem haben Semir, Martina und die anderen jede Menge Spaß. Sie sagen: „Ein Ehrenamt ist eine gute Sache. Man trägt Verantwortung und bekommt Selbstvertrauen." *JUMA* stellt die fünf vor: Semir, Martina, Arne, Sabrina und Anne.
– Semir, 18:
– Seit drei Jahren trainiere ich die kleinsten Kicker des Fußballvereins TuS Heven, zusammen mit meinem Co-Trainer Christian. Mir macht es riesig viel Spaß. Wir haben zwei Gruppen mit 34 Spielern. Die Begeisterung der Jungs ist toll. Die haben nie schlechte Laune. Sie sind immer gut drauf. Ich selbst spiele in einem anderen Verein Fußball. Trotzdem will ich hier Trainer bleiben. Ich profitiere von dem Kicken mit den Kurzen. Wir versuchen den Jungs „Fairplay" beizubringen. Unser Motto ist „Sich immer vertragen!"
– Martina, 17:
– Ich singe wahnsinnig gern. Seit über sieben Jahren bin ich im Chor des Ruhrgymnasiums. Irgendwann hat mich der Chorleiter angesprochen. Ich sollte mithelfen. Seitdem leite ich unsere Übungsgruppe. Außerdem mache ich Werbeplakate für unsere Auftritte. Ich gestalte sie am Computer. Dann gehen wir in Geschäfte. Wir bitten darum, dass man die Plakate aushängt. Wir singen klassische und moderne Musik: die „Carmina Burana" von Carl Orff, den „Messias" von Georg Friedrich Händel oder Stücke der „Beatles". Das Beste ist aber die Gemeinschaft unter uns 50 Leuten.
– Arne, 17:
– Ich bin in unserer evangelischen Kirchengemeinde aktiv. Seit zwei Jahren helfe ich bei Jugendfreizeiten. Dieses Jahr fahre ich mit 13- bis 17-jährigen Schülern nach Frankreich. Meine Freunde und ich bereiten die Fahrten vor. Wir entwerfen das Programm mit Liederabenden, Workshops, Spielen und Gottesdiensten. Wir kümmern uns um die Unterkunft, die Verpflegung, die Reiseapotheke, die Zimmerverteilung und den Spüldienst. Bei der Planung gibt es meistens viel zu lachen. Während der Reise ist man für vieles verantwortlich. Man muss auf vieles achten. Schön ist, dass man viele Leute und Landschaften kennen lernt. Selbst, wenn man vorher viel Arbeit hatte.
– Sabrina und Anne, beide 14:
– Wir betreuen die Mädchenturngruppe unseres Turnvereins „Blau-Weiß Annen". Das machen wir seit fast drei Jahren. Unsere „Babys" sind 6 bis 11 Jahre alt. 15 bis 20 Mädels kommen regelmäßig. Die Begeisterung der Kleinen ist klasse. Am schönsten finden sie das Turnen auf Bodenmatten, am Reck, am Stufenbarren und am Schwebebalken.
– Die Kleinen sind immer gut gelaunt. Sie erzählen uns viele Geschichten aus ihrem Alltag. Sie haben Vertrauen zu uns. Das ist die Belohnung für unsere Zeit und Mühe. Vielleicht sind wir bessere Ansprechpartner als die Erwachsenen. Wir möchten dieses Ehrenamt noch lange machen.

1b Lies jetzt den Artikel aus *JUMA* und vergleich ihn mit deinen Notizen. (AT3 Level 7)

Pupils read the article and compare it with the notes they made from the listening activity.

1c Wer ist das?

Pupils answer ten *wer?* questions on the article. Some questions have more than one answer.

Answers

1 Sabrina und Anne, **2** Semir, **3** Martina, **4** Arne, **5** Semir, **6** Arne, **7** Sabrina und Anne, **8** Martina, **9** Semir, Sabrina und Anne, **10** Martina

Ludwig: Coping with new vocabulary in a text

Point out Ludwig's strategies for coping with a reading text, reminding pupils that they often don't need to understand every word to do the activities. If they really need to know an unfamiliar word, they could use a dictionary or work with a friend who might know.

1d Beantworte die Fragen.

Pupils answer five comprehension questions in German on each of the teenagers in the article. They should answer in full sentences.

Answers

1 Er arbeitet mit Christian. **2** Ja. Die Arbeit gefällt ihm sehr gut. **3** Sie haben nie schlechte Laune. **4** Er spielt in einem anderen Verein. **5** Es heißt: „Always be tolerant", oder: „Always get along with each other". **6** Sie ist seit über sieben Jahren dort. **7** Sie leitet die Übungsgruppe. **8** Sie macht Werbeplakate. **9** Er singt klassische und moderne Musik. **10** Es gibt 50 Leute im Chor. **11** Er hilft in der evangelischen Kirchengemeinde. **12** Er fährt mit 13- bis 17-jährigen Schülern nach Frankreich.
13 Liederabende, Workshops, Spiele und Gottesdienste stehen auf dem Programm. **14** Er plant die Unterkunft, die Verpflegung, die Reiseapotheke, die Zimmerverteilung und den Spüldienst. **15** Es gefällt ihm, dass man viele

Leute und Landschaften kennen lernt. **16** Sie betreuen die Mädchenturngruppe ihres Turnvereins. **17** Sie machen das seit fast drei Jahren. **18** In der Gruppe sind 15 bis 20 Mädels im Alter von 6 bis 11. **19** Ihnen gefällt das Turnen auf Bodenmatten, am Reck, am Stufenbarren und am Schwebebalken. **20** Die Kinder haben Vertrauen zu ihnen.

1e Welchen Job findest du am interessantesten? Übersetze den Absatz ins Englische.

Pupils decide which piece of voluntary work they find the most interesting and then translate that paragraph into English.

2 Partnerarbeit. Übt Interviews mit den Jugendlichen aus dem Artikel. (AT2 Level 7)

Pupils work in pairs to conduct interviews with the teenagers from the article.

3 Was ist für dich ein idealer Job in Ehren? Schreib einen Absatz darüber für den Artikel. (AT4 Level 7)

Pupils write a paragraph about what would be ideal voluntary work for them.

Lernzieltest and Wiederholung (pp. 92–93)

Resources • Cassette C, Side B • Workbook pp. 48–50 • R & A File: Wortschatz pp. 99–100	Lernzieltest p. 101 Kontrolle 5 pp. 102–111 (including teacher's notes)

At the end of each chapter there is a revision unit for pupils to use before the assessment materials. The unit begins with a *Lernzieltest* (like the *Mini-Test*) for pupils to test themselves on key language from the chapter. This is also provided as a checklist for pupils to write on (R & A File p. 101) and some related gapped sentences are also provided on p. 50 of the Workbook.

If pupils are unsure of any of the language, they should be encouraged to revise the relevant unit in the chapter. A complete wordlist containing key words and phrases from the whole chapter is provided on the *Wortschatz* sheets (R & A File pp. 99–100).

Wiederholung provides pupils with revision exercises in the four skills. The listening exercises should be done in class, but the other exercises could be done either in class or for homework. Further revision exercises are provided on pp. 48–49 of the Workbook.

Wiederholung

Hören

1 Hör zu. Schreib die Tabelle ab und füll sie aus. (1–4) (AT1 Levels 5–6)

Pupils listen to four interviews with teenagers about their part-time work and note the details in a grid. Pupils need to listen out for the type of job, when it is done, what it is like and what each teenager is saving for.

Answers

	wo?	wann?	wie?	sparen?
1	Restaurant	samstags 10–4	interessant	Mofa
2	Babysitting	freitags 5–8	klasse	die Ferien
3	Supermarkt	jeden Tag 5–7	anstrengend	Computer
4	trage Zeitungen aus	jeden Tag 6–7	O.K.	Fahrrad

1 – Also, sag mal, hast du einen Job?
– Hmm, ja, ich arbeite im Restaurant.
– Ach, im Restaurant? Das finde ich sehr gut. Und wann arbeitest du dort?
– Meistens arbeite ich samstags von zehn Uhr bis vier Uhr, aber manchmal dauert es etwas länger.
– Aha. Und wie gefällt es dir dort?
– Na ja, eigentlich finde ich es sehr interessant.
– Das kann ich mir vorstellen. Und sag mal, sparst du denn dein Geld?
– Ja, ich würde mir gerne mal ein Mofa kaufen, aber dafür muss ich noch sehr viel arbeiten und es dauert noch ein bisschen.

2 – Und du? Sag mal, hast du denn auch einen Job?
– Ja, manchmal mache ich Babysitting.
– Aha, Babysitting. Das klingt schön. Und wie oft machst du das?
– Das mache ich immer freitags von fünf bis acht Uhr.
– Aha, freitags von fünf Uhr bis acht Uhr. Drei Stunden. Sehr gut. Und gefällt dir das?
– Ja, also, ich finde es klasse, aber letztes Wochende war es echt furchtbar, weil die Kinder sehr schlecht aufgelegt waren.
– O ja, das kann ich mir vorstellen. Aber sag mal, hast du dann große Pläne für dein Geld? Sparst du das Geld oder gibst du es gleich aus?
– Nein, also, ich spare für die Ferien. Im Sommer werde ich hoffentlich nach Spanien fahren, aber dafür werde ich wirklich eine ganze Menge Geld brauchen.

3 – Und du? Sag bloß, du machst auch Babysitting!
– Nein, ganz im Gegenteil. Ich arbeite im Supermarkt.
– Was? Wie bitte?
– Ich arbeite jetzt im Supermarkt.
– Ach, so. Aha. Aber sag mal, wann machst du das?
– Na ja, im Allgemeinen mache ich das jeden Tag von fünf Uhr bis sieben.
– Jeden Tag von fünf Uhr bis sieben Uhr. Und wie findest du das?
– Na ja, wie soll man das beschreiben? Es ist ziemlich ... anstrengend.
– Ja, das kann ich mir vorstellen. Und was machst du mit dem Geld? Sparst du dein Geld?
– Ja, also, mein Traum ist eigentlich ein Computer.

4 – Und du? Hast du auch einen Job?
– Na ja, ich trage Zeitungen aus. Das ist mir jetzt auch ein bisschen peinlich.
– Du trägst Zeitungen aus. Und wann trägst du Zeitungen aus?
– Na ... das ist – also ich muss immer so früh aufstehen. Ich mach das von sechs bis sieben Uhr.
– Von sechs bis sieben Uhr. Das ist ja schrecklich – so früh!
– Hmm, das ist O.K. Heute war es richtig cool, weil es so sonnig war. So einen Tag kann ich nicht vergessen.
– Das klingt doch gar nicht so uninteressant. Was machst du denn mit dem Geld, das du verdienst? Sparst du es oder sparst du es nicht?
– Ja, im Moment spare ich auf ein neues Fahrrad mit cooler Federung. Hoffentlich werde ich es mir Ende Mai leisten können.

Sprechen

2 Partnerarbeit. Mach Interviews mit folgenden Fragen. (AT2 Level 5)

Pupils conduct interviews about (imaginary) part-time work, using the questions provided.

Lesen

3 Lies die E-Mail und beantworte die Fragen. (AT3 Level 5–6)

Pupils read an e-mail from Kim about her new jobs and answer ten comprehension questions on it in German. They should answer in full sentences.

Answers

1 Sie trägt Zeitungen aus und sie macht Babysitting.
2 Am Wochenende muss sie um sieben Uhr aufstehen.
3 Sie muss immer pünktlich und freundlich sein. **4** Am Samstag ist sie vierzig Minuten zu spät zum Kiosk gekommen. **5** Sie hat einen zweiten Wecker gekauft.
6 Am Mittwochabend hat Kim Babysitting gemacht. Das Kind war krank und es hat den ganzen Abend geheult.
7 Beim Zeitungen-Austragen verdient sie mehr. **8** Sie wird eine neue Stereoanlage kaufen. **9** Sie braucht sie, weil ihre Stereoanlage sehr alt und fast kaputt ist.
10 Sie hatte eine Katastrophe mit der Suppe.

Schreiben

4 Schreib eine Antwort an Kim und vergleich sie mit deinem Partner / deiner Partnerin. Wer hatte die größte Katastrophe? (AT4 Levels 5–7)

Pupils write a reply to Kim in which they describe a catastrophic experience at work. Pupils then compare their replies to see who has the more catastrophic tale to tell.

EXTRA

The EXTRA pages at the back of the Pupil's Book are intended to provide consolidation/reinforcement activities (EXTRA A) and more challenging / extension activities (EXTRA B). The exercises concentrate on the skills of reading and writing only. They could be used for differentiated work in class or at home. The best place to use each activity is clearly indicated in these notes, just above the exercise rubric, e. g. [after pp. 80–81].

EXTRA A (p. 118)

[after pp. 80–81]

1a Sieh dir die Anzeigen an. Was passt zusammen? (AT3 Level 3)

Pupils read five newspaper job adverts and match them to the pictures.

Answers

1 d, **2** e, **3** a, **4** c, **5** b

1b Lies die Texte. Welcher Job passt für ihn/sie am besten? (AT3 Level 3)

Pupils read descriptions of five teenagers and decide which of the job adverts suits each person best.

Answers

a 3, **b** 2, **c** 1, **d** 4, **e** 5

[after pp. 86–87]

2a Sieh dir die Bilder an. Wer spricht? (AT3 Level 2)

Pupils read descriptions of what people are wearing and match them to the pictures.

Answers

1 b, **2** a, **3** b, **4** a, **5** c, **6** b, **7** d, **8** b

2b Zeichne und beschrifte ein Partyoutfit für dich. (AT4 Levels 3–4)

Pupils draw and write a description of their own party outfit – the more outrageous the better!

EXTRA B (p. 119)

[after pp. 80–81]

1a Lies die Texte und beantworte die Fragen. (AT3 Levels 4–5)

Pupils read three speech bubbles about teenagers' job opportunities and answer the questions. They need not answer in full sentences, although full sentence answers are provided here.

Answers

1 Er muss computererfahren sein, weil er einen Job im Internet hat. **2** Man besucht seine Website, wenn man etwas verkaufen oder kaufen will. **3** Er arbeitet jeden Tag vor der Schule und auch am Nachmittag und am Wochenende. **4** Er arbeitet in seinem Zimmer.
5 Sie kommt aus einem kleinen Dorf in Süddeutschland.
6 Es gibt keine Jobs für junge Leute im Dorf. **7** Sie wird ihre Kusine in München besuchen und sie werden beide in einem Friseursalon arbeiten. **8** Im Sommer arbeitet er im Supermarkt in der Stadt und im Winter arbeitet er an der Skischule. **9** Der Job gefällt ihm, weil er sehr sportlich ist und sehr gern Ski fährt. **10** Man muss immer sehr geduldig und pünktlich sein.

1b Schreib eine kurze Präsentation über deinen idealen Job. Lies sie der Klasse vor. (AT4 Levels 4–5)

Pupils imagine that they have the perfect job and write a presentation about it. The presentations can then be read out in class and the best job chosen.

[after pp. 86–87]

2a Sieh dir die Bilder auf Seite 118 Übung 2a an. Beschrifte sie. (AT4 Levels 3–4)

Pupils look at the pictures on page 118 and describe the outfits.

Answers

a Ich trage ein enges grünes T-Shirt, dicke Stiefel und eine Sonnenbrille. **b** Ich habe lange Haare. Ich trage einen gelben Rock, eine Perlenschnur, eine weiße Jacke, weiße Sandalen und eine Bluse mit Blumenmuster. **c** Ich trage braune Stiefel, ein langes blaues Kleid und große Ohrringe. **d** Ich trage einen gelben und grünen Hut, ein blaues T-Shirt, graue Schuhe und eine karierte Hose.

2b Zeichne und beschrifte ein Partyoutfit für dich wie auf Seite 118 Übung 2b. (AT4 Level 4)

Pupils draw and write a description of their own party outfit – the more outrageous the better!

Workbook

p. 41

1 (AT3 Level 4)

Nicola	Gartenarbeit	samstags, 10–3	sehr interessant
Michael	Supermarkt	in den Ferien	echt klasse
Kylie	Zeitungen	jeden Tag, 6–7 Uhr	O.K.
Tobias	Babysitting	freitags	ziemlich langweilig
Jasmin	Restaurant	am Wochenende	anstrengend

2 (AT4 Level 4)

individual answers

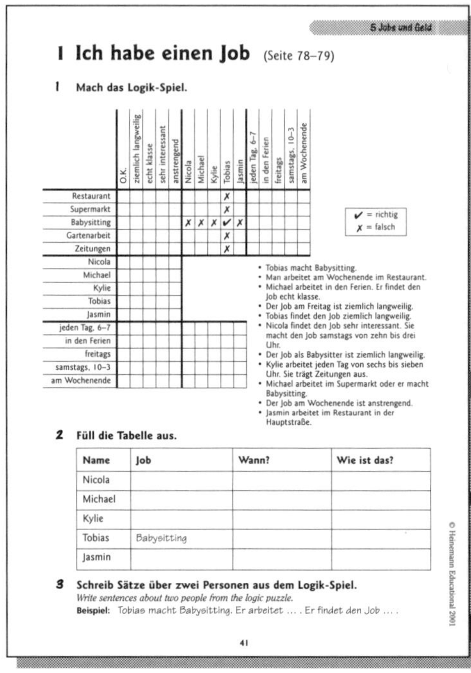
5 Jobs und Geld

1 Ich habe einen Job (Seite 78–79)

1 Mach das Logik-Spiel.

✔ = richtig
✗ = falsch

- Tobias macht Babysitting.
- Man arbeitet am Wochenende im Restaurant.
- Michael arbeitet in den Ferien. Er findet den Job echt klasse.
- Der Job am Freitag ist ziemlich langweilig.
- Tobias findet den Job ziemlich langweilig.
- Nicola findet den Job sehr interessant. Sie macht den Job samstags von zehn bis drei Uhr.
- Der Job als Babysitter ist ziemlich langweilig.
- Kylie arbeitet jeden Tag von sechs bis sieben Uhr. Sie trägt Zeitungen aus.
- Michael arbeitet im Supermarkt oder er macht Babysitting.
- Der Job am Wochenende ist anstrengend.
- Jasmin arbeitet im Restaurant in der Hauptstraße.

2 Füll die Tabelle aus.

Name	Job	Wann?	Wie ist das?
Nicola			
Michael			
Kylie			
Tobias	Babysitting		
Jasmin			

3 Schreib Sätze über zwei Personen aus dem Logik-Spiel.
Write sentences about two people from the logic puzzle.
Beispiel: Tobias macht Babysitting. Er arbeitet … . Er findet den Job … .

41

p. 42

1 **1** intelligent, **2** vernünftig, **3** sportlich, **4** pünktlich, **5** höflich, **6** fleißig, **7** freundlich

2 (AT3 Level 4)

1 intelligent, **2** pünktlich, **3** freundlich, **4** ordentlich, **5** computererfahren, **6** hilfsbereit, **7** vernünftig, **8** fleißig, **9** geduldig, **10** sportlich, **11** gut gelaunt

3 (AT4 Levels 4–5)

individual answers

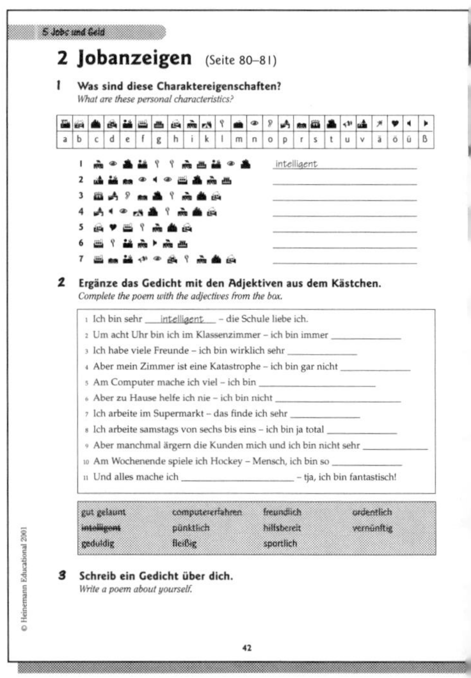
5 Jobs und Geld

2 Jobanzeigen (Seite 80–81)

1 Was sind diese Charaktereigenschaften?
What are these personal characteristics?

1 intelligent

2 Ergänze das Gedicht mit den Adjektiven aus dem Kästchen.
Complete the poem with the adjectives from the box.

1 Ich bin sehr intelligent – die Schule liebe ich.
2 Um acht Uhr bin ich im Klassenzimmer – ich bin immer ______
3 Ich habe viele Freunde – ich bin wirklich sehr ______
4 Aber mein Zimmer ist eine Katastrophe – ich bin gar nicht ______
5 Am Computer mache ich viel – ich bin ______
6 Aber zu Hause helfe ich nie – ich bin nicht ______
7 Ich arbeite im Supermarkt – das finde ich sehr ______
8 Ich arbeite samstags von sechs bis eins – ich bin ja total ______
9 Aber manchmal ärgern die Kunden mich und ich bin nicht sehr ______
10 Am Wochenende spiele ich Hockey – Mensch, ich bin so ______
11 Und alles mache ich ______ – tja, ich bin fantastisch!

gut gelaunt	computererfahren	freundlich	ordentlich
~~intelligent~~	pünktlich	hilfsbereit	vernünftig
geduldig	fleißig	sportlich	

3 Schreib ein Gedicht über dich.
Write a poem about yourself.

42

p. 43

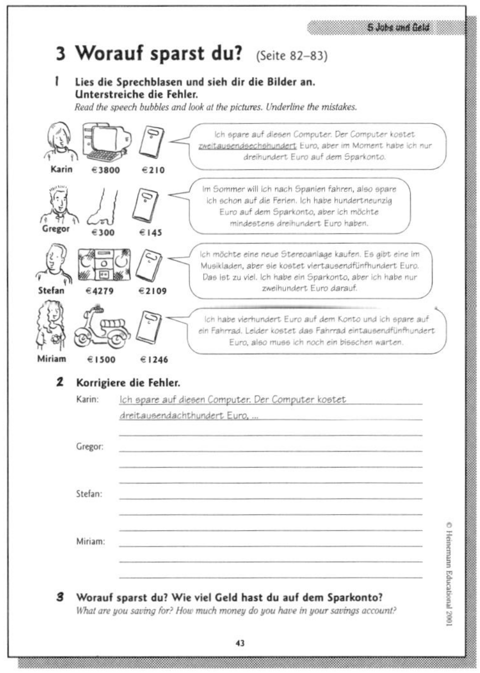

3 Worauf sparst du? (Seite 82–83)

1 Lies die Sprechblasen und sieh dir die Bilder an. Unterstreiche die Fehler.
Read the speech bubbles and look at the pictures. Underline the mistakes.

2 Korrigiere die Fehler.

Karin: Ich spare auf diesen Computer. Der Computer kostet dreitausendachthundert Euro, ...

Gregor:

Stefan:

Miriam:

3 Worauf sparst du? Wie viel Geld hast du auf dem Sparkonto?
What are you saving for? How much money do you have in your savings account?

43

1 & 2 (AT3 Level 4)

Karin: Der Computer kostet ~~zweitausendsechshundert~~ **dreitausendachthundert** Euro, aber im Moment habe ich nur ~~dreihundert~~ **zweihundertzehn** Euro auf dem Sparkonto.

Gregor: Im Sommer will ich nach ~~Spanien~~ **Italien** fahren, also spare ich schon auf die Ferien. Ich habe ~~hundertneunzig~~ **hundertfünfundvierzig** Euro auf dem Sparkonto … .

Stefan: … aber sie kostet ~~viertausendfünfhundert~~ **viertausendzweihundertneunundsiebzig** Euro. … Ich habe ein Sparkonto, aber ich habe nur ~~zweihundert~~ **zweitausendeinhundertneun** Euro darauf.

Miriam: Ich habe ~~vierhundert~~ **eintausendzweihundertsechsundvierzig** Euro auf dem Konto … .

3 (AT4 Levels 3–4)

individual answers

p. 44

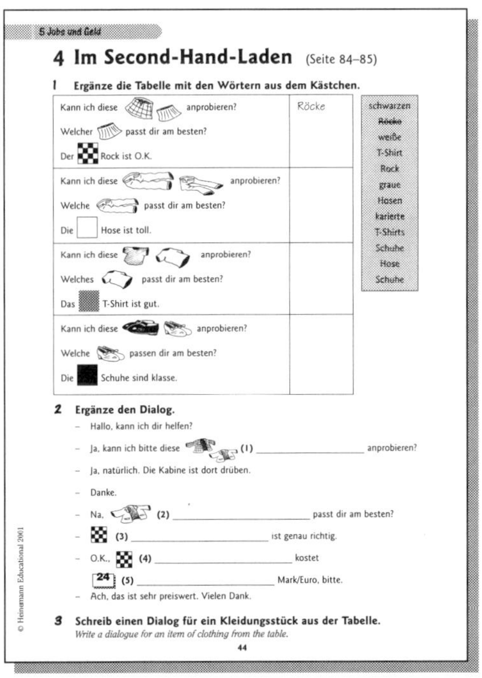

4 Im Second-Hand-Laden (Seite 84–85)

1 Ergänze die Tabelle mit den Wörtern aus dem Kästchen.

Kann ich diese anprobieren? Welcher passt dir am besten? Der Rock ist O.K.	Röcke
Kann ich diese anprobieren? Welche passt dir am besten? Die Hose ist toll.	
Kann ich diese anprobieren? Welches passt dir am besten? Das T-Shirt ist gut.	
Kann ich diese anprobieren? Welche passen dir am besten? Die Schuhe sind klasse.	

schwarzen, ~~Röcke~~, weiße, T-Shirt, Rock, graue, Hosen, karierte, T-Shirts, Schuhe, Hose, Schuhe

2 Ergänze den Dialog.

– Hallo, kann ich dir helfen?
– Ja, kann ich bitte diese (1) ______ anprobieren?
– Ja, natürlich. Die Kabine ist dort drüben.
– Danke.
– Na, (2) ______ passt dir am besten?
– (3) ______ ist genau richtig.
– O.K., (4) ______ kostet
24 (5) ______ Mark/Euro, bitte.
– Ach, das ist sehr preiswert. Vielen Dank.

3 Schreib einen Dialog für ein Kleidungsstück aus der Tabelle.
Write a dialogue for an item of clothing from the table.

44

p. 45

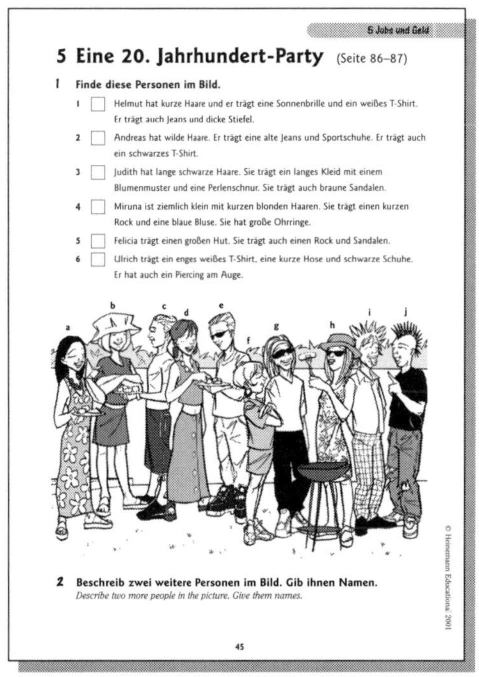

5 Eine 20. Jahrhundert-Party (Seite 86–87)

1 Finde diese Personen im Bild.

1 ☐ Helmut hat kurze Haare und er trägt eine Sonnenbrille und ein weißes T-Shirt. Er trägt auch Jeans und dicke Stiefel.
2 ☐ Andreas hat wilde Haare. Er trägt eine alte Jeans und Sportschuhe. Er trägt auch ein schwarzes T-Shirt.
3 ☐ Judith hat lange schwarze Haare. Sie trägt ein langes Kleid mit einem Blumenmuster und eine Perlenschnur. Sie trägt auch braune Sandalen.
4 ☐ Miruna ist ziemlich klein mit kurzen blonden Haaren. Sie trägt einen kurzen Rock und eine blaue Bluse. Sie hat große Ohrringe.
5 ☐ Felicia trägt einen großen Hut. Sie trägt auch einen Rock und Sandalen.
6 ☐ Ulrich trägt ein enges weißes T-Shirt, eine kurze Hose und schwarze Schuhe. Er hat auch ein Piercing am Auge.

2 Beschreib zwei weitere Personen im Bild. Gib ihnen Namen.
Describe two more people in the picture. Give them names.

45

1 Röcke, Rock, karierte; Hosen, Hose, weiße; T-Shirts, T-Shirt, graue; Schuhe, Schuhe, schwarzen.

2 (AT4 Levels 2–3)

1 Jacken, **2** welche Jacke, **3** Die karierte Jacke, **4** die karierte Jacke, **5** vierundzwanzig

3 (AT4 Level 4)

individual answers

1 (AT3 Level 3)

1 e, **2** j, **3** a, **4** f, **5** b, **6** c

2 (AT4 Level 4)

individual answers

p. 46

1 **a** Computer, **b** Walkman, **c** Sonnenbrille, **d** Hose, **e** Stereoanlage, **f** Fahrrad, **g** Kleid, **h** Handy, **i** Stiefel, **j** Sportschuhe, **k** CDs

2 (AT3 Level 4)

Suggested answers: **Amelie:** b, k, **Corinne:** h, **Peter:** c, d, i

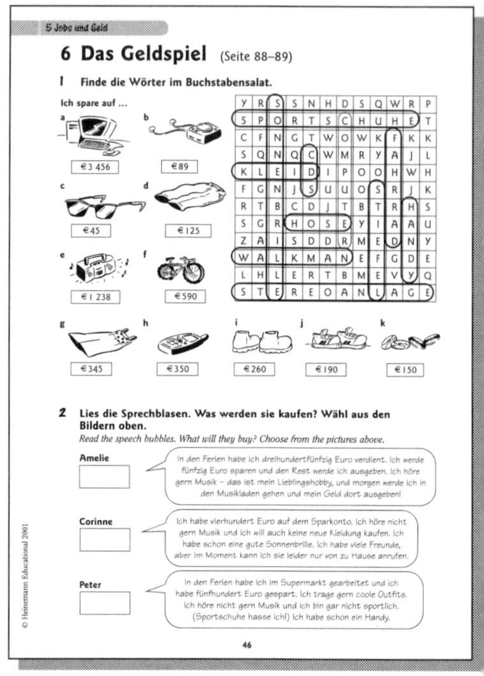

6 Das Geldspiel (Seite 88–89)

1 Finde die Wörter im Buchstabensalat.

Ich spare auf …

a €3 456
b €89
c €45
d €125
e €1 238
f €590
g €345
h €350
i €260
j €190
k €150

Y	R	S	S	N	H	D	S	Q	W	R	P
S	P	O	R	T	S	C	H	U	H	E	T
C	F	N	G	T	W	O	W	K	F	K	K
S	Q	N	Q	C	W	M	R	Y	A	J	L
K	L	E	I	D	I	P	O	O	H	W	H
F	G	N	J	S	U	U	O	S	R	J	K
R	T	B	C	D	J	T	B	T	R	H	S
S	G	R	H	O	S	E	Y	I	A	A	U
Z	A	I	S	D	D	R	M	E	D	N	Y
W	A	L	K	M	A	N	E	F	G	D	E
L	H	L	E	R	T	B	M	E	V	Y	Q
S	T	E	R	E	O	A	N	L	A	G	E

2 Lies die Sprechblasen. Was werden sie kaufen? Wähl aus den Bildern oben.

Read the speech bubbles. What will they buy? Choose from the pictures above.

Amelie

In den Ferien habe ich dreihundertfünfzig Euro verdient. Ich werde fünfzig Euro sparen und den Rest werde ich ausgeben. Ich höre gern Musik – das ist mein Lieblingshobby, und morgen werde ich in den Musikladen gehen und mein Geld dort ausgeben!

Corinne

Ich habe vierhundert Euro auf dem Sparkonto. Ich höre nicht gern Musik und ich will auch keine neue Kleidung kaufen. Ich habe schon eine gute Sonnenbrille. Ich habe viele Freunde, aber im Moment kann ich sie leider nur von zu Hause anrufen.

Peter

In den Ferien habe ich im Supermarkt gearbeitet und ich habe fünfhundert Euro gespart. Ich trage gern coole Outfits. Ich höre nicht gern Musik und ich bin gar nicht sportlich. (Sportschuhe hasse ich!) Ich habe schon ein Handy.

p. 47

1 **1** Welcher Rock passt dir am besten? Der blaue Rock ist zu lang, der gelbe Rock ist zu klein, aber der weiße Rock ist genau richtig!
2 Welche Jacke passt dir am besten? Die rote Jacke ist zu groß, die braune Jacke ist zu klein, aber die schwarze Jacke ist genau richtig!
3 Welches T-Shirt passt dir am besten? Das grüne T-Shirt ist zu groß, das schwarze T-Shirt ist zu kurz, aber das blaue T-Shirt ist genau richtig!

2 **1** Lisa trägt einen gelben Hut. **2** Dominik trägt einen großen Ohrring. **3** Jasmin trägt eine schwarze Sonnenbrille. **4** Peter trägt braune Sandalen. **5** Veronika trägt ein sehr enges T-Shirt.

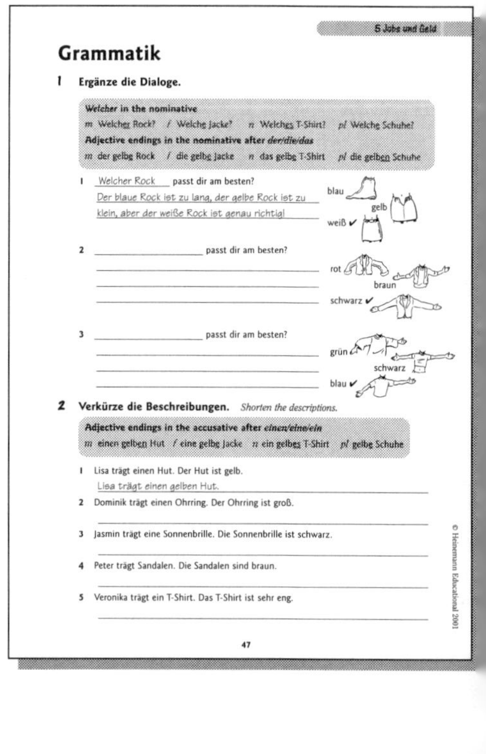

Grammatik

1 Ergänze die Dialoge.

***Welcher* in the nominative**
m Welcher Rock? *f* Welche Jacke? *n* Welches T-Shirt? *pl* Welche Schuhe?
Adjective endings in the nominative after *der/die/das*
m der gelbe Rock *f* die gelbe Jacke *n* das gelbe T-Shirt *pl* die gelben Schuhe

1 Welcher Rock passt dir am besten?
Der blaue Rock ist zu lang, der gelbe Rock ist zu klein, aber der weiße Rock ist genau richtig!

blau
gelb
weiß ✔

2 ______ passt dir am besten?

rot
braun
schwarz ✔

3 ______ passt dir am besten?

grün
schwarz
blau ✔

2 Verkürze die Beschreibungen. *Shorten the descriptions.*

Adjective endings in the accusative after *einen/eine/ein*
m einen gelben Hut *f* eine gelbe Jacke *n* ein gelbes T-Shirt *pl* gelbe Schuhe

1 Lisa trägt einen Hut. Der Hut ist gelb.
Lisa trägt einen gelben Hut.
2 Dominik trägt einen Ohrring. Der Ohrring ist groß.
3 Jasmin trägt eine Sonnenbrille. Die Sonnenbrille ist schwarz.
4 Peter trägt Sandalen. Die Sandalen sind braun.
5 Veronika trägt ein T-Shirt. Das T-Shirt ist sehr eng.

p. 48

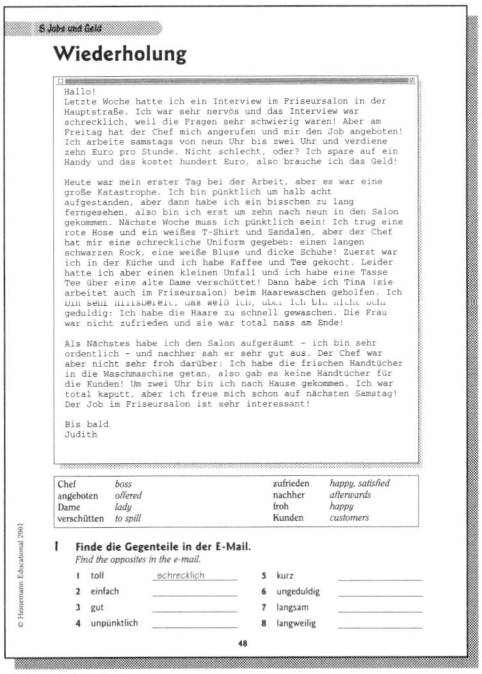

5 Jobs und Geld

Wiederholung

Hallo!
Letzte Woche hatte ich ein Interview im Friseursalon in der Hauptstraße. Ich war sehr nervös und das Interview war schrecklich, weil die Fragen sehr schwierig waren! Aber am Freitag hat der Chef mich angerufen und mir den Job angeboten! Ich arbeite samstags von neun Uhr bis zwei Uhr und verdiene zehn Euro pro Stunde. Nicht schlecht, oder? Ich spare auf ein Handy und das kostet hundert Euro, also brauche ich das Geld!

Heute war mein erster Tag bei der Arbeit, aber es war eine große Katastrophe. Ich bin pünktlich um halb acht aufgestanden, aber dann habe ich ein bisschen zu lang ferngesehen, also bin ich erst um zehn nach neun in den Salon gekommen. Nächste Woche muss ich pünktlich sein! Ich trug eine rote Hose und ein weißes T-Shirt und Sandalen, aber der Chef hat mir eine schreckliche Uniform gegeben: einen langen schwarzen Rock, eine weiße Bluse und dicke Schuhe! Zuerst war ich in der Küche und ich habe Kaffee und Tee gekocht. Leider hatte ich aber einen kleinen Unfall und ich habe eine Tasse Tee über eine alte Dame verschüttet! Dann habe ich Tina (sie arbeitet auch im Friseursalon) beim Haarewaschen geholfen. Ich bin sehr hilfsbereit, das weiß ich, aber ich bin nicht sehr geduldig: Ich habe die Haare zu schnell gewaschen. Die Frau war nicht zufrieden und sie war total nass am Ende!

Als Nächstes habe ich den Salon aufgeräumt – ich bin sehr ordentlich – und nachher sah er sehr gut aus. Der Chef war aber nicht sehr froh darüber: Ich habe die frischen Handtücher in die Waschmaschine getan, also gab es keine Handtücher für die Kunden! Um zwei Uhr bin ich nach Hause gekommen. Ich war total kaputt, aber ich freue mich schon auf nächsten Samstag! Der Job im Friseursalon ist sehr interessant!

Bis bald
Judith

Chef	*boss*	zufrieden	*happy, satisfied*
angeboten	*offered*	nachher	*afterwards*
Dame	*lady*	froh	*happy*
verschütten	*to spill*	Kunden	*customers*

1 Finde die Gegenteile in der E-Mail.
Find the opposites in the e-mail.

1 toll schrecklich	5 kurz
2 einfach	6 ungeduldig
3 gut	7 langsam
4 unpünktlich	8 langweilig

48

1a (AT3 Levels 5–6)
1 schrecklich, **2** schwierig, **3** schlecht, **4** pünktlich, **5** lang, **6** geduldig, **7** schnell, **8** interessant

p. 49

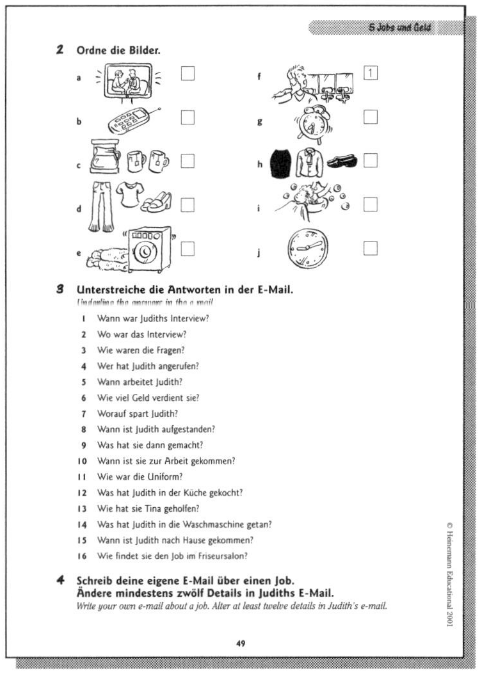

5 Jobs und Geld

2 Ordne die Bilder.

a, b, c, d, e, f 1, g, h, i, j

3 Unterstreiche die Antworten in der E-Mail.
Underline the answers in the e-mail.

1 Wann war Judiths Interview?
2 Wo war das Interview?
3 Wie waren die Fragen?
4 Wer hat Judith angerufen?
5 Wann arbeitet Judith?
6 Wie viel Geld verdient sie?
7 Worauf spart Judith?
8 Wann ist Judith aufgestanden?
9 Was hat sie dann gemacht?
10 Wann ist sie zur Arbeit gekommen?
11 Wie war die Uniform?
12 Was hat Judith in der Küche gekocht?
13 Wie hat sie Tina geholfen?
14 Was hat Judith in die Waschmaschine getan?
15 Wann ist Judith nach Hause gekommen?
16 Wie findet sie den Job im Friseursalon?

4 Schreib deine eigene E-Mail über einen Job. Ändere mindestens zwölf Details in Judiths E-Mail.
Write your own e-mail about a job. Alter at least twelve details in Judith's e-mail.

49

2 (AT3 Levels 5–6)
f, b, g, a, j, d, h, c, i, e
3 (AT3 Levels 5–6)
1 Letzte Woche, **2** im Friseursalon in der Hauptstraße, **3** sehr schwierig, **4** der Chef, **5** samstags von neun Uhr bis zwei Uhr, **6** zehn Euro pro Stunde, **7** ein Handy, **8** um halb acht, **9** ferngesehen, **10** um zehn nach neun, **11** schrecklich – einen schwarzen Rock, eine weiße Bluse und dicke Schuhe, **12** Kaffee und Tee, **13** beim Haarewaschen, **14** die frischen Handtücher, **15** Um zwei Uhr, **16** sehr interessant
4 (AT4 Levels 5–6)
individual answers

p. 50

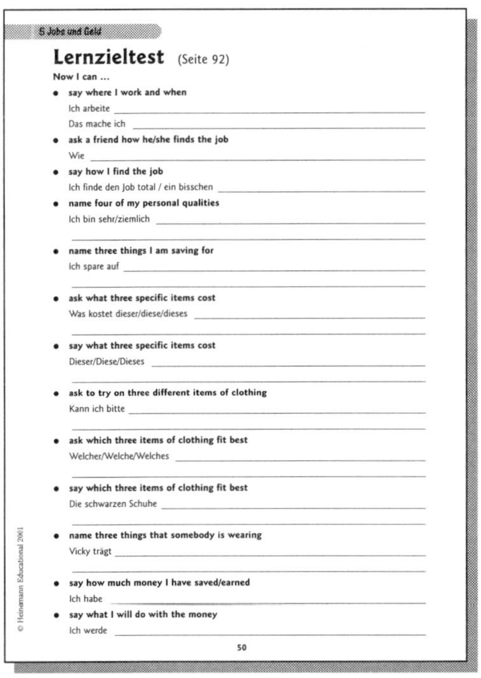

5 Jobs und Geld

Lernzieltest (Seite 92)

Now I can ...

- **say where I work and when**
  Ich arbeite
  Das mache ich
- **ask a friend how he/she finds the job**
  Wie
- **say how I find the job**
  Ich finde den Job total / ein bisschen
- **name four of my personal qualities**
  Ich bin sehr/ziemlich
- **name three things I am saving for**
  Ich spare auf
- **ask what three specific items cost**
  Was kostet dieser/diese/dieses
- **say what three specific items cost**
  Dieser/Diese/Dieses
- **ask to try on three different items of clothing**
  Kann ich bitte
- **ask which three items of clothing fit best**
  Welcher/Welche/Welches
- **say which three items of clothing fit best**
  Die schwarzen Schuhe
- **name three things that somebody is wearing**
  Vicky trägt
- **say how much money I have saved/earned**
  Ich habe
- **say what I will do with the money**
  Ich werde

50

individual answers

Resource & Assessment File

Arbeitsblatt 1
p. 89

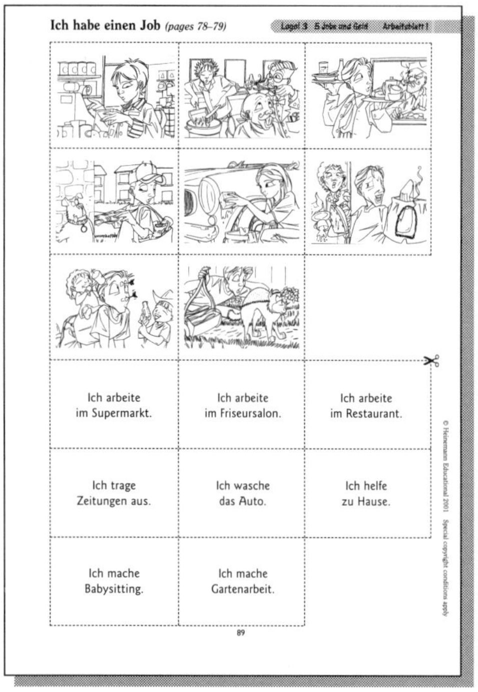
Ich habe einen Job *(pages 78–79)* Logo! 3 5 Jobs und Geld Arbeitsblatt 1

Ich arbeite im Supermarkt.	Ich arbeite im Friseursalon.	Ich arbeite im Restaurant.
Ich trage Zeitungen aus.	Ich wasche das Auto.	Ich helfe zu Hause.
Ich mache Babysitting.	Ich mache Gartenarbeit.	

© Heinemann Educational 2001. Special copyright conditions apply

89

Visuals of *Ich arbeite im Supermarkt. Ich arbeite im Friseursalon. Ich arbeite im Restaurant. Ich trage Zeitungen aus. Ich wasche das Auto. Ich helfe zu Hause. Ich mache Babysitting. Ich mache Gartenarbeit.*

Arbeitsblatt 2
p. 90

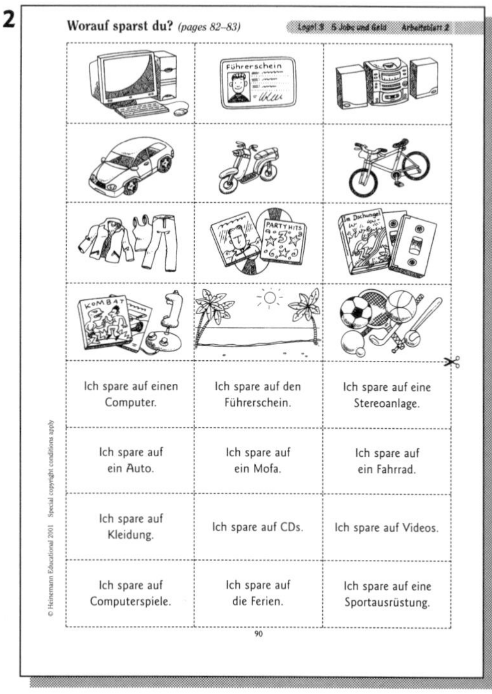
Worauf sparst du? *(pages 82–83)* Logo! 3 5 Jobs und Geld Arbeitsblatt 2

Ich spare auf einen Computer.	Ich spare auf den Führerschein.	Ich spare auf eine Stereoanlage.
Ich spare auf ein Auto.	Ich spare auf ein Mofa.	Ich spare auf ein Fahrrad.
Ich spare auf Kleidung.	Ich spare auf CDs.	Ich spare auf Videos.
Ich spare auf Computerspiele.	Ich spare auf die Ferien.	Ich spare auf eine Sportausrüstung.

© Heinemann Educational 2001. Special copyright conditions apply

90

Visuals of *Ich spare auf einen Computer, Ich spare auf den Führerschein, Ich spare auf eine Stereoanlage, Ich spare auf ein Auto, Ich spare auf ein Mofa, Ich spare auf ein Fahrrad, Ich spare auf Kleidung, Ich spare auf CDs, Ich spare auf Videos, Ich spare auf Computerspiele, Ich spare auf die Ferien, Ich spare auf Sportausrüstung.*

Arbeitsblatt 3
p. 91

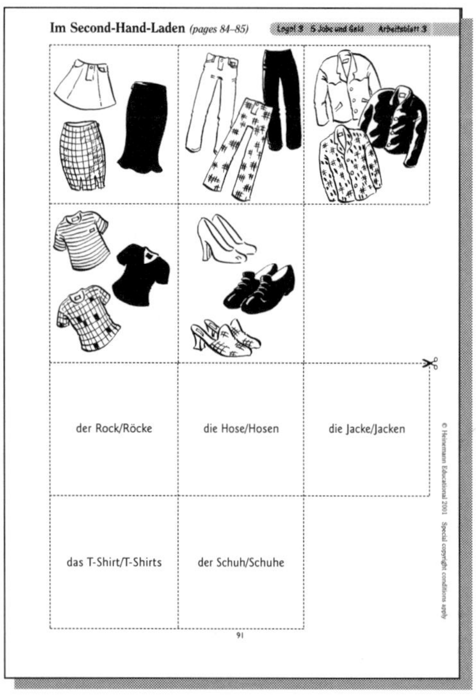
Im Second-Hand-Laden *(pages 84–85)* Logo! 3 5 Jobs und Geld Arbeitsblatt 3

der Rock/Röcke	die Hose/Hosen	die Jacke/Jacken
das T-Shirt/T-Shirts	der Schuh/Schuhe	

© Heinemann Educational 2001. Special copyright conditions apply

91

Visuals of *der Rock / Röcke, die Hose / Hosen, die Jacke / Jacken, das T-Shirt / T-Shirts, der Schuh / Schuhe*

Arbeitsblatt 4
p. 92

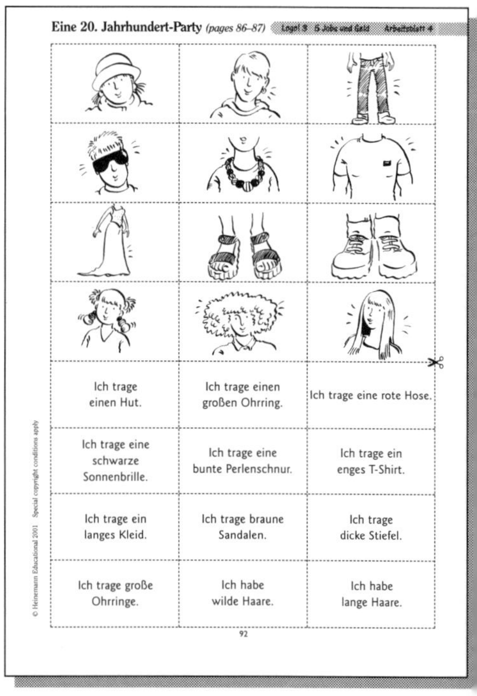
Eine 20. Jahrhundert-Party *(pages 86–87)* Logo! 3 5 Jobs und Geld Arbeitsblatt 4

Ich trage einen Hut.	Ich trage einen großen Ohrring.	Ich trage eine rote Hose.
Ich trage eine schwarze Sonnenbrille.	Ich trage eine bunte Perlenschnur.	Ich trage ein enges T-Shirt.
Ich trage ein langes Kleid.	Ich trage braune Sandalen.	Ich trage dicke Stiefel.
Ich trage große Ohrringe.	Ich habe wilde Haare.	Ich habe lange Haare.

© Heinemann Educational 2001. Special copyright conditions apply

92

Visuals of *Ich trage einen Hut, Ich trage einen großen Ohrring, Ich trage eine rote Hose, Ich trage eine schwarze Sonnenbrille, Ich trage eine bunte Perlenschnur, Ich trage ein enges T-Shirt, Ich trage ein langes Kleid, Ich trage braune Sandalen, Ich trage dicke Stiefel, Ich trage große Ohrringe, Ich habe wilde Haare, Ich habe lange Haare.*

Arbeitsblatt 5
p. 93

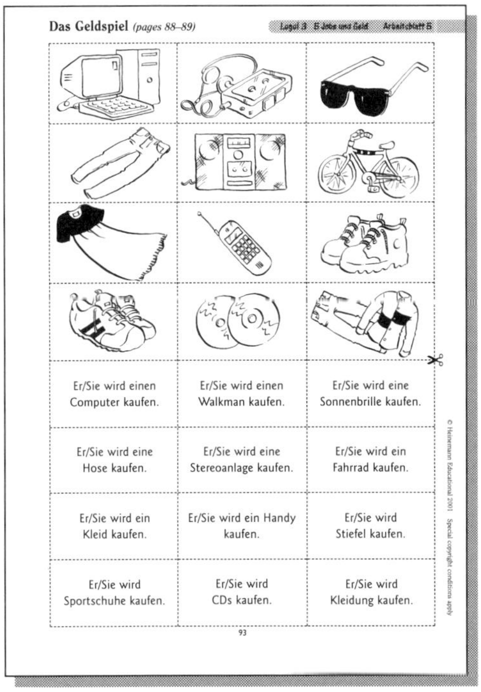

Das Geldspiel *(pages 88–89)* Logo! 3 5 Jobs und Geld Arbeitsblatt 5

Er/Sie wird einen Computer kaufen.	Er/Sie wird einen Walkman kaufen.	Er/Sie wird eine Sonnenbrille kaufen.
Er/Sie wird eine Hose kaufen.	Er/Sie wird eine Stereoanlage kaufen.	Er/Sie wird ein Fahrrad kaufen.
Er/Sie wird ein Kleid kaufen.	Er/Sie wird ein Handy kaufen.	Er/Sie wird Stiefel kaufen.
Er/Sie wird Sportschuhe kaufen.	Er/Sie wird CDs kaufen.	Er/Sie wird Kleidung kaufen.

93

Visuals of *Er/Sie wird einen Computer kaufen, Er/Sie wird einen Walkman kaufen, Er/Sie wird eine Sonnenbrille kaufen, Er/Sie wird eine Hose kaufen, Er/Sie wird eine Stereoanlage kaufen, Er/Sie wird ein Fahrrad kaufen, Er/Sie wird ein Kleid kaufen, Er/Sie wird ein Handy kaufen, Er/Sie wird Stiefel kaufen, Er/Sie wird Sportschuhe kaufen, Er/Sie wird CDs kaufen, Er/Sie wird Kleidung kaufen.*

Arbeitsblatt 6
p. 94

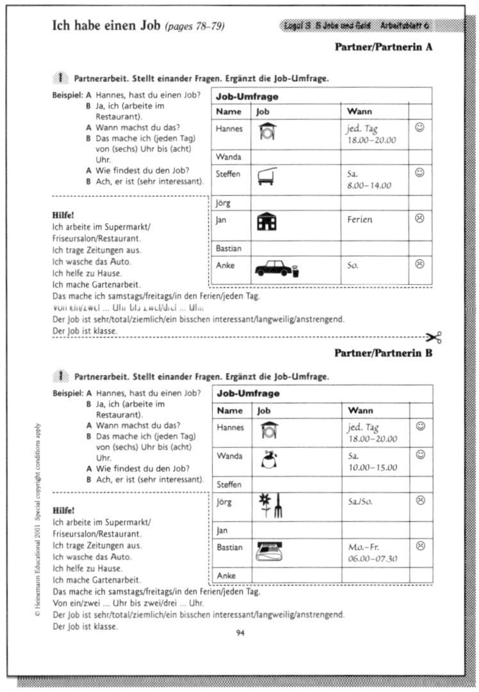

Ich habe einen Job *(pages 78–79)* Logo! 3 5 Jobs und Geld Arbeitsblatt 6

Partner/Partnerin A

1 Partnerarbeit. Stellt einander Fragen. Ergänzt die Job-Umfrage.

Beispiel: A Hannes, hast du einen Job?
B Ja, ich (arbeite im Restaurant).
A Wann machst du das?
B Das mache ich (jeden Tag) von (sechs) Uhr bis (acht) Uhr.
A Wie findest du den Job?
B Ach, er ist (sehr interessant).

Job-Umfrage

Name	Job	Wann	
Hannes		jed. Tag 18.00–20.00	☺
Wanda			
Steffen		Sa. 8.00–14.00	☺
Jörg			
Jan		Ferien	☹
Bastian			
Anke		So.	☹

Hilfe!
Ich arbeite im Supermarkt/Friseursalon/Restaurant.
Ich trage Zeitungen aus.
Ich wasche das Auto.
Ich helfe zu Hause.
Ich mache Gartenarbeit.
Das mache ich samstags/freitags/in den Ferien/jeden Tag.
Von ein/zwei ... Uhr bis zwei/drei ... Uhr.
Der Job ist sehr/total/ziemlich/ein bisschen interessant/langweilig/anstrengend.
Der Job ist klasse.

Partner/Partnerin B

1 Partnerarbeit. Stellt einander Fragen. Ergänzt die Job-Umfrage.

Beispiel: A Hannes, hast du einen Job?
B Ja, ich (arbeite im Restaurant).
A Wann machst du das?
B Das mache ich (jeden Tag) von (sechs) Uhr bis (acht) Uhr.
A Wie findest du den Job?
B Ach, er ist (sehr interessant).

Job-Umfrage

Name	Job	Wann	
Hannes		jed. Tag 18.00–20.00	☺
Wanda		Sa. 10.00–15.00	☺
Steffen			
Jörg		Sa./So.	☹
Jan			
Bastian		Mo.–Fr. 06.00–07.30	☹
Anke			

Hilfe!
Ich arbeite im Supermarkt/Friseursalon/Restaurant.
Ich trage Zeitungen aus.
Ich wasche das Auto.
Ich helfe zu Hause.
Ich mache Gartenarbeit.
Das mache ich samstags/freitags/in den Ferien/jeden Tag.
Von ein/zwei ... Uhr bis zwei/drei ... Uhr.
Der Job ist sehr/total/ziemlich/ein bisschen interessant/langweilig/anstrengend.
Der Job ist klasse.

94

Pairwork information-gap activity on job details.
AT2 Levels 4–5

Arbeitsblatt 7
p. 95

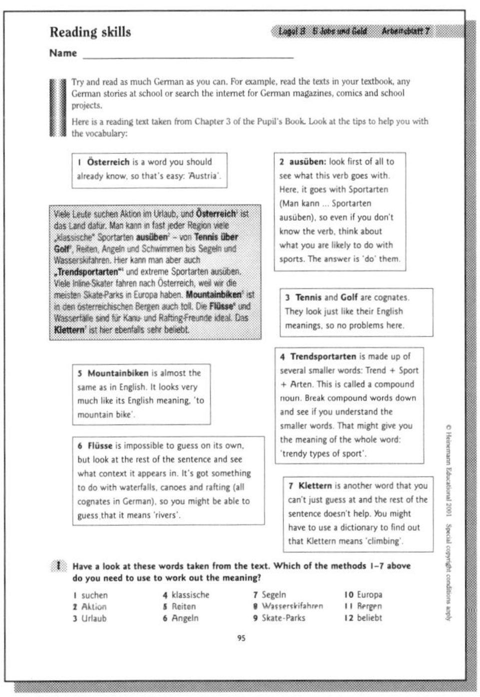

Reading skills Logo! 3 5 Jobs und Geld Arbeitsblatt 7

Name ____________________

Try and read as much German as you can. For example, read the texts in your textbook, any German stories at school or search the internet for German magazines, comics and school projects.

Here is a reading text taken from Chapter 3 of the Pupil's Book. Look at the tips to help you with the vocabulary:

Viele Leute suchen Aktion im Urlaub, und **Österreich**[1] ist das Land dafür. Man kann in fast jeder Region viele „klassische" Sportarten **ausüben**[2] – von **Tennis über Golf**[3], Reiten, Angeln und Schwimmen bis Segeln und Wasserskifahren. Hier kann man aber auch **„Trendsportarten"**[4] und extreme Sportarten ausüben. Viele Inline-Skater fahren nach Österreich, weil wir die meisten Skate-Parks in Europa haben. **Mountainbiken**[5] ist in den österreichischen Bergen auch toll. Die **Flüsse**[6] und Wasserfälle sind für Kanu- und Rafting-Freunde ideal. Das **Klettern**[7] ist hier ebenfalls sehr beliebt.

1 **Österreich** is a word you should already know, so that's easy: 'Austria'.

2 **ausüben:** look first of all to see what this verb goes with. Here, it goes with Sportarten (Man kann ... Sportarten ausüben), so even if you don't know the verb, think about what you are likely to do with sports. The answer is 'do' them.

3 **Tennis** and **Golf** are cognates. They look just like their English meanings, so no problems here.

4 **Trendsportarten** is made up of several smaller words: Trend + Sport + Arten. This is called a compound noun. Break compound words down and see if you understand the smaller words. That might give you the meaning of the whole word: 'trendy types of sport'.

5 **Mountainbiken** is almost the same as in English. It looks very much like its English meaning, 'to mountain bike'.

6 **Flüsse** is impossible to guess on its own, but look at the rest of the sentence and see what context it appears in. It's got something to do with waterfalls, canoes and rafting (all cognates in German), so you might be able to guess that it means 'rivers'.

7 **Klettern** is another word that you can't just guess at and the rest of the sentence doesn't help. You might have to use a dictionary to find out that Klettern means 'climbing'.

1 Have a look at these words taken from the text. Which of the methods 1–7 above do you need to use to work out the meaning?

1 suchen	4 klassische	7 Segeln	10 Europa
2 Aktion	5 Reiten	8 Wasserskifahren	11 Bergen
3 Urlaub	6 Angeln	9 Skate-Parks	12 beliebt

95

Advice on reading activities.

Grammatik 1
p. 96

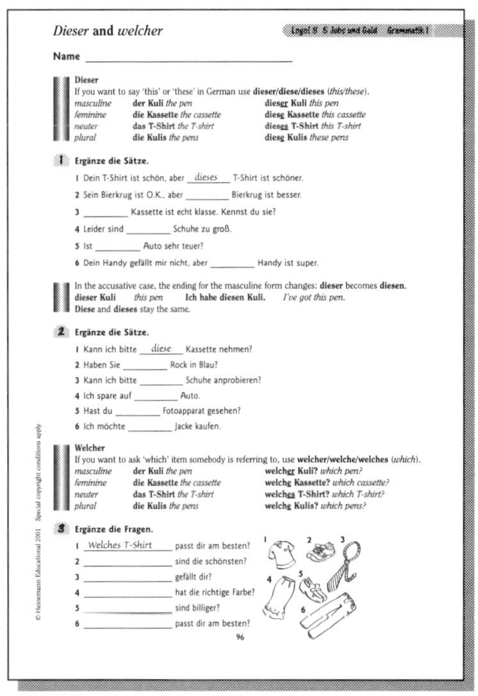

Dieser and *welcher* Logo! 3 5 Jobs und Geld Grammatik 1

Name ____________________

Dieser
If you want to say 'this' or 'these' in German use **dieser/diese/dieses** (*this/these*).

masculine	**der Kuli** *the pen*	**dieser Kuli** *this pen*
feminine	**die Kassette** *the cassette*	**diese Kassette** *this cassette*
neuter	**das T-Shirt** *the T-shirt*	**dieses T-Shirt** *this T-shirt*
plural	**die Kulis** *the pens*	**diese Kulis** *these pens*

1 Ergänze die Sätze.

1 Dein T-Shirt ist schön, aber *dieses* T-Shirt ist schöner.
2 Sein Bierkrug ist O.K., aber ________ Bierkrug ist besser.
3 ________ Kassette ist echt klasse. Kennst du sie?
4 Leider sind ________ Schuhe zu groß.
5 Ist ________ Auto sehr teuer?
6 Dein Handy gefällt mir nicht, aber ________ Handy ist super.

In the accusative case, the ending for the masculine form changes: **dieser** becomes **diesen**.
dieser Kuli *this pen* **Ich habe diesen Kuli.** *I've got this pen.*
Diese and **dieses** stay the same.

2 Ergänze die Sätze.

1 Kann ich bitte *diese* Kassette nehmen?
2 Haben Sie ________ Rock in Blau?
3 Kann ich bitte ________ Schuhe anprobieren?
4 Ich spare auf ________ Auto.
5 Hast du ________ Fotoapparat gesehen?
6 Ich möchte ________ Jacke kaufen.

Welcher
If you want to ask 'which' item somebody is referring to, use **welcher/welche/welches** (*which*).

masculine	**der Kuli** *the pen*	**welcher Kuli?** *which pen?*
feminine	**die Kassette** *the cassette*	**welche Kassette?** *which cassette?*
neuter	**das T-Shirt** *the T-shirt*	**welches T-Shirt?** *which T-shirt?*
plural	**die Kulis** *the pens*	**welche Kulis?** *which pens?*

3 Ergänze die Fragen.

1 *Welches T-Shirt* passt dir am besten?
2 ________ sind die schönsten?
3 ________ gefällt dir?
4 ________ hat die richtige Farbe?
5 ________ sind billiger?
6 ________ passt dir am besten?

96

Practice of *dieser* and *welcher*.

1 **1** dieses, **2** dieser, **3** Diese, **4** diese, **5** dieses, **6** dieses
2 **1** diese, **2** diesen, **3** diese, **4** dieses, **5** diesen, **6** diese
3 **1** Welches T-Shirt, **2** Welche Sportschuhe, **3** Welche Krawatte, **4** Welcher Rock, **5** Welche Schuhe, **6** Welche Hose

Grammatik 2 p. 97

Practice of adjective endings.

1 **1** Der grüne Rock ist zu lang. **2** Die schwarzen Schuhe sind zu groß. **3** Die braune Jacke ist zu teuer. **4** Das alte T-Shirt ist zu kurz. **5** Der karierte Schal ist schrecklich. **6** Die blauen Stiefel sind zu klein.

2 **1** Ich kaufe den blauen Pullover für Micki. **2** Ich kaufe das schwarze T-Shirt für meinen Bruder. **3** Ich kaufe den schönen Bierkrug für meinen Vater. **4** Ich kaufe die roten Schuhe für Hannes. **5** Ich kaufe den billigen Fotoapparat für Sandy. **6** Ich kaufe die gelbe Jacke für Karola.

3 **1** ein grüner Rock, **2** schwarze Schuhe, **3** eine braune Jacke, **4** ein altes T-Shirt, **5** ein karierter Schal, **6** blaue Stiefel

4 Verena trägt einen gelben Hut, ein langes Kleid, eine bunte Perlenschnur und rote Sandalen. Sie hat lange Haare.

Paul trägt eine schwarze Sonnenbrille, eine enge Hose und ein blaues T-Shirt. Er hat wilde Haare.

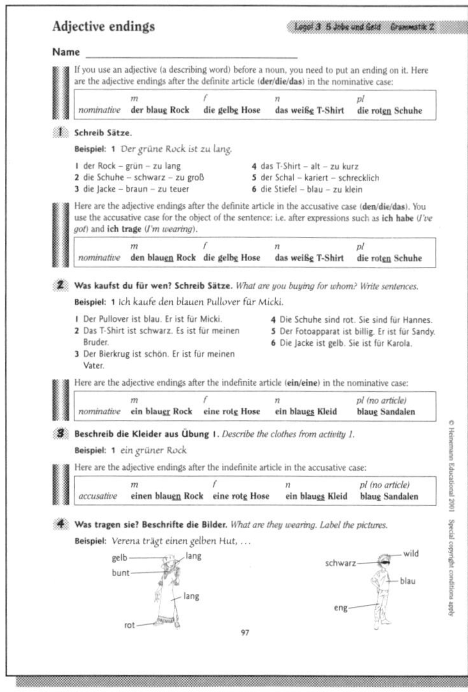

Adjective endings

Logo! 3 5 Jobs und Geld Grammatik 2

Name ____________________

If you use an adjective (a describing word) before a noun, you need to put an ending on it. Here are the adjective endings after the definite article (**der/die/das**) in the nominative case:

	m	*f*	*n*	*pl*
nominative	**der blaue Rock**	**die gelbe Hose**	**das weiße T-Shirt**	**die roten Schuhe**

1 **Schreib Sätze.**

Beispiel: 1 *Der grüne Rock ist zu lang.*

1 der Rock – grün – zu lang
2 die Schuhe – schwarz – zu groß
3 die Jacke – braun – zu teuer
4 das T-Shirt – alt – zu kurz
5 der Schal – kariert – schrecklich
6 die Stiefel – blau – zu klein

Here are the adjective endings after the definite article in the accusative case (**den/die/das**). You use the accusative case for the object of the sentence: i.e. after expressions such as **ich habe** (*I've got*) and **ich trage** (*I'm wearing*).

	m	*f*	*n*	*pl*
nominative	**den blauen Rock**	**die gelbe Hose**	**das weiße T-Shirt**	**die roten Schuhe**

2 **Was kaufst du für wen? Schreib Sätze.** *What are you buying for whom? Write sentences.*

Beispiel: 1 *Ich kaufe den blauen Pullover für Micki.*

1 Der Pullover ist blau. Er ist für Micki.
2 Das T-Shirt ist schwarz. Es ist für meinen Bruder.
3 Der Bierkrug ist schön. Er ist für meinen Vater.
4 Die Schuhe sind rot. Sie sind für Hannes.
5 Der Fotoapparat ist billig. Er ist für Sandy.
6 Die Jacke ist gelb. Sie ist für Karola.

Here are the adjective endings after the indefinite article (**ein/eine**) in the nominative case:

	m	*f*	*n*	*pl (no article)*
nominative	**ein blauer Rock**	**eine rote Hose**	**ein blaues Kleid**	**blaue Sandalen**

3 **Beschreib die Kleider aus Übung 1.** *Describe the clothes from activity 1.*

Beispiel: 1 *ein grüner Rock*

Here are the adjective endings after the indefinite article in the accusative case:

	m	*f*	*n*	*pl (no article)*
accusative	**einen blauen Rock**	**eine rote Hose**	**ein blaues Kleid**	**blaue Sandalen**

4 **Was tragen sie? Beschrifte die Bilder.** *What are they wearing. Label the pictures.*

Beispiel: *Verena trägt einen gelben Hut, …*

97

Grammatik 3 p. 98

Practice of prepositions.

1 **1** dem, **2** den, **3** dem, **4** der, **5** dem, **6** die, **7** der

2 **1** am, **2** ins, **3** unter die, **4** zwischen dem, dem **5** in die, **6** im, **7** neben dem

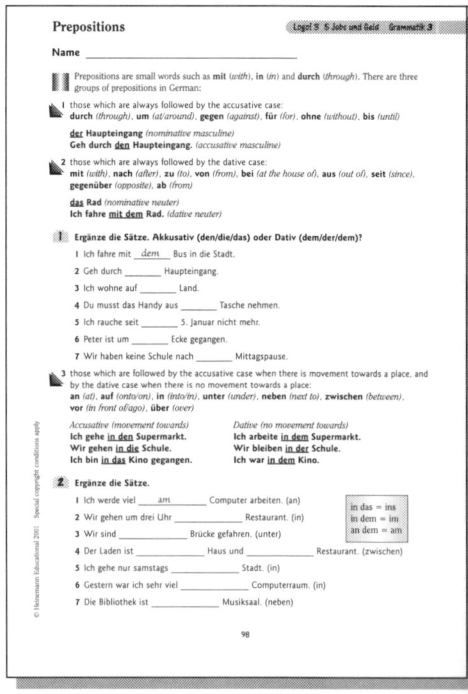

Prepositions

Logo! 3 5 Jobs und Geld Grammatik 3

Name ____________________

Prepositions are small words such as **mit** (*with*), **in** (*in*) and **durch** (*through*). There are three groups of prepositions in German:

1 those which are always followed by the accusative case:
durch (*through*), **um** (*at/around*), **gegen** (*against*), **für** (*for*), **ohne** (*without*), **bis** (*until*)

der Haupteingang (*nominative masculine*)
Geh durch den Haupteingang. (*accusative masculine*)

2 those which are always followed by the dative case:
mit (*with*), **nach** (*after*), **zu** (*to*), **von** (*from*), **bei** (*at the house of*), **aus** (*out of*), **seit** (*since*), **gegenüber** (*opposite*), **ab** (*from*)

das Rad (*nominative neuter*)
Ich fahre mit dem Rad. (*dative neuter*)

1 **Ergänze die Sätze. Akkusativ (den/die/das) oder Dativ (dem/der/dem)?**

1 Ich fahre mit *dem* Bus in die Stadt.
2 Geh durch ______ Haupteingang.
3 Ich wohne auf ______ Land.
4 Du musst das Handy aus ______ Tasche nehmen.
5 Ich rauche seit ______ 5. Januar nicht mehr.
6 Peter ist um ______ Ecke gegangen.
7 Wir haben keine Schule nach ______ Mittagspause.

3 those which are followed by the accusative case when there is movement towards a place, and by the dative case when there is no movement towards a place:
an (*at*), **auf** (*onto/on*), **in** (*into/in*), **unter** (*under*), **neben** (*next to*), **zwischen** (*between*), **vor** (*in front of/ago*), **über** (*over*)

Accusative (movement towards)	*Dative (no movement towards)*
Ich gehe in den Supermarkt.	**Ich arbeite in dem Supermarkt.**
Wir gehen in die Schule.	**Wir bleiben in der Schule.**
Ich bin in das Kino gegangen.	**Ich war in dem Kino.**

2 **Ergänze die Sätze.**

1 Ich werde viel *am* Computer arbeiten. (an)
2 Wir gehen um drei Uhr ______ Restaurant. (in)
3 Wir sind ______ Brücke gefahren. (unter)
4 Der Laden ist ______ Haus und ______ Restaurant. (zwischen)
5 Ich gehe nur samstags ______ Stadt. (in)
6 Gestern war ich sehr viel ______ Computerraum. (in)
7 Die Bibliothek ist ______ Musiksaal. (neben)

in das = ins
in dem = im
an dem = am

98

Wortschatz pp. 99–100 and Lernzieltest p. 101

These sheets are for revision at the end of the chapter. The *Wortschatz* sheets provide a list of all the key words and phrases from the chapter and the *Lernzieltest* gives a checklist of the areas covered, which pupils can check off as they revise.

6 Kein Problem (Pupil's Book pp. 96–109)

Topic area	Key language	Skills	Grammar	PoS
6.1 Meine Familie (pp. 96–97) Talk about your family	*Ich habe / Es gibt einen Vater/Stiefvater/Bruder/Halbbruder/Stiefbruder, eine Mutter/Stiefmutter/Schwester/Halbschwester/Stiefschwester, zwei Schwestern/Brüder/Halbschwestern/Halbbrüder/Stiefschwestern/Stiefbrüder. Wie findest du deinen/deine ...? Ich finde ihn/sie O.K., lustig, streng, nervig, altmodisch, nett, freundlich, launisch, doof, geduldig, gut gelaunt, klasse.*		Possessive adjectives, nom. and acc. Personal pronouns, acc.	1a, 2a
6.2 Zu Hause (pp. 98–99) Talk about what you are and aren't allowed to do at home	*Du darfst kein Piercing, keine Haustiere, keinen Job haben, nicht spät wegbleiben, keine laute Musik spielen, nicht bei Freunden übernachten, nicht allein in die Stadt fahren, keine Pommes essen, nicht am Vormittag fernsehen, nicht rauchen, oder? Doch ich darf ... . Stimmt, ich darf nicht/keine ... .*	Learning a short passage by recording it on tape (Teacher's Guide only)	*dürfen* + negatives: *kein/nicht*	2h, 3a
6.3 Probleme (pp. 100–101) Talk about problems	*Wenn ich ein Problem, Liebeskummer, Zoff mit den Eltern habe, down bin, die Schule schwierig finde, meine Freunde Drogen nehmen, meine Freunde mich ärgern, bin ich down/traurig, höre ich laute Musik, mache ich eine Radtour, mache ich nicht mit, spreche ich mit meinen Freunden / dem Lehrer, esse ich nichts.*		*wenn* + verb to the end (revision) *mit* + dative	3b, 4c, 4d
6.4 Die Zukunft (pp. 102–103) Talk about your resolutions	*Ich werde nicht rauchen, ein bisschen Geld wegschenken, mehr lesen, meine Hausaufgaben rechtzeitig machen, einen Job finden, ein Instrument lernen, umweltfreundlicher leben, nicht launisch sein, zu Hause mehr helfen, früher ins Bett gehen.*	Building up longer sentences	Future tense (revision) *weil* + verb to the end (revision)	1c, 2f, 5f
6.5 Liebe Ellie (pp. 104–105) Write a letter of introduction Interview an older person	Revision of language from Logo! 3	Making notes and listening more than once to the recording	*Sie/du/ihr* (revision)	2d, 2e, 2i, 5h
Lernzieltest und Wiederholung (pp. 106–107)	Revision			2a, 5d
Wörter (pp. 108–109)	Word list			
Extra (pp. 120–121)	Differentiated reading and writing			3e

1 Meine Familie (pp. 96–97)

Pupils will learn how to:
- talk about their family

Key language

Ich habe / Es gibt ...
- einen (Stief-)Vater
- einen (Halb-/Stief-) Bruder
- eine (Stief-)Mutter
- eine (Halb-/Stief-) Schwester
- zwei (Halb-/Stief-) Schwestern
- zwei (Halb-/Stief-) Brüder

Wie findest du deinen/deine ... ?
Ich finde ihn/sie ...
- O.K./lustig/nett/ freundlich/geduldig/ gut gelaunt/klasse streng/nervig/ altmodisch/launisch/ doof

Grammar focus
- possessive adjectives, nominative and accusative
- personal pronouns, accusative

Resources
- Cassette C, Side B
- Workbook p. 51
- R & A File: Grammatik 1 (p. 116)

This chapter focuses mainly on teenagers' home life and families and the problems and conflicts they may encounter there.

This unit revises family vocabulary from Logo! 2 and introduces adjectives to describe family members. Brainstorm family vocabulary with the class and write it on the board/OHT. Then add any new words from the list above and ask the pupils if they can work them out.

1a Hör zu und wiederhole. (AT1 Level 3)
Pupils listen to the recording and repeat the four teenagers' descriptions of their families.

- Meine Eltern gehen mir auf die Nerven. Ich finde sie zu streng und altmodisch.
- Ich verstehe mich nicht gut mit meinem Stiefbruder. Ich finde ihn so doof.
- Ich komme gut mit meiner Halbschwester aus. Ich finde sie sehr nett und geduldig.
- Mein Vater geht mir oft auf die Nerven. Ich finde ihn sehr launisch und nervig.

1b Schreib sechs Fragen für deinen Partner / deine Partnerin auf. Tauscht dann die Fragen und beantwortet sie. (AT4 Levels 2–3)
Pupils write questions about the four families. They then answer their partner's questions.

2a Such dir die Familienwörter oben aus und ordne sie.
Pupils categorise the words for family members according to number and gender.

Answers

der	die	die	die	die
Vater	Schwester	Brüder	Schwestern	Eltern
Stiefbruder	Stiefmutter	Stiefbrüder		
Bruder	Halbschwester			
Halbbruder	Mutter			
Stiefvater	Stiefschwester			

2b Partnerarbeit. Person B macht das Buch zu. (AT2 Levels 3–4)
One pupil closes his/her book and the other pupil questions him/her about the four families introduced in activity 1a above. Once an incorrect answer has been given, pupils swap roles.

Grammatik: 'his' and 'her'
This grammar box summarises the possessive adjectives *sein* and *ihr*. Point out to pupils that they need to agree with the noun they go with, and that they follow the same pattern as *ein* and *mein*. Give pupils a list of nouns and ask them to change *der/die/das* to *sein* and *ihr*: e.g. *der Fußball = sein/ihr Fußball, die Kassette = seine/ihre Kassette, das Buch = sein/ihr Buch* and *die Kinder = seine/ihre Kinder*. Pupils could also make a list of the family members from activity 1a, using *sein* and *ihr* appropriately in their descriptions, e.g.: *Ihre Eltern heißen Jörg und Katrina. Ihre Brüder heißen ... .*

Refer to p. 124 of the Pupil's Book for further information. More practice of this grammar point is also provided on Grammatik 1 (R & A File p. 116).

3 Hör zu und mach Notizen. Positiv oder negativ? (1–4) (AT1 Level 4)
Pupils listen to the four teenagers from activity 1a describing their families. They write down as many details in note form as possible. They then decide whether each person is given a positive or negative description.

Answers

1 Meike: Eltern – streng, altmodisch ☹, Brüder – nett, freundlich ☺, Schwester – launisch ☹; **2 Ingrid:** Vater – nett, geduldig ☺, Stiefmutter – lustig ☺, Stiefbruder – doof ☹, Bruder – lustig ☺, Halbbruder – O.K. ☺; **3 Patrick:** Mutter – streng ☹, Stiefvater – echt klasse, gut gelaunt ☺, Stiefschwester – klasse ☺, Stiefbrüder – nervig ☹, Halbschwester nett, geduldig ☺; **4 Latze:** Vater – launisch, nervig ☹, Schwestern – super, echt klass ☺

1, Meike – Meine Eltern gehen mir auf die Nerven. Ich finde sie zu streng und altmodisch. Ich habe zwei Brüder, Frank und Felix, und sie sind meistens sehr nett und freundlich. Meine Schwester Iris ist vierzehn

Jahre alt und sie geht mir total auf die Nerven. Sie ist so launisch!

2. Ingrid – Meine Eltern gehen mir nie auf die Nerven. Mein Vater ist immer sehr nett und geduldig und meine Stiefmutter ist sehr lustig. Aber mein Stiefbruder geht mir total auf die Nerven. Ich finde ihn so doof! Ich habe auch einen Bruder, Oliver, und ich finde ihn sehr lustig. Mein Halbbruder, Daniel, ist nur ein Jahr alt und er ist O.K.

3. Patrick – Meine Mutter geht mir oft auf die Nerven, weil sie so streng ist, aber Thomas, mein Stiefvater, ist echt klasse und immer gut gelaunt. Meine Stiefschwester ist auch klasse, aber meine Stiefbrüder gehen mir dauernd auf die Nerven. Sie sind sehr nervig. Meine Halbschwester geht mir aber nicht auf die Nerven. Ich finde sie sehr nett und geduldig.

4. Latze – Mein Vater geht mir oft auf die Nerven. Ich finde ihn sehr launisch und nervig. Meine Schwestern sind aber super – ich finde sie echt klasse!

4 Lies den Artikel und such dir Wörter zu folgenden Themen aus. (AT3 Level 4)
Pupils read the text about Patrick's family and note any words which correspond to four given categories.

Answers
1 sieben, vierzig, fünfundvierzig, eine, zwei; **2** Mutter, Stiefvater, Stiefschwester, Stiefbrüder, Halbschwester; **3** nett, intelligent, geduldig; **4** schlecht gelaunt, streng

Pupils make up further questions for a partner, based on Patrick's text.

5a Erfinde eine Familie für eine Seifenoper. Mach eine Liste.
Pupils work out a list of family members and their corresponding characteristics for a soap opera.

5b Partnerarbeit. Vergleicht eure Seifenoper-Familien. (AT2 Levels 4–5)
Pupils compare their soap opera families.

6 Beschreib deine Seifenoper-Familie mit so vielen Details wie möglich. Patricks Text oben hilft dir dabei. (AT4 Levels 4–5)
Pupils write a text to describe their soap opera family and how its members get on with each other.

Grammatik: 'him', 'her', 'them'
This grammar box shows the third person accusative case pronouns, which pupils will need to use when they are saying how they find other people. Point out that it is only the masculine *er* which changes in the accusative case – to *ihn*. Pupils might see a parallel here with the definite article change from *der* to *den*.

R Refer to pp. 124–125 of the Pupil's Book for further information. More practice of this grammar point is also provided on Grammatik 1 (R & A File p. 116).

R Further practice of this unit's language is to be found on p. 120 of the Pupil's Book, activity 1.

E Further practice of this unit's language is to be found on p. 121 of the Pupil's Book, activity 1.

2 Zu Hause (pp. 98–99)

Pupils will learn how to:

- talk about what they are and are not allowed to do at home

Key language
Du darfst keinen/keine/kein ... , oder?
Doch, ich darf (einen/eine/ein) ...
Stimmt, ich darf keinen/keine/kein ...
  Piercing haben
  Haustiere haben
  Job haben
  laute Musik spielen
  Pommes essen
Du darfst nicht ... , oder?
  spät wegbleiben
  bei Freunden übernachten
  allein in die Stadt fahren
  am Vormittag fernsehen
  rauchen
Doch, ich darf ...
Stimmt, ich darf nicht ...

Grammar focus

- *dürfen* + negatives: *kein/nicht*

Skill focus

- learning a short passage by recording it (Teacher's Guide only)

Resources

- Cassette C, Side B
- Workbook p. 52
- R & A File: Arbeitsblatt 1 (p. 112), Grammatik 2 (p. 117)

This unit focuses on house rules and what pupils are and are not allowed to do at home. Before pupils tackle the unit, ask them to write down ten things they are not allowed to do at home. Then introduce the new vocabulary, using a copy of the visuals on Arbeitsblatt 1 (R & A File p. 112) on an OHT. Ask pupils to compare these rules to the ones they wrote down. You could then rank the visuals on the board/OHT, according to how many pupils have that rule at home.

For further oral practice, give each pair of pupils a copy of the visuals to cut up and place face-down on the desk. They put a cross on half of the cards and a tick on the other half. One pupil then turns over a card and the other pupil asks: *Du darfst nicht/keinen/keine/kein ... , oder?* The first pupil replies in the negative, if there is a cross on the card: *Stimmt, ich darf nicht/keinen/keine/kein ...* and in the positive if there is a tick: *Doch, ich darf ...* .

1a Hör zu und wiederhole. Was passt zusammen? (1–10) (AT1 Levels 2–3)

Pupils listen to and repeat ten statements, which they then match to the correct pictures.

Answers

1 e, **2** j, **3** c, **4** g, **5** i, **6** a, **7** d, **8** h, **9** f, **10** b

1 – Ich darf nicht bei Freunden übernachten.
2 – Ich darf kein Piercing haben.
3 – Ich darf nicht spät wegbleiben.
4 – Ich darf keine Pommes essen.
5 – Ich darf nicht am Vormittag fernsehen.
6 – Ich darf keine Haustiere haben.
7 – Ich darf keine laute Musik spielen.
8 – Ich darf nicht rauchen.
9 – Ich darf nicht allein in die Stadt fahren.
10 – Ich darf keinen Job haben.

1b Hast du die gleichen Regeln? Schreib Sätze. (AT4 Level 3)

Pupils write sentences to say whether they have the same rules at home or not. This would also be a good time for pupils to add any other rules of their own which might not be mentioned here.

R Practice of using negatives in sentences with *dürfen* is provided on Grammatik 2 (R & A File p. 117).

2 Hör zu und mach Notizen. Was darf man (nicht) machen? (1–10) (AT1 Level 3)

Pupils listen and make notes about what a teenager is and is not allowed to do at home.

Answers

1 Musik ✗, **2** am Vormittag fernsehen ✓, **3** bei Freunden übernachten ✓, **4** Pommes essen ✓, **5** in die Stadt fahren ✗, **6** spät wegbleiben ✗, **7** rauchen ✗, **8** Job ✓, **9** Haustiere ✓, **10** Piercing ✓

1 – Darfst du laute Musik spielen?
– Nein, das darf ich nicht machen. Meine Eltern sind ziemlich streng.
2 – Und darfst du am Vormittag fernsehen?
– Ja, klar! Das darf doch jeder, oder?
3 – Darfst du bei Freunden übernachten?
– Ja, aber nur am Wochenende oder in den Ferien.
4 – Und darfst du Pommes essen?
– Pommes essen? Ja, ich darf Pommes essen!
5 – Und darfst du allein in die Stadt fahren?
– Nein, das darf ich nicht.
6 – Darfst du spät wegbleiben?
– Nein, ich muss immer um neun Uhr zu Hause sein.
7 – Und darfst du rauchen?
– Nein. Rauchen darf ich natürlich nicht.
8 – Darfst du einen Job haben?
– Ja, wenn ich will. Aber ich will keinen Job haben.
9 – Und darfst du Haustiere haben?
– Ja, wir haben einen Hund und eine Katze.
10 – Und darfst du ein Piercing haben?
– Ja, wenn ich will.

3 Partnerarbeit. Rate mal, was dein Partner / deine Partnerin machen darf! (AT2 Levels 3–4)

Pupils firstly guess what house rules their partner has and then ask each other questions to see whether they guessed correctly. You might wish to revise the structure *du darfst* + infinitive at the end, by looking back at chapter 2 unit 3 (pp. 28–29), where *dürfen* was encountered in the *man darf* form.

4 Lies den Text. Schreib Sätze für Ingrid. (AT3 Levels 5–6)

Pupils read Ingrid's text and then write a sentence for each picture, saying whether she is allowed to do the activity or not.

Answers

1 Ingrid darf ein Piercing haben. **2** Ingrid darf einen Job haben. **3** Ingrid darf keine Pommes essen. **4** Ingrid darf nicht rauchen. **5** Ingrid darf nicht allein in die Stadt fahren. **6** Ingrid darf nicht spät wegbleiben. **7** Ingrid darf keine laute Musik spielen. **8** Ingrid darf am Vormittag fernsehen. **9** Ingrid darf keine Haustiere haben. **10** Ingrid darf bei Freundinnen übernachten.

5 Was darfst du zu Hause machen? Was darfst du nicht machen? Schreib einen Text und nimm ihn auf Kassette auf. (AT4 Levels 4–5, AT2 Levels 4–5)

Pupils write a text to explain what they are and are not allowed to do at home. Encourage pupils to give their opinion of each rule and to use constructions with *weil* and *wenn* if possible.

Pupils record their text on cassette to help them to memorise it. If pupils make any subsequent amendments to the text, they can re-record the updated version and memorise it once more.

3 Probleme (pp. 100–101)

Pupils will learn how to:
- talk about problems

Key language
Wenn ich ein Problem habe, ...
Wenn ich Liebeskummer habe, ...
Wenn ich Zoff mit den Eltern habe, ...
Wenn ich down bin, ...
Wenn ich die Schule schwierig finde, ...
Wenn meine Freunde Drogen nehmen, ...
Wenn meine Freunde mich ärgern, ...
bin ich traurig.
höre ich laute Musik.
mache ich eine Radtour.
mache ich nicht mit.
spreche ich mit meinen Freunden.
spreche ich mit dem Lehrer
esse ich nichts.

Grammar focus
- *wenn* + subordinate clause word order (revision)
- *mit* + dative

Resources
- Cassette C, Side B
- Workbook pp. 53, 56

This unit covers some common teenage problems. The language is presented firstly via three problem letters to a teenage magazine and then via some illustrations of the problems. You may want to read the texts with the class first and ask them to explain the gist of each problem. You could give each pair of pupils one of the problem letters to look at further. Give them five minutes to work out what it is about and then they can share ideas with other groups or the whole class.

1a Lies die Briefe. Finde die Sätze auf Deutsch in den Briefen. (AT3 Level 5)

Pupils read the problem letters to a teenage magazine and find the specified German expressions in them.

Answers

1 ... jetzt geht er mit meiner besten Freundin aus. **2** Ich habe Liebeskummer. **3** ... das kann ich nicht ausstehen. **4** Ich bin noch in ihn verknallt ... , **5** ... ich darf keine Freunde einladen. **6** Wenn das so weitergeht, werde ich weglaufen. **7** Wenn sie ihr Geld bekommt, kauft sie immer nur Zigaretten damit. **8** Letzte Woche hat mein Freund Schluss mit mir gemacht ...

1b Lies die Briefe und beantworte die Fragen.

Pupils answer seven *warum?* questions about the letters. As in the example, pupils can start each answer with *weil*, rather than giving a full sentence. Remind them that the verb goes to the end after *weil*.

Answers

1 Weil sie ihm nicht zuhört. **2** Weil sie das cool findet. **3** Weil sie so streng und altmodisch sind. **4** Weil ihre Eltern Popmusik nicht mögen. **5** Weil er sie zu launisch und kindisch findet. **6** Weil sie so traurig ist. / Weil sie ihn mit ihrer Freundin zusammen sieht. **7** Weil sie noch in ihn verknallt ist.

2 Hör zu. Was ist das Problem? (1–6) (AT1 Level 4)

Pupils listen and identify what the problem area is for each speaker. Pupils could listen again and note down as many details as possible about the problems, if they need further listening practice.

Answers

1 Liebeskummer, **2** Familie, **3** Tabak, **4** Freunde, **5** Liebeskummer, **6** Familie

1 – Ach, ich habe ein Problem! Ich bin ... in Sandra verknallt, ja, aber sie geht leider viel lieber mit meinem besten Freund aus.
2 – Also, ich habe ein Problem! Ein ziemlich großes Problem – denn mein Stiefvater geht mir total auf die Nerven. Ich kann ihn nicht ausstehen, er ist so streng und launisch.
3 – Mein Problem ist, dass ich einfach zu viel rauche. Ich weiß, dass das eigentlich ziemlich doof ist, und ich will es auch nicht. Aber ich kann machen, was ich will: Ich kann nicht aufhören. Das ist wie eine Sucht. Zigaretten brauche ich einfach.
4 – Ja, ich habe echt ein Problem. Ich – ich habe einfach keine Freunde in der Schule. Ich komme dahin und die ignorieren mich alle. Ich – ich bin nett und ich bin freundlich und ich rede mit denen, aber die mögen mich alle nicht.
5 – Ach, ich bin furchtbar deprimiert. Ich habe ein Problem. Ich liebe ein Mädchen in der Klasse, aber sie sagt, sie würde mich nicht lieben. Ich wäre ihr irgendwie zu anstrengend.
6 – Kann ich mal mit dir reden? Ich habe ein Problem. Meine Mutter hat einen neuen Freund und er ist total doof und unsympathisch. Was soll ich bloß machen? Ich mag ihn einfach nicht.

3 Was passt zusammen? Schreib Sätze. (AT3 Level 3)

Pupils read the problems listed and look at the illustrations to complete the *wenn* sentences with the words in the clouds. Remind pupils of the change in word order after *wenn*. If necessary, refer them to the section which covers this on p. 133.

Answers

1 Wenn ich Zoff mit den Eltern habe, bin ich traurig. **2** Wenn meine Freunde Drogen nehmen, mache ich nicht mit. **3** Wenn meine Freunde mich ärgern, mache ich eine Radtour. **4** Wenn ich down bin, höre ich laute Musik. **5** Wenn ich ein Problem habe, spreche ich mit meinen Freunden. **6** Wenn ich die Schule schwierig finde, spreche ich mit dem Lehrer / der Lehrerin. **7** Wenn ich Liebeskummer habe, esse ich nichts.

Pupils complete each sentence with their own ideas.

An exercise on word order is provided on page 56 of the Workbook.

4 Partnerarbeit. Bereitet eine Radiosendung über Jugendprobleme vor. Nehmt sie dann auf Kassette auf. (AT2 Levels 4–6)

Pupils work in pairs to prepare a radio broadcast about teenage problems. Encourage pupils to expand from the sentences presented at the top of the page and to use their own ideas and solutions to problems.

Grammatik: *mit* + dative

This grammar box points out that the preposition *mit* is always followed by the dative case. Pupils have already met this with modes of transport: *mit dem Auto, mit der Straßenbahn,* etc. Here the possessive adjective *mein* (masculine) becomes *meinem*, *meine* (feminine) becomes *meiner* and *meine* (plural) becomes *meinen*.

5 Schreib einen Problembrief wie auf Seite 100. (AT4 Levels 4–6)

Pupils write a problem letter to a teenage magazine about a problem of their choice. The letters on page 100 will help them to structure their work.

MINI-TEST

At the end of the third unit in every chapter, there is a *Mini-Test*. This is intended as a half-way checkpoint for pupils to check that they are familiar with the key language of the chapter so far. Pupils could revise the language with a partner in class or for homework.

4 Die Zukunft (pp. 102–103)

Pupils will learn how to:
- talk about their resolutions

Key language	**Grammar focus**
Ich werde … nicht rauchen. ein bisschen Geld wegschenken. mehr lesen. meine Hausaufgaben. rechtzeitig machen. einen Job finden. ein Instrument lernen. umweltfreundlicher leben. nicht launisch sein. zu Hause mehr helfen. früher ins Bett gehen.	• future tense (revision) • *weil* + subordinate clause word order (revision) **Skill focus** • constructing longer sentences **Resources** • Cassette C, Side B • Workbook pp. 54, 56 • R & A File: Arbeitsblatt 2 (p. 113)

This unit focuses on looking ahead and making resolutions for the future. The future tense is revised here, along with vocabulary which pupils have met in other contexts throughout Logo! 3. Introduce the new vocabulary orally, using the visuals on Arbeitsblatt 2 (R & A File p. 113) on an OHT to reinforce the future tense structure, asking e.g.: *Was werde ich machen?*

For further oral practice, give each pair of pupils a set of the visuals on Arbeitsblatt 2 to cut up and place in a pile face-down on the desk. One pupil takes a card and the other pupil tries to guess which one he/she has chosen by making statements: *Ich werde …* . The other pupil replies *Nein* until the card is guessed correctly.

1a Hör zu und wiederhole. Meike, Ingrid, Patrick und Latze haben ihre Pläne für die Zukunft diskutiert. Hier sind ihre Ideen … (AT3 Level 3)
Pupils listen to and repeat the teenagers' resolutions.

– Ich werde nicht rauchen.
– Ich werde ein bisschen Geld wegschenken.
– Ich werde mehr lesen.
– Ich werde meine Hausaufgaben rechtzeitig machen.
– Ich werde einen Job finden.
– Ich werde ein Instrument lernen.
– Ich werde umweltfreundlicher leben.
– Ich werde nicht launisch sein.
– Ich werde zu Hause mehr helfen.
– Ich werde früher ins Bett gehen.

1b Hör zu. Was werden Meike, Ingrid, Patrick und Latze machen? (1–4) (AT1 Levels 5–6)
Pupils listen to the recording and note down which teenager has made which of the resolutions from activity 1a.

Answers
1 Meike: h, d; **2** Ingrid: i, f; **3** Patrick: e, g, c; **4** Latze: a, j, b

1 – Meike, sag mir doch mal, was du machen wirst.
– Ja, also, ich will in Zukunft nicht mehr so launisch sein.
– Nicht mehr so launisch sein. Gut! Und was noch?
– Ich will auch meine Hausaufgaben rechtzeitig machen.
– Wieso? Machst du das normalerweise nicht?
– Nein, ich bin damit immer spät dran.
2 – Ingrid, was hast du dir vorgenommen?
– Also, ich werde zu Hause mehr helfen, so abwaschen, Zimmer aufräumen und auf den Kleinen aufpassen.
– Abwaschen, Zimmer aufräumen, auf den Kleinen aufpassen. Sehr gut!
– Ja, und dann habe ich mir überlegt, dass ich gerne ein Instrument lernen möchte.
– Das ist ja interessant. Und welches?
– Na ja, ich weiß noch nicht, vielleicht Klavier oder Klarinette oder so.
3 – Na, Patrick? Erzähl mir, was du dir vorgenommen hast.
– Ach, also, ich habe viel vor. Als Allererstes will ich mir allerdings einen Job suchen. Und ich werde auch einen finden.
– Und was für einen Job möchtest du finden?
– Ja, schwierig. Ich weiß noch nicht. Vielleicht in irgendeinem Café.
– Das ist wirklich gut. Und sonst noch was?
– Ja, ich habe mir auch vorgenommen, viel umweltbewusster und umweltfreundlicher zu leben.
– Das finde ich wirklich richtig gut, und das ist auch sehr wichtig.
– Das ist total wichtig. Und ich will auch mehr lesen. Ich will noch klüger und schlauer werden.
4 – Und Latze, was wirst du machen?
– Ja, das sage ich gern. Als Erstes habe ich mir vorgenommen, nicht zu rauchen.
– Ich hoffe, das hältst du durch. Das finde ich wirklich sehr sehr sehr gut.
– Ja, und außerdem habe ich mir noch vorgenommen, mal früher ins Bett zu gehen. Das habe ich immer nicht so eingehalten.
– Warum denn nicht? Na ja, und was sonst noch?
– Hmm, zu guter Letzt, hmm, ja … Was mache ich? Ich glaube – ja: ich werde noch ein bisschen Geld wegschenken.
– Geld wegschenken? Das ist wirklich eine sehr originelle Idee.

2a Wie findest du die Ideen oben? Ordne sie von 1 (der besten Idee) bis 10. (AT4 Level 2)
Pupils rank the resolutions in their personal order of importance.

2b Partnerarbeit. (AT2 Level 3)
Pupils discuss their lists to see whether they have the same order.

3a Lies die Texte. Wer hat die meisten Informationen im Text geschrieben? (AT3 Level 5)

Pupils read three texts written by the teenagers to explain their resolutions. Pupils say which text has provided the most information.

Answers

Latze's text

Ludwig: Constructing longer sentences

Go through Ludwig's advice, relating the points he makes to Latze's text. Ask pupils to pick out examples in the text. Compile a class checklist on the board/OHT of things to include in a text to make it more interesting. Encourage pupils to have the checklist to hand whenever they do written work and to include as many of the ideas as possible.

3b Füg den Texten von Meike und Patrick weitere Informationen hinzu. (AT4 Levels 4–6)

Pupils work on Meike's and Patrick's texts to try to improve them by using some of the methods suggested in Ludwig's advice.

4 Bilde weil-Sätze.

Pupils construct *weil* sentences, both to reinforce this sentence structure and to illustrate how *weil* sentences can improve the flow of writing.

Answers

1 Ich werde umweltfreundlicher leben, weil ich das wichtig finde. **2** Ich werde einen Job finden, weil ich auf die Ferien spare. **3** Ich werde ein Instrument lernen, weil ich musikalisch bin. **4** Ich werde zu Hause mehr helfen, weil meine Mutter das anstrengend findet. **5** Ich werde keine Drogen nehmen, weil ich das doof finde. **6** Ich werde viel Fußball spielen, weil das mein Lieblingssport ist.

Wiederholung: *weil* + verb to the end

This grammar revision box reminds pupils of subordinate clause word order after *weil.*

An exercise on word order is provided on page 56 of the Workbook.

5a Was wirst du in Zukunft machen? Schreib einen Text und benutz die Wörter rechts mindestens einmal im Text. (AT4 Levels 4–6)

Pupils write a text about their resolutions for the future, using each of the conjunctions provided at least once.

▶ 5b Partnerarbeit. Vergleicht eure Texte. Wer hat den interessantesten Text geschrieben? (AT2 Levels 4–6)

Pupils work in pairs to compare their texts and discuss who has written the more interesting piece. Some example sentences are provided in the speech bubbles. You could also have a class session to compile any useful structures for all pupils to note for future use.

R Further practice of this unit's language is to be found on p. 120 of the Pupil's Book, activity 2.

E Further practice of this unit's language is to be found on p. 121 of the Pupil's Book, activity 2.

5 Liebe Ellie (pp. 104–105)

Pupils will learn how to:
- write a letter of introduction
- interview an older person

Key language	Resources
Revising the vocabulary and structures covered in Logo! 3	• Cassette C, Side B • Workbook pp. 55, 57 • R & A File: Arbeitsblatt 3 (p. 114)
Grammar focus • *du, ihr* and *Sie* (revision)	
Skill focus • making notes and listening more than once to the recording	

This unit presents an example of an informal letter giving personal information. Pupils then practise the *Sie* form of address in interviewing an older person. Most of the vocabulary should be familiar to pupils.

1a Lies den Brief. In welchem Absatz schreibt Patrick über: (AT3 Levels 5–6)

Pupils read the letter and identify the paragraph in which Patrick talks about each of the specified aspects of his life.

Answers

1 b, **2** a, **3** c, **4** b, **5** e, **6** a, **7** d, **8** e

1b Beantworte die Fragen. (AT3 Levels 5–6)

Pupils answer eight comprehension questions in German on Patrick's letter. They need not use full sentences in their answers, although full sentence answers are provided below.

Answers

1 Er wohnt in München. **2** Er liest gern Sportbücher und Comics. **3** Er sieht gern Actionfilme und Krimis. **4** Er spielt Fußball, Tennis und Handball und fährt Ski. **5** Er bekommt meistens gute Noten. **6** Er mag Kunst, Deutsch und Geschichte. **7** Er mag Englisch nicht, weil es sehr schwierig ist. **8** Er hat Gartenarbeit gemacht.

2 Hör zu. Mach Notizen über Ingrid, Latze und Meike. (1–3) (AT1 Level 5)

Pupils listen to Ingrid, Latze and Meike giving details about themselves. They note down information in six categories for each speaker. If pupils need further support for this task, you could provide a more structured answer grid for them to copy out and fill in:

a Name … ; Alter … ; Kommt aus … ; Wohnt in …
b Familienmitglieder … (Mutter, Bruder, Stiefvater, usw.)
c Hobbys … (fernsehen, Musik, Kino, Tennis, usw.)
d Schulfächer … (Sport, Kunst, Musik, usw.) ☺, ☹
e Job … ; spart auf …
f Charaktereigenschaften … (pünktlich, geduldig, lustig, usw.)

Answers

1 a Ingrid, 14 J., kommt aus Österreich, wohnt in München, **b** Vater, Stiefmutter, Bruder, Halbbruder, Stiefbruder, **c** Musik, fernsehen, **d** Geschichte ☺, Biologie ☹, **e** spart auf die Ferien, **f** intelligent, lustig, freundlich
2 a Latze, 15 J., kommt aus Köln, wohnt in München, **b** Vater , 2 Schwestern, **c** einkaufen, Tennis, lesen, Ski fahren, **d** Sport ☺, Mathe ☹, **e** Job im Supermarkt, spart auf eine Stereoanlage, **f** pünktlich und geduldig
3 a Meike, 14 J. kommt aus Hamburg, wohnt in einem kleinen Dorf auf dem Land, **b** Eltern, 2 Brüder, Schwester, **c** Musik, Kino, Computerspiele, im See baden, **d** Englisch ☺, Erdkunde ☹, **e** spart auf Kleidung, **f** hilfsbereit, umweltfreundlich und fit

1 – Hallo. Ich heiße Ingrid und ich bin vierzehn Jahre alt. Ich komme aus Österreich und jetzt wohne ich in München. München ist eine sehr schöne Stadt und es gefällt mir hier sehr. Ich wohne mit meinem Vater und meiner Stiefmutter, meinem Bruder, meinem Halbbruder und meinem Stiefbruder. Das ist schon viel, nicht? Mein Vater, meine Mutter, mein Bruder, mein Halbbruder und mein Stiefbruder! Ich habe nicht viele Hobbys, aber ich höre gern Musik und ich sehe gern fern. In der Schule ist mein Lieblingsfach Geschichte. Biologie gefällt mir nicht, weil das so langweilig ist. Im Moment spare ich auf die Ferien. Ich bin ziemlich intelligent, lustig und freundlich!

2 – Hallo. Ich heiße Latze und ich bin fünfzehn Jahre alt. Ich komme aus Köln und jetzt wohne ich in München. Ich wohne hier mit meinem Vater und meinen zwei Schwestern, Lotte und Sophie. Ich habe viele Hobbys: Ich gehe gern einkaufen, ich spiele gern Tennis und ich lese gern. Ich fahre auch gern Ski. In der Schule ist mein Lieblingsfach Sport – das finde ich immer lustig. Ich finde Mathe sehr schwierig, also mag ich es nicht. Ja, Mathe finde ich schrecklich! Ich habe einen Job im Supermarkt und im Moment spare ich auf eine Stereoanlage. Ich bin immer sehr pünktlich und geduldig.

3 – Hallo. Ich heiße Meike und ich bin vierzehn Jahre alt. Ich komme aus Hamburg und jetzt wohne ich in einem kleinen Dorf auf dem Land. Ich wohne hier mit meinen Eltern, meinen zwei Brüdern und meiner Schwester. Ich höre gern Musik und ich gehe gern ins Kino. Ich spiele auch gern Computerspiele und im Sommer bade ich gern im See. In der Schule ist mein Lieblingsfach Englisch – das finde ich sehr nützlich und interessant. Ich finde Erdkunde sehr kompliziert und langweilig, also mag ich die Erdkundestunden gar nicht. Im Moment spare ich auf Kleidung, weil ich immer neue Kleidung brauche. Ich bin sehr hilfsbereit, umweltfreundlich und fit!

Ludwig: Making notes and listening more than once to the recording
Ludwig reminds pupils just to write notes as they listen, and then to listen a second time to fill any gaps.

Before pupils do activity 3, invite them to ask you the key questions in the clouds about yourself and to make notes about your answers. These could be about an imaginary famous person if you don't want them to be about you.

3 Partnerarbeit. Erfindet Radiointerviews mit einer berühmten Person und nehmt sie auf Kassette auf. (AT2 Levels 4–6)
Pupils invent radio interviews with a famous person (living or dead), using the *Sie* form in their questioning. Pupils might need to research the details of a famous person on the internet or in the library before they do this task.

Pupils ask these key questions of other German speakers in the department. They could record their interviews on cassette and note the answers afterwards.

Wiederholung: 'you'
This grammar revision box reminds pupils of the three forms for 'you' in German. Make sure that pupils are familiar with the appropriate situations for each one.

4 Schreib einen Brief an Patrick oder Ellie und stell dich vor. Gib so viele Details wie möglich. (AT4 Levels 4–6)
Pupils write a letter to Patrick or Ellie, giving as many details as possible about themselves.

A crossword on the perfect tense summarising work in the whole of Logo! 3 is provided on page 57 of the Workbook.

For further oral practice of the language of the unit, pupils could do the pairwork activity on Arbeitsblatt 3 (R & A File p. 114).

Lernzieltest and Wiederholung (pp. 106–107)

Resources
- Cassette C, Side B
- Workbook pp. 58–60
- R & A File: Wortschatz pp. 119–120

Lernzieltest p. 121
Kontrolle 6 pp. 122–132 (including teacher's notes)

At the end of each chapter there is a revision unit for pupils to use before the assessment materials. The unit begins with a *Lernzieltest* (like the *Mini-Test*) for pupils to test themselves on key language from the chapter. This is also provided as a checklist for pupils to write on (R & A File p. 121) and some related gapped sentences are also provided on p. 60 of the Workbook.

If pupils are unsure of any of the language, they should be encouraged to revise the relevant unit in the chapter. A complete wordlist containing key words and phrases from the whole chapter is provided on the *Wortschatz* sheets (R &A File pp. 119–120).

Wiederholung provides pupils with revision exercises in the four skills. The listening exercises should be done in class, but the other exercises could be done either in class or for homework. Further revision exercises are provided on pp. 58–59 of the Workbook.

Wiederholung

Hören

1 Hör zu und mach Notizen. (1–10) (AT1 Level 3)

Pupils listen to ten teenagers and note down which family member is mentioned each time and which characteristic is attributed to him/her.

Answers

1 Stiefmutter – launisch, **2** Stiefvater – lustig, **3** drei Brüder – sehr nervig, **4** Schwester – launisch, **5** Mutter – freundlich, **6** Vater – altmodisch, **7** Halbbruder – nett, **8** Stiefschwester – streng, **9** Halbschwester – gut gelaunt, **10** Bruder – geduldig

1 – Meine Stiefmutter geht mir total auf die Nerven. Sie ist total launisch und das kann ich nicht ausstehen.
2 – Ich habe einen Stiefvater und ich finde ihn sehr lustig.
3 – Ich habe drei Brüder und alle drei finde ich sehr nervig.
4 – Meine Schwester ist sieben Jahre älter als ich und sie ist so launisch.
5 – Alle meine Freunde finden meine Mutter sehr freundlich. Ich auch!
6 – Mein Vater geht mir immer auf die Nerven, weil er so altmodisch ist. Er trägt noch Kleidung aus den sechziger Jahren.
7 – Mein Halbbruder ist sechs Jahre alt und ziemlich nett.
8 – Wenn meine Stiefschwester zu Hause ist, darf ich nichts machen. Sie ist so streng.
9 – Ich komme sehr gut mit meiner Halbschwester aus, weil sie immer gut gelaunt ist.
10 – Ich mag meinen Bruder sehr, weil er sehr geduldig ist und mir bei den Hausaufgaben viel hilft.

2 Hör zu und mach Notizen. Was darf Georgia nicht machen? (AT1 Levels 5–6)

Pupils listen to Georgia describing what she is not allowed to do at home, and make notes.

Answers

ein Piercing haben, laute Musik spielen, Pommes oder Schokoladenpudding essen, rauchen, am Vormittag fernsehen

Hallo, mein Name ist Georgia und meine Eltern sind total streng. Das geht mir dauernd auf die Nerven, aber was kann man dagegen machen? Zum Beispiel bin ich gestern in die Stadt gefahren und ich habe ein Piercing bekommen. Meine Mutter hat das gesehen und hat sich furchtbar geärgert. Und warum? Weil ich kein Piercing haben darf! Mensch, ich bin sechzehn Jahre alt. Alle dürfen das machen, nur ich nicht. Das finde ich total unfair. Ich habe danach im Zimmer Musik gehört, aber zehn Minuten später ist mein Vater ins Zimmer gekommen: „Georgia, stell bitte die Musik leise", hat er gesagt: „Das ist viel zu laut, wir werden alle furchtbare Kopfschmerzen kriegen." Also, keine laute Musik für mich! Zu Mittag gab's wieder Salat und Kartoffeln zu essen. Bei uns darf man nie etwas Leckeres wie Pommes oder Schokoladenpudding essen. Meine Mutter ist ein totaler Fitnessfan und alles muss gesund sein. Letzten Monat habe ich Hausarrest gehabt, weil meine Mutter eine Schachtel Zigaretten in meiner Tasche fand. Sie war sehr böse und es gab furchtbaren Krach. Rauchen ist verboten, weißt du. Rauchen – das darf man nicht! Während des Hausarrests habe ich viel mit unserer Katze gespielt und ich habe auch viel ferngesehen. Ich habe sogar am Vormittag ferngesehen – das darf man bei uns eigentlich nicht, aber meine Eltern waren oft im Garten und sie haben mich nicht erwischt! Nächsten Samstag gibt es eine Party bei meiner besten Freundin und ich werde bei ihr übernachten – ich freue mich irrisinnig darauf, weil ihre Eltern sehr nett und locker sind. Bei ihr darf man fast alles machen!

Sprechen

3 Partnerarbeit. Seht euch die zwei Info-Karten an (Seite 107). Übt Interviews und erfindet noch drei Details für jede Person. (AT2 Levels 4–6)

Pupils use the information on the cue cards (p. 107) to conduct interviews, using the *Sie* form of address. The questions in speech bubbles will help them with the interview. Pupils must also invent three further details for each person.

Lesen

4 Lies den Brief und beantworte die Fragen. (AT3 Levels 5–6)

Pupils read a problem letter to a magazine and answer six comprehension questions on it in German. They need not answer in full sentences, although full sentence answers are provided below.

Answers

1 Sie geht ihm auf die Nerven, weil sie immer so launisch ist. **2** Sie ist launisch, weil sie mit einer neuen Clique in der Schule herumgeht. **3** Er war im Zimmer, um an Hannahs Computer zu spielen. **4** Er hat eine Schachtel Zigaretten und eine kleine Flasche Wodka gefunden. **5** Er kann mit seiner Mutter oder mit seiner Schwester reden. **6** Sie wird Ärger bekommen, wenn sie mit der Clique weiter herumgeht.

Schreiben

5 Schreib einen Brief an „Tante Pauline“ über folgendes Problem. (AT4 Levels 4–6)

Pupils write a problem letter to a magazine, using one of the suggestions provided in the clouds.

► EXTRA

The EXTRA pages at the back of the Pupil's Book are intended to provide consolidation/reinforcement activities (EXTRA A) and more challenging / extension activities (EXTRA B). The exercises concentrate on the skills of reading and writing only. They could be used for differentiated work in class or at home. The best place to use each activity is clearly indicated in these notes, just above the exercise rubric, e. g. [after pp. 96–97].

EXTRA A (p. 120)

[after pp. 96–97]

1a Was passt zusammen? (AT3 Level 2)

Pupils match descriptions of family members to pictures.

Answers

1 d, **2** e, **3** c, **4** g, **5** b, **6** f, **7** a

1b Beschreib deine Familie. (AT4 Levels 3–4)

Pupils describe their own or an imaginary family.

[after pp. 102–103]

2a Lies die Texte. Richtig oder falsch? (AT3 Level 5)

Pupils read an article about teenagers' plans for the future and decide whether the sentences are true or false.

Answers

1 falsch, **2** richtig, **3** richtig, **4** falsch, **5** richtig, **6** falsch, **7** falsch, **8** richtig

2b Such dir die Verben aus dem Text heraus und ergänze die Tabelle.

Pupils complete a table with expressions from the article in the present, perfect and future tense.

Answers

Präsens	Perfekt	Zukunft
ich rauche, finde, spare, räume ... auf, das ... ist sie findet	ich habe ... gemacht, gespart	ich werde ... rauchen, machen, finden, helfen, abwaschen, arbeiten

2c Beantworte die Fragen für dich. (AT4 Levels 4–5)

Pupils answer questions about their plans, using the future tense.

EXTRA B (p. 121)

[after pp. 96–97]

1 Lies die Sprechblasen und schreib Sätze. (AT4 Levels 3–4)

Pupils read the speech bubbles and describe the families.

Answers

Jens hat einen Stiefbruder, aber er findet ihn doof und launisch. **Maria** hat eine Stiefmutter und sie findet sie gut gelaunt und geduldig. **Peter** hat Halbbrüder und er findet sie nett und freundlich. **Werner** hat eine Schwester, aber er findet sie altmodisch. **Lisa** hat einen Bruder und sie findet ihn echt klasse. **Eddie** hat eine Mutter, aber er findet sie sehr streng. **Dagmar** hat einen Vater und sie findet ihn nett und geduldig.

[after pp. 102–103]

2a Lies den Text und wähl die richtige Antwort aus. (AT3 Levels 5–6)

Pupils read a text in which Anita talks about her relationship with her family and the rules at home. Pupils then answer some multiple-choice questions on the text.

Answers

1 c, **2** b, **3** a, **4** a, **5** b, **6** a, **7** c, **8** b, **9** c

2b Such dir die Verben aus dem Text heraus und ergänze die Tabelle.

Pupils complete a table with expressions from the text in the present, perfect, imperfect and future tenses.

Answers

Präsens	Perfekt	Imperfekt	Zukunft
ich heiße, bin, habe, komme aus, finde, darf, muss; er ist, hat, darf; sie ist; wir wohnen	ich bin mitgefahren, habe gefunden, geredet; sie sind gefahren	er war	ich werde treffen; er wird machen, bleiben, sein; es wird sein

2c Wie ist deine Familie? Was für Probleme hast du? Schreib einen kurzen Text wie Anitas und benutz die Verben aus der Tabelle oben. (AT4 Levels 4–6)

Pupils write a text about their own or an imaginary family, giving details of family members, whether they get on and what house rules there are.

Workbook

p. 51

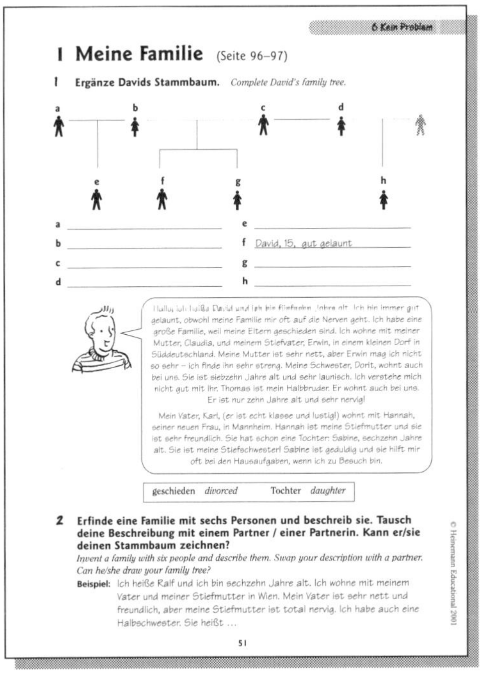
6 Kein Problem
1 Meine Familie (Seite 96–97)
1 Ergänze Davids Stammbaum. Complete David's family tree.
2 Erfinde eine Familie mit sechs Personen und beschreib sie. Tausch deine Beschreibung mit einem Partner / einer Partnerin. Kann er/sie deinen Stammbaum zeichnen?
Invent a family with six people and describe them. Swap your description with a partner. Can he/she draw your family tree?
51

1 (AT3 Level 5)
a Erwin, streng, **b** Claudia, sehr nett, **c** Karl, echt klasse und lustig, **d** Hannah, sehr freundlich, **e** Thomas, 10, sehr nervig, **f** David, 15, gut gelaunt, **g** Dorit, 17, sehr launisch, **h** Sabine, 16, geduldig
2 (AT4 Levels 4–5)
individual answers

p. 52

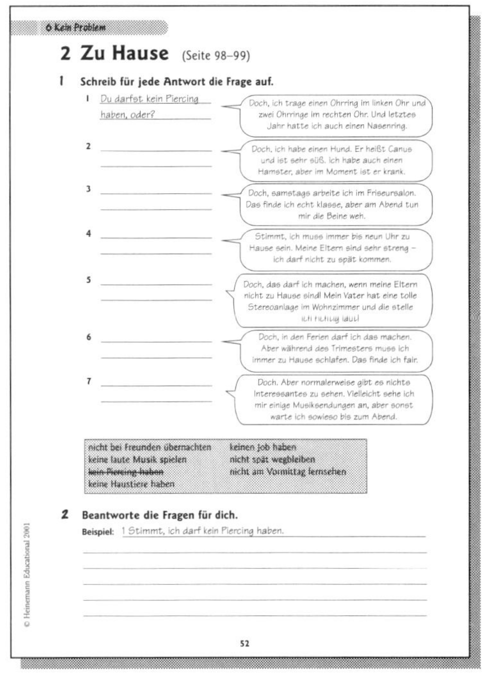
6 Kein Problem
2 Zu Hause (Seite 98–99)
1 Schreib für jede Antwort die Frage auf.
2 Beantworte die Fragen für dich.
52

1 (AT3 Levels 4–5)
1 Du darfst kein Piercing haben, oder? **2** Du darfst keine Haustiere haben, oder? **3** Du darfst keinen Job haben, oder? **4** Du darfst nicht spät wegbleiben, oder? **5** Du darfst keine laute Musik spielen, oder? **6** Du darfst nicht bei Freunden übernachten, oder? **7** Du darfst nicht am Vormittag fernsehen, oder?
2 (AT4 Level 4)
individual answers

p. 53

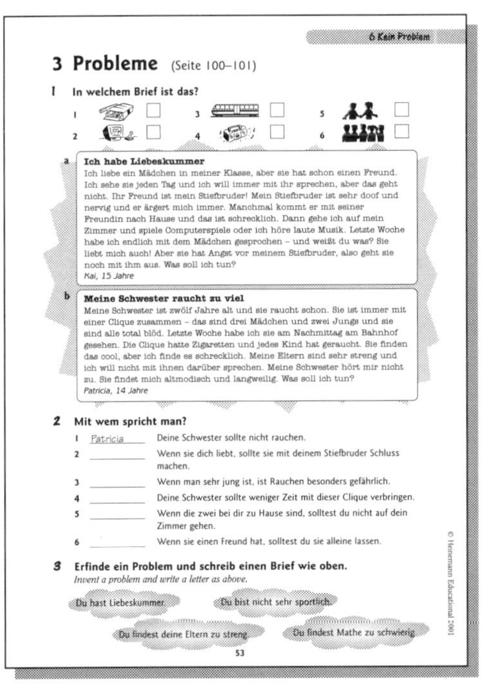
6 Kein Problem
3 Probleme (Seite 100–101)
1 In welchem Brief ist das?
2 Mit wem spricht man?
3 Erfinde ein Problem und schreib einen Brief wie oben.
Invent a problem and write a letter as above.
53

1 (AT3 Level 5)
1 b, **2** a, **3** b, **4** a, **5** a, **6** b
2 (AT3 Level 5)
1 Patricia, **2** Kai, **3** Patricia, **4** Patricia, **5** Kai, **6** Kai
3 (AT4 Levels 5–6)
individual answers

p. 54

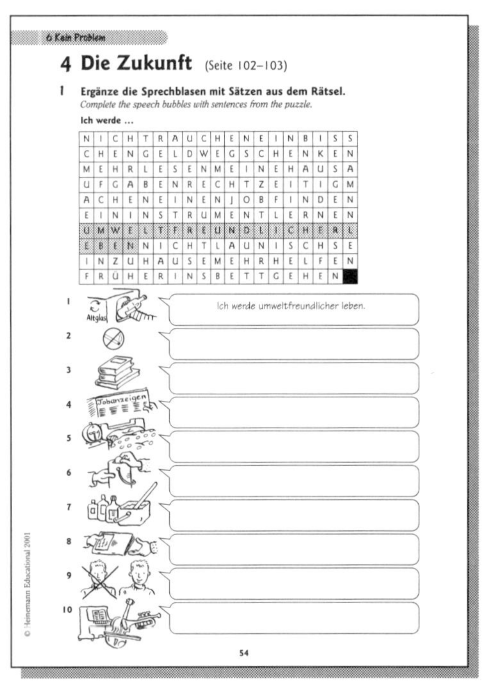
6 Kein Problem
4 Die Zukunft (Seite 102–103)
1 Ergänze die Sprechblasen mit Sätzen aus dem Rätsel.
Complete the speech bubbles with sentences from the puzzle.
54

1 (AT4 Level 3)
1 Ich werde umweltfreundlicher leben. **2** Ich werde nicht rauchen. **3** Ich werde mehr lesen. **4** Ich werde einen Job finden. **5** Ich werde früher ins Bett gehen. **6** Ich werde ein bisschen Geld wegschenken. **7** Ich werde zu Hause mehr helfen. **8** Ich werde meine Hausaufgaben rechtzeitig machen. **9** Ich werde nicht launisch sein. **10** Ich werde ein Instrument lernen.

p. 55

1 (AT3 Levels 4–5)

1 den 21. Juni, **2** Lieber, **3** Brief, **4** Fußball, **5** Mutter, **6** Bruder, **7** Fußball, **8** Park, **9** sehe ... fern, **10** Computerspiele, **11** schwimmen, **12** Vater, **13** echt klasse, **14** zwanzig Mark, **15** Mofa, **16** gespart, **17** Zug, **18** Großmutter

2 (AT3 Levels 4–5)

1 Er wohnt in Hamburg. **2** Es ist sehr laut, weil es so viel Verkehr im Stadtzentrum gibt. **3** Im Sommer geht er gern schwimmen. **4** Er arbeitet in einer Autowerkstatt. **5** Er hat zweihundert Mark gespart. **6** Er fährt nach Berlin, um seine Großmutter zu besuchen.

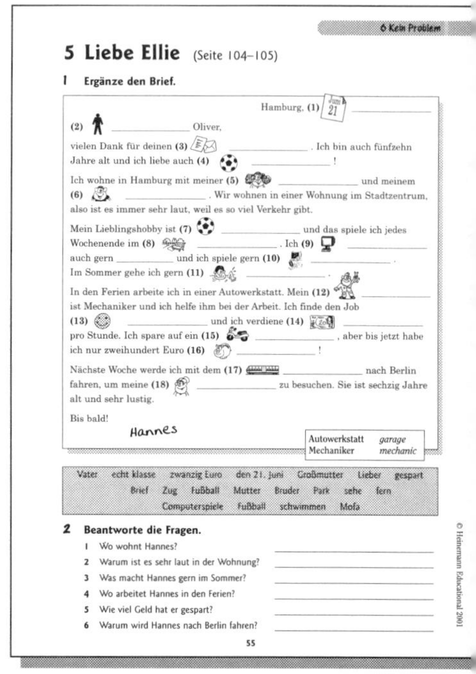
6 Kein Problem

5 Liebe Ellie (Seite 104–105)

1 Ergänze den Brief.

Hamburg, **(1)** ______

(2) ______ Oliver,

vielen Dank für deinen **(3)** ______. Ich bin auch fünfzehn Jahre alt und ich liebe auch **(4)** ______!

Ich wohne in Hamburg mit meiner **(5)** ______ und meinem **(6)** ______. Wir wohnen in einer Wohnung im Stadtzentrum, also ist es immer sehr laut, weil es so viel Verkehr gibt.

Mein Lieblingshobby ist **(7)** ______ und das spiele ich jedes Wochenende im **(8)** ______. Ich **(9)** ______ auch gern ______ und ich spiele gern **(10)** ______. Im Sommer gehe ich gern **(11)** ______.

In den Ferien arbeite ich in einer Autowerkstatt. Mein **(12)** ______ ist Mechaniker und ich helfe ihm bei der Arbeit. Ich finde den Job **(13)** ______ und ich verdiene **(14)** ______ pro Stunde. Ich spare auf ein **(15)** ______, aber bis jetzt habe ich nur zweihundert Euro **(16)** ______!

Nächste Woche werde ich mit dem **(17)** ______ nach Berlin fahren, um meine **(18)** ______ zu besuchen. Sie ist sechzig Jahre alt und sehr lustig.

Bis bald!

Hannes

Autowerkstatt	*garage*
Mechaniker	*mechanic*

Vater echt klasse zwanzig Euro den 21. Juni Großmutter Lieber gespart Brief Zug Fußball Mutter Bruder Park sehe fern Computerspiele Fußball schwimmen Mofa

2 Beantworte die Fragen.

1 Wo wohnt Hannes?
2 Warum ist es sehr laut in der Wohnung?
3 Was macht Hannes gern im Sommer?
4 Wo arbeitet Hannes in den Ferien?
5 Wie viel Geld hat er gespart?
6 Warum wird Hannes nach Berlin fahren?

55

© Heinemann Educational 2001

p. 56

1 **1** Wenn ich Liebeskummer habe, schreibe ich an eine Zeitschrift. **2** Wenn ich die Schule schwierig finde, bleibe ich zu Hause. **3** Wenn ich Zoff mit den Eltern habe, übernachte ich bei einer Freundin. **4** Ich bin nicht fit, weil ich keinen Sport treibe. **5** Ich habe keine Freunde, weil ich unfreundlich bin. **6** Ich spare mein Geld, weil ich einen Computer kaufen will. **7** Ich fahre nach Frankreich, um Französisch zu lernen. **8** Ich fahre nach Spanien, um Madrid zu besichtigen.

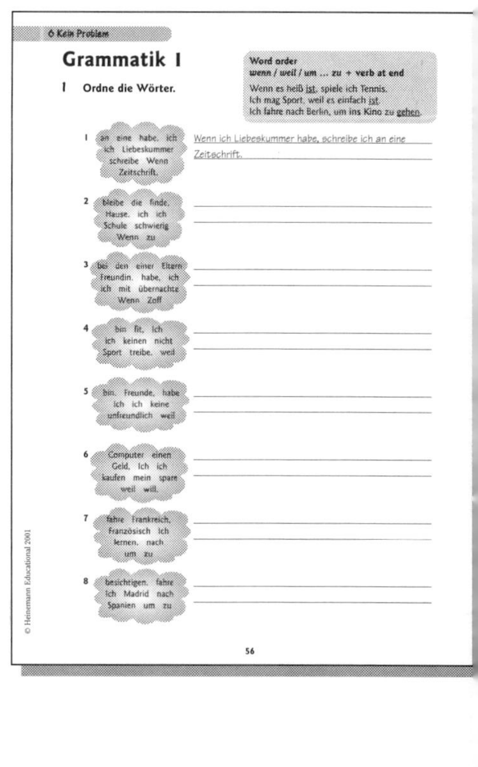
6 Kein Problem

Grammatik 1

1 Ordne die Wörter.

Word order
wenn / weil / um ... zu + verb at end
Wenn es heiß ist, spiele ich Tennis.
Ich mag Sport, weil es einfach ist.
Ich fahre nach Berlin, um ins Kino zu gehen.

1 an eine habe. ich ich Liebeskummer schreibe Wenn Zeitschrift. — Wenn ich Liebeskummer habe, schreibe ich an eine Zeitschrift.
2 bleibe die finde. Hause. ich ich Schule schwierig Wenn zu
3 bei den einer Eltern Freundin. habe, ich ich mit übernachte Wenn Zoff
4 bin fit, ich ich keinen nicht Sport treibe. weil
5 bin. Freunde, habe ich ich keine unfreundlich weil
6 Computer einen Geld, Ich ich kaufen mein spare weil will.
7 fahre Frankreich, Französisch Ich lernen. nach um zu
8 besichtigen. fahre Ich Madrid nach Spanien um zu

56

© Heinemann Educational 2001

p. 57

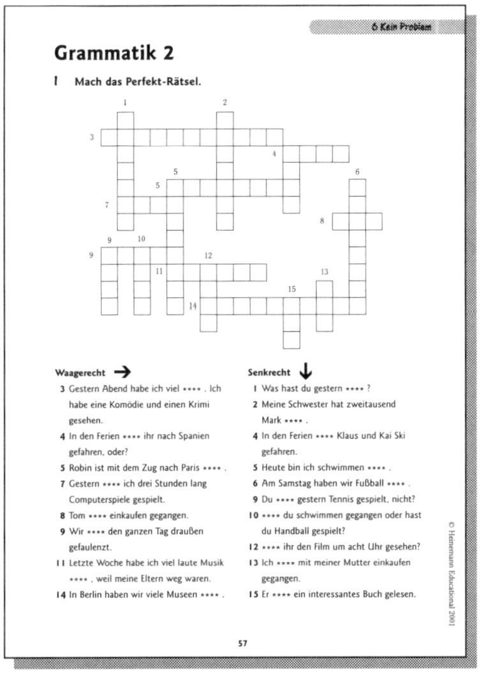
6 Kein Problem

Grammatik 2

1 Mach das Perfekt-Rätsel.

Waagerecht →
3 Gestern Abend habe ich viel •••• . Ich habe eine Komödie und einen Krimi gesehen.
4 In den Ferien •••• ihr nach Spanien gefahren, oder?
5 Robin ist mit dem Zug nach Paris •••• .
7 Gestern •••• ich drei Stunden lang Computerspiele gespielt.
8 Tom •••• einkaufen gegangen.
9 Wir •••• den ganzen Tag draußen gefaulenzt.
11 Letzte Woche habe ich viel laute Musik •••• , weil meine Eltern weg waren.
14 In Berlin haben wir viele Museen •••• .

Senkrecht ↓
1 Was hast du gestern •••• ?
2 Meine Schwester hat zweitausend Mark •••• .
4 In den Ferien •••• Klaus und Kai Ski gefahren.
5 Heute bin ich schwimmen •••• .
6 Am Samstag haben wir Fußball •••• .
9 Du •••• gestern Tennis gespielt, nicht?
10 •••• du schwimmen gegangen oder hast du Handball gespielt?
12 •••• ihr den Film um acht Uhr gesehen?
13 Ich •••• mit meiner Mutter einkaufen gegangen.
15 Er •••• ein interessantes Buch gelesen.

© Heinemann Educational 2001

57

p. 58

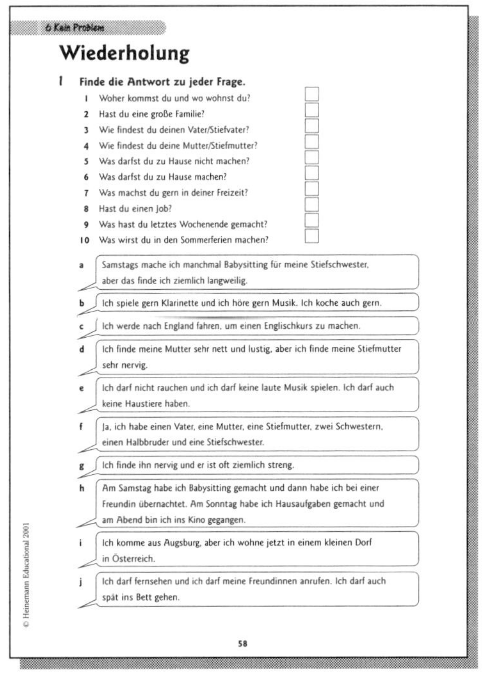
6 Kein Problem

Wiederholung

1 Finde die Antwort zu jeder Frage.

1 Woher kommst du und wo wohnst du?
2 Hast du eine große Familie?
3 Wie findest du deinen Vater/Stiefvater?
4 Wie findest du deine Mutter/Stiefmutter?
5 Was darfst du zu Hause nicht machen?
6 Was darfst du zu Hause machen?
7 Was machst du gern in deiner Freizeit?
8 Hast du einen Job?
9 Was hast du letztes Wochenende gemacht?
10 Was wirst du in den Sommerferien machen?

a Samstags mache ich manchmal Babysitting für meine Stiefschwester, aber das finde ich ziemlich langweilig.
b Ich spiele gern Klarinette und ich höre gern Musik. Ich koche auch gern.
c Ich werde nach England fahren, um einen Englischkurs zu machen.
d Ich finde meine Mutter sehr nett und lustig, aber ich finde meine Stiefmutter sehr nervig.
e Ich darf nicht rauchen und ich darf keine laute Musik spielen. Ich darf auch keine Haustiere haben.
f Ja, ich habe einen Vater, eine Mutter, eine Stiefmutter, zwei Schwestern, einen Halbbruder und eine Stiefschwester.
g Ich finde ihn nervig und er ist oft ziemlich streng.
h Am Samstag habe ich Babysitting gemacht und dann habe ich bei einer Freundin übernachtet. Am Sonntag habe ich Hausaufgaben gemacht und am Abend bin ich ins Kino gegangen.
i Ich komme aus Augsburg, aber ich wohne jetzt in einem kleinen Dorf in Österreich.
j Ich darf fernsehen und ich darf meine Freundinnen anrufen. Ich darf auch spät ins Bett gehen.

© Heinemann Educational 2001

58

1 Waagerecht: **3** ferngesehen, **4** seid, **5** gefahren, **7** habe, **8** ist, **9** haben, **11** gehört, **14** besichtigt
Senkrecht: **1** gemacht, **2** gespart, **4** sind, **5** gegangen, **6** gespielt, **9** hast, **10** bist, **12** habt, **13** bin, **15** hat

1 (AT3 Level 4)
1 i, **2** f, **3** g, **4** d, **5** e, **6** j, **7** b, **8** a, **9** h, **10** c

p. 59

6 Kein Problem

2 Beantworte die Fragen für dich.

1 Woher kommst du und wo wohnst du?
2 Hast du eine große Familie?
3 Wie findest du deinen Vater/Stiefvater?
4 Wie findest du deine Mutter/Stiefmutter?
5 Was darfst du zu Hause nicht machen?
6 Was darfst du zu Hause machen?
7 Was machst du gern in deiner Freizeit?
8 Hast du einen Job?
9 Was hast du letztes Wochenende gemacht?
10 Was wirst du in den Sommerferien machen?

© Heinemann Educational 2001

59

p. 60

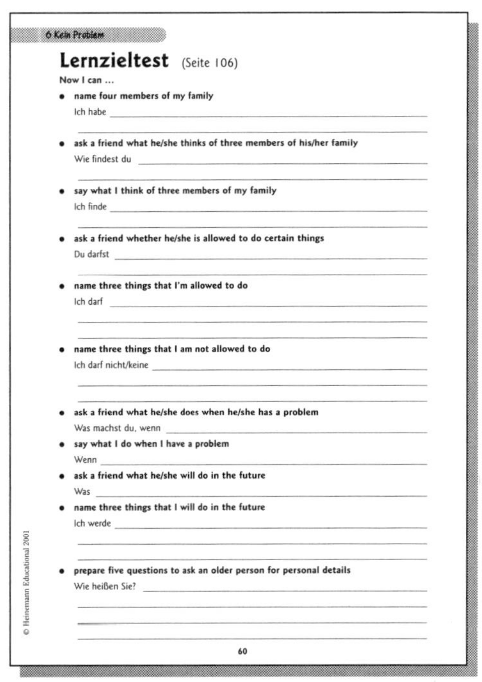
6 Kein Problem

Lernzieltest (Seite 106)

Now I can ...

- name four members of my family
  Ich habe
- ask a friend what he/she thinks of three members of his/her family
  Wie findest du
- say what I think of three members of my family
  Ich finde
- ask a friend whether he/she is allowed to do certain things
  Du darfst
- name three things that I'm allowed to do
  Ich darf
- name three things that I am not allowed to do
  Ich darf nicht/keine
- ask a friend what he/she does when he/she has a problem
  Was machst du, wenn
- say what I do when I have a problem
  Wenn
- ask a friend what he/she will do in the future
  Was
- name three things that I will do in the future
  Ich werde
- prepare five questions to ask an older person for personal details
  Wie heißen Sie?

© Heinemann Educational 2001

60

2 (AT4 Levels 4–5)
individual answers

individual answers

Resource & Assessment File

Arbeitsblatt 1
p. 112

Zu Hause *(pages 98–99)*   Logo! 3 6 Kein Problem Arbeitsblatt 1

ein Piercing haben	Haustiere haben	einen Job haben
spät wegbleiben	laute Musik spielen	bei Freunden übernachten
allein in die Stadt fahren	Pommes essen	am Vormittag fernsehen
	rauchen	

112

Visuals of *ein Piercing haben, Haustiere haben, einen Job haben, spät wegbleiben, laute Musik spielen, bei Freunden übernachten, allein in die Stadt fahren, Pommes essen, am Vormittag fernsehen, rauchen*

Arbeitsblatt 2
p. 113

Die Zukunft *(pages 102–103)*   Logo! 3 6 Kein Problem Arbeitsblatt 2

Ich werde nicht rauchen.	Ich werde ein bisschen Geld wegschenken.	Ich werde mehr lesen.
Ich werde meine Hausaufgaben rechtzeitig machen.	Ich werde einen Job finden.	Ich werde ein Instrument lernen.
Ich werde umweltfreundlicher leben.	Ich werde nicht launisch sein.	Ich werde zu Hause mehr helfen.
	Ich werde früher ins Bett gehen.	

113

Visuals of *Ich werde nicht rauchen, Ich werde ein bisschen Geld wegschenken, Ich werde mehr lesen, Ich werde meine Hausaufgaben rechtzeitig machen, Ich werde einen Job finden, Ich werde ein Instrument lernen, Ich werde umweltfreundlicher leben, Ich werde nicht launisch sein, Ich werde zu Hause mehr helfen, Ich werde früher ins Bett gehen*

Arbeitsblatt 3
p. 114

Liebe Ellie *(pages 104–105)*   Logo! 3 6 Kein Problem Arbeitsblatt 3

Partner/Partnerin A

Dialog 1
Du bist Reporter/Reporterin. Mach ein Interview mit Bastian Burger oder Bettina Burger.

Beispiel: A Wie heißen Sie?
B Ich heiße (Bastian Burger).

Fragen:
Wie heißen Sie?
Wie alt sind Sie?
Haben Sie eine große Familie?
Was sind Ihre Hobbys?
Was haben Sie am Wochenende gemacht?
Wo arbeiten Sie?
Wie viel Geld verdienen Sie?
Worauf sparen Sie?
Was für Charaktereigenschaften haben Sie?
Was werden Sie nächstes Jahr machen?

Dialog 2
Du bist Gabriella Lohnert oder Michael Lohnert. Beantworte die Fragen deines Partners / deiner Partnerin.

Name: Gabriella Lohnert / Michael Lohnert
Alter: 28
Familie: Vater, 3 Brüder
Hobbys: fernsehen, lesen, reisen
Wochenende: fernsehen, schwimmen, Kino
Arbeit: in Kalifornien
Geld: €25 000 im Monat
Sparen: Auto
Charaktereigenschaften: sportlich, geduldig, freundlich
Nächstes Jahr: in London arbeiten

Erfindet weitere Personen und macht weitere Interviews.
Invent more people and carry out more interviews.

Partner/Partnerin B

Dialog 1
Du bist Bastian Burger oder Bettina Burger. Beantworte die Fragen deines Partners / deiner Partnerin.

Name: Bastian Burger / Bettina Burger
Alter: 31
Familie: Mutter, 1 Schwester, 1 Bruder
Hobbys: Ski fahren, Fußball spielen, ins Kino gehen
Wochenende: Ski fahren, lesen, nach New York fahren
Arbeit: in Berlin
Geld: €23 000 im Monat
Sparen: Haus in Los Angeles
Charaktereigenschaften: sportlich, gut gelaunt, ordentlich
Nächstes Jahr: nach Australien fahren

Dialog 2
Du bist Reporter/Reporterin. Mach ein Interview mit Gabrielle Lohnert oder Michael Lohnert.

Beispiel: A Wie heißen Sie?
B Ich heiße (Gabrielle Lohnert).

Fragen:
Wie heißen Sie?
Wie alt sind Sie?
Haben Sie eine große Familie?
Was sind Ihre Hobbys?
Was haben Sie am Wochenende gemacht?
Wo arbeiten Sie?
Wie viel Geld verdienen Sie?
Worauf sparen Sie?
Was für Charaktereigenschaften haben Sie?
Was werden Sie nächstes Jahr machen?

Erfindet weitere Personen und macht weitere Interviews.
Invent more people and carry out more interviews.

114

Pairwork interviews with an older person.
AT2 Levels 4–5

Arbeitsblatt 4
p. 115

Writing skills   Logo! 3 6 Kein Problem Arbeitsblatt 4

Name ______________________

Writing German can range from writing one-word answers to full sentences and even to whole passages. If you prepare your written German work on a computer, it is much easier to correct mistakes and re-draft the text at a later stage.

Always read through any written work to check the following points:

1 Check that all nouns have capital letters (**Frau**, **Klassenzimmer**, **Italien**).
2 Check that **ich** has no capital letter (unless it starts the sentence).
3 Check that all spellings are correct – if you're not sure, use a dictionary.
4 Check that the grammar is correct – if you're not sure, use the grammar section.
5 Check that the punctuation is correct (commas before **weil**, **wenn**, **aber**).
6 Check that the text makes sense.
7 Check that you have written all you want to.

1 Have a look at this piece of writing. Find and correct the following:

1 Four spelling mistakes **2** Two grammar mistakes **3** Two punctuation mistakes

Ich heiße Andreas. Ich bin fünfzehn jahre alt Ich bin östereicker. Ich wohnst in Graz.

Im Winter schneit es oft. Dann fahren ich Ski. Im Sommer ist es heiß und sonnig.

Dann gehe ich swimmen. Viele Touristen kommen nach Österreich.

Sie fahren Ski und gehen vandern. Ich liebe Österreich weil es so schön ist.

Once you are happy that your piece of written work is correct, see if you can make it more interesting and a little longer.

- Try to add some adjectives, such as **groß**, **schwarz**, **lustig** or **interessant**.
- Words like **und** (*and*) and **aber** (*but*) are quick and easy ways of making longer sentences.
- You could also join two shorter sentences together with **weil** (*because*), **wenn** (*if*) or **um ... zu** (*in order to*).

2 Can you rewrite the following text, making it longer and more interesting? Try to lengthen the sentences and add a few more details.

Servus! Mein Name ist Mathias. Ich bin nicht gesund. Ich esse gern Pommes. Gestern bin ich in die Stadt gefahren. Ich hatte Hunger. Ich bin in mein Lieblingsrestaurant gegangen. Sie hatten nur Apfelstrudel. Sie hatten keine Pommes für mich. Das war blöd. Ich habe mich geärgert. Dann bin ich zu McDonalds gegangen. Ich habe zehn Portionen Pommes bekommen. Bravo!! Ich habe alles in fünf Minuten gegessen!

115

Advice on writing activities.

1 *Correct version of text*: Ich heiße Andreas. Ich bin fünfzehn Jahre alt. Ich bin Österreicher. Ich wohne in Graz. Im Winter schneit es oft. Dann fahre ich Ski. Im Sommer ist es heiß und sonnig. Dann gehe ich schwimmen. Viele Touristen kommen nach Österreich. Sie fahren Ski und gehen wandern. Ich liebe Österreich, weil es so schön ist.
2 *individual answers*

Grammatik 1 p. 116

Practice of pronouns.

1 **1** Ich finde ihn lustig. **2** Ich finde sie O.K. **3** Ich finde sie streng. **4** Ich finde ihn klasse. **5** Ich finde dich langweilig. **6** Ich finde es zu groß. **7** Ich finde sie toll. **8** Ich finde euch lustig.

2 **1** ihm, **2** mir, **3** ihr, **4** uns

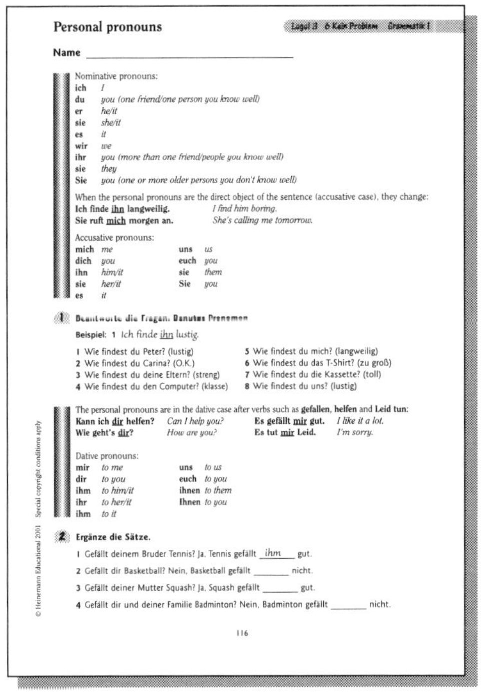

Personal pronouns

Logo! 3 6 Kein Problem Grammatik 1

Name ______________________

Nominative pronouns:

ich *I*
du *you (one friend/one person you know well)*
er *he/it*
sie *she/it*
es *it*
wir *we*
ihr *you (more than one friend/people you know well)*
sie *they*
Sie *you (one or more older persons you don't know well)*

When the personal pronouns are the direct object of the sentence (accusative case), they change:

Ich finde ihn langweilig. *I find him boring.*
Sie ruft mich morgen an. *She's calling me tomorrow.*

Accusative pronouns:

mich	*me*	**uns**	*us*
dich	*you*	**euch**	*you*
ihn	*him/it*	**sie**	*them*
sie	*her/it*	**Sie**	*you*
es	*it*		

1 **Beantworte die Fragen. Benutze Pronomen**

Beispiel: 1 *Ich finde ihn lustig.*

1 Wie findest du Peter? (lustig)
2 Wie findest du Carina? (O.K.)
3 Wie findest du deine Eltern? (streng)
4 Wie findest du den Computer? (klasse)
5 Wie findest du mich? (langweilig)
6 Wie findest du das T-Shirt? (zu groß)
7 Wie findest du die Kassette? (toll)
8 Wie findest du uns? (lustig)

The personal pronouns are in the dative case after verbs such as **gefallen**, **helfen** and **Leid tun**:

Kann ich dir helfen? *Can I help you?* **Es gefällt mir gut.** *I like it a lot.*
Wie geht's dir? *How are you?* **Es tut mir Leid.** *I'm sorry.*

Dative pronouns:

mir	*to me*	**uns**	*to us*
dir	*to you*	**euch**	*to you*
ihm	*to him/it*	**ihnen**	*to them*
ihr	*to her/it*	**Ihnen**	*to you*
ihm	*to it*		

2 **Ergänze die Sätze.**

1 Gefällt deinem Bruder Tennis? Ja, Tennis gefällt *ihm* gut.
2 Gefällt dir Basketball? Nein, Basketball gefällt ________ nicht.
3 Gefällt deiner Mutter Squash? Ja, Squash gefällt ________ gut.
4 Gefällt dir und deiner Familie Badminton? Nein, Badminton gefällt ________ nicht.

116

Grammatik 2 p. 117

Practice of negatives.

1 **1** Ich darf keine Maus haben. **2** Ich darf keine Sportschuhe haben. **3** Ich darf keinen Computer haben. **4** Ich darf keine Katze haben. **5** Ich darf kein Handy haben. **6** Ich darf keine Ohrringe haben.

2 **1** Nein, ich darf nicht allein in die Stadt fahren. **2** Nein, ich darf nicht bei Freunden übernachten. **3** Nein, ich darf nicht fernsehen. **4** Nein, ich darf nicht rauchen. **5** Nein, ich darf nicht in die Disco gehen. **6** Nein, ich darf nicht schwimmen gehen.

3 **1** Das stimmt nicht. Ich habe keine Haustiere. **2** Das stimmt nicht. Ich gehe nie ins Kino. **3** Das stimmt nicht. Ich wohne nicht auf dem Land. **4** Das stimmt nicht. Ich habe keine Schwestern. **5** Das stimmt nicht. Ich höre nicht gern Musik. **6** Das stimmt nicht. Ich habe nichts gekauft. **7** Das stimmt nicht. Ich darf nicht rauchen. **8** Das stimmt nicht. Ich spiele nie Fußball. **9** Das stimmt nicht. Ich lese keine Sportbücher. **10** Das stimmt nicht. Ich esse nie Pommes.

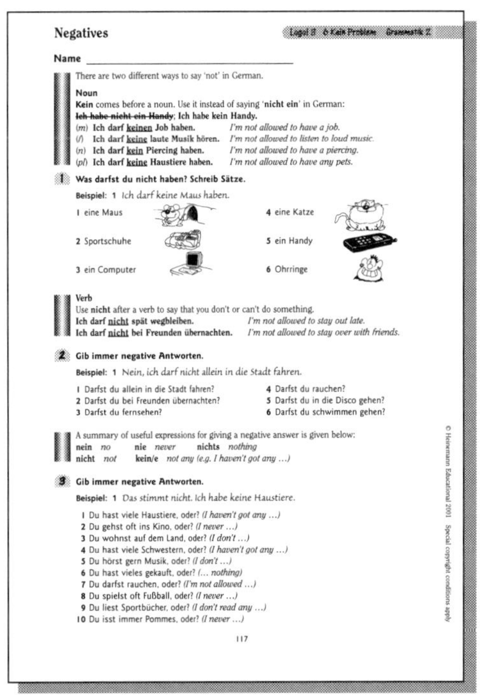

Negatives

Logo! 3 6 Kein Problem Grammatik 2

Name ______________________

There are two different ways to say 'not' in German.

Noun

Kein comes before a noun. Use it instead of saying '**nicht ein**' in German:

~~**Ich habe nicht ein Handy**~~; **Ich habe kein Handy.**

(*m*) **Ich darf keinen Job haben.** *I'm not allowed to have a job.*
(*f*) **Ich darf keine laute Musik hören.** *I'm not allowed to listen to loud music.*
(*n*) **Ich darf kein Piercing haben.** *I'm not allowed to have a piercing.*
(*pl*) **Ich darf keine Haustiere haben.** *I'm not allowed to have any pets.*

1 **Was darfst du nicht haben? Schreib Sätze.**

Beispiel: 1 *Ich darf keine Maus haben.*

1 eine Maus
2 Sportschuhe
3 ein Computer
4 eine Katze
5 ein Handy
6 Ohrringe

Verb

Use **nicht** after a verb to say that you don't or can't do something.

Ich darf nicht spät wegbleiben. *I'm not allowed to stay out late.*
Ich darf nicht bei Freunden übernachten. *I'm not allowed to stay over with friends.*

2 **Gib immer negative Antworten.**

Beispiel: 1 *Nein, ich darf nicht allein in die Stadt fahren.*

1 Darfst du allein in die Stadt fahren?
2 Darfst du bei Freunden übernachten?
3 Darfst du fernsehen?
4 Darfst du rauchen?
5 Darfst du in die Disco gehen?
6 Darfst du schwimmen gehen?

A summary of useful expressions for giving a negative answer is given below:

nein *no* **nie** *never* **nichts** *nothing*
nicht *not* **kein/e** *not any (e.g. I haven't got any …)*

3 **Gib immer negative Antworten.**

Beispiel: 1 *Das stimmt nicht. Ich habe keine Haustiere.*

1 Du hast viele Haustiere, oder? *(I haven't got any …)*
2 Du gehst oft ins Kino, oder? *(I never …)*
3 Du wohnst auf dem Land, oder? *(I don't …)*
4 Du hast viele Schwestern, oder? *(I haven't got any …)*
5 Du hörst gern Musik, oder? *(I don't …)*
6 Du hast vieles gekauft, oder? *(… nothing)*
7 Du darfst rauchen, oder? *(I'm not allowed …)*
8 Du spielst oft Fußball, oder? *(I never …)*
9 Du liest Sportbücher, oder? *(I don't read any …)*
10 Du isst immer Pommes, oder? *(I never …)*

117

Grammatik 3 p. 118
Practice of possessive adjectives.
1 **1** Sein Vater ist streng. **2** Seine Mutter ist nett. **3** Sein Bruder ist intelligent. **4** Seine Schwestern sind lustig. **5** Sein Großvater ist freundlich.
2 **1** Ihre Großmutter ist lustig. **2** Ihr Stiefvater ist O.K. **3** Ihre Mutter ist gut gelaunt. **4** Ihr Stiefbruder ist launisch. **5** Ihre Halbschwester ist nervig.
3 Paul findet seinen Vater streng, seine Mutter nett, seinen Bruder intelligent, seine Schwestern lustig und seinen Großvater freundlich. Verena findet ihre Großmutter lustig, ihren Stiefvater O.K., ihre Mutter gut gelaunt, ihren Stiefbruder launisch und ihre Halbschwester nervig.
4 **1** ihrer, **2** seinen, **3** meiner, **4** meinem, **5** seinem, **6** deiner, **7** ihrem, **8** deinen

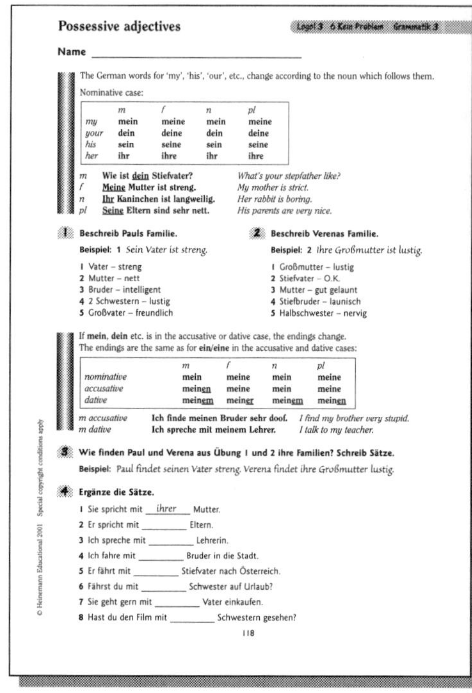
Possessive adjectives — Logo! 3 6 Kein Problem Grammatik 3

Name ____________________

The German words for 'my', 'his', 'our', etc., change according to the noun which follows them.
Nominative case:

	m	*f*	*n*	*pl*
my	**mein**	**meine**	**mein**	**meine**
your	**dein**	**deine**	**dein**	**deine**
his	**sein**	**seine**	**sein**	**seine**
her	**ihr**	**ihre**	**ihr**	**ihre**

m **Wie ist dein Stiefvater?** *What's your stepfather like?*
f **Meine Mutter ist streng.** *My mother is strict.*
n **Ihr Kaninchen ist langweilig.** *Her rabbit is boring.*
pl **Seine Eltern sind sehr nett.** *His parents are very nice.*

1 Beschreib Pauls Familie.
Beispiel: 1 *Sein Vater ist streng.*
1 Vater – streng
2 Mutter – nett
3 Bruder – intelligent
4 2 Schwestern – lustig
5 Großvater – freundlich

2 Beschreib Verenas Familie.
Beispiel: 2 *Ihre Großmutter ist lustig.*
1 Großmutter – lustig
2 Stiefvater – O.K.
3 Mutter – gut gelaunt
4 Stiefbruder – launisch
5 Halbschwester – nervig

If **mein**, **dein** etc. is in the accusative or dative case, the endings change.
The endings are the same as for **ein/eine** in the accusative and dative cases:

	m	*f*	*n*	*pl*
nominative	**mein**	**meine**	**mein**	**meine**
accusative	**meinen**	**meine**	**mein**	**meine**
dative	**meinem**	**meiner**	**meinem**	**meinen**

m accusative **Ich finde meinen Bruder sehr doof.** *I find my brother very stupid.*
m dative **Ich spreche mit meinem Lehrer.** *I talk to my teacher.*

3 Wie finden Paul und Verena aus Übung 1 und 2 ihre Familien? Schreib Sätze.
Beispiel: *Paul findet seinen Vater streng. Verena findet ihre Großmutter lustig.*

4 Ergänze die Sätze.
1 Sie spricht mit *ihrer* Mutter.
2 Er spricht mit ________ Eltern.
3 Ich spreche mit ________ Lehrerin.
4 Ich fahre mit ________ Bruder in die Stadt.
5 Er fährt mit ________ Stiefvater nach Österreich.
6 Fährst du mit ________ Schwester auf Urlaub?
7 Sie geht gern mit ________ Vater einkaufen.
8 Hast du den Film mit ________ Schwestern gesehen?

118

Wortschatz pp. 119–120 and Lernzieltest p. 121
These sheets are for revision at the end of the chapter. The *Wortschatz* sheets provide a list of all the key words and phrases from the chapter and the *Lernzieltest* gives a checklist of the areas covered, which pupils can check off as they revise.